WORKSHOP OF **Revolution**

WORKSHOP OF
Revolution

Plebeian Buenos Aires and the
Atlantic World, 1776–1810

Lyman L. Johnson

Duke University Press
Durham and London
2011

© 2011 Duke University Press

All rights reserved

Printed in the United States of America on acid-free paper ∞

Designed by Heather Hensley

Typeset in Monotype Fournier by Tseng Information Systems, Inc.

Library of Congress Cataloging-in-Publication Data appear on
the last printed page of this book.

for Sue

Contents

Preface

The complex story I tell in this book pulls together research conducted in Argentina, Spain, and the United States over more than two decades. I did not begin with the intention of writing a book that would recast the first stages of the independence movement in Argentina. Instead, I pursued a series of economic and social historical topics focused on Buenos Aires during the late colonial and early national periods. I began with craft organization and later examined wage and price history, demography, and slavery. During most of this long intellectual migration, my research was related and interdependent but not integrated in the service of a single objective.

This changed when, after spending six months in the Archivo General de la Nación in Buenos Aires collecting wealth data from the probate inventories of the Rosas period for a different project, I took some time away from numbers to sample late colonial era *audiencia* cases. I soon stumbled on the criminal cases that now serve as the explanatory fulcrum of this book, chapter 5, "The French Conspiracy of 1795." This purported conspiracy to raise a slave rebellion in Buenos Aires not only provided powerful backward linkages to the economic and demographic changes that had transformed the Buenos Aires plebe in the previous decade, but it also served to illuminate the plebe's role in the transformative events of 1806–1810. The result is the book outlined below, a book intended to reinterpret and reframe the origins of popular support for independence in this crucial Spanish colonial capital city and to place May 25, 1810, firmly in the context of Atlantic history.

My assumption is that the *porteño* plebe experienced the city and its economy through the mediation of physical settings and the rhythms of demographic change. Chapter 1 begins with a discussion of the built environment, the physical settings for work, family life, and leisure that framed the economic and social interactions of the plebe and helped guide the development of class consciousness. Plebeian experiences were also framed by a dynamic and ever-changing demography, a city population continually transformed by free migration and the slave trade. The chapter concludes with a broadly focused examination of the skilled crafts that focuses on the changing ethnic and racial origins of artisans found in censuses and matriculations.

Chapter 2 places the colonial plebe in the social and cultural structures that guided both individual life trajectories and collective actions. I argue that artisan crafts and lesser-skilled trades (cart drivers, slaughter yard laborers, and porters, for example) served as vectors inculcating the values and norms of masculine culture while at the same time transmitting skills and experiences crucial to the working lives of plebeians. To illuminate these connections, I examine apprenticeship, the culture of honor, and male sociability and leisure, including sport and gaming. These foundational social and cultural venues, I argue, sustained and nursed the plebeian values and behaviors visible in every significant political contest during the last decades of the colonial era in Buenos Aires.

Chapters 3 and 4 examine the plebe in action by closely following the three-decade long struggle to create guilds of shoemakers and silversmiths in Buenos Aires. I locate these collective actions in the context of the city's growing integration in the Atlantic economy and the effects of this integration on local manufacturing and services. These guild efforts began with broad support among artisans and with the encouragement of municipal and colonial authorities. Despite initial successes, both efforts to establish traditional corporate structures succumbed to the corrosive effects of colonial ethnic and racial factionalism. The ambition of immigrant master artisans to replicate Iberia's craft organization failed comprehensively in Buenos Aires. Their defeat marked the first appearance of an assertive and politically sophisticated group of black and *casta* craftsmen who not only outmaneuvered and ultimately defeated their European rivals in these crafts, but successfully contested the power of the *cabildo*, audiencia, and viceroy in Buenos Aires.

Chapter 5 explores a little-known and seldom-discussed event in the history of colonial Buenos Aires, the so-called French Conspiracy.[1] In 1795 Viceroy Nicolás de Arredondo appointed a local judge to investigate rumors of a planned slave insurrection. Scores of artisans and laborers were eventually arrested and two were tortured. While there is little evidence of a genuine conspiracy, the case illuminates both the political world of late colonial artisans and shopkeepers and the heightened fear of racial and class violence among the colonial governing class. It also indicates the many ways in which the powerful revolutionary ideas of the era penetrated the protective carapace of Spanish censorship and informed plebeian understandings of political legitimacy and class hierarchy.

In chapters 6 and 7 I use a broad mix of price, wage, and wealth measures to situate the plebe in the late colonial economy of Buenos Aires. I provide price estimates for basic commodities and apartment rentals and calculate a cost of living index, providing a tool for judging the impact of price history on plebeian lives. I use probate inventories and testaments to develop measures of average wealth for both skilled indoor and outdoor trades. These same records permit a tentative estimation of the distribution of wealth assets among production and consumption goods in the estates of artisans, small manufacturers, and laborers. Social historians have long assumed that Spanish immigrants enjoyed privileged access to opportunity and material benefits in the colonies. They also presume that the skilled trades that produced luxury goods had higher status and higher incomes than outdoor trades like carpentry or bricklaying. I use the best measure of material success, the wealth held at the time of death, to test these assumptions. In this rapidly growing viceregal capital, the native born and members of outdoor trades were more likely to acquire substantial wealth than European immigrants in the prestigious trades.

In chapter 7 I provide estimates of median wages for a range of skilled and unskilled laborers in Buenos Aires and show wages that rose dramatically in the last two decades of the colonial period. The rich records for Buenos Aires also permit a confident estimation of earnings for distinct skill levels within trades as well as the calculation of averages for broadly defined occupations. Among my findings is that artisans and laborers often elected leisure rather than work when presented with options. Finally, I use my indices of wages and prices to calculate a real-wage index that suggests the last decade of Spanish rule began with a deep and punishing contraction in the plebe's standard of living.

Chapter 8 connects this history to the large events that pulled Buenos Aires loose from the Spanish Empire and suggests that the experiences of plebeians were crucial to the development of popular political culture. The surrender of Buenos Aires to General Beresford in 1806 began an unforeseen transformation of the plebe as thousands rallied to the popular resistance and then, after victory, entered the militia.[2] This militarization eventually included the majority of the city's artisans and laborers, distorting the labor market, driving up wages, and drawing the plebe more actively into politics. I argue that the earlier collapse of the guild system and the steep decline in real wages after 1802 prepared the ground for these large changes. With few collective protections against economic hard times, the military emergency was both threat and promise for the plebe.[3] The hierarchies and collective ethos of military units mimicked the organization and social functions of the defunct guild order, providing an alternative integration in the urban civic order, while more predictably providing similar levels of income. Mobilized as members of militia units or present in popular demonstrations, the plebe would be visibly active in every large event from 1806 to 1810.

The obvious result of my long intellectual trajectory is an accumulated debt owed to numerous friends, colleagues, archivists, librarians, universities, and foundations. Now, as this book is published, I am provided with the opportunity to recognize the generosity and support of the numerous institutions that provided access to document collections and published materials or that supported my travel and research. It is also an opportunity to thank the many friends, colleagues, and editors who read drafts, suggested sources, raised issues of method and interpretation, tracked down citations, and, perhaps most importantly, provided the enthusiasm, interest, and engagement that has sustained my lonely hours in front of a computer monitor. If I have not included your name in the paragraphs that follow, please believe that I have remembered the kindness and intelligent guidance that is such an important part of our shared lives in this profession.

The Archivo General de la Nación (AGN) in Buenos Aires is a remarkable place. It was housed in an already decrepit building when I requested the first bundle of documents in the 1970s. The sad decline of this once grand building serves as a metaphor for the mismanagement and corruption that has blighted so much of Argentina's history during my career. There have been periods without elevator service and without photocopying services, even days without lights. Through it all, in periods with enlightened and visionary archival administration and in periods when this foundational institution of intellectual life was run by political appointees little concerned with conserving the nation's patrimony, the archive's professional staff have worked near miracles in conserving documents and making them available to scholars. While there was never adequate funding, the staff always did their best to make my visits productive. Over the years there has been such turnover in administration and staff, as the institution sought to react to budget pressures and political interference, that any attempt to recognize individually those who have aided my work would necessarily leave many out. Let me just say that this book is rooted in that collection and every chapter has depended upon the efforts of these professionals to support the discovery and conservation of Argentina's history in extremely difficult circumstances. I am very grateful. In Argentina I am also grateful to the staff of the Archivo Historico de la Provincia de Buenos Aires in La Plata for their assistance in accessing colonial era audiencia records.

I am also grateful for the efforts of the administration and staff of the Archivo General de las Indias in Seville, Spain. Nearly every historian of colonial Spanish America spends time in this remarkable setting, and all recognize the high standard of professionalism and the competence with which the staff services requests. Similarly, the staffs of the National Archives and Library of Congress Hispanic Division in Washington have striven to meet my every request for assistance, as have the librarians at University of North Carolina, Chapel Hill; Duke University; and the University of North Carolina, Charlotte.

I owe a special debt to the John Carter Brown Library (JCBL) in Providence, Rhode Island. At a moment when my tasks seemed insurmountable, the JCBL provided a six-month fellowship funded by the National Endowment for the Humanities and access to its wonderful collection of early publications from the Río de la Plata. The JCBL's staff provided me with crucial guidance in the collection as well as generous support and encouragement in my efforts to finish this book.

No Latin American historian can succeed without the support of foundations and government agencies as well as the resources of the universities that employ us. This project has been supported by three fellowships from the National Endowment for the Humanities, by a Senior Fulbright Fellowship, as well as by a series of summer grants from the American Philosophical Society, the Southern Regional Education Board, and the Foundation of the University of North Carolina, Charlotte. I would have had no hope of fully excavating the rich documentation this book is based on without this generous financial support.

My interest in the porteño plebe began as a graduate student at the University of Connecticut while working with the late Hugh Hamill. Hugh's enthusiasm for my research and his conviction that I had something important to say was crucial to me. Throughout my career I have tried to treat my own students with the warm encouragement that Hugh so reliably provided to me. Susan Socolow, Ken Andrien, Jerry Dávila, Herb Klein, and the anonymous readers provided by Duke University Press read the entire manuscript, and the version you have before you has been enriched by their comments and suggestions. Many other friends and colleagues have read chapters or sections of chapters, and their comments have helped me to focus my argument and improve my style. I especially want to acknowledge Ann Twinam, Donna Guy, David Holtby, and Mark Burkholder, who all, at crucial times, helped urge me forward. Two talented economic historians now deceased, Enrique Tandeter and Robert Gallman, generously read my discussions of wages, prices, and wealth holding at an early stage and guided me to the acquisition of new quantitative skills. Jenna Duncan provided crucial assistance in preparing the illustrations and maps found in this book, and I am grateful for her skill, patience, and generosity. Gabriela Braccio, Gustavo Paz, and Jorge Troisi generously tracked down archival material for me in Buenos Aires and La Plata when I was unable to travel. I am very grateful for their intelligence, determination, and archival skills.

This book is dedicated to my wife, Sue Johnson, who has accompanied me on numerous research trips and read hundreds, if not thousands, of drafts over the years. Her advice was always generous and sound, but, more importantly, her great patience with my passion for this project and the innumerable evenings, weekends, and whole summers it has consumed ultimately made this book possible. My children, Eliza, Ned, and Ben, played a crucial role as well by reminding me, gently and lovingly, that a sensible person ultimately must place career and professional achievement at the service of family. If this book has taken longer than it should have, I want you to know that I would not have traded one additional minute of time away from my family to have completed it sooner.

Introduction

On December 15, 1806, the pardo shoemakers Mariano Camara and Juan Josef Frutos wrote to the *fiscal* of the *audiencia* of Buenos Aires to protest a recent decision by one of the city's two alcaldes. The alcalde had assessed every shoemaker in the city sixteen and a half pesos to liquidate the accumulated legal costs associated with a long and unsuccessful effort to create a guild of shoemakers.[1] Camara and Frutos complained that they were not even apprentices seventeen years earlier when a group of master shoemakers, no longer active in the trade, incurred the first of these legal fees.[2] In many ways this is an unexceptional case, two men of humble circumstances appealing to Spanish colonial authorities to void an unfavorable judgment by a municipal officer. Historians of Spanish America have long used cases like this to suggest the myriad ways that indigenous groups, slaves, and free plebeians skillfully used Spanish law and legal institutions to protect customary practices or historic rights, demonstrating in the accumulation of examples the possibilities for human agency in a range of Spanish colonial settings.

While identifying themselves by *calidad* and occupation, traditional markers for social status in the Spanish colonies, Camara and Frutos simultaneously sought to escape consequences that attached to another important component of identity and status for the urban plebe, membership in a corporate craft organization. The back story to their appeal reveals a broad swath of the plebeian experience in late colonial Buenos Aires. The leaders of this craft first proposed the creation of a guild to Viceroy Juan José Vértiz y Salcedo (viceroy, 1778–1784) in 1779 but quickly dropped this idea in the face of unanticipated opposition from the cabildo. The shoemakers renewed their effort in 1788 when the first legal fees were assessed, but every attempt to write a constitution or elect guild officers led to conflicts within the craft and, in many cases, to heated confrontations with cabildo officers and eventually with the highest ranks of the Spanish colonial bureaucracy. No event was more important to this cycle of conflict than the 1793 decision by black and casta shoemakers to create a separate and racially segregated guild of their own. Excluded from guild offices and subjected to punitive fees and inspections by the Iberian immigrants who controlled the recently formed united guild, these humble artisans pursued their objective relentlessly, despite rejection by every level of the vice-regency's government. They would eventually appeal their case directly to the king.[3] In the end, ethnic and racial conflict among the shoemakers wrecked craft solidarity and wore out the patience of previously supportive colonial officials, leading in 1799 to a comprehensive rejection of traditional corporate craft organization by colonial authorities.[4] Camara and Frutos were the predictable products of this history, two skilled men with no direct experience with guilds forced to defend their individual savings from the burdensome and expensive legal legacy of an earlier generation's pursuit of the corporate ideal.

The rich cache of documents produced by the shoemakers reveals that members of this trade, as well as other artisans, often interacted with colonial administration in predictable ways, manipulating the prejudices of officials or exploiting the rivalries among colonial institutions as they sought to achieve their objectives. These documents also illuminate the highly charged and unpredictable ways that metropolitan understandings of race and ethnicity intersected with the social and cultural expectations and practices developed in the increasingly unstable, fluid, and contentious setting that was late colonial Buenos Aires. In this city traditional craft identity, buttressed by recruitment and training regimes long-established in Iberia, had survived in rough equilibrium with the powerful centrifugal effects of colonial racial and ethnic practice, but the rising tide of European immigration and the parallel development of the African slave trade after 1790 undercut the fragile compromises and convenient social fabrications that had made this tenuous balance sustainable.[5] Simultaneously, deepening integration in Atlantic commerce increased the city's vulnerability to the disruptions occasioned by a cycle of wars, starting with the American Revolution and continuing to the end of the Napoleonic period. These potent demographic, economic, and geopolitical forces made the social arrangements of 1776 unsustainable in 1800.

The timing of the appeal filed by Camara and Frutos in December 1806 situates these two men and the plebe more generally at a moment when transformative political and economic forces began to crest in Buenos Aires. Less than six months earlier, a small British force led by William Carr Beresford had captured Buenos Aires without meeting serious military resistance. Both the Spanish viceroy, Rafael de Sobremonte (viceroy, 1804–1807), and the Spanish garrison behaved badly in the face of this challenge. In the wake of the humiliating surrender that followed, Santiago de Liniers, a French nobleman serving in the Spanish Navy, cobbled together a popular volunteer force that returned the city to Spanish rule supported by a popular uprising. As a new, larger British force gathered in the estuary, the cabildo and militia officer corps recruited a new, much larger militia force and mobilized popular support to defend the city while at the same time marginalizing both the Spanish viceroy and audiencia. By the time these local forces defeated the second British expedition in July 1807, the Buenos Aires plebe was militarized.[6]

In this new era of almost continuous emergency, militia membership came to supplement or, in some cases, displace traditional plebeian identities that had previously attached to craft, workshop, ethnicity, or neighborhood. When the cabildo and military leadership decided to call militia units to active service in anticipation of the second invasion, they agreed to pay wages that in many cases surpassed those earned by plebeians in the civilian sector, accelerating the plebe's attachment to this popular new force. By 1810, militia regiments, marked off by unique uniforms, rituals, and values, had come to overshadow, without completely replacing, the traditional institutions and associations that had long-organized the Buenos Aires plebe.

A gravely weakened Spanish colonial administration and the appearance of a militarized urban population led inexorably to a political transformation of unforeseen scale and consequence. As the chapters that follow make clear, the plebeians of Buenos Aires were familiar with using an impressive array of political and legal tools to protect established rights and privileges or pursue new collective objectives like creating a guild of shoemakers. Addressing authorities directly or through their *apoderados*, artisans and laborers habitually evoked established colonial traditions or metropolitan practices as precedents, using the distinctive nomenclature and historic role of guilds and religious brotherhoods to remind local authorities of an idealized European corporate social order. The role of good government, they asserted, was to replicate this ideal.

The structure of this dialogue, artisans and other laborers addressing colonial authorities through the traditional forms of collective, corporate identity, could not survive the internal conflicts that fractured the shoemakers and other crafts in the 1790s and the mounting presence of slaves in all the city's skilled trades. As Spanish colonial institutions in the South Atlantic weakened under the sequential onslaught of two British attacks on Buenos Aires followed by the French invasion of Spain itself, local political power shifted decisively to the cabildo and the militia officer corps. Operating in uncharted territory after the decision to depose Viceroy Sobremonte in 1807, the leaders of these institutions routinely sought the massed support of the plebe, now redefined in the argot of the Atlantic's revolutionary age as "the people." These often cynical mobilizations did nothing to ameliorate the consequences that attended the debilitation of the craft tradition and increased competition from European manufactures, and, as a result, the plebe would enter the new political era threatened by the rising tide of Atlantic trade and dependent on military wages.

I began this book with the intention of writing a social history of the city's artisan population focused on the skilled trades alone.[7] Although artisans have remained at the center of my project, years of research have made it clear that artisans and other skilled tradesmen lived their lives in a much broader and more complex social and economic environment that included free laborers and slaves.[8] As the colonial era drew to a close in Buenos Aires, apprenticeships and less formal mechanisms of recruitment and training continued to define identity in narrow, craft-based ways for many. Similarly, seniority and skill, reinforced by wage differentials, continued as key determinants in masculine estimations of social place and hierarchy. Nevertheless, the complex functioning of local and international markets combined with the city's limited housing options, tight array of physical settings for leisure activities, and, especially after 1806, militia memberships to forge a much broader secondary identity as plebeians.[9]

Colonial-era records demonstrate clearly the web of residential, commercial, employment, and leisure experiences that integrated the lives of artisans, petty merchants, laborers, and even slaves in Buenos Aires. Men from different crafts or from different ranks and skill levels within single crafts were mixed together with laborers and even slaves in shared residences, gaming and drinking establishments, and, increasingly, in the workplace. In construction and port activities, for example, few employers recruited narrowly among traditionally trained and organized artisans. Instead, slaves and free men, whites, castas, and blacks, artisans and laborers, immigrants and the native born worked side by side. Even though wage differentials and job security continued to manifest the residual authority of traditional craft-based labor organization in Buenos Aires, the ability of master craftsmen to control the local labor market was much diminished by 1800.

In fact, master artisans were themselves often the agents of change. In traditional skilled trades like baking, shoemaking, metal trades, and apparel making, master artisans purchased slaves or hired lesser-skilled laborers to prepare materials, move finished goods to market, or to sell goods to the public in the city's markets in increasing numbers after 1790. This transformation advanced even more rapidly in the construction trades, where a majority of workers were laborers, not artisans trained in traditional ways. In late colonial Buenos Aires, skills were losing value and the established boundaries that separated artisans and laborers were collapsing as a series of wars brought the Spanish monopoly trade system to its knees and placed many local artisans and manufacturers in direct competition with a Europe well into the first stage of industrialization. Shoemaking, the city's largest trade, felt this competition more directly than most when, less than three years after Mariano Camara and Juan Josef Frutos wrote to the fiscal to protest the fees assessed by the alcalde, Viceroy Baltasar Hidalgo de Cisneros (viceroy, 1809–1810) opened Buenos Aires to British shipping. The first British vessel to legally unload goods disembarked 19,000 pairs of British factory-made shoes, effectively killing a year's demand for the common shoes worn by the plebe.[10]

While I focus on the experiences of the laboring men of late colonial Buenos Aires, sensible historians realize that they cannot disaggregate the lives of men and women without doing injury to the lived experiences of the past. Young men entering the trades depended on fathers and mothers for the advice, small loans, and connections that would launch their independent lives. In a city with large numbers of female-headed households, the role of mothers was even more consequential than in more-established and stable cities of the Spanish colonial world. Once married, plebeian husbands and wives functioned as economic units, pooling inheritances, earnings, skills, and labor power to make their way, a point I emphasize in my discussion of wealth, income, and material culture. If this study concentrates on the most masculine precincts of skilled and unskilled manual labor, it will hopefully serve as an invitation to colleagues to more fully engage the world of working women as well.[11]

My intention from the beginning has been to recover as fully as possible the lives of colonial-era working men and do justice to their struggles and achievements. The world of work was necessarily at the center of my enterprise, and I examine closely the ways that recruitment, training, and employment defined lives and connected individuals to the larger economy. This meant in practice that I had to carefully define and preserve boundaries between occupations, skill levels, and incomes. At the same time, my research made clear that over time the declining authority of craft organizations, the integration of less-skilled laborers in job sites previously controlled by artisan crafts, and the expanded slave trade obscured these boundaries. In creating a sensible template to use when deciding whether individuals or groups were in or out of my study I paid close attention to the ways that lives intersected in residential and leisure settings as well as in the economy. The backgrounds of marriage partners, wealth and income levels, and the assignment and manipulation of racial and ethnic identities all proved useful in focusing my research. While artisans, common laborers, and slaves are the focus of my study, I also explore the experiences of *pulperos*, other petty retailers, and some small-scale manufacturers as well. As a result, I do not use the word *plebe* to suggest a single uniform experience or a single structural relationship with the local and Atlantic economies or with the colonial social order. Instead, I emphasize the fluid and complex nature of class identity in this preindustrial setting.

While my examination of the late colonial plebe of Buenos Aires remains rooted in the concrete experiences of men and women who depended on the strength of their backs and arms and the skills of their hands, I strive to illuminate the ways these lives were affected by the large and powerful forces transforming the Atlantic world in the late eighteenth and early nineteenth centuries.[12] As I pursued this more ambitious goal, I was encouraged to find numerous intersections between my original interests and the larger political and economic topics that dominate the recent historiography of the

Atlantic world in the early nineteenth century, including free migration, the African slave trade, and the violent political beginnings of the revolutionary era.[13] At the same time, I realized that the reaction of the *porteño* plebe to these transformative forces illuminated the transition to independence in previously unappreciated ways.[14]

I have situated the plebe in a research design that integrates economic, political, and social history. This meant exploring sources and methods not traditionally attached to Spanish colonial social history, for example, the careful accumulation and analysis of wage and price records and probate inventories. Even in my use of more traditional sources, like criminal, census, and notary records, I have sought to satisfy expectations of representativeness and inclusiveness sensibly asserted by social scientists. When I turned to colonial notary copybooks to examine the topics of manumission, apprenticeship, and wealth holding, for example, I examined every surviving volume and extracted every manumission case, every apprenticeship, and every testament. Similarly, I went through the entire censuses of 1778 and 1810 to locate every artisan, every colonial treasury account, and every convent and hospital account book to track every wage payment or purchase of common consumption. While time consuming, this thoroughness permits me to write with some confidence about changes in material conditions and social organization across this crucial period.

This idiosyncratic odyssey is, perhaps, not a sensible way to write a book or organize a career, but, retrospectively, I am grateful that the passage of years, the discovery of new sources, and the acquisition of some new quantitative skills have prepared me to write a book very different from my initial intention, a book that reflects the dynamism and complexity that framed the lives of late colonial plebeians. My ambition is to place the porteño plebe in motion, to write a history that reveals more fully than previous studies the ways in which laboring men and their families calculated and acted upon the opportunities and threats that attended the rapid rise of this South Atlantic colonial city. In pursuing this end, I hope that I have forced the revision of many assumptions about the colonial history of Buenos Aires.

Late colonial Buenos Aires, among the Spanish colonial cities most transformed by the Bourbon project and among those most completely integrated into the Atlantic World in 1800, was the first Spanish American city of consequence to establish effective political independence. In this large and dramatic political moment, the porteño plebe played an active and influential role. Yet, among historians of late colonial Spanish America, Buenos Aires has attracted little attention outside Argentine academic circles.[15] The great viceregal capitals of Lima and Mexico City dominate the literature of the late colonial period, but Bogotá, Caracas, and Quito have also found a better-established place in the historical literature of this period than has Buenos Aires. This hierarchy of scholarly attention seems instinctively correct to anyone who has visited these cities in modern times. The colonial past is hardly present in modern Buenos Aires. All that is left of the city that existed in 1810 are a few late colonial churches, a handful of colonial-era residences, and the cabildo building, a once imposing building now comically trimmed to half its original size to facilitate the construction of two diagonal streets more than a century ago. If compared with the surviving glories of the past retained by Spain's other colonial capitals, the architectural legacy of colonial Buenos Aires seems to justify its marginalization in the historiography. In fact, late-eighteenth-century Buenos Aires, despite its elevation as a viceregal capital, was a city of modest pretensions, as was pointed out by foreign visitors who often remarked on the poverty of the ecclesiastical establishment and the lack of grandeur in the buildings of the colonial government.[16]

As a result, the city hardly appears in the large historical narratives of the Spanish colonial era that are dominated by Mesoamerican and Andean events and themes. When Buenos Aires does appear in this larger story it is at the very end of the colonial period, introduced narrowly in brief descriptions of the British invasions of 1806 and 1807 or the political events of May 1810. Colonial Río de la Plata specialists in Argentina, Europe, and the United States have had little success in inserting this regional history into the broad discussion of the Spanish Empire. The emergence of Atlantic history in the last decade, however, has provided a new, more hospitable context for connecting the history of Buenos Aires and the colonial Río de la Plata to the concerns of a much broader community of scholars.

The city grew rapidly after 1776 when the Crown established the Viceroyalty of Río de la Plata and made Buenos Aires its capital. Population expanded from roughly 25,000 in 1776 (about the size of New York City in 1775) to more than 60,000 in 1810 (about the size of Lima at that time). This rapid population growth resulted primarily from immigration. Free immigrants from Europe and the interior of the viceroyalty arrived in large numbers after 1780 as the economy expanded employment opportunities and commercial volume. Slave trades with Brazil and directly with Africa also increased dramatically after 1780 and rose to their peaks after 1795. Every city block, work place, market, and apartment house mixed these human ingredients with the native born in unpredictable ways, facilitating cultural exchange, challenging traditional ideas about race and identity, and producing a proliferating series of tensions and conflicts that marked plebeian life in the last decades of Spanish rule.

The city's dependence on these continuing streams of international and regional migrants affected the full array of urban social arrangements. This was a young population and a very masculine population, at least until the 1790s when the migration of young women from provincial towns and the viceroyalty's interior provinces steeply increased. Colonial censuses reveal both large numbers of female-headed households and large numbers of apartments packed with single men. Although the physical city expanded steadily, this fluid and restless urban population relentlessly pressed against the space provided by the built environment.

Across more than three decades, a smaller, but still substantial, outmigration mimicked the rhythms and pace of in-migration to Buenos Aires and the surrounding region. While large numbers of free migrants from the interior and Europe arrived, put down roots (marrying, purchasing houses, or opening shops and small factories) and stayed, many others decided to move on after testing their chances in the city. These free out-migrants, mostly men in their teens and twenties, had arrived in Buenos Aires, worked for months or even years, and then decided to move on to Alto Peru, Chile, or, in many cases, Montevideo across the estuary. Some returned home to Europe or to distant interior cities and towns.

While the constraints of their legal condition prevented slaves from following this restless circulation, the slave trade itself imitated in broad outline the movement of free laborers. Until the 1790s, Buenos Aires merchants bought slaves imported from Brazil or Africa and then resold the majority to purchasers in Alto Peru, Chile, and Paraguay or to the viceroyalty's interior provinces, especially Córdoba. By the end of that decade, however, the vast majority of slaves imported to estuary ports were retained in urban Buenos Aires by a growing economy and by the rising return on investment offered to local slave owners by rising local wages. Nevertheless, fluctuations in regional economic performance continued to move slaves back and forth between urban and rural economic sectors throughout this period.

This powerful ebb and flow of population affected wages, real estate values, and the pace of local agricultural expansion. It also powerfully affected the organization of work in Buenos Aires. Nearly all the cities of the Spanish New World evolved some version of the guild-based manufacturing system developed in early-modern Iberia.[17] This system was most completely replicated in the richest viceregal capitals, Mexico City and Lima, but its essential elements can be identified in smaller and poorer places like Guatemala City, Quito, and other second-tier colonial cities. In each of these colonial venues Spanish immigrant craftsmen served as vectors for the transmission and implantation of the essential cultural and economic structures associated with this tradition. These immigrant artisans introduced craft technologies, found the necessary raw materials, recruited and trained apprentices and journeymen, and formulated guild regulations. They also formed cofradías (lay brotherhoods) that organized collective participation in secular and religious festivals and provided an array of spiritual and social welfare benefits. The prior experiences and official ideology of the colonial administrative class predisposed officials to promote and sponsor guilds and cofradías, but the long-term vitality of these institutions in American urban settings depended, at least initially, on the wealth, connections and determination of the European-born segment of the artisan community. Where guilds and cofradías were established, natives, slaves, and free castas eventually constituted majorities within these artisanal institutions, a process that deeply altered and invigorated in unpredictable ways the American variants of these Iberian institutions, even where European immigration continued.

The presence of a critical mass of European-trained craftsmen occurred late in the history of colonial Buenos Aires. It was only with the creation of the viceroyalty that local demand for the products and services of skilled craftsmen reached the level that would sustain a traditionally organized artisan community and attract large numbers of Spanish and other European craftsmen. As a result, the effort to create guilds and establish cofradías began well after the powerful economic and ideological forces that would ultimately sweep away these institutions and values had already gathered on the European flank of the Atlantic Basin.[18]

Even as recently arrived European artisans initiated efforts in Buenos Aires to create guilds and strengthen other elements of traditional labor organization, the plebe was being transformed by a booming South Atlantic slave trade and a dramatically increased volume of free casta migrants from the cities and towns of the viceregal interior. Neither population arrived with strong attachments to the guild tradition. Inevitably, craft standards and training regimes in colonial Buenos Aires were soon complicated by rising levels of ethnic tension and disputes over craft standards. Transplanted from societies where guilds still routinely demanded proof of *limpieza de sangre*, Spanish and other European immigrant artisans once in Buenos Aires and engaged in the drafting of guild regulations were pulled in the direction of racial discrimination like moths to a flame. This inclination to "colonize" the workshops and markets of Buenos Aires was predictable, despite the late date of these guild initiatives. The resourceful and determined resistance of black and casta artisans to racial domination in the trades of Buenos Aires demonstrates the limits and vulnerabilities present in the presumed hierarchies of race and ethnicity in this colonial city.

This is not a book about gender, but, because it is impossible to write a book about workingmen in the Iberian Atlantic and ignore masculinity and the culture of honor, these topics inform nearly every section of the book. Years ago when traveling with a friend in rural Catamarca we came across a country bricklayer and his young apprentice on their way to a job at a distant estancia. As was still the custom in this region, the man and boy traveled on horseback. In lonely places like this empty countryside travelers pause to enjoy conversation whenever possible and we spent a half hour exchanging the bits and pieces of who we were and what we were doing. In the course of our conversation this artisan told us that the boy's mother, a local widow, had "given" him the boy "to make him a man." In the previous weeks prior to this trip I had worked through scores of apprenticeship contracts in the national archive in Buenos Aires and this conversation served as a revelation. Apprenticeship and less-formal mentoring structures passed on much more than craft skills; young men and boys acquired masculine identity and skill simultaneously, and once acquired these values and behaviors guided the life trajectories of laboring men.

In late colonial Buenos Aires, boys entered the skilled trades or sought work as laborers at very young ages. It was not uncommon for parents, guardians, or slave owners to place boys as apprentices before their tenth birthday. Most boys from poor families went into the streets at similar ages to seek work as *jornaleros* (day laborers), accompanying fathers, uncles, or older male neighbors to the markets and worksites where jobbers hired laborers. Once pulled within these orbits, boys learned values and behaviors that would inform their decisions and actions during the remainder of their lives. They learned what they should say to other males without provoking violence and learned what they could not tolerate in the words and actions of other males without losing face. They learned the value of courage as well as the need to recognize situations that demanded the performance of deference, for example, when confronted by members of the *gente decente* or by their masters. They apprehended the crucial importance of skill and competence in fixing the place of men among workmates and neighbors. In their integration into the world of work, they learned to be men. But this was a prickly business where many challenges and insults could not be tolerated without being shamed. The defense of honor, a first order lesson along the way to manhood, was a dangerous burden.

We should presume that these values, often interrogated by historians in relationship to violent crime or the physical abuse of women, were present in more politicized environments as well. Certainly the language and aggressive behaviors of porteño artisans during disputes over guild formation or in confrontations with authorities over standards and prices reveal their sensitivity to presumed insult and their refusal to accept domination by others, providing a recurring script of plebeian protest and violence to the end of the colonial period. It is also clear that the citywide revulsion and anger that followed the surrender of Buenos Aires to General Beresford in 1806 was at its roots the collective experience of shame. This powerful sentiment pulled nearly the entire laboring class into the armed uprising that returned the city to Spanish rule forty-five days later and found expression in the angry popular demonstrations that soon demanded the destitution of Viceroy Sobremonte. Numerous contemporary sources remarked that the crowds of plebeians gathered in front of the cabildo had extravagantly insulted the viceroy as a coward and traitor. Once mobilized and militarized the Buenos Aires plebe helped propel the city to effective independence in May 1810. As the plebe found its voice in the demonstrations and armed actions along this route, the language of popular political ambitions borrowed heavily from the vocabulary of masculine honor.

I am firmly convinced that historians cannot adequately capture the history of workingmen, indeed the history of the popular classes generally, without locating these lives within the economic contexts that were so influential in determining their life trajectories.[19] I believe it a great misfortune that so many Latin American historians interested in the popular classes have failed to situate their research within the economic structures that framed those lives.[20] The rhythms of fiscal regimes, the ebb and flow of commercial traffic, and the long arc of mining production are all crucial to our efforts to understand the Spanish colonial economy but are too often present only as stage props in the social history of our field. As we have pursued the lives of market women, laborers, artisans, and slaves as they struggled to survive in difficult conditions, we have not committed ourselves to connect these lives to the large forces that held the power to shape opportunities and distribute resources as well as to crush aspirations. As I developed this project, I paused to improve my statistical skills and spent more than two additional years in archival research to develop wage and price series from surviving records. I then undertook a systematic exploration of colonial-era probate records to calculate measures of average wealth for the colonial plebe. Recognizing that many readers drawn to my topic may have limited experience with economic history, I have struggled to make my results accessible and useful to colleagues less patient with graphs and tables.

My close analysis of employment records reinforced earlier conclusions drawn from more traditional social historical records like criminal cases and the reports of colonial officials; the plebeians of Buenos Aires invented, enforced, and defended their own hierarchies of skill, physical competence, income, age, and race. Some of this is obvious. Masters insisted on the subordination of the journeymen and apprentices they employed. Some skilled trades, silversmiths for example, regarded other trades, like shoemaking and carpentry, as inferior. Some artisans died rich while most died poor. Some artisans and laborers married, but many more remained too poor to afford the housing and provisioning that a family demanded. These distinctions and hierarchies, presumed or real, were fiercely defended through legal actions, face-to-face arguments, or, sometimes, violence. While it is often useful to employ broadly conceived terms like subaltern, a term with many advocates, or even plebeian, the contemporary category I use in this study, we must recognize the importance of difference and hierarchy to the men and women who bore the weight of this society on their shoulders. This is why we must test the interpretive insights we presume when we use broad occupational categories, like baker, carpenter, or bricklayer, found in censuses or official reports to define social standing or wealth. Plebeians were sophisticated social observers, sensitive to differences and hierarchies largely invisible in these sources. The category-subverting reality of their lives requires us to honor their understandings.

In the course of this analysis, I insert the individual and collective experiences of artisans and laborers in late colonial Buenos Aires within the powerful mechanisms of production and exchange that revolutionized the Atlantic economy between 1750 and 1850. In Buenos Aires, opportunities to find work, earn adequate wages, save, and achieve social mobility all depended on the city's ability to benefit from its position as a point of exchange that connected Atlantic commerce, Andean mining, the expansive farms and ranches of the Río de la Plata, and local artisanal production. While networks of friends and family were crucial to the daily business of finding work and securing shelter, this larger economy could determine life trajectories in unpredictable ways. Skill and experience had value only in relationship to the city's need for labor. This brief survey suggests that the city's economy and population pulsed reciprocally with the rhythm of Atlantic events. The intensifying pace of warfare following 1789 repeatedly constricted the trade of the city and slowed the flow of immigration. These large forces pushed prices and wages higher with the more rapid upward movement of prices undermining the hard-won material well-being of the plebe. Periods of peace, on the other hand, brought bulging ships filled with goods to estuary ports and led to lower prices, as well as to an increased pace of free immigration and slave imports. Municipal and colonial fiscal establishments were cyclically beneficiaries and victims of these events as well. Like the major port cities of Anglophone North America and the Caribbean, the Buenos Aires economy moved in close syncopation with the Atlantic economy while local colonial administration and popular political understandings were compelled to react to the powerful events that shook Europe and the Caribbean.[21]

Artisans and laborers as well as slaves followed these system-shaking events in France and Saint-Domingue in formal and informal ways with the literate minority sharing pamphlets and periodicals from Europe and the illiterate majority sharing news and gossip heard from arriving ship crews and from migrating laborers from Europe or other American colonies, especially Brazil. In urban markets, taverns, billiard parlors, and food stalls, slaves as well as free artisans and laborers eagerly discussed and debated news from these distant foci of revolutionary change.[22] Horror and anticipation contested for purchase across the city.[23] While an adventurous and bold few said that Robespierre could "rule the world" and others hinted darkly that the Spanish could usefully imitate the French, many members of the plebe expressed horror and rage over France's attack on Spain and the apparent excitement of servile insurrection in the Caribbean by the partisans of liberty. That single word, *liberty*, had become by 1795 a shorthand evocation of the spirit of this new age, leading to arrests and judicial tortures in Buenos Aires.[24]

While war between Spain and revolutionary France unleashed powerful political forces in Buenos Aires and led ultimately to the arrest of scores of artisans, the global contest between Napoleonic France and England after 1803 would prove much more consequential for the city and its plebe. With Spain pulled into an asymmetrical alliance with Napoleonic France, Buenos Aires became the target for an English attack in 1806. Left nearly defenseless by the viceroy's decisions to flee the city, save the colonial treasury, and evacuate his most effective troops, remaining Spanish officers surrendered Buenos Aires to an English force of fewer than 1,600. This event set in motion the militarization of the plebe, a second British invasion, the removal of the viceroy by the actions of a popular assembly, and the first appearance of a Romantic style of popular political representation, a vocabulary of gestures and ritualized interactions with the plebe first rehearsed in Buenos Aires by Santiago de Liniers, that would cumulatively propel the city towards the creation of a junta in May 1810.

This book is an effort to broadly explore the colonial plebe of Buenos Aires, an effort to place that plebe at the center of the history of this city and nation. The instrumental events of 1810 were not at root a plebeian insurrection, but the history of the late colonial plebe transforms our understandings of these events. Traditional forms of artisan organization were lost in a series of complex confrontations fought across ethnic and racial lines by 1800. Many skilled trades confronted the effects of direct competition with distant manufactures as the city was incrementally opened to trade neutrals and allies after 1796; the opening of the port to direct trade with Britain in 1809 culminated rather than initiated this competition. The growing volume of slaves also unsettled the organization of work and the structures of recruitment and employment. By 1810, there was little left of associations of mutuality and identity that had previously bound the plebe to the colonial state. The colonial sources have proven rich and varied, and the voices of these humble men and women are clear and convincing as they explain their world to us.

I | Plebeian City

Late Colonial Buenos Aires

In February 1772, the slave Gregorio Ygnacio de Echeverria appealed to the *alcalde de segundo voto*, who served as *defensor de pobres, indios y esclavos*, to intervene in what had become for him an impossible situation. Twenty years earlier, Gregorio's mother, a free morena, had given his original master a 150 peso down payment toward his manumission. They had agreed that Gregorio's future wages in the building trades would provide the remaining 190 pesos. His original master put this agreement in doubt when he sold Gregorio to Nicolás Zarco, who owned a small brickyard. Even though Gregorio served as the brickyard's supervisor, his new master beat him in front of the other slaves and free laborers when he sought to clarify his legal status. When this humiliation failed to quiet Gregorio's protests, Zarco turned again to the whip. Unwilling to live with this treatment, Gregorio ran away.

From his hiding place, Gregorio protested to the defensor that after twenty years in the "most subordinated servitude," he was now "compensated with ever harsher punishments and harder labors." He begged the defensor "to avoid the fatal consequences" of sending him back into the hands of his enemy. While the defensor did not return Gregorio to Zarco, he forced Gregorio to pay the full 190 pesos for manumission without any recognition of the terms of the original agreement between his mother and first master or his twenty years of labor.[1]

Like Zarco, many artisans and small manufacturers in late colonial Buenos Aires owned slaves. While most owned only one or two slaves, the most successful owned more than ten.[2] The majority of these masters and slaves worked and lived together, sharing hard labor, humble housing, and rough meals. In most cases, there were few differences in the material circumstances of masters and slaves. Many slave owners were castas or, in a small number of cases, recently freed former slaves. In this case, Gregorio lived in Zarco's humble *rancho*, with its straw roof and mud walls, and shared sleeping quarters and meals with a mixed crew of free laborers and slaves. Nevertheless, Gregorio's long struggle to escape bondage reminds us that the differences between slavery and freedom were very consequential.

Nicolás Zarco was not a rich or important person, but he was able to control his slave's life in arbitrary and cruel ways as he obstructed Gregorio's struggle to gain freedom. If the defensor found a way for Gregorio to escape his captivity, he also took care to protect Zarco's property rights in the process. Slavery allowed men like Zarco to build their businesses and multiply their wealth, but it simultaneously eroded the egalitarian and corporatist underpinnings of traditionally organized skilled trades. Artisans and small manufacturers as well as many petty retailers funded their growing dependence on slave labor by discounting the once valuable coinage of corporate ideals.

In the late colonial period, the Buenos Aires plebe expanded in numbers and complexity in a built environment that flexed and strained to keep up with population growth and a surging local economy. The city's streets, plazas, and markets framed the search for work and leisure, creating small worlds where artisans and laborers worked, found friendship, and began families. The city's physical spaces, workshops, houses, and apartments, pushed the men and women of the laboring class together or pulled them apart, strengthening, or sometimes subverting, the social boundaries of occupation, skill level, marital status, ethnicity, and legal condition.

The city's fluid and dynamic demography, its constantly changing mix of origins, identities, and skills, also framed the lives of artisans and laborers. The decision of the Spanish Crown to create the Viceroyalty of Río de la Plata and make Buenos Aires its capital in 1776 initiated a long period of demographic growth and economic expansion. In this environment of scarce labor and high wages, the city attracted large numbers of free migrants from the interior and from Europe, and these new arrivals in turn challenged existing understandings of racial and ethnic identity negotiated in the less dynamic decades before their arrival. The growing importation of slaves after 1780 supplemented this stream of free labor, and this expanded slave trade eventually transformed the local labor market, placing slaves in nearly every craft — and calling into question the very viability of traditional artisanal forms.

The Cityscape

In 1780 Buenos Aires was the least distinguished viceregal capital in Spain's American empire. According to the city census of 1778, it was a city of approximately 25,000 inhabitants, although Spanish officials and visitors often claimed the city population was larger. It was also an immigrant city. African slaves, recently freed blacks (mostly recent arrivals), and casta migrants from the interior provinces or from more distant Spanish colonies constituted nearly 35 percent of the urban population and an even larger percentage of the populations of nearby small towns scattered across the countryside. Another 20 percent of the city's residents were European immigrants, mostly Spaniards but hundreds of Portuguese and Italians as well. While the city experienced steady immigrant-driven population growth from the 1770s to the end of the colonial period, it sent a reciprocal stream of out-migrants in search of better prospects across the river to Montevideo, along the much longer riverine routes to Santa Fe or Paraguay, or overland to Chile and the Andean provinces. Like in the better-known modern era of immigration in the late nineteenth century and early twentieth, Buenos Aires in the eighteenth century and early nineteenth both attracted waves of migrants and served as an important source of migrants across the whole Río de la Plata region.

Contraband trade dominated the city's early history.[3] In fact, it was the Spanish Crown's desire to stem the illegal flow of Andean silver through Buenos Aires to European rivals that led to the decision to create the Viceroyalty of Río de la Plata.[4] Over the next thirty-five years, the presence of a viceroy, an *audiencia*, an enlarged colonial bureaucracy, and an enhanced coast guard, naval force, and garrison failed to suppress the long-established willingness of the local merchant community to bend the law or the eagerness of Spanish officials to line their pockets.[5] By the last decade of the colonial period, changes in commercial policy permitted by a Spanish Crown facing enormous fiscal pressures pushed the door further open.[6] The era's succession of wars disrupted Atlantic trade and forced the Spanish Crown to grant neutral ships access to Buenos Aires. The Crown also permitted local merchants to purchase foreign vessels to use in neutral trade as well as in the African slave trade. In practice, these measures served as a thin disguise for a dramatic expansion of contraband trade.[7] Across the long sweep of the colonial period, smuggling and official corruption created a resilient legacy of freewheeling commerce and lax official oversight.[8]

With the possible exception of the small army of cart drivers and muleteers recruited in the small towns and villages of the viceroyalty's interior, the physical city impressed few visitors. Passengers arriving from Europe, Brazil, or the Caribbean disembarked in one of three inconvenient locations. The deepwater port of Montevideo was the most secure regional harbor, but goods and passengers arriving there had to be carried more than 140 miles to Buenos Aires in small boats. Some large vessels chose to anchor in deep water well off the Buenos Aires riverfront and land their cargos and passengers via a system of small boats and wagons. Smaller ships with shallow drafts could enter the Riachuelo. Once ashore there, however, passengers faced a long, muddy transit to the city.

Thomas Falkner reported in 1774 that "Buenos Ayres (properly speaking) has no port, but only an open river, exposed to all the winds. [This is] because the shallowness of the coast obliges ships to come to anchor three leagues from the land."[9] Twenty years later, another British traveler reiterated that no ship "can approach nearer the town than three or four leagues."[10] As a result, small boats carried passengers, their bags, and freight in the initial stage of disembarkation, and then, as the shore rose up to meet them, people and goods were transferred to rough, horse-drawn carts mounted on huge wheels to traverse the last hundreds of yards to shore.[11]

Whatever appearance of urban grandeur strangers thought they had glimpsed in the distance from shipboard was erased incrementally by the town's humble built environment. At the riverbank, the customs house and walls of the decrepit fort framed a first glance of the city's central political and commercial precinct. The modest physical presence of Spanish imperial authority, municipal governance, and ecclesiastical power were arrayed around the central plaza, the Plaza Mayor. The cabildo was located opposite the fortress at the far side of this large and open plaza.[12] On the cabildo's left flank was the still unfinished cathedral. If the cabildo expressed local political ambitions and the merchant elite's growing sense of self importance and power, the unfinished cathedral and the relative obscurity and small size of the city's convents and parish churches suggested a church

FIGURE I Shallow water forced ships arriving in Buenos Aires to anchor well offshore and transfer passengers and goods to small boats and then to wagons like the one pictured here.
Source: Gregorio Ibarra, *Trajes y costumbres de la Provincia de Buenos Aires* (Buenos Aires: César Hippoly te Bacle y compania, 1833).

establishment weakened decades earlier by the expulsion of the Jesuits and now constrained in its ambitions by limited funds.

Across the expanse separating the authority of the viceroy from that of the town council sprawled the busy public market with neighboring food stalls, cafes, *confiterías*, and taverns.[13] At best, municipal regulation and local custom proved to be a poor defense for the boundary between the seat of local authority, the cabildo, and the organized chaos of the city's major market. The commerce of the Plaza Mayor routinely pushed its way into the ground floor of the cabildo building and even onto the steps of the cathedral. During the rainy season, butchers routinely relocated their stocks of beef and pork to the hallways of the cabildo from their stalls in the plaza, leading the councilors to complain that blood and offal were destroying the building's tile floors.[14] This was simply one symptom of the city's lack of hygiene and cleanliness. Until 1800, there was no organized effort to remove the piles of waste accumulated in the plaza by the end of a market day. The powerful odors of spoiled meats, fruits, and vegetables left behind by market venders combined with the equally powerful smells from the nearby pastures that hosted the thousands of grazing oxen, horses, and mules used to move carts and wagons to city markets. The casual, uninhibited use of city streets as garbage dumps or worse pushed the raw, exterior world of decay and waste through the doors and windows of even the richest households.[15]

The city's jail was located behind the cabildo, and the cries of poor prisoners begging for a crust of bread or a small coin assailed pedestrians on their way to and from the market. Subsistence for prisoners was provided by leftovers from city convents and day-old or spoiled bread donated by bakers because the municipal authorities provided no budget for prisoners' meals. When finally forced to confront the near starvation afflicting its prisoners, the cabildo hired a stonemason to place a grilled window at ground level to facilitate their begging.[16]

A short distance away from this intersection of commerce and politics were the temporary encampments of cart drivers and muleteers who connected the capital with its dependencies in the interior of the viceroyalty. The cabildo repeatedly attempted to ban the passage of large carts drawn by teams of four to eight oxen. These awkward but durable conveyances hauled the goods the city required from Córdoba, Mendoza, Salta, and other points to the north and west, but they had a destructive impact on streets and plazas. Each prohibition faced massive complaints from merchants and petty retailers who resented the complications imposed on deliveries.

As a compromise, the city initially permitted smaller, lighter carts pulled by only two oxen as well as horse carts and mule teams to enter the city center. This expedient ultimately failed because three or four of the smaller carts were necessary to carry the goods brought from the port at Riachuelo or from the interior by a single large cart, and, as a result, transportation costs increased and traffic congestion intensified around the Plaza Mayor.[17] In the end, the cabildo agreed to permit large carts on the streets in the early morning and at dusk. This schedule forced cart drivers, muleteers, and the laborers they employed to remain in the center until the markets closed. They spent hours napping or talking in the shelter of the carts' great bulk as they waited for return cargos. The English visitor John Mawe dismissed these porters and carters as "idle and dissolute," and claimed that "when they have a little money, they drink and gamble, and when penniless, they sometimes betake themselves to pilfering."[18]

During the heat of the day laborers and drivers wandered off to join un-

FIGURE 2 The Plaza Mayor in Buenos Aires, location of the city's largest market. The Recova, the arched building in the background, bisected the plaza. Its interior spaces housed the shops of artisans and petty merchants. Source: Emeric Essex Vidal, *Picturesque Illustrations of Buenos Ayres and Monte Video, Consisting of Twenty-four Views* (London: R. Ackermann, 1820).

employed artisans and day laborers in the taverns and gaming places along the narrow streets that led away from the river. The transportation sector was essential to the city's economy, but authorities relentlessly held to the opinion that the hundreds of temporary sojourners present in the city on any day were essentially lawless and lazy. Police officials interpreted the time spent by crews waiting to accumulate cargos for return trips as idleness providing an opportunity for criminality. While the hundreds of drivers and peones who lounged around the carts or congregated in the pulperías scandalized the city's *gente decente*, the days or weeks (often months) of dangerous and exhausting work needed to bring cargo to Buenos Aires from the interior was little appreciated by city residents.

The layout of the city was organized in the familiar grid pattern that framed Spanish urbanization across much of the continent.[19] Despite the appearance of order conferred by the grid, the built environment had developed with little guidance and few restraints in Buenos Aires. Before 1776, individual property owners routinely sought to increase the size of their residences and commercial buildings by ignoring regulations intended to maintain the width of streets, stealing up to a vara (32.9 inches) or sometimes more of living or working space from the public way. As a result, in parts of the city center, it was impossible for two carts to pass at once. More-ephemeral intrusions contributed to urban congestion as well. Carpenters, furniture makers, and smiths often moved their work into the street to escape the confines of small rented spaces. Bakers, brickmakers, and millers routinely stacked wood and charcoal for furnaces and ovens as well as other supplies in the street, interfering with the passage of pedestrians and cart traffic. In the warmer months, artisans in the indoor trades, tailors, shoemakers, and even silversmiths often escaped the dark and airless interior spaces of their shops by moving tables and benches into the street, taking advantage of sunlight and cleaner air.[20]

At midcentury, most of the private residences in Buenos Aires had been constructed from adobe, and the majority had straw roofs. One Jesuit passing through the city in 1729 wrote, "the houses are low, of a single floor, and the majority is made of raw earth. Each [is] a rectangle of four walls without a single window, receiving whatever light possible through the open door."[21] As the city grew and prospered after 1776, urban construction became more substantial and better regulated. City authorities began to require building permits by 1788 and carefully scrutinized the design and location of new construction in the city center.[22] As the city's wealth grew, property owners tore down older structures in the blocks surrounding the Plaza Mayor and replaced them with flat-roofed brick buildings, many with a second story. One English resident in 1797 found "the middle of the city . . . better, and some of the principal streets [had] a show of opulence and taste that [was] very agreeable."[23] However, even during the long era of expansion in the 1780s and early 1790s, some rundown or abandoned buildings remained to blight the city center.

The Jesuits claimed that they had introduced brick and tile making to the city as a necessary support for the construction of their college.[24] Whether they deserved the authorship of this innovation or not, we know that by 1780 local artisans produced brick in large volume. In fact, brick manufacturers along with the city's bakers maintained the largest workforces in the city, employing both slaves and free laborers. In many cases, slaves were in charge of the day-to-day operations of these substantial businesses.[25] The mounting volume of brick production in Buenos Aires lowered prices and eventually allowed householders of modest resources to build two-story residences imitating contemporary metropolitan Spanish styles.[26] Travelers to Buenos Aires in the 1790s favorably noted that the brick buildings nearest the Plaza Mayor were whitewashed and that some of the streets were paved, although imperfectly, with brick or stone.[27]

Despite repeated campaigns mounted to force the paving of city streets in the decades that followed the creation of the viceroyalty, most streets were still unpaved at the end of the colonial period. The blocks closest to the Plaza Mayor were the only predictable exceptions. Viceroy Nicolás de Arredondo admitted to his successor in 1795 that most streets remained unpaved, and, as a result, most streets were subject to flooding in the winter and blanketed by dust in the summer.[28] Some prosperous householders outside the city center privately paid to pave a walkway in front of their homes, but this meant in practice that fifty or a hundred yards of paving could quickly give way to five blocks of muck and refuse. The cabildo's effort to enforce the paving of crosswalks at corners as a less costly alternative to paving the entire city fell victim to the high cost of labor and the poor quality of the work done by prisoners used to reduce the expense. At the end of the colonial period, after four decades of population growth and commercial expansion, it was still impossible to walk ten blocks from the central plaza in any direction on stone or brick paving.

The city's largest homes had two or three interior patios and extended the width of a city block with doors facing both front and back streets. Some had heavy double doors set in impressive masonry frames topped by crenellated arches that, in a few instances, displayed family crests. Interior rooms opened onto the patios and connected internally without hallways. Merchants and the top echelon of the colonial political establishment owned these residences and maintained large households that included free and slave dependents as well as family members. However, even in the homes of wealthy merchants, it was common to dedicate space on the lower floor to commerce. The absence of decent hotels or inns in Buenos Aires also meant that wealthy residents sometimes rented rooms to visiting merchants or to Spanish officials.[29] A few affluent homes used the second patio as a garden. More commonly, dependents lived in rooms that opened onto the second patio where kitchens were also located. In the largest homes, a third patio faced the back street and sometimes housed stables or a small number of fruit trees. In two-story homes, the proprietor's family lived above the clutter of commerce and household necessity at street level. These large residences were not monuments to class or race segregation; they were instead settings within which slaves, free servants, temporary laborers, artisans, commercial apprentices, and renters routinely interacted, in predictably deferential ways, with the city's richest merchants and officials.

Smaller, one-story homes were far more common in the city. Even well established members of the merchant class often lived in one-story residences. Master artisans, pulperos, and other petty retailers did as well. These groups generally preferred corner locations. These *esquinas* featured a front door turned forty-five degrees to face two intersecting streets, giving maximum access to pedestrian traffic. In esquinas the door was cut at waist level and fitted with a shelf so the merchant, retailer, or artisan could engage clients passing in the street from the shelter of his shop. As a result, small crowds of customers periodically massed at these doorways, producing additional congestion in the narrow streets. In most cases, the families of pulperos and artisans lived in a single room located behind the retail space of the esquina. In these venues, commerce and family life intersected throughout the day. All across the city, private and public space were permeable and necessarily ambiguous venues.

Multifamily residences were increasingly common in the late colonial city. First generation structures were in most cases the former homes of once wealthy families now broken up into small apartments and single rooms. A new generation of purpose-built, multifamily residences was in service in Buenos Aires by the late 1780s. In an era of steeply rising real estate prices that closed off home ownership to all but the most prosperous plebeians, speculators were able to harvest high rents from the city's fast growing population. Typically, renters had only a single room with access to additional shared living space in the patio and, perhaps, to an oven or open fire for cooking. By 1800, groups of single laborers or artisans, often as many as five or six, shared twenty-by-twenty-foot rented rooms in many multifamily residences. In this environment, privacy was an impossible dream, but thousands lived in worse conditions. Many poor urban residents paid a small amount to sleep in the shelter of the open interior patio in one of these buildings. Some poor families constructed ranchos, adobe or mud and wattle walls covered by a straw roof, on the southern and eastern flanks of the city to escape the high rents and real estate costs of the urban center. The city's poorest residents slept rough under the *portales* of the cabildo or in doorways near the market. Limited housing options and high rents effectively placed a brake on family formation for the poor, since family life required at least minimal privacy.

The Plaza Mayor fronting the fortress remained the ceremonial center of the city. It was the major market, and all major religious and civic festivals were organized and performed there until the end of the colonial period. It was here that the viceroy, archbishop, audiencia, and cabildo displayed whatever public grandeur they could muster in the seldom-realized intention of awing the urban masses.[30] However, the heavy use and constant pressure exerted by merchants, their customers, and suppliers had begun to wear down the plaza's public face by the 1780s. Residents had cut down the trees planted in the time of the Jesuits, and cartwheels and pedestrian traffic had deeply scared the unpaved earth of the plaza. Even as late as 1802, Viceroy Joaquín del Pino y Rozas was still pushing the cabildo to find a sanitary and hygienic venue for the city's butchers who sold meat in the Plaza Mayor and left behind blood and waste.[31]

From the time of Viceroy Juan José de Vértiz y Salcedo (viceroy, 1778–1784), various schemes were proposed to beautify and reorganize the Plaza Mayor.[32] The danger of fires and the desire to remove refuse and fuel from the streets led the cabildo to pressure bakers, millers, and brick makers to relocate at some distance from the Plaza Mayor. The most ambitious urban improvement was the proposal, first made in the 1780s, to construct a Recova, a covered, two-story retail space. The proposal was universally viewed as the best way to organize and order the congested and unprotected retail of the city center while at the same time producing a new source of rental income for the cabildo. In the end, limited funds and a lack of disciplined leadership slowed the construction of the Recova until the last decade of the colonial era.[33]

Disputes over the quality of the masonry and carpentry accompanied the final stage of construction in the period 1803–1804.[34] Once completed, the Recova bisected the Plaza Mayor, splitting the cabildo from the fortress and viceroy's residence. Because the city only began to impose regulations on brick and tile manufacturers after 1800, the walls of the Recova, like most large structures in the city, rose and fell like ripples on the surface of a lake stirred by a breeze.[35] Despite the slow-motion construction process, the poor quality of the construction, and the relatively high rents the cabildo charged, tenants for the commercial spaces of the Recova appeared immediately. Most were artisans who served high-end consumers or specialized retailers who could afford the rent.

As the urban population accumulated rapidly after 1776, the market located in the Plaza Mayor no longer met the needs of a populace increasingly clustered on the periphery of the old city center. As a result, municipal authorities developed secondary markets to serve emerging neighborhoods. The first was Plaza Chica located near the Church of Santo Domingo. While much smaller than the sprawling two-block long Plaza Mayor, Plaza Chica eventually rivaled the central market in the value of its commerce.[36] Many of the city's most significant import and export merchants clustered along its margins, and many of the most successful artisans in luxury trades were located on nearby streets. The cabildo then developed Plaza Nueva, soon to become the major market and distribution point for cart and wagon traffic. The cabildo established a fourth market in 1785, Plaza Monserrat. The cabildo undermined the plaza's early commercial vitality by selecting this as site of the city's first permanent bullring. These boisterous festivals with the attendant drinking and gambling caused many merchants to relocate, driving down rents and attracting large numbers of poor, free black artisans and laborers.[37] As this community developed, it served as host to black *cofradías* as well as to less formal performances of African drumming and dancing.[38] Once established as the center of Afro *porteño* culture, the cabildo targeted Monserrat for intensified police patrols and imposed harsh regulations. Only when authorities relocated the bullring to a new location in the Retiro a decade later did Monserrat regain its status as a vital part of the city's retail life, drawing millers and bakers to relocate near this important market for shipments of wheat sent from the *chacras* of the neighboring countryside.[39] As the city population grew and humble new neighborhoods appeared on the periphery of the developed center, a number of smaller, less regulated markets, called *plazuelas*, were established.

The People of Late Colonial Buenos Aires

In 1744, thirty-two years before the city's elevation as a viceregal capital, municipal census takers counted 11,600 inhabitants. It is clear that from this date the population of Buenos Aires increased steadily until the end of the colonial period. The rate of growth and actual size of the population is more difficult to determine. The census of 1778 counted 24,363 inhabitants. Parts of the 1810 census are lost so demographers and historians generally presume the total found in surviving census tracks, 42,872, represents a significant undercount of the urban population. We should probably view the "complete" 1744 and 1778 censuses as rough estimates as well, rather than as comprehensive population counts. We know that modern censuses compiled by trained experts in rich industrialized nations undercount the poorest sectors of the population by as much as 4 or 5 percent.[40] The census takers of eighteenth-century Buenos Aires certainly missed the mark by a larger margin. One commentator in 1783 claimed a city population of "30 to 40 thousand souls."[41] In 1795, Viceroy Nicolás de Arrendondo claimed in his *Memoria* that Buenos Aires was a "city that could count in a day a population of 60,000 souls."[42] A little more than a decade later in 1806, the cabildo of Buenos Aires indicated in a letter to the king that the city population was 70,000.[43] Almost at the same time, Sir Home Popham, commander of the British naval force that attacked Buenos Aires in 1806, reported to his superiors that the city had a population of 70,000, and Gonzalo Doblas, who helped plan the defense of the city against Popham's attack, asserted this same number.[44] All of these informed estimates suggest that the city population had to have been significantly larger than the 42,872 found in surviving portions of the 1810 census.

We can be confident that the city's most affluent families located in substantial residences in the urban center were the most likely to be counted in the colonial censuses. Census takers were also likely to count the slaves and free dependents of affluent families accurately. The city's large population of day laborers, artisans (especially the poorest journeymen), as well as the substantial floating population of ship crews, cart drivers, and soldiers were much less likely to show up in census counts. These groups found shelter in ranchos constructed in the sprawling suburbs, in shared rooms at the back of shops, stables, brickyards, and bakeries, and in the patios and hallways of downtown apartment blocks. Few colonial-era census takers reliably located and counted these men and women.

Figure 3 provides two estimates of urban population for the census years of 1744, 1778, and 1810. The first estimates are those provided by the census counts. For the second estimate I used the baptismal records found in parish records to calculate the likely population size necessary to produce the number of births recorded by ecclesiastical authorities in each census year, a statistic called crude birthrate (number of live births per one thousand inhabitants).[45] It is sensible to assume that the process of recording

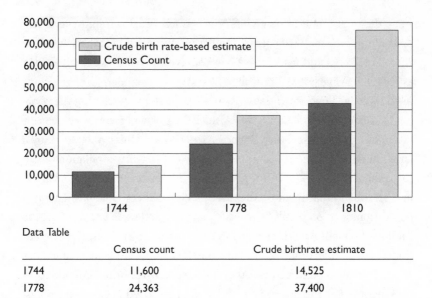

Data Table

	Census count	Crude birthrate estimate
1744	11,600	14,525
1778	24,363	37,400
1810	42,872	76,450

FIGURE 3 Population estimates for Buenos Aires in 1744, 1778, and 1810. Source: The 1744 census is found in Universidad de Buenos Aires, *Documentos para la historia Argentina*, vol. 10, "*Padrones de la ciudad y campaña de Buenos Aires (1726–1810)*" (Buenos Aires, 1820), 328–506. The 1778 census is published in the same collection, vol. 11, *Territorio y población, Padron de la ciudad de Buenos Aires* (Buenos Aires, 1919). The 1810 census is not published. The manuscript is found in AGN, Buenos Aires, Argentina, *Padron de habitantes de la ciudad de Buenos Aires, 1810*, 11-10-7-7. The estimation of baptisms is from Alberto B. Martínez, *Historia demográfica de Buenos Aires*, vol. 3, Dirección General de Estadística Municipal (Buenos Aires, 1910).

baptisms in the city parishes was more likely to be accurate than were contemporary census counts, although some small percentage of births in this observant Catholic colony may have escaped this ecclesiastical ritual.[46] If we presume the population counts of the three censuses are accurate, then the crude birthrates based on parish records were 50 per thousand (1744), 61 per thousand (1778), and 71 per thousand (1810). This means that in 1744 when there were 581 baptisms Buenos Aires had a crude birthrate comparable to the highest rates found in modern Africa, an unlikely but not easily dismissed possibility. The 3,058 baptisms of 1810, however, would have required an impossibly high crude birthrate of 71 per thousand, if the census count of 42,872 was accurate. This seems highly implausible when late-eighteenth-century Spain had a crude birthrate of 42 per thousand, France 32 per thousand, and Ireland 33 per thousand.[47]

If we assume a crude birthrate for late colonial Buenos Aires similar to that established for Spain in this same period, 40 per thousand, then we can estimate the urban population size most likely to produce the number of baptisms recorded in parish records in 1744, 1778, and 1810. I provide the results of these calculations in the right-hand columns of figure 3.[48] While these estimates may be a little high, there is virtually no likelihood that the census counts that have provided the basis for nearly every demographic analysis of colonial Buenos Aires were accurate. The population had to be substantially greater than the census counts to produce the number of births recorded by ecclesiastical authorities. It seems reasonable to assume that the potent combination of administrative changes (creation of Viceroyalty of Río de la Plata), trade liberalization (*comercio libre* and later trade with neutrals), and the broad expansion of Atlantic markets in the eighteenth century led to potent demographic, as well as economic, expansion in Buenos Aires. Our evidence suggests that the crude birthrate-derived population estimates in figure 3 most accurately represent this demographic trajectory.[49]

Free Immigrants and Migrants

Free and forced immigration were the principal sources of population growth in late colonial Buenos Aires. Demographers and historians have not yet fully explored these important topics, but the slave trade has attracted much more attention in recent decades than free immigration. Colonial censuses permit us to construct a much more detailed, if still incomplete, outline of the origin and volume of immigrants from Spain and other European nations than of migrants from the interior of the viceroyalty and other South American colonies. Spanish authorities more reliably counted migrants who embarked in Spain or disembarked in Montevideo, Buenos Aires, or other estuary ports than those who entered the region via terrestrial or riverine routes from Paraguay, Córdoba, Salta, or Alto Peru.[50] Only those migrants who stayed in Buenos Aires long enough to be included in period censuses or who married, died, or were arrested appear in surviving records. Because Spaniards dominated the colonial civic and military bureaucracies and religious establishments as well as both retail and wholesale trade the documentary legacy of this population is rich and deep. Free migrants from the interior of the viceroyalty or from other South American colonies were overwhelmingly poor castas who remain a shadowy presence in the records.[51]

In addition to the settled and visible Spaniards that inhabited the hierarchies of church, state, and commerce, there was a larger, less rooted Spanish population that included the enlisted ranks of navy and army as well as short-term residents associated with Atlantic commerce. The proximity of Brazil and the long history of Buenos Aires as the most important contraband entrepôt in Spanish South America help explain the presence of a very substantial Portuguese population in Buenos Aires. These two groups, Spaniards and Portuguese, controlled most of the region's imports and exports as competitors and as coconspirators in the subversion of Spanish commercial laws.[52] Less visibly, these two groups also provided the majority of the city's most successful artisans and petty merchants. The census of 1744 indicated that 25 percent of the urban population whose birthplace was known were immigrants from Europe and, among these European immigrants, 70 percent were Spaniards. By 1810 the percentage of Europeans had fallen slightly to 22 percent with the percentage of Spaniards among all Europeans rising to 77 percent.[53]

While migrants from the Andean north, Paraguay, and the near interior cities of Córdoba and Santa Fe had long found their way to Buenos Aires to seek opportunity, what had been a trickle before 1776 grew to flood tide with the economic expansion of the last decades of the colonial period. A census of tailors compiled in 1780, for example, registered apprentices José Antonio Vasquez from Paraguay and Pedro Nolasco of Córdoba living with the porteño master Gregorio Andujar near Plaza Monserrat. Across the city, the journeymen José Guillermo of Alto Peru shared a room near the Franciscan convent with Simón Villafaña from Tucumán.[54] Evidence of this increase in the number of migrants from interior provinces is unambiguously present in period censuses as well, but because of the inconsistent and unreliable ways colonial census takers recorded place of birth, census summaries must be used with care.[55] Among those for whom birthplace was recorded, the locally born accounted for 50 percent of the population in 1744 and 43 percent in 1810. While the Iberian Spanish population grew in number across the period, as a proportion of the city population it remained constant at 17 percent. The population of free migrants from the interior and from other Spanish colonies, on the other hand, grew from 25 to 36 percent among those whose origin was recorded by city census takers.

Because of Marisa M. Díaz's careful examination of matrimonial registers from the colonial parishes of Buenos Aires, we can discuss the free migrant population with much greater confidence than was possible when colonial censuses served as our primary sources. Men constituted the majority of migrants from the interior with the exception of the 1790s, when the volume of female migration overtook the volume of men. After 1800 the scale of male migration returned to earlier levels, again eclipsing female levels. As is generally true in all migratory streams, the majority of these late colonial migrants were young adults, with 58 percent of female migrants and 55 percent of males under the age of thirty.[56] Both the rising volume of migration and the relative youth of this population explain the growing percentage of migrants among marriage partners recorded in parish registers. The percentage of migrants marrying fluctuated between 5 percent and 15 percent of all those married in the city of Buenos Aires until 1790 when it moved upward, stabilizing between 20 percent to 30 percent until the beginning of the independence era in 1810.[57]

Paraguay remained the most important source of male migrants to Buenos Aires to the end of the colonial period. City censuses compiled in 1778 and 1810 indicate that nearly 40 percent of male migrants originated in this province. Parish records reinforce the 1779 estimate but suggest that Paraguay's share had fallen to 21 percent of all male migrants by 1810. According to the censuses, Córdoba was the most important source of female migrants to Buenos Aires throughout the late colonial period, providing roughly 25 percent of all female migrants. Parish matrimonial registers suggest a different story. These records indicate that Córdoba contributed roughly 24 percent of all female migrants in 1744 and 1779. But, by 1810, female migrants from rural districts closer to Buenos Aires surpassed Córdoba, accounting for 44 percent of female migrants.[58]

The rising tide of internal migrants is perhaps the best sociological proxy for measuring the economic expansion centered in Buenos Aires after 1776. The decisions of free adults, both men and women, to migrate to Buenos Aires from the interior of the viceroyalty were little affected by the impact of Atlantic warfare on commerce and shipping levels, events that were central to the decisions of potential European immigrants. Internal migrants, especially those living along the densest commercial and informational routes that connected Alto Peru and Paraguay to Buenos Aires, also had access to better quality and more recent intelligence about labor demands and wage rates in Buenos Aires than did potential European immigrants. The fact that nominal wages rose steadily in Buenos Aires even as war restricted

FIGURE 4 Laundresses, many of them free blacks, carried laundry through the streets to wash in the shallow water near the fort and viceroy's residence in the city center. Source: Gregorio Ibarra, *Trajes y costumbres de la Provincia de Buenos Aires* (Buenos Aires: César Hippolyte Bacle y compania, 1833).

the Atlantic commercial corridor explains why by 1810 the city's population of internal migrants was growing much faster than arrivals from Europe.

Between 1744 and 1810 the black and casta population of Buenos Aires grew relative to the number of criollos and Europeans.[59] Parish records make it clear that this rearrangement was not the result of a significant decline in the fertility of criollos or European immigrant populations. Instead, the growing importance of the African slave trade and an expanded migration from the interior adjusted ethnic and racial balances in the city. Pardos and morenos as well as Indians and mestizos numerically dominated migration from interior provinces, but the racial character of internal migration is not fully visible in period censuses. In fact, census takers classified 72 percent of male internal migrants and 64 percent of female migrants as white. In the matrimonial registers analyzed by Díaz, however, a clear majority of both male and female migrants from interior provinces were nonwhites, 65 percent and 58 percent, respectively.[60] The young average age of internal migrants and their high fertility rate, including births out of wedlock, quickly multiplied the effect of migration on urban racial distributions.

While it is clear that employment opportunities and the rising wages of the less skilled drew migrants to Buenos Aires, colonial authorities consistently identified migrants as lazy or alternatively as dangerous and criminal. These dismissive criticisms were most common after 1790 when the wave of migration crested. For example, the cabildo's *procurador síndico general* in a letter to the viceroy in 1791 expressed his judgment that, "the multitude of poor beggars that we observe in the city are *foresteros* of the interior provinces and the major part are no more than lazy bums who have chosen this mode of life to avoid work."[61] The cabildo revealed growing fears of this population, both established migrants from the interior as well as the transients who carried the products of the campo and more distant regions to the city in carts and mule trains, in a series of punitive police regulations. This fear of migrants explained in large measure the efforts to ban or limit the access of carts to the center city. It also informed the decision to recruit *alcades de barrio* to police the poor suburbs and encampments of muleteers and carters in the near countryside. The cabildo's numerous efforts to overcome what it saw as rural labor shortages during harvest season by rounding up "beggars," the "unemployed," prisoners, and other members of the urban poor, most casta migrants, were indirectly justified by this same antimigrant prejudice.[62]

Slaves and the Slave Trade

While the accumulating political importance and expanding economic vitality of Buenos Aires after 1776 attracted thousands of free immigrants, these same forces underwrote vast new investments in slaves. Slaves in significant numbers had been imported prior to the momentous changes of the late eighteenth century. Before 1776, however, the merchants of Buenos Aires transferred the majority of imported slaves to destinations in the silver-producing regions of the Andes or, in smaller numbers, to Chile or Paraguay via intermediary markets. After 1780, the numbers of slaves retained by the city of Buenos Aires increased steadily, reaching a peak in the early 1800s when the city became the major recipient of African slaves in Spanish South America.[63]

The Spanish Crown had granted monopoly control of the slave trade to Buenos Aires before 1750 to a succession of foreign companies, including the French Guinea Company and, after the War of Spanish Succession, the British South Sea Company. During the period of the French and British monopolies, approximately 14,000 slaves legally entered Buenos Aires. As had been true in the seventeenth century, merchants in Buenos Aires sold the majority of these slaves to secondary markets. Of the approximately 11,000 slaves imported by the British monopoly between 1715 and 1738 only 30 percent, or approximately 3,300, remained in Buenos Aires and its rural hinterland.[64]

The legal importation of slaves grew after 1750, but it was only after 1790 that the trade reached its apogee in the Río de la Plata. From 1770 to 1779, local merchants imported only 475 slaves and a similar level of importations continued to the mid-1780s. Although European wars disrupted Atlantic commerce repeatedly, during the years 1790–1806 slave imports to Buenos Aires increased as Spain permitted local merchants to begin a direct trade with Africa and then granted permission to neutral nations to import slaves.[65] During the long period of nearly constant warfare after 1790, foreign slave ships captured off the coast of Africa by local privateers also contributed to the rising tide of slave imports.

As a result, an explosive growth in slave imports occurred between 1791 and 1800 when at least 18,282 slaves arrived in Montevideo and Buenos Aires from Brazil and Africa. Approximately 15,566 slaves arrived directly from Africa and another 7,722 slaves from Brazil between 1801 and the first British invasion in 1806, a staggering 24,146 slaves imported in five years.[66] While the dense succession of late colonial wars interrupted the African slave trade after this date, significant numbers of slaves continued to be imported. As a result, somewhere between 80 and 90 percent of all legally registered slave imports arrived in Buenos Aires during the final fifteen years of the colonial period.[67] Actual slave imports were probably much higher. Some scholars have suggested that slave imports totaled between 40,000 and 50,000 as contraband supplemented rising legal imports.[68]

The slave trade with Brazil expanded first during the 1790s and then continued, despite the burgeoning direct trade with Africa, to the end of the colonial period. Historians using Brazilian sources estimate that as many as 100,000 slaves were sent to the Río de la Plata from the 1740s to 1806, but this number seems very high given the numbers of slaves found in censuses and other enumerations.[69] Whether this estimate is reliable or not, the importance of Brazil was confirmed in 1795 when Viceroy Arredondo noted that 2,689 slaves had been legally imported between February 11, 1792, and March 16, 1795, and that 2,264 (84 percent) of these slaves had been imported from Brazil with the remainder arriving from Africa.[70] As demand grew in Buenos Aires during the 1790s, legal and contraband slave imports from Brazil totaled something like 10,000 to 15,000, and this volume was maintained during the next decade.[71]

The size of the urban slave population grew dynamically as a result, despite the continuing sale of slaves to the interior provinces and other Spanish colonies. The last colonial-era city censuses capture the results of mounting slave imports. The incomplete and flawed censuses of 1806 and 1807 identified 6,650 blacks and mulattoes in an urban population of 25,404 (26 percent). The better quality, but still incomplete, census of 1810 registered 9,615 blacks and mulattoes in a population of 32,558 (29 percent). An effort to reconstruct the census of 1810 by Emilio Ravignani produced the same proportion, 29 percent or 11,837 blacks and mulattoes in an urban population he estimated at 40,398.[72] Since the population was probably at least 20,000 larger than Ravignani's estimate, we should assume a similarly larger population of free blacks and slaves. During this same period, the percentage of slaves among all black and mulatto residents rose from 75 percent to 86.3 percent, indicating that as slave imports increased the majority of recent arrivals now remained in the city or the nearby countryside.[73]

Most visitors claimed a much larger slave and free black population for the city than was suggested in official records. Around midcentury, Padre Charlevoix estimated Buenos Aires to have a population of 16,000 and claimed that three quarters were "mestizos, negroes y mulattoes." A couple of decades later, Concolorcorvo (Alonso Carrió de la Vandera) asserted that "half" the urban population was either "negro or casta" in a total population of roughly 22,207.[74] Alexander Gillespie, an officer in the English invasion force led by Beresford in 1806, claimed that only 20 percent of the urban population was "white," "the rest being a compound breed throughout various stages of connexion, and progressive changes, from the Negro to the hue of the clearest European."[75] Even the surviving sections of the census of 1810 indicated that 45 percent of the urban population was non-white with pardos and morenos providing roughly 80 percent of the population of color.[76]

As recently arrived Africans became an ever-larger presence in the streets and other public places of Buenos Aires in the 1780s, the cabildo and colonial authorities expressed growing concern for public order and safety. Slaves had been part of the city's social and cultural mix since its origins without provoking expressions of anger and fear, but this changed as the volume of the slave trade spiked and as the slave population became more culturally distinct, more African. Many Spanish and criollo residents regarded African diet, language, dress, and social and religious practices as odd, uncivilized, and sometimes threatening.[77] The common Atlantic trade practice of branding slaves on the chest or face combined with these cultural differences to distinguish and separate newly arrived slaves from the locals. While Spain ultimately banned branding in 1784, slaves brought to the city by French, Dutch, or American merchants or slaves imported from Brazil continued to arrive with these outward signs of this cruel trade until the end of the colonial period.[78]

Despite the fears generated by this rising tide of slave imports, slaves became a central prop of the local economy. Slaves provided much of the city's occasional labor. They were present in nearly every artisan trade and were crucial to small retail, managing the stalls in the city's markets and peddling everything from thread to bread and milk door to door.[79] Nearly every householder with pretensions to membership in the *gente decente* owned one or more slaves. This included the very humble homes of many impoverished widows and the elderly. In many ways, slaves were more completely integrated as a physical presence in colonial porteño society than were poor free migrants from the interior. While the elite worried about slavery's potential to undermine public order and increase property crime, they aggressively sponsored (and profited from) the expansion of the African and Brazilian slave trades.

This perceived threat to public order was in reality a complex of fears. Free residents of Buenos Aires saw the slave trade and slaves themselves as threats to public health and hygiene. The cabildo made repeated attempts to regulate the slave pens where arriving slaves were held awaiting sale. These dreadful places were initially located near the disembarkation point at Riachuelo until authorities forced their relocation across the city to Retiro.

Worried about the spread of disease, the cabildo ordered that slave importers bathe captives upon arrival as a health measure. In the city itself, slaves were kept together in smaller numbers for inspection and sale. Municipal authorities uniformly regarded these smaller, urban slave pens as unhealthy and disease ridden and finally ordered them from the city center.[80] These same regulations made clear that city authorities understood that greedy and irresponsible slave traders were ultimately the vector transmitting these threats to the public. In 1804, the year of maximum volume in the slave trade to Buenos Aires, the cabildo expressed its outrage over slave importers who shamelessly discarded the bodies of slaves who had succumbed to disease while awaiting sale in city streets without any "concern for the claims of the church, charity or public hygiene."[81]

Slaves and the Buenos Aires Labor Market

Travelers visiting Buenos Aires as well as informed local residents drew attention to two central features of the local slave regime. First, although there were some substantial slave holdings in the city, as was true in all the Spanish American capitals, there were very large numbers of slave owners in late colonial Buenos Aires who owned only a single slave. A small number of wealthy individuals, including wholesale merchants and high-ranking royal officials, had substantial slaveholdings but seldom owned more than ten slaves. Many of the city's largest slave-holdings belonged to a handful of successful artisan manufacturers (especially bakers and owners of brick factories) who each owned on average more than thirty slaves.[82]

Second, men and women of very modest means collectively owned large numbers of slaves in late colonial Buenos Aires. Householders with only one or two slaves owned a majority of the city's slaves. As one visitor put it in 1794, "you should know that there are an increased number of slaves in the city and many families have no property other than their slaves . . . these the law obligates to provide their owners with a daily payment."[83] Many owners, in fact, were completely dependent on the wages of their slaves. A year later, another visitor remarked that the slaves of poor masters were "obligated by law to contribute their wages to their masters." He noted that "many slaves earned their wages delivering water or as laborers working for blacksmiths or other artisans."[84] Legal cases brought to the courts by slaves seeking their freedom or a *papel de venta* (a court order allowing a slave to locate a new owner willing to pay his or her assessed value) corroborate this generalization. In 1796, for example, the slave María Justa sought to buy her freedom, but her owner's demand for 400 pesos frustrated her efforts. When pressed to explain this punitive amount, the owner Doña Victoria Díaz stated that she was "poor and completely dependent" on the earnings of her slave.[85]

A variety of colonial-era sources corroborate the facts presented in this single case. It was common for slave owners to acknowledge unambiguously to authorities their dependence on the earnings of one or more slaves. As a result of this dependence, many slaves gained freedom conditionally, burdened by the requirement that they continue to make weekly or monthly cash payments during the owner's lifetime.[86] The city's political institutions clearly recognized the importance of these transfer payments as well. The shoemakers had submitted a guild constitution to the town council that prohibited slaves from attaining the rank of master in 1789. The cabildo responded by asserting the importance of slave wages to families and individuals of limited means, summarily rejecting the proposed guild constitution, and singling out the proposed limitation to the advancement and earnings of slaves. This, the councilors noted, "is prejudicial to the Republic, it being apparent that there are many widows and families in this city that sustain themselves with the daily wages of their slaves."[87]

As slave arrivals increased after 1790, slave prices declined thus drawing a larger pool of potential buyers into the market. In 1802 Buenos Aires's first periodical, *Telégrafo Mercantil*, offered the following short summary of the city's slave market: "Every day there arrives in our port a frigate with three or four hundred slaves to be disembarked on our shores. With notice of the arrival, people who wish to begin living a lazy life congregate to seek those who will work in their place. To accomplish this end, each comes with one or two thousand pesos to spend, departing for their home very satisfied. Within a few days they obligate their new slaves to walk the streets to find a day's labor that will pay four or five reales."[88] We know that "three or four hundred slaves" did not arrive daily in 1802. Despite this obvious exaggeration, it is clear from period accounts that as the volume of slave imports rose and as opportunities for hiring out increased in the heated Buenos Aires labor market, slave ownership became more common among people of modest means.

It also seems unlikely that slave owners sent a majority of recent arrivals from Africa or Brazil into the local labor market with the minimal cultural equipment suggested in the *Telégrafo Mercantil* article, but we must assume the practice was common enough that the writer and others noticed. Unable to speak Spanish and without knowledge of local wage and price custom or knowledge of monetary values, a recent arrival was certain to be a target for abuse and fraud. The likelihood that unassimilated and inexperienced slaves would be unable to locate employment at standard rates and would fail to provide their owners the expected return on invested capital was a more pressing concern. It might be useful to assume that the self-interest of slave owners, except those completely overtaken by sloth or completely absorbed in their own affairs, led most to supervise the employment terms of newly arrived slaves. Indeed, notary copybooks suggest that in longer labor contracts employers of hired slave labor commonly paid wages, minus estimated living expenses, directly to slave owners.

These same records indicate that it was more common for owners to place slaves as apprentices or as unskilled helpers with established artisans or lesser-skilled wage earners like whitewashers or teamsters than to send newly purchased slaves out on their own. At the cost of some lost income, these slave owners were able to delegate direct supervision of their slaves to employers for a period of weeks or months in the case of lesser-skilled occupations or up to two to six years for apprentices in skilled trades. As was the case with free apprentices, these slaves lived in the home of a master who provided room and board and, sometimes after the first year, a small wage. Although less formal arrangements were the norm in the brick kilns, bakeries, stockyards, and construction gangs that employed thousands of the city's workers, it was also customary for slaves in these occupations to share meals and sleeping arrangements with free workmates. In late colonial Buenos Aires, nearly every workplace integrated free and slave workers.[89]

Since the youngest, least-skilled slaves had only limited earning potential, slave owners sought to reduce the cost of skill acquisition and subsistence by transferring these burdens to an employer. As slaves gained experience and acquired skills, their income potential grew. Owners generally responded to a slave's enhanced earning potential by granting greater freedom to negotiate employment and determine living arrangements. For thousands of slaves in late colonial Buenos Aires, one central condition of their legal status was the requirement to provide weekly, or less commonly monthly, cash payments to owners.

By 1800 nearly every manual occupation, every skill level, and nearly every job site in the city hosted an integrated workforce of slave and free laborers that included both African-born slaves and free casta migrants from interior provinces. Racial affinity and racial discrimination played an important role in distributing workers among employers, but a close examination of censuses and guild matriculations reveal a deep interpenetration of black and white and slave and free labor. In the brickyards and bakeries that employed large numbers of workers, every employer in Buenos Aires mixed free and slave labor. Among artisans, slave and free laborers worked together in all but the smallest shops that employed only one or two apprentices or journeymen. Some master artisans gained economies of scale by purchasing and training slaves in their own trades. Once these slave artisans were in place, their masters enjoyed a competitive advantage relative to master artisans who hired smaller numbers of free journeymen. As a result, the most prosperous artisans in many trades were those who owned large numbers of slaves. In 1810, for example, 45 shoemakers owned 109 slaves and 21 bakers owned 247 slaves.[90]

While many master artisans owned the slave apprentices and journeymen they employed, it was more common for masters to employ slaves who hired out their own time or were placed by their owners. There were also many examples in late colonial Buenos Aires where slaves, who had achieved the rank of journeyman or master, directed the labor of free apprentices or laborers and even used corporeal punishment to discipline them.[91] This was therefore an artisan culture where many slave journeymen arranged their own labor contracts and where some slaves that were master artisans trained and supervised free apprentices. In this environment, the distinction between a free and a coerced laborer was seldom visible in the tasks performed.

At the same time that the mounting labor demands of this rapidly expanding urban economy promoted the expansion of slaveholding in Buenos Aires, a steady stream of enslaved men and women gained their freedom through manumission and entered the pool of free labor. Between 1776 and 1810, 1,356 slaves gained manumission. The pace of manumission quickened as the slave population grew in the 1790s and 1800s, with 54 percent of all manumissions granted in the last ten years of the colonial period. The ability of slaves to earn wages and accumulate savings was the key ingredient in this process.[92] In late colonial Buenos Aires, 67 percent of male manumissions and 57 percent of female manumissions were the result of self-purchase or purchase by parents in the case of a child. Adult slaves in prime working years, fifteen to forty-five years of age, purchased 66 percent of all manumissions.

Two things seem obvious. First, a substantial number of slaves, as individuals and as families, were able to accumulate significant amounts of cash. Second, this was only possible if large numbers of slaves contracted their own time and received wages for their work. For men this commonly meant work as day laborers or artisans, and for women this meant market work or employment as washerwomen or tailors. Of all the occupations that employed slaves, the artisan trades provided the highest incomes. Given that manumissions cost on average 250 pesos, this expenditure was the equivalent of 200 days of work for a journeyman earning 10 reales a day.

In effect, large numbers of those in bondage operated with substantial independence in the local labor market, seeking work and negotiating wages with little direct supervision by their owners. The expanding economy of late colonial Buenos Aires produced seemingly contradictory results relative to our common assumptions about the competition between slave and free labor. The long period of sustained labor demand and high wages initiated by imperial reforms made the purchase of large numbers of costly slaves feasible. This same expansion also produced significant opportunities for manumission as many slaves were integrated in the economy as wage earners.

The Late Colonial Artisan Community

Any effort to estimate the size of the working population of a late-colonial Spanish city must confront the weakness of the surviving documents and the unreliable character of the broad generalities offered by visitors and Spanish officials. Félix de Azara, for example, claimed that "the arts and trades [in Buenos Aires] are reduced to only the indispensable and are exercised only by some poor Spaniards arrived from Europe and by the people of color."[93] There were no attempts by either the municipal or the colonial governments to count the lesser-skilled population of *jornaleros* and peones. We do know, however, that the municipal government repeatedly took emergency action to meet harvest labor shortages in the nearby wheat-growing region by emptying the city jail, mobilizing "vagrants, lazy people, and malefactors," and forcibly gathering Indians from distant Guaraní missions. City authorities used similar coercive methods to pave the center city streets, pick up garbage, and move freight to and from the ports. If we cannot know how many men and women made up the large class of lesser-skilled laborers, both slave and free, we can assert confidently that for more than two decades employers and colonial administrators complained relentlessly that the numbers were too small and that wages (and slave prices) were too high as a result.

We can discuss the size, occupational distributions, origins, and skill levels of the city's artisan community with much greater confidence. This task is easier because Viceroy Juan José de Vértiz y Salcedo, the same viceroy who initiated efforts to pave and illuminate city streets, improve the port, regulate cart traffic, and even build the city's first theater, also promoted the organization of artisan trades. He published a *bando* in 1780 that ordered the members of all artisan trades to report to the city's notaries and register as a preliminary to the formation of guilds. In the end, only two crafts attempted to organize, but the craft censuses provide a firm foundation for an analysis of this sector.

Table 1 summarizes the surviving matriculations of artisans and adds census data for two additional crafts for a total of sixteen trades.[94] There were 1,133 artisans counted in these documents. The shoemakers were by far the largest group with 354 operatives. Carpenters, tailors, and the related trades of bricklayers and masons were the next largest groups. What this suggests immediately is that the skilled trades of Buenos Aires primarily serviced basic consumer needs and that construction crafts, rather than the luxury trades, were the most prosperous. With the exception of the silversmiths, a trade that in Buenos Aires included workers in precious and semi-precious stones and goldsmiths, the powerful artisan corporations devoted to the production of elite goods that dominated Lima and Mexico City were absent from the landscape of skilled trades in colonial Buenos Aires. In this viceregal capital, the outdoor trades, bricklayers, carpenters, and smiths, were wealthier and more numerous than were the traditionally more prestigious indoor trades like the silversmiths.

The growth of the city's artisan trades depended on three migratory streams, free migrants from Europe and the interior, forced migrants from Africa, and the recruitment of the locally born. Since most internal and international migrants arrived in their late teens or twenties, the importance of immigration to the skilled trades gave this population a youthful character with approximately 80 percent of all artisans less than forty years

TABLE 1 Artisan population by craft and rank (1780)

Trade	Masters	Journeymen	Apprentices	Totals
Leather trades	20	11	0	31
Wood trades	35	13	5	53
Masons	23	71	9	103
Barber surgeons	69	7	4	80
Caulkers	1	24	2	27
Carpenters	76	93	30	199
Ship carpenters	1	38	3	42
Bakers	41	0	0	41
Silversmiths	30	16	0	46
Tailors	58	87	12	157
Shoemakers	130	165	59	354
Total	484 (43%)	525 (46%)	124 (11%)	1133 (100%)

Sources: The matricula of *tallistas, carpinteros, estatuarios, silleteros, toneleros, aserradores y peineros* is in AGN, División Colonia, Sección Gobierno, Tribunales, leg. 13, exp. 15. The matricula of *albañiles* is in AGN, División Colonia, Sección Gobierno, Tribunales, leg. 66, exp. 37; and *barberos* in AGN, División Colonia, Sección Gobierno, Interior, leg. 9, exp. 5. *Sastres* are found in AGN, División Colonia, Sección Gobierno, Justicia, leg. 9, exp. 177. *Lomilleros, zapateros,* and other leather trades are in AGN, División Colonia, Sección Gobierno, Interior leg. 9, exp. 5. *Calafates* and *carpinteros de ribera* are in AGN, División Colonia, Sección Gobierno, Tribunales, leg. 13, exp. 15. I have added *panaderos* and *plateros* from the census of 1778 to these matriculations to produce this table. The census in found in Universidad de Buenos Aires, *Documentos para la historia Argentina,* Facultad de Filosofía y letras, 24 tomos (1913–), vol. 11, *Territorio y población, passim.*

of age in 1780. The influence of European immigrants was most visible at the top of the craft structure among masters. Only 35 percent of the city's 413 master artisans were locally born. There were 191 European immigrants (46 percent of total) among the masters. Spanish immigrants with 29 percent of all masters (118) nearly matched the number of native porteños (144) and surely had a superior position to the locals in terms of client base and income. Free casta migrants from the interior (52) and free blacks and slaves (28) filled the remaining master ranks.

The locally born did dominate some trades: 50 percent of master bakers, 61 percent of master masons and bricklayers, 48 percent of master shoemakers, and 36 percent of master carpenters were porteños. Spaniards controlled the master ranks in other trades. In port-related trades, for example, 79 percent of all ship carpenters and 85 percent of caulkers were Spanish immigrants. There were more Spaniards than locally born masters among the skilled wood trades (furniture makers, framers, turners, and barrel makers) and barber surgeons as well. The only trades where migrants from the interior predominated were low-status leather trades like tanning and saddle making that had strong positions in the economies of the interior provinces.

FIGURE 5 Many artisans carried their wares through the streets looking for
customers. In this illustration a candlemaker carries his production to market.
Source: Gregorio Ibarra, *Trajes y Costumbres de la Provincia de Buenos Aires* (Buenos Aires:
César Hippolyte Bacle y compania, 1833).

The locally born dominated the lower guild ranks. The majority of apprentices and journeymen were porteños, with 64 percent of the former
rank and 72 percent of the latter. At the rank of journeyman, Europeans
were found in roughly equal numbers with blacks (both slave and free)
and casta migrants. Among apprentices, European immigrants provided
an inconsequential 7 percent of operatives, while blacks and castas contributed 26 percent. The pattern revealed in the documents was that European artisans immigrated to Buenos Aires as either journeymen or masters.
Once established, they recruited and trained apprentices and journeymen
from the local population, supplementing this pool with smaller numbers

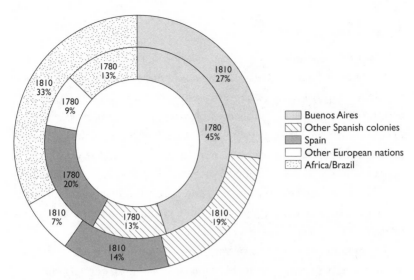

FIGURE 6 Origins of Buenos Aires artisans in 1780 and 1810. Source: The 1778 census is published in Universidad de Buenos Aires, *Documentos para la historia Argentina*, vol. II, *Territorio y población, Padron de la ciudad de Buenos Aires* (Buenos Aires, 1919). The 1810 census is found in AGN, Buenos Aires, Argentina, *Padron de habitantes de la ciudad de Buenos Aires, 1810*, II-10-7-7.

of free migrants from the interior and slaves. Contemporary commentators claimed that the presence of large numbers of blacks and castas in the Buenos Aires crafts kept white parents from apprenticing their sons, fearing a loss of status. One actually claimed white apprentices "would learn faster than rude castas" who, he claimed, were better suited to agriculture.[95] Evidence suggests that an English observer came closer to the mark when he claimed in 1807 that, "Spaniards despise these trades, and cannot stoop to work along with Negroes or mulattos."[96]

In the years 1780–1810, the rhythms of free migration and the slave trade transformed the ethnic and cultural character of the skilled trades of Buenos Aires as figure 6 demonstrates clearly. The percentage of porteños in artisan trades fell steeply in these three decades from 45 percent to 27 percent. The percentage of Spaniards and other European immigrants in the crafts fell similarly from 20 percent to 14 percent and from 9 percent to 7 percent, respectively. Free migrants from the interior of the viceroyalty and other Spanish colonies, the majority being castas, increased from 13 percent to 19 percent. The presence of slave and free blacks in the skilled trades was altered most dramatically by 1810, rising from 13 percent in 1780 to 33 percent in 1810.

Conclusion

Following the creation of the Viceroyalty of Río de la Plata in 1776, the city of Buenos Aires enjoyed both rapid economic growth and a dramatic population expansion. Historians focused on port activity, export volume, commercial taxes, and the growing prosperity of the commercial elite have long acknowledged the scale and persistence of economic growth, despite the negative effects of wartime disruptions to trade and the variability of agricultural and grazing sector performance. The population estimates produced here, based on crude birthrates, now make clear that the rate of population growth after 1780 was also a major contributor to the economic expansion.

The mounting force of these transformative powers constantly pressed against the city's existing built environment, creating an ongoing competition for residential and commercial space and pushing up real estate values and rents. The accumulating wealth in private hands, especially in the hands of the commercial sector tied to long-distance trade, and the ambitions of the municipal and colonial governments organized and financed the expansion of the physical city. Nevertheless, despite new commercial spaces and new housing, the city's built environment contained the growing population and economy like an ill-fitting suit. The costs associated with this scarcity burdened the plebe disproportionally. High residential rents forced many artisans and laborers to defer marriage into their thirties or even forties. Some, especially the poorest, never married. Similarly, the high cost of commercial space, the inescapable expense of becoming an independent master, or opening a factory proved an insurmountable obstacle to the ambitions of many skilled journeymen who sought to escape the status of wage laborer.

While the expansion of the built environment always lagged behind the demands of a growing population and economy, Buenos Aires in 1810 was a much larger and more imposing city than in 1776. The actions of municipal and colonial governments played a central role as they improved the number and grandeur of public spaces. They also devoted resources to improving the city's infrastructure, expanding the grid, paving streets, and developing new plazas. They transformed the Plaza Mayor by the construction of the Recova that briefly satisfied the need for new commercial space. At the same time, merchant capital financed the construction of numerous new residential and commercial buildings that provided new settings for plebeian employment, housing, and social life, but in an enduring situation of residential and commercial real estate scarcity, the plebeian population restlessly churned within the built environment.

Buenos Aires was already an immigrant city at the end of the colonial period. In the skilled trades the arrival of hundreds of European immigrant artisans, mostly masters or experienced journeymen, lifted local skill levels and set in motion efforts to create formal guilds. Simultaneously, the quickly established market dominance and social prominence of these recent arrivals threatened the established locally born master artisans and their ambitious journeymen. The fact that many European masters presumed that local credentials and training were inferior and that most local competitors were therefore "false masters" meant that every step towards the development of traditional craft corporations was fraught with conflict. Because the frontier separating native and immigrant masters had a racial character as well, local artisans routinely understood even the most oblique references to *limpieza de sangre* by immigrants as a direct threat to their status. Could the artisans of Buenos Aires sustain craft traditions of recruitment and training in an environment defined by tensions that attached so predictably to European immigration?

When local wages and employment opportunities surged past those found in less dynamic Spanish colonial settings, the migration of growing numbers of free casta artisans and laborers from the viceregal interior and from more distant South American colonies complicated both the local labor market and the social settings of plebeian life. As this migratory stream crested after 1790, both municipal and viceregal authorities had come to see this fast-growing casta population as a threat to public order and property and imposed a broad range of draconian police and labor regulations that affected the plebe. But the dramatic expansion of the slave trade in the late colonial period would prove to be an even more potent transformative force.

While the city's fast-growing slave population multiplied the productive potential of shops, factories, and service providers, it was also one of many sources of instability and conflict. Many artisans found the means to benefit from the growing slave trade. They purchased slaves and trained them in their trades, multiplying their ability to produce and distribute goods and hedging against the rising wages paid to free laborers. Even more artisans as well as many owners of bakeries, brick kilns, and slaughter yards trained and employed the slaves of others. This practice allowed them to avoid the very substantial cost of purchasing slaves while still harvesting the marginal benefits of lower labor costs and reducing the disruptive effects of workplace turnover among free laborers and artisans.

Plebeian incomes increased steadily in Buenos Aires from the 1780s to the end of the colonial period, but competition for housing, even competition for space in the streets and plazas of the city, increased in a parallel manner. As a result, workingmen and their families continued to be thrown together in uncomfortable residential arrangements with little privacy and very few comforts. European immigrants, migrants from the viceroyalty's interior, and slaves were also integrated in ever more complex ways in the workshops, small factories, bakeries, and brick kilns, as were the work crews that moved goods, built housing, and cleaned streets. In this way, the built environment and the rapidly changing mix of ethnicities, races, and legal conditions framed individual life trajectories, including employment, advancement, access to housing, and opportunities to begin families or maintain less formal social linkages in unpredictable and sometimes combustible ways. Skills, language, cuisine, and understandings of social place and honor had to be negotiated or reinvented as European immigrants, migrants from the interior, and slaves mixed with the natives. While artisans and laborers worked out local accommodations over craft standards, recruitment, employment conditions, and training, the steady flow of laborers at various skill levels, market dynamism, the actions of colonial government, and the unpredictable nature of Atlantic trade intensified the potential for conflict.

In the absence of formal guilds, the most senior and wealthiest artisans and small manufacturers came to depend completely on the colonial and municipal governments to set and enforce standards. These elite members of the laboring classes could not control recruitment, training, or advancement in their crafts. Many European-trained masters watched in horror as their journeymen opened shops and claimed to be masters without passing formal examinations. While elements of the organizational and cultural forms of Europe were in place in Buenos Aires before 1776, the social architecture of the urban plebe remained fluid and conflicted.

2

The Structures of a Working Life
Masculinity, Sociability, Skill, and Honor

At around eight in the evening on August 14, 1786, Juan Montanche, a journeyman bricklayer, entered a *pulpería* located near the Convent of the Catalinas. He asked for a quarter-real's worth of cheese and a quarter real of bread. At the end of the transaction Montanche claimed the young shop assistant, Vicente Buzeta, had shortchanged him, and a heated argument ensued. The issue was not merely who was telling the truth or who was honorable; it was also about who could compel agreement. As the discussion grew in intensity, Montanche drew his knife and attacked the unarmed counterman, cutting his face and puncturing his stomach. The wounded victim finally wrestled his attacker to the ground and called for help.

Testimony presented by the victim and other shopkeepers from the neighborhood suggested that Montanche was a troublesome customer who often alleged that he had been shortchanged and commonly abused the credit custom of shop owners. Wouldn't a man who routinely tried to cheat in petty business dealings expect disagreement and confrontation? What made this particular exchange so dangerous? There was certainly a racial dimension to the confrontation; the attacker was a dark-skinned casta migrant from the interior, and Buzeta, the shop assistant, was a Spanish immigrant. Montanche ignored this difference in his testimony to the investigating judge and focused instead on Buzeta's allegation that he had lied, in effect claiming to unmask him.[1] The young shop assistant's charge of dishonesty delivered in a public place had shamed Montanche and forced him to react. Just as no man in this culture could permit another man to call him a coward or a woman, no man could passively accept being branded a thief or a liar without losing face.

This violent confrontation reveals some of the foundational elements of late colonial plebeian society. Men left home as young boys or adolescents and entered a masculine world dominated by older men who instructed them, worked with them, and mediated their acceptance in masculine venues of sport and leisure. This was a rough and sometimes violent environment where adherence to cultural norms, including a prickly sense of personal honor and a willingness to defend it, served as the basis for finding friends and thwarting rivals. Apprenticeships, work sites, and the shared accommodations common to members of this class were the classrooms and proving grounds of masculinity.

Every young artisan or laborer entering adulthood had served similar periods of tutelage and discipline in a workplaces, shared residences, drinking places, gaming houses, and sports venues. They learned when to joke or tease and they learned what words or actions were likely to provoke violence or lead to vengeance. In late colonial Buenos Aires few members of the propertied classes would have recognized any plebeian's claim to honor, although some plebes did assert it. Yet the prickly refusal of colonial plebeians to accept insult or bullying, their refusal to be shamed, is evident everywhere in period documents. Despite the risks and dangers, joking, teasing, physical challenges, and athletic competition were the foundation of masculine sociability. The social tools and cultural meanings that workingmen acquired as a result of these social interactions infused the world of work. They also provided the collective ideals and values that gave meaning to participation in craft organizations or in collective political life.

The Social Origins of Cultural Practice

The artisans, laborers, and petty merchants of Buenos Aires constituted a broad, diverse, and hierarchically arranged social category. A significant minority of master artisans owned slaves and in many of these cases earned incomes similar to those earned by mid-rank military officers or lower level colonial bureaucrats.[2] The poorest laborers and artisans, on the other hand, lived desperate lives, barely able to pay for food and shelter. We might therefore sensibly dismiss the idea that this was a single class with a formally constructed idea of itself and its social position. Certainly, we cannot assert a narrow description of income and wealth, material conditions, family organization, or ethnic identity that would encompass the lives and experiences of every peddler, artisan, laborer, or small manufacturer in late colonial Buenos Aires. Nevertheless, this largely masculine stratum of colonial society viewed itself as sharing foundational characteristics and experiences.

The thousands of men organized by the artisan crafts of late colonial Buenos Aires, as well as a larger number of men employed in less skilled construction and transportation trades, shared a set of experiences and values acquired during their recruitment, training, and first work experiences. While an immigrant silversmith from Spain certainly saw himself as the social superior of a casta bricklayer trained in Buenos Aires, both men had entered their careers as young boys or teenagers placed in the care of older craftsmen by parents or guardians.[3] During their working lives, both had acquired skills and played, prayed, learned about sex, and gotten drunk in the company of older men already established in their trades. As boys both had eaten their meals in the company of established artisans and laborers who presumed the right to tell them what to do, to criticize their manners or skills and, on occasion, to bully or physically discipline them. As young men, they had slept where the older men had allowed them and eaten what their masters or employers, or even older workmates, left when they were finished. Employers and older workmates routinely assigned them the dirtiest jobs, and if they took too long or failed, had then severely disciplined them. Along the way these young men learned to model the behaviors and embrace the values that served as the foundation of this very masculine precinct within Spanish American colonial society. The guild systems of the richest Spanish colonial cities, like Mexico City and Lima, formally institutionalized the values and practices of this tradition.[4] Without a developed guild system in Buenos Aires, the transmission of values and behaviors was necessarily less formal and less predictable. This was, at its base, a turbulent and sometimes brutal world, but it was also a world with clear, if sometimes unenforced, rules.

The Vocational Formation and Cultural Initiation of the Laboring Class

While families were crucial to the life experiences of plebeians, we need to remind ourselves that the modern family, despite the news media's overwrought coverage of presumed crisis, is typically stronger, better financed, and more influential in the lives of its members than were families of the pre-industrial era. Certainly, family influence over the lives of children endures much longer now than in the past. In the preindustrial era the male children of artisans, laborers, and slaves left home, entered a trade, or sought wages in casual labor as preteens, some leaving home as young as seven or eight years old. With the exception of elite and professional men, nearly every male was fully engaged in the workforce in some way by his early teens. This pattern was also the norm in retail commerce where apprenticeships were the accepted entry portal for careers.[5] While often kept closer to home, young girls were also active in the economy at an early age as they accompanied mothers or grandmothers to work in markets or worked alongside mothers who prepared food for sale in the streets or worked as laundresses, seamstresses, or servants.

Birth families were certainly very important for transmitting values and providing material and emotional resources to artisans and laborers. But young men and boys learned the essential skills and practices of their crafts as well as the values and beliefs that framed individual and collective action while apprentices or in less formal training environments. While master artisans or mentors in more casual settings were central to this process, workmates and the comrades who shared rooms and meals played crucial roles. The passions, beliefs, and collective obligations that provided the deep context for class action and simultaneously guided individual career pathways were often rooted in the serial experiences of the highly masculine environments that framed work and leisure.

In Spain and in the major political centers of colonial Spanish America, many apprentices came from the families of guild masters and their promotion to journeyman and later master were pro forma rituals.[6] A less formal and much more fluid system of recruitment and training emerged in Buenos Aires where artisans only established two guilds and these guilds functioned only briefly. In Europe and in the major viceregal capitals of Spanish America, apprenticeship was typically a conservative and static mechanism for perpetuating privilege.[7] In the most powerful guilds few apprentices drawn from families outside the craft could achieve advancement to the rank of master because of burdensome examination fees and the high cost of tools, materials, and shop rentals.[8] In Spain's American colonies a regime of racial and ethnic discrimination routinely complicated these practices and restrained the progress of indigenous, casta, and black apprentices.[9]

FIGURE 7 A baker mounted on a mule passes by a busy *pulpería* as he delivers bread to market.
Source: C. E. Pellegrini, *Recuerdos del Río de la Plata* (Buenos Aires: Libreria L'Amateur, 1969). Published with the permission of the publisher, Librería L'Amateur, Buenos Aires.

Without formal guilds to enforce recruitment and skill requirements, apprenticeships in late colonial Buenos Aires could not be required for young men entering the skilled trades.[10] Instead, most apprenticeships were arranged between parents (or guardians) and masters without the formality of a contract. The skilled crafts were also unable to impose an examination system on journeymen who claimed the rank of master. In this little-policed environment apprentices could, and did, claim to be journeymen, and journeymen could, and did, claim to be masters without penalty. Despite their inability to control recruitment and promotion within their crafts, immigrant masters from Spain and other European nations as well as many locally recruited masters still accepted and trained locally born apprentices in traditional ways.

In response to migration from the viceroyalty's interior and the growing slave trade, the number of blacks and castas entering the skilled trades increased after 1776. According to the 1780 craft matriculations, 40 percent of all apprentices in Buenos Aires were identified as pardos or morenos and another 7 percent as mestizos.[11] As we will see later, the actual percentages were much higher. Furthermore, 73 percent of the pardo and moreno apprentices were slaves.[12] Although most masters provided housing, food, clothing, and religious instruction for their apprentices, regardless of color or legal status, mounting racial and ethnic divisions within the artisan trades in Buenos Aires worked to loosen the traditional bonds between masters and apprentices. These powerful solvents undermined traditional collegial ties while promoting prejudice, discrimination, and, in some cases, violence.

An apprenticeship contract was only legally enforceable if recorded by a notary. Between 1775 and 1810 the notaries of Buenos Aires recorded only 139 apprenticeship contracts despite the dynamic growth of the skilled trades.[13] It is therefore clear that parents, guardians, and even civil authorities arranged a much larger number of apprenticeships outside this contractual system. We know there were at least 124 apprentices in Buenos Aires in 1780, just under 12 percent of the 1,045 artisans registered by municipal notaries in response to Viceroy Vértiz's order. Given the procedures followed to register the city's artisans, we know that colonial officials failed to count every artisan and, in at least four cases, failed to enroll whole crafts (the silversmiths, bakers, blacksmiths, and arms makers). It seems safe to assume that the combination of undercounting and the missing craft matriculations meant that something like 10 to 30 additional apprentices were present in Buenos Aires in 1780. This means that the 139 apprenticeship contracts found in notary records over thirty-four years represent a fragment of the total number of apprenticeships for the period.

We can demonstrate this using the carpenters as an example. Authorities counted 30 apprentices in this trade in the 1780 matriculation, but city notaries only recorded 3 apprenticeship contracts for the entire period of 1775 to 1810.[14] If we assume from these contracts that the average apprenticeship lasted about four years, it seems safe to estimate a minimum of 200 apprentices were employed by this trade alone during the viceregal period, and something like 1,100 to 1,250 apprentices were employed by all the Buenos Aires skilled trades in the same period, rather than the 139 apprentices recorded by notaries.[15]

The cost of the notary's services, typically eight reales or about four days labor for an unskilled worker, may have suppressed the number of formal contracts. However, without guilds to enforce this traditional training arrangement there were no penalties for parents or guardians who agreed to

TABLE 2 Distribution of apprenticeship contracts by craft, 1775–1810

Occupation	Number of cases	Average age of apprentices	Average length of contract
Lamp maker	1	9	4
Carpenter	3	13	6
Bricklayer	4	13	4.5
Silversmith	7	13.7	5.6
Blacksmith	3	14	4.6
Shoemaker	85	14	3.8
Barber surgeon	4	14	6.4
Tailor	18	12.4	5
Hat maker	2	12	4
Saddle maker	1	10	5
Cooper	1	20	4
Wig maker	1	13	3
Chair maker	5	13	3.6
Button maker	3	13	4
Painter	1	13	4
Total	139	13.3	4.2

Sources: This table is based on the universe of apprenticeship cases found in the seven notary copybooks for Buenos Aires, 1775–1810. AGN, Escribanía, Registros 1–7.

less formal arrangements with masters who, in turn, found it attractive to limit the obligations and costs of a formal agreement with the parents of an apprentice. This combination of self interest and cost trimming explains why there were only thirteen apprenticeship contracts formalized in the city of Buenos Aires between 1775 and 1789 (slightly less than one per year), even though the artisan matriculation of 1780 counted a total of 124 apprentices. With the temporary institutionalization of a shoemaker's guild early in the 1790s, the total number of apprenticeship contracts rose to seventy-eight between 1790 and 1799 (approximately eight per year). Indeed, fourteen of the total of sixteen apprenticeship contracts recorded in 1793 were for shoemaking, as were all thirteen contracts registered in 1794 and nine of the ten contracts recorded the following year.

Table 2 displays the distribution of the 139 formal apprenticeship contracts among the city's artisan trades. Other than the shoemakers whose experience was exceptional, only the tailors, with a total of 12 contracts, seem to have maintained some commitment to traditional apprenticeship without establishing some form of rudimentary guild. Yet even in this craft there were no contracts before 1790, and there was only one year with more than a single apprenticeship (1805 with 2 contracts). This does not mean that the cabildo or agents of the colonial government had given up on traditional apprenticeships as a curative for a range of perceived social problems. As late as 1808, long after the city's artisans had given up on creating guilds, the alcalde of the second vote proposed that the cabildo require neighborhood police officials to conduct a census of poor boys as a preliminary to placing them in apprenticeships. This, he claimed, would both end the city's scarcity of labor that retarded the progress of the trades and put a stop to the "disorders and laziness" that afflicted the poor.[16]

The contracts found in notary records typically provide the age when a young man began an apprenticeship as well as the apprenticeship's term. As a group, apprentices were young adolescents who averaged thirteen years of age. While masters accepted a small number of older boys and even a few young adults as apprentices, this was not common. There were only nine cases of older apprentices with the oldest of these a twenty year old. The average length of the apprenticeship period was 4.2 years. However, a substantial number of contracts required a longer service. In fact, seventeen contracts called for 6 or more years of service as an unpaid apprentice. Apprentice silversmiths regularly served 6 years before becoming journeymen, while contracts of 8 and 9 years were common for barber surgeons. Generally, the length of an apprenticeship appears tied to the age of the boy, with the youngest boys serving the longest apprenticeships.

In many outdoor trades traditional apprenticeships nearly disappeared in the late colonial period as master artisans and the owners of small factories (brickyards, bronze foundries, and bakeries among others) integrated younger, less skilled workers into their worksites without recourse to traditional apprenticeships or, alternatively, purchased slaves to fill these spots. These less skilled workers, both slave and free, could be employed as needed and then more easily released in response to fluctuating labor demands than could traditional journeymen or apprentices with formal contracts. Among masons and stonecutters, trades with 103 total members in 1780, there was not a single apprentice registered in 1780.[17] Instead, the masters in these well-compensated trades had introduced a range of low-skill positions to fill the jobs previously assigned to apprentices. It may be that some of these "*obreros, peones,* and *jornaleros,*" eventually identified themselves as journeymen after they had acquired the essential skills and experiences, but there is little evidence for this.[18]

Only a small minority of apprentices came from intact nuclear families.

TABLE 3 Relationship of adult signatory to apprentice

Relationship	Number	Percentage of all cases
Father and mother	8	6.6
Father	29	23.9
Mother	48	39.7
Guardian	11	9.1
Alcalde	10	8.3
Slave owner	11	9.1
Adult apprentice	4	3.3
Total	121	100%

Source: AGN, Escribanía, Registros 1–7.

Fathers, or fathers and mothers together, signed only 37 of 121 contracts.[19] As shown in Table 3, mothers alone, either widows or women living as heads of household, signed 48 contracts, 40 percent of the total. Guardians or distant kin signed 11 apprenticeship contracts for young boys, and the city alcalde serving as *defensor de menores* signed 10 contracts. Boys placed by the defensor or other municipal authorities were typically orphans or delinquents. For example, one of the city's alcaldes placed the young, free moreno Josef Nicolás Cevallos as apprentice bricklayer in 1787 while the young man served a jail sentence for theft.[20] Finally, slave owners signed a total of 11 contracts to place slaves as apprentices with master artisans. Hundreds of slaves purchased directly by artisans became apprentices without this formality.

These records make it clear that apprenticeships were very often a form of refuge for sons of fractured or fragmented families or boys at risk as a result of lawbreaking. Alcaldes could, and sometimes did, remove boys from irresponsible or exploitive parents and place them with masters to try to protect them.[21] In these cases masters became surrogate fathers or guardians, exercising substantial authority and responsibility for overseeing a young man's transition to manhood and citizenship in addition to supervising his training in the trade. In the worst cases some masters exploited and brutalized the boys placed in their care, forcing colonial authorities, when alerted to the mistreatment, to intervene and place the apprentice with another master.[22] More commonly, however, abused apprentices took matters into their own hands by finding another master, leaving the craft entirely or fleeing the city. In these cases the absence of strong guilds limited the ability of abusive or incompetent masters to control or retain unhappy apprentices.

Some contracts provided a frank discussion of the reason why a parent, guardian, or defensor de menores arranged an apprenticeship. Maria de Carmen Lledras, for example, acknowledged her thirteen-year-old son's illegitimate birth and candidly admitted her inability to financially support him.[23] Micaela Reyes apprenticed her son Antonio because "my blind husband is unable to provide for the family."[24] Antonio Rocha placed his twelve-year-old son, José Domingo, with the master shoemaker, Pedro de la Rosa, to "free him from laziness and bad habits."[25] The contracts make clear the difficult personal and material circumstances that afflicted many members of this class. The guardian of the eleven-year-old Juan Escobar placed him with a shoemaker because "his mother has died and his father's whereabouts are unknown." The guardian agreed to the master's requirement that the boy would complete his full apprenticeship term even if his father returned to the city.[26]

Contracts often required that a master treat his apprentice "as his own son," a formula that suggested the master's obligation to supply both material and emotional needs.[27] Masters, on the other hand, sought to limit their financial obligations and assure discipline. The master shoemaker José Labrador, who trained many apprentices in this period, always stipulated a clear division of clothing costs with parents or guardians.[28] Roughly a third of contracts mandated that parents and the master share the cost of maintaining the apprentice. In these cases the responsibilities of the parents were concentrated during the first half of the contract when the work of the apprentice was least profitable, while the master took responsibility for the second half of the contract. For example, the master shoemaker Josef Alberto Vazquez, a colleague of José Labrador, agreed to "educate, dress and feed (the boy) as his own son" and "correct him with all human moderation." Similarly, Labrador promised to provide food, shelter, and "clean clothes" for his apprentice Pantaleon Costane. Most masters were less generous.[29]

The master shoemaker Juan Bautista de Esmit, for example, agreed to bear the full costs of clothing, feeding, and sheltering his apprentice, the slave José, but stipulated that in case of grave illness all medical costs were to be paid by José's owner.[30] The guardian of the apprentice tailor Mateo Ximenez agreed that in the event of a serious illness his master could return the boy to his parents for care in their home.[31] It was also customary for masters to provide some religious instruction and, in some cases, rudimentary schooling. Marco Rondón, a master chainmaker, committed himself in 1807 to provide regular religious instruction for his apprentice, the orphan Valentín Peralta.[32] In 1805 a master tailor committed to pay for one year of primary education for his apprentice, the twelve-year-old Bartolo José Velásquez, in what was for Buenos Aires a very unusual contract.[33]

The right of masters to use corporal punishment to enforce rules was one of the logical results of this transfer of responsibility from parents to master. Yet it was not unusual for parents to add the proviso that they had the right to suspend the contract if the master treated their son cruelly.[34] Fear that a master might mistreat his apprentice or fail to provide medical care during an illness led parents, guardians, or the alcalde to reserve the right to suspend the contract and place the boy with another master. Many stipulated the right to end the contract if the master provided inadequate training. However, it is worth noting that only one surviving case suggests that a parent or other signatory abrogated a contract and ended an apprenticeship in these circumstances.[35] Nevertheless, a master's authority, and that of journeymen in the master's shop, to physically enforce standards overshadowed whatever residual parental authority was claimed in a contract. This authority was signaled in contracts by a standard provision that required parents to return their son to his master if he ran away.

Most formal apprenticeships required that master craftsmen provide apprentices with all the skills necessary to become a journeyman within the agreed contract period.[36] Some agreements stated that the master train the boy without withholding any of the "secrets or knowledge" of the profession. In European nations with strong guilds artisans usually referred to these essential skills as "mysteries," but regardless of the terminology nearly all traditionally trained artisans understood that the conservation and transmission of craft knowledge dignified their labor and protected their incomes.[37] The dignity of their craft was rooted in the mastery of skills. It was these skills that conferred agency (a word they would not use) in their lives, providing each craftsman with a platform of physical competence that located him in the social universe of his class.

Leaving Home and Finding Your Way

Not only did young men leave their families early to work or learn a trade, but once employed they tended to postpone marriage and the formation of families until well established in their careers. This meant that most artisans and laborers married in their late twenties or thirties, if ever. The 1780 survey of artisan crafts provided numerous examples of middle-aged bachelors sharing housing with workmates. For example, the master *cedazero* (artisan who made tools used in slaughter yards) Juan Ventura Toledo and the master *peinero* (comb maker) Antonio Ravina shared a rented room with other artisans, despite the fact that each had twenty-three years of experience in his craft.[38] As apprentices and journeymen, artisans commonly spent decades of their lives outside the structures of family life. Most shared rented rooms or, in harder times, made due sleeping in hallways, patios, or storerooms. In 1780 three single bricklayers born in Buenos Aires, Bernardo Sosa; his bother, José Benito Sosa; and a workmate, Juan Roberto Rodríguez, shared a room rented from an impoverished widow in the neighborhood of Piedad.[39] Arrangements like this were not narrowly limited to the unmarried, since many artisans and laborers working in Buenos Aires had left their wives and children behind when they migrated. For example, the immigrant tailor Cayetano Gutierrez, who had left his wife behind in Spain when he sailed for Buenos Aires, shared a room near the Merced Church with the tailor Tadeo Castro, a single, criollo migrant from Potosí.[40] These common housing arrangements were the predictable result of the ebb and flow of migration and the city's difficult housing market. While artisans typically arranged their work lives within a single trade and laborers found employment within a cluster of related jobs, they all moved in much more complex rhythms outside of work. Friendships and more casual relationships blossomed in taverns, *pulperías*, and the numerous venues of sport, gambling, and leisure. While work tended to organize men in hierarchies of skill and age, housing arrangements like these suggest the larger, less visible, plebeian identity that transcended the narrow world of work.

More typical for housing arrangements in Buenos Aires was the cluttered two-room apartment shared by eleven journeyman tailors in Calle Santisima Trinidad. In this case the roommates ranged from eight to twenty-nine years of age and included recent immigrants from Spain and Portugal, migrants from Corrrientes and Santa Fe in the interior, as well as three native sons of Buenos Aires.[41] Nearby, the master carpenter Ramón Caseras of Montevideo shared a rented room with three other carpenters, the journeymen Luis Ambrosio of Buenos Aires, Juan Viera of Portugal, and the apprentice Joseph Cuello of Buenos Aires. These residential clusters built around a shared trade were very common, but if we enlarge our

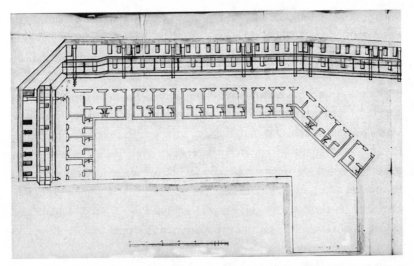

FIGURE 8 Architectural drawing of a proposed two-story apartment building. While the individual apartments were small, only well-established master artisans could afford the rent. Published with the permission of the AGN, Buenos Aires, Argentina.

frame of analysis from rooms or apartments to city blocks or streets, we see more completely the rich integration of the laboring class by origins, race, craft, and age. The 1790 census of artisans provides a useful snapshot of a single Buenos Aires block that housed two silversmiths, two master carpenters, a journeyman carpenter, two barber surgeons, two tailors, three shoemakers, and four laborers (jornaleros). In this same document we find a single master carpenter and a married master barber surgeon, whose wife remained in Spain, sharing an apartment with a widowed master tailor, his single journeyman, and young apprentice.[42] While it is certain that individual crafts and trades provided central pillars of plebeian identity, the complex, integrated nature of plebeian housing in Buenos Aires suggests the existence of a broader class identity that was reinforced by leisure activities experienced in the pulperías or sporting and gambling venues of neighborhoods.

But these living arrangements were generally short term and unstable. Individual laborers and artisans passed from one rented room or apartment to another, from one cuartel or parish to another, or from Buenos Aires to other colonial cities, seeking marginal advantages in living and working conditions and wages. The historians of colonial Spanish America have never adequately appreciated this social dynamism and fluidity. An example of this complex ebb and flow is revealed if we extract all the artisans registered in the Buenos Aires city census of 1778 and compare this population with the list of artisans compiled by city notaries in the craft matriculations ordered by Viceroy Juan José de Vértiz y Salcedo two years later.[43] Slightly less than 45 percent of the artisans found in the 1778 census were present in the craft-based lists produced just two years later. Because there were differences in the methods applied to these counts, we certainly cannot presume that every artisan recorded in the 1778 census but missing in the 1780 census left the city, looking to improve his prospects, to escape his debts, or to embark on an adventure. Nevertheless, the pattern of restless movement that characterized this class should be obvious.[44] The Buenos Aires plebe existed in a state of continuous movement and renewal. Roots were shallow, and the winds were strong.

While a large minority of the native born entered trades as young men and then remained in Buenos Aires for the remainder of their working lives, this was always a highly mobile population little constrained by family obligations, property ownership, or loyalty to employers. Marriage to a local woman and the creation of a family rooted only a small minority of European immigrants and migrants from the interior provinces once in Buenos Aires. The character of the local labor market clearly contributed to the restless habits of this mobile class. While some laborers and journeymen experienced stable employment for months at a time, it was more common for artisans and laborers to work for a single employer for only days or weeks. For example, during a seven-month period in 1780, the colonial government employed twenty-five different journeymen bricklayers to repair a seawall. Only one man worked all seven months while the majority, fifteen, worked only a single month on this project.[45] Whenever the end of a job coincided with some savings accumulation, laborers and artisans balanced the need to search for employment in Buenos Aires with the ever-present seduction of hitting the road.

Because wages were high in late colonial Buenos Aires (relative to Spain and other Spanish colonies) artisans or laborers as individuals or as groups could quickly collect the resources to cross the estuary to Montevideo, to go up river to Asunción, or even to undertake the much more arduous trek to Potosí. The experience of traveling with friends and workmates, seeking employment, and sharing rooms and meals while on the move had long been an essential element of European artisan life, but historians have largely ignored the importance of this practice for the Spanish colonies. This was the case with Sebastián Lincel y Ortega and Patricio Molina, two journeymen tailors, who arrived together in Buenos Aires after meeting in Córdoba where they stopped to replenish their pocketbooks by working for six months. Once in Buenos Aires they roomed together near the Plaza Mayor, sometimes finding opportunities to work together.

Once the lives of artisans or laborers intersected as they moved between cities or among employers, residential settings, and leisure activities, bonds were forged that could last a lifetime.[46] When in 1795 judicial authorities asked the French-immigrant baker Juan Luis Dumont how he knew the tailor Andres de Espelan, another French immigrant, he replied that they had met first in Cádiz before immigrating. When Espelan eventually arrived in Buenos Aires, Dumont was already established. Reunited, Dumont offered his old friend a place to stay, lent him money, and then introduced him to his friends.[47] The versions of masculine culture transmitted through apprenticeships and less formal introductions to the world of work were essentially uniform across the large distances of the Spanish imperial system and were locally renewed and revised in the social intersections imposed by the sometimes harsh realities of work, housing, and leisure in Buenos Aires.

Marriage and Family

When artisans and laborers married they pulled loose (rather than completely withdrew) from the matrix of skill acquisition and fellowship that framed their formative years as men and as workers. The distance that marriage put between a man and his workmates and companions was an effective marker of this transition. Among the 921 masters and journeymen registered in Buenos Aires in 1780, only 43 percent were married. Master artisans, older and wealthier as a group, were more likely than journeymen to be married, 52 percent to 36 percent respectively. Yet, the fact that 48 percent of masters in Buenos Aires were unmarried distinguishes this colonial case from that of Europe, where nearly all masters were married or widowed.[48] While most male plebeians deferred marriage until they were thirty years old or older and many never married, there were powerful material inducements to eventually marry. Marriage to the widow of a master or a small shopkeeper was a time-honored means of accelerating the transition from journeyman to master or to economic self-sufficiency, since a widow was able to offer her deceased husband's tools, materials, and shop as a de facto dowry to an ambitious suitor. These kinds of transferable assets held the promise of advancement and enhanced earnings for both immigrant and native journeymen.

Among master artisans, those born in Buenos Aires and those born in the interior of the Viceroyalty of Río de la Plata were the least likely to marry. European immigrants, on the other hand, were the most likely to marry. While 43 percent of *porteño* masters married, 47 percent of Spanish immigrants married. Immigrants from other European nations were even more likely to marry than Spaniards: 71 percent of Portuguese immigrants and 61 percent of immigrants from other European nations were married in 1780. Even slaves who gained the rank of master were more likely to marry (with 80 percent) than were free masters born in Buenos Aires.[49]

Spanish law helped to create these patterns. Immigrants from outside the Spanish Empire, especially those who entered Buenos Aires without legal permission for residence, could legalize their residency status by marriage to a local woman. There were other advantages as well.[50] While single men born in Buenos Aires or the nearby countryside were able to count on their birth families and networks of long-established friends for small loans, business referrals, and, in hard times, food and shelter, European immigrants and migrants from interior provinces could only replicate these support mechanisms through marriage to a local woman, creating in effect a parallel set of social assets that imitated the emotional and economic endowments available naturally to the native born.[51]

Like marriage, we can use homeownership as a marker for rootedness and commitment to the local community. In 1780 only 26 percent of all master artisans owned their own homes, and, surprisingly, journeymen were just as likely to own a home as were masters. Silversmiths and other skilled artisans who serviced the upper end of the consumer market were, in fact, among the least likely to purchase a home. On the other hand, homeownership among artisans and less skilled laborers in the less prestigious building trades like carpentry, bricklaying, and masonry was common. This was probably because men in these trades could trim costs by doing the work themselves, but we must suspect that cultural factors played a role as well. In 1780 three-quarters of all master bricklayers and stone masons owned their homes as did nearly half of all master carpenters. The city's largest artisan trade, shoemaking, displayed the more universal pattern with only 16 percent of masters owning homes.[52]

Among less skilled laborers, marriage and homeownership were more predictably associated, suggesting that physical mobility was more common for artisans who could shop their skills in nearly any of the viceroyalty's urban settings than for laborers who were generally unable to differentiate themselves from competitors by demonstrating unique skills. The unskilled workers who did the brutal and dangerous work of the city's slaughter yards, for example, had a much higher incidence of both marriage and home ownership than did the city's most skilled artisans. Nearly all these laborers were locals or recent immigrants from nearby provinces of the viceroyalty. Of the 128 workers employed in slaughtering in 1788, 100 were married and among them 78 owned a home.[53]

The social and occupational trajectories of both laborers and artisans followed similar paths. They entered the world of work as boys and deferred marriage to their late twenties or thirties. Many never married, forging instead a series of casual or short-term relationships with women in multiple locations. One consequence of this pattern was that many of their sons and daughters were born out of wedlock, the mothers becoming heads of household and disguising the illegitimacy of children by claiming to be widows.[54] Many marriages subsequently fractured as men moved on in search of better opportunities, promising to later send for wives or families. Some never reestablished contact while many others maintained only episodic contacts. Plebeian marriages, marriages serially disrupted by travel in search of employment, were necessarily fragile and sometimes violent. Some women sought divorce or other forms of separation from abusive or incompetent husbands. This led the bishop of Buenos Aires to write to the Council of the Indies in 1780 to ask that a Casa de Recogimiento be created to "control women who live as libertines or solicit divorce for frivolous pretexts."[55]

In 1792 the shoemaker José Manuel de los Santos murdered his wife. While the prisoner awaited the resolution of his case the alcalde embargoed and inventoried his goods. The goods had little value but the alcalde sought to protect the meager legacy due the prisoner's four minor children, who were soon to be orphans.[56] While there were few spousal murders, jealousy and violence were common in marriages routinely assaulted by the effects of poverty, separation, and long working hours. The probate process often revealed these tensions. In 1781 the probate of the criollo blacksmith Josef de Viera Lobo demonstrated that he was a man of substantial property. At the time of his death he owned his shop, his home, and four slaves. He had four thousand pesos in silver coins and was owed two thousand five hundred pesos by the estate of a customer. Even in death Viera Lobo attempted to maintain his power over his wife, stipulating in his will that if she remarried then 20 percent of her inheritance was to be transferred to the surviving children.[57]

Honor and the Construction of Masculinity

While still in their early teens, apprentices and young laborers entered a world of work and leisure in which they struggled to master skills and gain some measure of independence and autonomy. Older, more experienced men dominated this world and in formal and less structured ways they passed on the values and behaviors that attached to masculinity. Young men were expected to be deferential but not craven or cowardly. At first they had little freedom, but as they learned skills, earned wages, and gained size and strength, it was expected that they would become more assertive and less willing to accept insults and physical challenges. In the language of this class they learned to act like men. That is, they sought to enhance and protect their honor. Honor in this context was not understood to be merely correct behavior. It was a defensible claim to social authority, the ability to compel or command others.[58] Put another way, it was an ambition to dominate others and the fear of humiliation at the hands of others.

Few members of the colonial elite or less prestigious colonial middling groups believed that laborers and artisans could have honor, although there were some exceptions.[59] The most successful members of the most prestigious crafts like silversmiths and jewelry makers were assumed to have honor as were the wealthiest bakers and small manufacturers, two groups that owned substantial property that included slaves. Nevertheless, the fact that even these affluent artisans worked with their hands or routinely conducted retail trade directly with the public limited their claims to honor and status. These limitations can be viewed clearly in the exclusion of artisans, even the most affluent, from significant public office, although a small number of artisans did serve as *alcaldes de barrio*, unpaid neighborhood police officials, in Buenos Aires.[60]

Race reinforced the common prejudice against manual labor. By the 1790s many trades in Buenos Aires had black and mixed-race majorities, but even in white-dominated trades, like silversmiths and shipyard workers (caulkers and ship carpenters), casta minorities were highly visible. The combination of significant numbers of free black and casta artisans as well as the growing presence of slaves in artisan trades depreciated the reputation of the manual arts generally and separated all but a handful of artisans and laborers from the culture of honor.[61] In March 1806 this was remarked upon in a long article published in *Seminario de Agricultura, Industria y Comercio*, the city's lone periodical at this time. The anonymous author began by expressing pride in the city's affluence and dynamism. He then asked rhetorically why there were so many "sterile and unemployed" workers. In effect, he asked how abundant opportunity could coincide so comfortably with "complete laziness." The author's explanation was that propertied men and women who "sought to maintain themselves without work" had profited from the increased importation of slaves and their employment in artisan trades. The labor of the slaves, he asserted, "earned something more than the interest owed on the borrowed funds used to purchase them." As the city employed slaves in greater numbers, Spaniards (used in this case to include the white, native born) refused to apprentice their sons in trades where slaves were present in large numbers. Could the sons of free men and women enter trades as apprentices without surrendering their claims to honor, the author asked.[62] The solution, he claimed, was to enforce the separation of freemen and slaves in a limited number of masters' shops.

While few artisans or laborers directly claimed to have honor, the values and related behaviors of this cultural system had penetrated nearly every level of masculine society. Plebeians were every bit as sensitive to the experience of shame and humiliation as were members of the elite and professional classes. Artisans and laborers often used violence or, in some cases, brought criminal charges for the offense of *malas palabras* to avenge insults. For example, in 1793 when Bernardino Luque called the wife of the shoemaker Andres Morales "a fox and a whore," Morales went to court and forced a retraction and apology.[63]

These patterns of provocation and violent response dominated the relationships of even the youngest members of the working class in late colonial Buenos Aires. While at work or during leisure activities young men were subject to severe discipline and humiliating corporeal punishments by both employers and older workmates. At the same time they were ceaselessly admonished to "act like men," to respond to insult and challenge. Masculine relationships were constructed in the dangerous arena of teasing and challenging taunts that sorted out leaders and followers (machos and their victims), but not every jest or prank required a violent response. If the challenger used the right tone and avoided the most provocative topics, playful banter helped to build intimacy and friendship. Every young man needed to learn to distinguish between what could be tolerated and what could not. Failure to recognize the line between affectionate teasing and insult was dangerous because it inevitably led to loss of reputation or to confrontation and violence.

In July 1783 a group of three friends, the fourteen-year-old apprentice shoemaker José de la Cruz and two of his workmates, crossed paths with Ygnacio, an eighteen-year-old wagoneer's helper. José's friends included an older pardo apprentice and a young Spanish boy (*mozo*). The three boys were on their way to a fandango in the Retiro neighborhood, having already visited a pulpería where each boy had had at least two brandies. Trouble began with an exchange of insults in the street. Ygnacio pushed the youngest and smallest of José's group to the ground and walked off, returning within minutes with two allies. As the confrontation heated up, Ygnacio threw a brick at José who responded by pulling out a small knife and stabbing Ygnacio in the chest. His honor protected, José de la Cruz and his two friends left Ygnacio bleeding in the street and went to the dance. Later arrested by an alcalde de barrio, José showed no remorse, stating simply that he had responded naturally to Ygnacio's insults and assault.[64] The court exonerated him.

Honor also had a specific sexual and gender character. Mediterranean codes of honor had provided the foundation for the system of honor found in late colonial Buenos Aires, although important differences appeared in response to local conditions and experiences.[65] In important ways a man's honor depended on the sexual behavior and moral reputation of his female relatives, especially his wife. As a result, words or actions that challenged the reputation of a wife, daughter, or mother often provoked a violent response. Among plebeians the weakness or even temporary absence of a father or husband could put a woman at risk. Demeaning comments, allegations of promiscuity, and sexual assaults roiled the lives of unprotected plebeian women, who were forced by their employment to conduct their daily lives in streets and markets. Masculine culture judged that a man's failure to act with proper courage and physical skill was, in effect, an admission that his wife or other female family members were undefended. His cowardice and incompetence, manifested as a failure to avenge being shamed or

FIGURE 9 Interior of pulpería. The artist represents the mix of activities and customers common in the neighborhoods of laborers and artisans. Source: Gregorio Ibarra, *Trajes y costumbres de la Provincia de Buenos Aires* (Buenos Aires: César Hippolyte Bacle y compania, 1833).

humiliated, was often interpreted to mean that liberties could be taken with his female relatives.

Even among friends and kinsmen, jests, pranks, and roughhousing could provoke violence. On October 17, 1793, the master shoemaker José Escobar, a pardo immigrant from the Canaries, invited his journeyman Justo Gorordo, two other journeymen shoemakers, and a soldier to his rented room after an evening drinking at a pulpería. Friendly banter and teasing led to rough horseplay. Eventually, the three younger men began fighting in earnest. When Escobar tried to intervene, Gorordo lost his temper and slashed his employer's arm with a knife.[66] Why would Gorordo attack his employer and occasional drinking associate rather than one of the three men with whom he had been fighting? While denying that he had cut Escobar, Gorordo still complained that his employer's intervention in the fight was an act of disloyalty. In the culture of honor, he seemed to say, failure to support a friend in whatever circumstance was a form of betrayal.

Because most single laborers and artisans shared rooms with workmates or, in many cases, with near strangers, there was little privacy. Once an argument had begun or insults were exchanged, combatants found it diffi-cult to walk away and cool down. Despite the apparent intimacy of these housing arrangements, few members of this class knew their neighbors and workmates well. The combination of residential patterns that provided little privacy and the restless mobility of the Buenos Aires plebe proved an explo-sive environment for the values of the culture of honor.

The growing prosperity of Buenos Aires after 1776 led to a building boom that promoted the construction trades and local brick factories. The owners were generally men and women of modest means, most working alongside their slaves and free laborers. This was hard, dirty work that paid little for experience or skill. Laborers were paid the least amount possible and workforces ebbed and flowed in response to changing demand. Workers were universally poor, few were married, and employment was unstable. Brickyards well exemplify the pattern of fluid employment and forced inti-macy, and a murder committed at a brick factory in 1780 illuminates the connection between these characteristics and masculine violence.

With the owner of the factory away from Buenos Aires on business, his ten employees and an acquaintance from a nearby farm spent the morn-ing gambling at cards. In the course of the card game, the young farm-worker began to argue with an older man, Ramón, over a bet. As the two men argued, one of the other brickyard laborers, Joseph, intervened, calling Ramón "a shit from Santiago del Estero" and "a son of a whore who had been thrown out of the tent." Ramón replied in kind calling Joseph "a son of a whore." Bricks followed insults, until Ramón pulled a knife and fatally stabbed Joseph through the heart.

After the arrest of the perpetrator, testimony provided to authorities by witnesses revealed the easy cohabitation of familiarity and anonymity among the plebe. None of the witnesses knew the last name of either vic-tim or perpetrator even though they had shared meals and living quarters in a small shed on the factory grounds for weeks. When asked by the in-vestigator to provide the racial identity of the perpetrator and victim they proved equally incompetent, variously identifying each as mestizo, casta, and pardo. Without supervision the workers, comfortable in the superficial intimacy of their circumstances, had left their work at the brick factory and begun a daylong card game that ultimately led to the clumsy effort at cheat-ing and to the verbal challenge and insults that precipitated the homicide.[67]

While the colonial elite assumed the dominance of free, white Europeans, the world of artisans and laborers confounded these expectations routinely. Many recently arrived European journeymen worked for criollo or even casta masters in many trades. It was not uncommon in Buenos Aires for black and casta master artisans to supervise white apprentices. Among laborers like long-distance cart drivers it was not uncommon for an experienced slave to supervise mixed crews of slaves and free laborers. Nevertheless, whites and light-skinned castas presumed their superiority to free blacks and slaves, especially in casual situations. Slaves, black freemen, Europeans, criollos, and castas also lived together in diverse and unpredictable ways.[68] Yet race was a central component of social identity, and prejudice and discrimination were common. This combination of pervasive integration in work, housing, and social life and the presumption of clear racial hierarchy led inexorably to conflict as plebeians struggled to sort out their sense of proper order.

In the surviving criminal records for the period, there are only a few homicides where the victim was white and the perpetrator black. There are even fewer cases where a white took the life of a black in a private quarrel. Generally speaking, homicides and assaults in Buenos Aires linked perpetrators and victims from the same or proximate racial and class categories. In fact, the majority of both homicides and assaults involved castas or blacks. Inhibited from freely protecting their honor from the taunts and insults of whites, young black freemen often vented their anger and frustration on targets less comprehensively protected by law and custom — slaves.

It is among these marginalized groups, that the interplay of masculine values and anxiety about status produced its most dangerous content.[69] Free blacks (both pardos and morenos) and other castas operated within the same system of masculine values as their white peers, that is, a masculine culture of honor derived largely from Mediterranean Europe. Even male slaves sought to achieve some approximation of this ideal. Yet, in their daily undertakings, black and casta males, free and especially slave, were compelled to accept a set of legal restraints and social presumptions that conflicted with their need to protect personal honor against insults and physical challenges. In this social system, the position of a black freeman or male slave was nearly intolerable, since neither was sanctioned to unambiguously assert the pride and aggressiveness that were at the center of male culture.[70]

Shoemaking was the most completely integrated artisan occupation in colonial Buenos Aires. At the time of the creation of the Viceroyalty of Río

FIGURE 10 A broom maker sells his wares in the street. Source: Gregorio Ibarra, *Trajes y costumbres de la Provincia de Buenos Aires* (Buenos Aires César Hippolyte Bacle y compania, 1833).

de la Plata in 1776, there were already a large number of successful black masters in this trade. The shop of the pardo master shoemaker José Antonio Orrega was not unusual: he employed five journeymen, two apprentices, and a slave helper. This group included two whites, four free pardos, a mestizo, and the moreno slave owned by someone else.[71] Testimony later provided to investigators makes it clear that few of the workers knew each other well. Almost no one could provide the last name of any of his workmates. Still, it appears that José Antonio Orrega's shop was an easygoing workplace characterized by constant banter and playful jests. On October 30, 1777, the journeyman Matheo Troncoso's repeated taunts provoked the moreno slave Casimiro Falcon to respond in kind. As the exchange heated up, insults flew back and forth. When Troncoso, a free pardo, threw a shoe, the slave Casimiro grabbed a stool and a sharp tool. Troncoso then pulled his knife and stabbed the slave twice, nearly killing him. Following the investigation, Troncoso agreed to pay Casimiro's owner for lost wages, medical costs, and court fees.

Similarly, in 1780, the free pardo, journeyman carpenter Terbacio seriously wounded José, a slave of the master carpenter Domingo Garay. Again the attack was preceded by what appeared to be jests and harmless taunts exchanged by workmates. As was customary, the slave José had prepared yerba, Paraguayan tea, for his master's employees at midmorning. When he asked the journeyman Terbacio for an unfinished board to use as a serving tray, Terbacio refused. Insults were exchanged until the pardo journeyman, enraged by what he took to be the presumption of the slave, struck a near mortal blow with his chisel.[72] Despite society's use of laws and less formal devices to define and enforce hierarchies of race and status, the everyday understanding of hierarchy among plebeian men — the ability of one man to compel the subordination of another — was forged dialectically in sometimes violent contests of strength and will.

Late-eighteenth-century Buenos Aires was an immigrant city, free immigrants arrived from Europe and the interior of the viceroyalty and slaves were brought to the city by the growing African trade. As a result, the working class was fluid in nature with large numbers of young men entering the city's labor force for brief periods on their way to other colonial cities, the agricultural frontier, or the Atlantic trade system. Males of this youthful and highly mobile plebeian world were united by a desire to protect themselves from insult and intimidation and were only slightly constrained by the relatively small number of older experienced men willing to stifle the passion and aggressiveness of young apprentices and laborers. Because they lived surrounded by strangers, deprived of privacy, and unconstrained by obligations to family, young men often found the burden of defending their honor heavy indeed.

Public Representations and the Private
World of Friendship and Leisure

Despite the absence of formal guilds, the skilled craftsmen of Buenos Aires still understood themselves and represented themselves to authorities with the nomenclature and rhetoric of the fully formed European model that few knew through direct experience. They referred to themselves as masters or journeymen and routinely expressed pride in this tradition of skilled work when addressing the cabildo or the colonial government. These institutions in turn acknowledged these claims on status and privilege by permitting, even encouraging, the retention of a vestigial guild structure that allowed minimal elements self-governance and a limited participation in the city's civic and religious life.[73] Artisans were particularly visible in the civic and religious rituals and festivals that gave outward expression to the society's ideal of organic hierarchical order.[74]

The cabildo facilitated these forms of participation in the rituals of urban life by identifying one or more senior masters in the most-skilled crafts as a *maestro mayor*, charging them with organizing participation in religious and civic festivals, resolving disputes within the trade, and supervising the examination system for apprentices and journeymen. While the selection of these craft representatives was useful to the political authorities, their ability to exercise actual influence among their peers by enforcing compliance with craft standards was very limited. Religious *cofradías* and *hermandades*, however, were common in Buenos Aires and attracted many artisans, laborers, and slaves. Unlike cities with fully developed guild systems, the porteño versions of these organizations seldom recruited their members from a single craft and none had an endowment of any consequence.[75] Nevertheless, cofradías and hermandades helped to organize the life of the plebe, giving dignity and purpose to collective life. If these elemental structures used to guide the skilled workers of Buenos Aires proved a weak prop for controlling recruitment, training, or standards, they were substantial enough to organize participation in public festivals.[76]

Both local and imperial authorities and foreign visitors to Buenos Aires routinely offered two critical assessments of the local labor market and the character of the plebe. Nearly all expressed frustration with a labor market characterized by labor scarcity and high wages.[77] These same commentators often claimed the plebe was sunk in sloth and addicted to games, drunkenness, and casual crime. Félix de Azara, for example, noted "the repugnance felt for work is always stronger in America than in other parts."[78] Located at the intersection of these two claims was the assumption that the labor shortage resulted from lazy and irresponsible plebeians withholding their labor while using the unnaturally high wages of the city to fund their leisure.

These beliefs provided the logic for an array of repressive, if mostly inef-fective, police and labor policies generated by both municipal and colonial authorities. Typical of these measures was a 1790 *bando* published by Vice-roy Nicolás de Arredondo that stated, "it is necessary to eliminate the idle-ness of certain people. Vagrants should be persecuted and punished without delays, because their hands have to be applied to productive activities for their own benefit and for the common good."[79]

Beginning in the 1780s the physical settings of working-class leisure and conviviality, like the city's gaming and drinking establishments, were regulated by a strict licensing regime that included limiting hours of opera-tion and controlling the plebe's preferred forms of entertainments.[80] By the 1790s the cabildo focused its attention on the city's growing slave popu-lation, banning dances, drumming, and other social activities organized by the city's growing number of African fraternal organizations.[81] At the same time, municipal and colonial authorities increasingly subjected free laborers to punitive criminal penalties for theft, fencing stolen merchandise, and minor acts of violence. Most typically, authorities used terms of forced labor to discipline the plebe. In a world where authorities viewed plebeian sociability as sloth and plebeian sport as criminality, repression and com-pulsion were inevitable. By 1800 the wheat harvest as well as most public improvements depended on forced labor drafts taken from the city jail or recruited by police sweeps of taverns and gaming establishments. This form of forced labor offered the secondary benefit of reduced costs, since pris-oners worked "for food and without wage."[82]

These draconian restrictions on the mobility, work patterns, and leisure of the plebe were of limited efficacy, forcing the cabildo to attempt effec-tive compliance through a series of legal refinements and improved law en-forcement. While the elite and other propertied groups sought to impose discipline and direction on a contentious plebe thought to be seduced into idleness by the ready availability of work and by the abundance of relatively cheap food, the plebe invented an ever-changing array of tactics to neutral-ize or limit the effectiveness of these controls. Cultural and labor policies were therefore an effort to deny the plebe the two essential benefits that logically followed from an economy where labor supply trailed the rate of economic expansion, high wages, and access to leisure. In the end neither the imposition of social controls on free laborers nor an increasing recourse to the African slave trade succeeded in disciplining the plebe or repressing this assertive culture rooted in a blend of African, European, and local traditions.

Bullfighting was the most popular blood sport in colonial Buenos Aires, and it attracted both the plebe and the elite. Municipal authorities first held staged bullfights in Buenos Aires in the middle of the seventeenth century. In the late colonial period it remained the most popular mass entertainment but was substantially altered. Originally, the elite had both organized and performed in these events while the plebe watched. As late as the 1770s young men from the city's propertied class fought bulls from horseback, demonstrating skills associated with the warrior culture they presumed justified their high status.[83] In the late eighteenth century this sport was professionalized, and the nature of both elite and plebeian participation radically transformed.[84] Permanent bullrings constructed by profit-seeking investors replaced the temporary bullrings created in the Plaza Mayor by earlier generations at the same time that professional toreros replaced elite amateurs.[85]

With these changes in place, the relationship between bullfight crowds, overwhelmingly composed of the paying urban masses, and performers, paid experts recruited from plebeian ranks, changed.[86] Plebeians discarded earlier inhibitions as they became a central, even defining, part of the performance, shouting out their opinions of both bulls and toreros. While the viceroy, members of the audiencia, and cabildo were almost always present at the bullring, as were members of the commercial elite and other propertied groups, the demonstrative reactions of the plebe framed opinion and gave these events their essential character.[87] When bulls failed to display courage and aggression the crowd typically demanded that firecrackers be attached to the banderillas to provoke them. The crowd mercilessly tormented toreros, banderilleros, and picadores who proved clumsy, craven, or timid in the ring and, in some cases, later in the streets.[88] It is clear that by the late 1790s when the new bullring in Plaza Monserrat was fully operational, the collective pleasure, anger, or hilarity of boisterous and exuberant crowds of plebeians defined the experience of the privileged groups so visibly present in the more expensive and protected seats.

While connections are not obvious, it is clear that the popular classes increasingly influenced the spectacle of the bullring, paralleling the incremental process in which slaves and free laborers insinuated themselves into the porteño experience of carnival. As early as the 1770s colonial administrators and ecclesiastical authorities began to criticize what they saw as scandalous behavior during carnival. No longer safely contained within the walls of elite residences, carnival had begun to take on a riotous public character. Wealthy families had moved their evening parties and dances away from their city homes to country estates, and participants had begun to affect costumes and wear masks. During the day groups of young pranksters, men and women, took over windows and rooftops to throw water bombs, typically eggshells filled with perfumed water, or small bags of flour at passersby. At the time, the most aggressive of these rampaging parties were made up entirely of women. The city specifically banned throwing "eggs, water, or flour" in 1792 under penalty of a twenty-five peso fine. These status-bending and rule-breaking enthusiasms ultimately infected the celebration of Christmas as well. Viceroy Arredondo, concerned throughout his viceregency with order, reacted by ordering that "families and individuals" return to their homes following religious ceremonies under threat of incarceration, "regardless of their status."[89] Over time the plebe insinuated itself into these customs, giving a sharp edge to previously tame practices.[90] Black men and women, their faces whitened by flour paste, increasingly asserted the right to participate in these comic "attacks" launched in the streets of the city center.

Simultaneously authorities responded to growing fears provoked by dances organized by African slaves. Slaves and free blacks located their dances at *tambos* secured for this purpose on the suburban fringes of the city, and loud drum music drove the dancers. The cabildo and police authorities saw these assemblies as threatening and the dancing as lascivious and overtly sexual, but this alone did not move them to act. Rather it was the undeniable fact that these dances attracted growing numbers of free blacks, castas, and even "decent" men and women. During his term, Governor Juan José de Vértiz y Salcedo, later the second viceroy of the Río de la Plata, attempted to suppress both the masked balls and the African dances.[91] Once these ineffective efforts to control the city's black population were initiated, they were repeated by Vértiz y Salcedo's successors with little effect to the end of the colonial period.

By the end of the 1780s the elite and plebeian traditions had begun to meld in Buenos Aires. The plebe, like the elite, began to participate in carnival in disguise and began to playfully attack authority and hierarchy. The elite, like the plebe, began to experiment with African rhythms and the public suggestion of sexuality. The cultural boundaries of class and race were less clearly drawn and less reliably defended in these circumstances. What is clear is that the plebe recognized that certain venues, the bullring or city streets during carnival, allowed them to temporarily suspend controls. Individuals disguised by masks or blackened by soot or hidden in large crowds could make scandalous or defamatory statements not safely expressed elsewhere. Within limits, they could challenge, torment, confront, or even assault, with bags of flour or with water bombs, the powerful. Despite oft-repeated efforts to control or ban these "excesses" outright, these ritual challenges to established authority endured. In 1795 Viceroy Nicolás de Arredondo banned again "the sport [of throwing] water, flour, eggs and other things" during carnival as the fears generated by the French Revolution and the Haitian Revolution gave the drums, masks, and loud, riotous confrontations in the streets a darker more overtly political coloration.[92]

The collective personality of the plebe as manifested in crowd behavior at the bullring or in the city streets during carnival or other festival days was rooted in a rich network of friendship, leisure, and work experience that attached the lives of artisans and laborers to each other and to the cityscape. Given that a majority of the city's artisans and laborers at any time were single men and given that few had long-term employment or fixed residence, rich layers of friendship and attachment, ranging from intimate to casual, were created during a working life. Over a relatively short period each individual worked with scores of men and lived with scores more. The absence of privacy and lack of comfort in the rooms and sheds they inhabited pushed them into the streets and from the streets to taverns, pulperías, and gaming places where associations proliferated. In these venues a secondary masculine hierarchy was established. If skill levels, seniority, race, and wealth organized the hierarchy of work, the hierarchy of leisure was based on athleticism, vivacity, and generosity with one's friends and workmates. Men with a few reales in their pockets treated friends and acquaintances to wine or *aguardiente*, bought roasted chickens and salads to share, or wagered on athletic contests or games of chance.[93] Openhandedness was respected, and meanness was the butt of jokes and pranks.

Cockfighting, a blood sport like bullfighting, was set in more intimate locales, purpose-built sheds or small buildings equipped with rings and seats or open lots or patios were temporarily appropriated for these contests. By the end of the eighteenth century a small number of men had begun to breed fighting cocks in the city and the nearby countryside, and promoters were competing for the patronage of the enthusiasts. The plebe's passion for gambling, more than the spectacle itself, drove the popularity of cock-fighting. Despite the relative poverty of this class, gambling was attached to nearly every leisure activity or sport. Card and dice games were everywhere. In 1780 the bishop complained in a letter to the Council of the Indies that gambling was the "ruin of the residents," claiming "even children ten years of age gambled." [94] While billiards tables were located in the cafes that served the wealthy and gender-segregated card games gave pleasure in the homes of elite and middling groups, artisans and laborers found their pleasures elsewhere. [95] A majority of *pulperos* provided tables for cardplayers. To police authorities the combination of gambling and drink in the pulperías served as an open invitation to the plebe to plan thefts and fence stolen goods. In 1790 Viceroy Nicolás de Arredondo expressed this opinion neatly, offering intensified regulation as "the immediate remedy for the disorders and excesses that are committed in pulperías." [96] He required pulperos to immediately register and pay for a license to operate in the city limits. [97] His analysis and remedy were not unique since authorities at every level viewed pulperías as venues of masculine violence and property crime, citing as evidence that most of the city's murders and assaults were committed in or near pulperías. [98]

A handful of local entrepreneurs built *canchas de bolos*, a form of lawn bowling, where competitors displayed their skills while onlookers placed bets. [99] Authorities saw this game and the bets it attracted as particularly dangerous, threatening "families" and provoking slaves to run away from masters and workers to embrace idleness. According to the cabildo the players were "lazy, vagabonds, and delinquents." [100] Periodic efforts to repress the sites were then predictably relaxed when connected investors sought licenses. In 1796, for example, a militia captain, Don Carlos Pereda, petitioned the cabildo to open a "cancha" in Plaza Nueva, but, despite his status, was turned down on the advice of the *procurador* because of the "robberies and dangers that would result, prejudicing the Republic." [101]

Pelota, a form of modern handball, was often played on purpose-built courts, a *fronton*, but it was more common for players to improvise a court wherever they found flat ground and a brick wall. Skilled players drew crowds and hotly contested games lasted hours. Bochas, modern boche ball, was an open air relative of bolos, that gained great popularity in Buenos

Aires. Pulperos built many of the most popular canchas as a way of gaining larger clienteles for their dry goods, food, and drink. Skilled players, scheming with unacknowledged partners who placed wagers, easily manipulated both of these games of skill.[102] The explosive mix of sport, wagers, and the suspicion of cheating were a predictable antecedent to violence. The response of city authorities was to limit the number and hours of pulperías, frontons, boche courts, and gaming places.[103] The inefficacy of these regulations and restrictions is demonstrated by the regularity with which they were repeated by the cabildo. As the costs of defense rose in the first decade of the nineteenth century, the municipality reversed course in order to impose new revenue-generating taxes on these gaming and drinking establishments. The effect was immediate as the number of cafes, canchas, and *billares* increased 30 percent in the next year.[104]

The vitality and endurance of these props to conviviality and leisure suggest in turn their importance to the laboring classes, especially to single men in the early stages of their careers. In these settings reputation was as likely to rest on accomplishment and skill in games or on generosity with friends and casual acquaintances as it was on skill within a craft. Buying wine for mates, sharing your winnings, or paying for a meal created the expectation of reciprocal generosity when jobs were hard to find or when illness or bad luck wiped out savings. These were also the social contexts where artisans or laborers commonly went to borrow money to purchase materials or tools or to purchase a home when marrying or starting a family. These places and the social networks they sustained served also as intelligence networks where laborers and artisans learned about local wage custom, gained referrals for jobs, and found places to stay and to get a meal.

Conclusion

In many ways late colonial Buenos Aires was a typical Spanish colonial city, but the anomalies are worth examining. Even as late as the 1790s, its political status as a viceregal capital and its commercial dynamism was of such a recent vintage that there was little political experience to rely on in a crisis or, alternatively, commercial momentum to carry the city forward in a period of interrupted trade or natural disaster. The city was rich and yet vulnerable; it was dynamic and yet its confidence was easily shaken. The laboring core of the population, the individuals and families that produced and moved goods, built and repaired the city's buildings, and conducted the retail commerce, had a mixed and contradictory character as well. Free and slave laborers worked side by side in activities as diverse as paving the streets, unloading arriving vessels, clearing the muck from stables, as well as producing the expensive silver objects that graced elite tables. The mix of Europeans, criollos, castas, and Africans in plebeian ranks was typical of Spanish colonial cities, but the power and authority of Spanish masters in artisan trades, retail commerce, and manufacturing was weaker and more easily challenged in Buenos Aires than in the most mature viceregal capitals. This population was also highly fluid and mobile, characteristics that weakened guild formation and undermined other traditional plebeian hierarchies of seniority, skill, race, and wealth. This mobility and plasticity help explain the plebe's low marriage rates as well as in its constant fluctuation in employment and residence. The cumulative effect of these characteristics was that most plebeians were only weakly connected to the city, to their employers, to their neighbors, or, in many cases, to their trades.

Despite these contradictions and the mobility and tentativeness that underlay all plebeian relationships, the artisans and laborers of late colonial Buenos Aires managed to forge a distinctive local culture. They built their friendships quickly, binding themselves together in work and leisure by privileging generosity, openness, and candor. They saw skill and physical mastery as valuable and defended themselves fiercely when diminished, threatened, or insulted by the words or actions of others. This masculine culture was warm and dangerous, spontaneous and guarded, and the workings of the porteño economy reinforced these characteristics.

As the city and regional economies expanded after 1780, wages were pushed upward for both skilled artisans and lesser-skilled laborers, but rents and the cost of living also rose rapidly, effectively denying workingmen the expected benefits of their income. In this environment workingmen, especially single men, often took their wage premiums in the form of greater independence, leisure, or both. The culture of honor provided the values that gave cultural meaning to these decisions. With subsistence easily provided, men routinely walked away from abusive or difficult employers; they stayed home on Mondays or came to work late; when bored, angry, or frustrated they crossed the estuary to look for work in Montevideo or sailed up river to Asunción. While the economy made it very difficult to save, purchase property, or begin a business, it simultaneously made it easy to assert independence.

3

Remembered Scripts and Atlantic Colonial Realities

The Shoemakers and Silversmiths of Buenos Aires

After work on April 30, 1779, seventy-one shoemakers met in the patio of an apartment block close to the Plaza Mayor to discuss creating a guild. While most were masters, a handful of journeymen mingled on the fringes of the assembly. The tone of the meeting was open and friendly, reflecting the fact that the shoemakers had already made the most important decisions in a series of casual conversations and smaller meetings held in the residences of the most-established masters or in *pulperías* and other public places where artisans came together after work.[1] The shoemakers had determined to create a guild before calling the general meeting.

A small group of recent immigrants from Spain had initiated this effort, but they had found many local-born allies. There were seventeen Spaniards as well as a small number of French, Portuguese, and Italian masters at the meeting, but the majority were native born. Established shoemakers like Manuel Borges, with twenty-five years of experience in his trade, and Eusebio Calvo, with forty years of experience, had always practiced their trade in Buenos Aires and had no prior, direct experience with a guild. But both men supported the initiative and brought their journeymen to the meeting. Even younger craftsmen like José Antonio de Arce, a *porteño* who had been a master for less than a year, were present in numbers.

It took the shoemakers less than an hour to agree to seek official support from Viceroy Juan José Vértiz y Salcedo (viceroy, 1778–1784). Forty-two of those who endorsed this petition were illiterate and signed with a mark. The document reflected the group's belief that a guild would allow them to regulate the volatile city market and enhance their collective social status. The petition's language closely followed the boosterism current in the public statements of the viceroy and other Spanish officials, who were simultaneously promoting an array of local improvements that included street paving and illumination, the establishment of an orphanage, and the sponsorship of theatrical productions. No one present could have anticipated that this objective, floated naively on their collective ambition, would propel this craft across three decades of destructive and costly conflict to its near extinction in the years following independence.

A second porteño craft, the silversmiths, followed a parallel but distinct path towards the same objective. Silversmiths began their quest for a guild from a stronger position, one rooted in the society's presumption that the "nobility" of their materials and the generally higher status of their clientele indicated the honor and elevated social position of the operatives themselves.[2] Perhaps because of this small advantage, relative to the shoemakers, the silversmiths did not initially seek to establish a guild. Instead, they sought limited official support for essential guild tasks like collecting dues to fund collective participation in religious and civic festivals and enforcing an examination system for journeymen seeking to become masters. Only in the 1790s would colonial authorities begin to force the silversmiths to imitate shoemakers by writing a guild constitution and acquiring official sanction. The troubled course of these two organizational efforts illuminates in surprising detail the economic and social realities experienced by skilled laborers in this fast-growing Atlantic Basin city.

The Initial Effort to Create a Guild of Shoemakers

The shoemakers immediately hired the attorney Dr. Vicente Cañete to represent them.[3] He drafted a single letter to the viceroy in which he summarized the problems afflicting the shoemakers and sought to justify the creation of a guild, asserting that "the growth, prosperity, and happiness of Republics precisely depends on the corporations dedicated to the development of industry, agriculture, and other occupations." He cleverly lubricated his request by servicing the elite's low opinion of the Buenos Aires plebe, claiming that the guild, once organized, would provide "a useful occupation to the large numbers of vagrants who threaten public order." The presumption that Buenos Aires suffered a plague of beggars and vagrants had long informed the actions of the cabildo, serving to justify the conscription of free laborers during harvest or for public works projects as well as the compulsory employment of prisoners in these tasks.

More to the point, Cañete detailed for the viceroy the difficult conditions in which the city's shoemakers exercised their craft. Because they lacked the protective carapace of a traditional guild, he stated, shoemakers faced depressed conditions and unfair competition.[4] The city's legitimate master shoemakers lived with intense price-cutting competition from the "multitude of individuals claiming to be masters who open public shops without skills superior to those of apprentices." As the number of false masters rose, he reminded authorities, the city predictably suffered from a proliferation of consumer frauds.[5]

While European immigrants provided the craft's leadership, Cañete's proposed guild organization suggests that the local-born majority had organized themselves to influence the process, avoiding a narrow imitation of Spanish practice.[6] To control costs, the shoemakers suggested only two guild officers who would have the power to assess fines, embargo inferior merchandise, and even close the shops of chronic offenders. These officers would also review the credentials of masters and institutionalize a fee-based examination process for prospective masters. This was not a fully developed draft constitution, but was instead the beginnings of what the craftsmen saw as a process of negotiation with colonial authorities. In exchange for some marginal improvements in consumer protection, the shoemakers wished to protect the economic prospects of legitimate masters or, more precisely, the men who currently claimed that status.

Shoemakers and other artisans in late colonial Buenos Aires had long used the traditional nomenclature of the European guild system, identifying themselves as masters, journeymen, and apprentices. They also used the word guild when they discussed collective participation in religious and civic celebrations with authorities, even though they lacked the capacity to enforce either standards or hierarchical discipline. In this city ambitious journeymen and sometimes even apprentices routinely claimed the status of master and opened shops in competition with former employers. The racial and religious restrictions that framed recruitment and promotion opportunities within artisan organizations in Europe and in some of the older areas of Spain's American empire were also unenforceable in Buenos Aires. As a result, the majority of shoemakers in Buenos Aires in 1779 were native non-whites recruited and trained in the relaxed tradition of the city. While the seventy-one masters that addressed themselves to the viceroy railed against "false" masters, only a minority had bona fide credentials.

The only enforceable regulations imposed on the shoemakers as this process began were annual *aranceles*, lists of maximum retail prices for shoes and boots determined by the cabildo.[7] Intended to protect consumers from price gouging, these price ceilings combined with the cost-cutting competition of journeymen and apprentices to undermine the economic viability of the craft. Immigrant artisans, accustomed to European norms, resented the resulting economic pressures more than did native-born masters. These immigrant artisans were impatient with what they saw as lax standards and undisciplined recruitment mechanisms in Buenos Aires, but they also needed the support of native masters to establish a guild.[8] The native born realized that corporate discipline and enforceable standards were not merely ideals; potentially, they were weapons that could be used to eliminate competitors.[9] Nevertheless, men with dubious credentials or no credentials at all were present at the meeting on April 30, 1779, and openly supported the decision to create a guild. This support may have been in part the rote endorsement of an organizational form that was characteristic of the European urban economy, but it was also the result of a cold calculation made by weak and vulnerable men looking to deflect the potential consequences of new rules and regulations away from themselves from inside the guild.[10]

In response to this appeal, Viceroy Vértiz ordered the cabildo to formulate regulations for the shoemakers.[11] The cabildo in turn delegated this task to Regidor Gregorio Ramos Mexía.[12] He reported on October 12, 1779, that he had been unable to make progress because of the uncooperative and self-interested actions of the shoemakers. He complained to his colleagues that the shoemakers had provided inappropriate or spurious fragments of Spanish guild constitutions, rather than legitimate guild constitutions that might serve as a model for Buenos Aires. Impatient with this process, Ramos Mexía complained to his colleagues that they could hope for little from "a craft in which drunkenness and other vices are so deeply rooted."[13]

The regidor's undisguised dismissal of the collective character of this craft reflected the widely held opinion of his class. Few master shoemakers were men of property, and most journeymen lived lives no better than those of common laborers. Recently, authorities had arrested and jailed a number of shoemakers for begging. In fact, just two years earlier the city's elite had followed closely the arrest and punishment of two journeymen shoemakers,

Thomás, the moreno slave of Don José Lorente, and Nicolás López, a free pardo, who had been arrested for robbing the shop of another shoemaker. The two journeymen stole two pairs of shoes and a few shoemaking tools that they then fenced to a *pulpero* for the paltry sum of eleven reales. Once in custody, they admitted to additional thefts. After hearing the evidence, the presiding alcalde sentenced Thomás to one hundred lashes and the pardo freeman, Nicolás López, to death.[14] When Ramos Mexía dismissed the shoemakers as lacking the cultural qualities and dependability of Spanish artisans, his opinion found immediate purchase among his colleagues on the cabildo.

Despite his mandate to submit a draft constitution "with all possible speed," the regidor only completed his task on July 19, 1780.[15] Frustrated and angry with the shoemakers, Ramos Mexía produced a document designed to protect society from what he took to be their natural viciousness and incompetence by granting intrusive supervisory powers to the cabildo. While accepting Dr. Cañete's suggestion that two *maestros mayores* supervise standards and hierarchical discipline, he denied the membership the opportunity to elect these officers and instead gave the cabildo authority to appoint both officials. He urged his colleagues to select "the most decent and moderate individuals in the guild, those with the best reputations and most respected ability." His language suggested clearly that in such a dissolute group there would be few candidates.[16] Ramos Mexía wanted to further restrain the anarchic impulses of the shoemakers by making one of the cabildo's alcaldes the "director" of the guild with authority to audit guild funds and accounts. Under his plan, the shoemakers would pay fifty pesos annually to support the cost of this intrusive supervision of guild affairs.[17]

Ramos Mexía and the shoemakers agreed on the issue of enforcing craft standards. The regidor's draft constitution charged guild officers with policing standards and enforcing guild price lists through monthly *visitas* (inspection visits) to the shops of all shoemakers.[18] Guild officials would be empowered to assess fines and even seize the tools and close the shops of chronic offenders.[19] The maestros mayores were also to be given responsibility for the supervision of recruitment and the instruction of apprentices and journeymen, mandating six years of experience to take the examination for master. Apprenticeships would be closely regulated, "whoever would like to learn this occupation ought to register with the director of the guild and, if the son of a family, have the consent of his father, of his grandparents or guardians, and if a slave, the consent of his owner."[20] In order to maintain high recruitment standards and encourage the masters to supervise closely the behavior of their young charges, masters would be required to deposit a sum of money with the guild treasurer as a guarantee for the good conduct of each new apprentice.[21] It is no surprise that Ramos Mexía and the shoemakers who led the guild effort sought to impose financial obstacles for the rank of master, requiring in the case of the regidor the payment of forty-one pesos, an astronomical figure given that wages seldom surpassed four reales per day.[22] The draft provided that sons and sons-in-law of guild members, on the other hand, would pay 50 percent of this total, intentionally transforming the status of master into a form of hereditary endowment.[23]

Without concessions this proposal would have found few supporters among the native majority in the trade. This is why the immigrant masters, even those contemptuous of local training and standards, agreed to accept the credentials of everyone who currently claimed to be a master without scrutiny. Ramos Mexía, with the support of craft leaders, also placed no racial or ethnic restrictions on either recruitment or mobility within the trade. In a city where race and ethnicity had always had a fluid character, neither the regidor nor the European masters pushing for organization was willing to provoke division over these issues.[24] Despite these concessions and broad internal agreement in the trade, the shoemakers abandoned their effort soon after the regidor sent his draft constitution to the *sindico procurador* on July 19, 1780.[25] They would not try again until the silversmiths had gained the support of the colonial bureaucracy for their guild.

Shadow to Substance: The Guild of Silversmiths

While the shoemakers were the first to seek permission to create a guild in Buenos Aires, the city's silversmiths had already evolved an informal corporate structure. Their incremental development of guild functions, each sanctioned by custom or by the focused decisions of municipal authorities, permitted this craft's leaders to collect dues, organize participation in civic and religious festivals, and provide general supervision of recruitment and product standards.[26] While their dependence on the colonial state ultimately distorted the development of the guild, in the early 1780s when the shoemakers initiated their efforts the silversmiths were already exercising effective guild authority based on the support of the local authorities.[27]

Their craft structure imitated only in outline the mature institutions long in place in Lima or Mexico City. The guilds of silversmiths in these colonial centers were among the first Spanish economic institutions organized in the New World.[28] In both cases silversmiths had quickly evolved guild organizations that rivaled the authority exercised by contemporary Spanish corporations.[29] The wealth of their religious confraternities and the power and influence of their corporate officials placed them on a social plane with merchants and imperial bureaucrats.[30] As a result, colonial authorities granted them the right to carry swords and use the honorific *don*. Some of their children even rose to prominence in the institutions of church and state.[31] They were the aristocracy of the colonial artisan class.

Colonial records reveal the much humbler history of this trade in Buenos Aires, where only fifteen masters pursued this craft in 1748.[32] Eight of the craft's eleven masters identified by birthplace were Europeans, five of these Spaniards. The first efforts to assert the basic elements of corporate organization were provoked by the aggressive actions of the local government and later by the first appearance of chauvinist factionalism within the craft. In 1753 the alcalde of the second vote, Don Luis Aurelio de Zavala, demanded that the silversmiths contribute to the celebration of Corpus Christi as members of a "mechanical art," but the master silversmiths replied by citing Spanish precedent that they were a "liberal" art. This led to an angry face-to-face meeting with the alcalde, resulting in his decision to arrest five of the masters.[33] Threatened with additional arrests, the silversmiths named two masters, Miguel Moreno Reyes and Baltasar de Quiros, to appeal to the captain general.[34] This extraordinary meeting and the consequent nomination of the two *apoderados*, was, in effect, the first appointment of craft officials. The captain general responded favorably to the apoderados' petition and recognized the craft's status as a liberal art, ordering the release of the imprisoned masters.

It would prove much more difficult to quiet ethnic conflict once it appeared. In 1757 a group of Spanish masters undertook an aggressive campaign to eliminate Portuguese and other foreign masters from the craft. Rather than appeal to authorities, Spanish masters and journeymen took direct action by gathering in front of the shop of Manuel Pintos, a Portuguese immigrant, and angrily demanding that he shutter his shop or show his license to reside in the city. Pintos appealed to the alcalde of the first vote for protection, and the Spanish masters took their case to the full cabildo, requesting that it "deport from this city all members of this profession who are not Spaniards and not permit any individual to open a public shop if he has not been officially examined as a master."[35] While the cabildo ignored the request for deportations, it acceded to the demand that all silversmiths within its jurisdiction present "certification of examination to the alcalde."[36] This assault on the presence of foreign masters predicted the future trajectory of ethnic conflict in this craft.

The imposition of an examination system supported by the cabildo decades later proved crucial to the expansion of guild authority. Juan Antonio Callejas y Sandoval, an immigrant from Valladolid and one of the city's most prosperous silversmiths, served as the craft's *mayordomo* for nearly two decades. Already claiming this as his title, in February 1785 he petitioned the governor intendant, Francisco de Paula Sanz, to enforce the guild's requirement that members pay weekly dues of one real, since some members resisted this requirement. His exchange with authorities suggests that the informal and incremental development of the craft up to this point had led to a confused blending of guild and lay brotherhood functions. The mayordomo informed Paula Sanz that dues covered expenses associated with the annual celebration of the feast day of their patron saint, Saint Eloy, on the first Sunday of December. Callejas y Sandoval went on to claim that the excesses and irregularities of his predecessors had undermined this practice in recent years with "excess solemnity and superfluous expenses that included sung masses" in these celebrations. Previous officers, he claimed, had been seduced into fiscal irresponsibility "because no one wants to defer to another in the ostentation and magnificence of this celebration that has already become an act of extravagance and vanity."[37]

According to Callejas y Sandoval, the membership sustained this mounting extravagance with difficulty.[38] He claimed that his predecessor as mayordomo, Cipriano Rodríguez, had been forced to pay for some of the festival costs personally because the craft treasury was empty. Unwilling to absorb the loss, Rodríguez attempted to coerce the membership to reimburse him by removing and hiding the silver miter and staff used to decorate the image of Saint Eloy. Despite pleas, he had kept both objects and even threatened to sell them to cover his costs. In the end, the guild recovered these valuable articles by bringing the case to the civil magistrates and having Rodríguez threatened with jail.[39] With this recent embarrassment on the table, Callejas y Sandoval requested the governor intendant to order the silversmiths to restrain their observance of the feast day and commit themselves to "deference and moderation," limiting their observance to a single mass "without refreshments, fireworks, or music."[40] Paula Sanz acceded to this request on December 9, 1785.

Callejas y Sandoval addressed a new petition to the *audiencia* in January 1786, reiterating his complaint that some members still refused to pay dues. He claimed that "this congregation," suggesting again that he directed a *cofradía* (religious confraternity), not a guild, was dedicated to the celebration of the feast day of Saint Eloy that had been in existence since 1743.[41] The reply of the audiencia's *fiscal* was completely unanticipated; he dismissed the request out of hand, noting that because the brotherhood was not a "true and formally sanctioned cofradía or congregation as required by royal law," it was improper to require the payment of dues.

This decision meant that the craft's leaders would now have to seek formal recognition by the colonial bureaucracy or lose control over the increasingly factionalized silversmiths.[42] While Callejas y Sandoval and his predecessors used the terms guild and cofradía when addressing authorities, the silversmiths had never formally established either form of craft organization. They held regular meetings, elected officers, collected dues, celebrated the feast day of their patron, and supervised, on an informal basis, examinations and craft standards. But the fiscal now made it clear that craft leaders could not enforce any of these functions without sanction from colonial authorities. The silversmiths would need to follow the path taken by the shoemakers in 1779. Within a year Callejas y Sandoval requested that the colonial administration formally recognize the right of the guild to set policies for apprenticeship and regulate standards within the trade.[43]

Paula Sanz, a reliable friend of corporate organization, responded favorably on April 18, 1788. His *bando* asserted without qualification that no one could exercise the trade of silversmith or sell silver to the public who had not served five years of apprenticeship and two years as a journeyman with a licensed master. He also ordered all silversmiths to observe and obey the ordinances that guild members would draft now and submit to the cabildo. Anyone who violated the decree by opening a public shop without fulfilling the vocational prerequisites was to be subject to a fine and the loss of all tools and materials.[44] While this decision did not establish a formal guild, it gave Callejas y Sandoval and his supporters within the craft ad hoc authority to impose their standards and practices on reluctant colleagues. Paula Sanz had provided guild leaders with a potentially controversial authority, the novel practice of forcing compliance with yet unwritten ordinances. Since the bando did not clearly specify the standards and quality that silversmiths needed to meet, the natural legacy of this document was a proliferation of civil suits and appeals to the colonial bureaucracy. The bando of 1788 did not institute a major transformation in the relationship between the silversmiths and the bureaucracy; it formalized and embellished the old relationship, infusing it with greater promise and greater risk.

The Social Topography of Artisan Mobilization

Colonial sources permit a broad examination of these crafts in the years immediately following the creation of the Viceroyalty of Río de la Plata: a citywide census compiled in 1778 and the general matriculation of artisan crafts ordered by Viceroy Vértiz on July 31, 1780.[45] While the 1780 matriculation of shoemakers survives, the contemporary record for the silversmiths is lost. As a result, a comparison of demographic character between the two crafts must rely on the city census conducted two years earlier. *Alcaldes de barrio* and their lieutenants compiled the census by going through the city block by block, sometimes using a single informant to identify all the residents of a household or even a group of households. These officials proved most diligent, and therefore most reliable, in the city center, which was inhabited by the city's more affluent individuals and families. They were least careful in the poorest neighborhoods and shantytowns on the fringes of the city. We must presume that both the census and guild matriculation probably undercounted the poor black and casta laboring class, especially single men living in nontraditional housing.

Census takers identified 100 silversmiths and 241 shoemakers in 1778. Members of both crafts were distributed across every urban census track, but nearly 75 percent of the two crafts lived in the six *manzanas* (city blocks) that ringed the Plaza Mayor. The city census takers did not identify the craft rank of artisans but did record occupation, age, and marital status for most. In most cases they also noted household and family size as well as the number of free servants and slaves when present in a household. Census takers also indicated what contemporaries called color or calidad for all the silversmiths and 226 of the 241 shoemakers. They assigned a single category, Español, to identify both European Spaniards and criollos, thus suggesting that color was a more important marker than birthplace. This was true as well for less privileged sectors of society. Indios and mestizos, like pardos

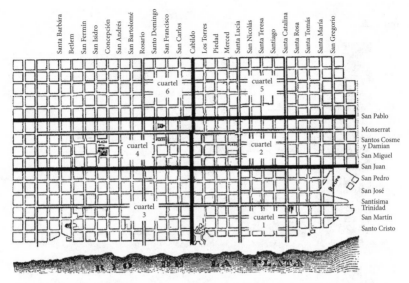

FIGURE II Buenos Aires city plan with street names and census *cuarteles*, 1778. Source: Published with the permission of the AGN, Buenos Aires, Argentina.

and morenos, were almost universally identified without reference to origins. Enumerators did carefully distinguish between free and slave, but not between those carried to Buenos Aires from Africa and their American-born progeny. The two crafts are compared in figure 12.

Census enumerators in 1778 identified 92 percent of silversmiths and 63 percent of shoemakers as whites or Españoles. Only a handful of pardos or morenos were identified among the silversmiths, but these fast-growing porteño populations contributed 33 percent to the craft ranks of the lower status and poorer shoemakers. Mestizos contributed to the final 2 percent of the silversmiths, and mestizos and indios combined made up the last 4 percent of shoemakers. The census takers took care to indicate ownership of slaves in the households of artisans. Fourteen of the one hundred silversmiths owned a total of thirty-two slaves, including one slave identified as a practicing silversmith and two slaves trained in other skilled crafts. Twenty-nine of the slaves owned by silversmiths were household servants or worked outside their masters' households as day laborers. Nearly all the silversmiths who owned slaves were European immigrants, like the Spanish-born Callejas y Sandoval who eventually owned nine slaves.[46]

The connections between the shoemakers and slavery were more important and complex than those found among the silversmiths. Shoemakers

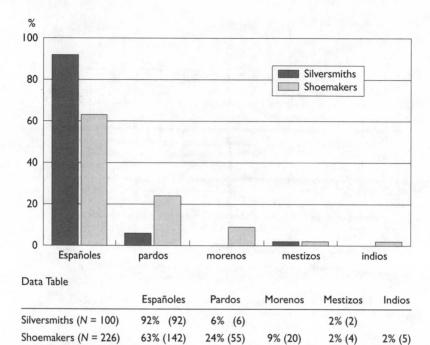

Data Table

	Españoles	Pardos	Morenos	Mestizos	Indios
Silversmiths (N = 100)	92% (92)	6% (6)		2% (2)	
Shoemakers (N = 226)	63% (142)	24% (55)	9% (20)	2% (4)	2% (5)

FIGURE 12 Racial composition of silversmiths and shoemakers (1778). Source: Universidad de Buenos Aires, *Documentos para la historia Argentina*, vol. II, *Territorio y población, Padron de la ciudad de Buenos Aires . . .*

owned fewer slaves, twenty-six, but a much larger percentage, 50 percent, had been trained in their owners' craft. In fact, eleven of the shoemakers enumerated in the census were slaves. The larger presence of slaves in craft ranks connected logically to the larger presence of free black and mulatto shoemakers relative to the silversmiths. Nearly all of the forty-nine free, black master and journeymen shoemakers had begun their training as slaves and then purchased their freedom from their savings.[47]

The 1780 artisan matriculation is a more dependable source than the 1778 census for exploring the relationship between race and ethnicity and craft status, since each artisan personally appeared before one of the cabildo's *escribanos* to enroll.[48] These face-to-face encounters were likely to produce a more reliable, if still imperfect, result. The matriculation of silversmiths is lost, but the 1780 craft matriculation of shoemakers provides the birth-place for Europeans, criollos, Indians, and mestizos. Nevertheless, as with the census, escribanos seldom assigned the birthplace of pardos and mo-renos, whether slave or free. Instead, they utilized the everyday nomenclature of calidad then in use in Buenos Aires (pardo, moreno, or, in a few cases, chino) to describe black artisans. While useful we cannot assume that escribanos applied these categories uniformly.[49]

The 1780 matriculation provides race and ethnic identities for 128 more shoemakers than had the census of 1778. The 354 shoemakers registered in 1780 were overwhelmingly American born. Porteños made up 50 percent (177) of this craft. Another 13 percent (45) were migrants from other American colonies, the majority of these castas. Only 16 percent (57) of the city's shoemakers were European immigrants, with 25 of these from Spain. The remaining 21 percent (75) were morenos and pardos, 48 slaves and 27 free-men. There were 6 Brazilians among the blacks and mulattoes, and they may have been escaped slaves, since Spanish law granted freedom to escaped slaves entering Spanish territory from the Portuguese possessions.[50]

These proportions varied from rank to rank. Among masters the propor-tions of porteños and other American born closely tracked the group's craft-wide distribution with 48 percent (62) and 11 percent (15) respectively. Only 9 masters were free pardos and morenos. European immigrants made up 34 percent (44) of all masters, but the presence of Europeans dramatically di-minished and the presence of pardos and morenos dramatically increased at the lower ranks. Among the 165 journeymen shoemakers only 6 percent (10) were European born. Porteños and migrants from other American colonies contributed 47 percent (78) and 16 percent (26) respectively to the number of journeymen shoemakers. Even at this early date the effect of the slave trade on this craft was visible, as 31 percent of the journeymen shoemakers (51) and 25 percent of apprentice shoemakers (25) were pardos or morenos. While the matriculation found four times as many slaves as freemen among black and mulatto apprentices, more than half of all black masters and jour-neymen were free. This reinforces the assumption that wages could act as a powerful solvent dissolving the chains of captivity imposed by the slave trade.[51]

Sixty-eight journeymen, or 41 percent of the total, had fewer than five years of experience in 1780. This means that more than half of the jour-neymen, 59 percent, had more than the minimum experience proposed in 1779 as a prerequisite for taking the examination for master. It is interesting to note that immigrants from Spanish colonies, Brazil, and Europe all had higher percentages at the upper end of the experience scale then did the na-tive born. This suggests that experienced shoemakers with few prospects for advancement to the master rank at home emigrated in larger numbers than did younger colleagues with better prospects. It also suggests that even in the relaxed craft environment of Buenos Aires, where there were no guilds to scrutinize credentials or enforce standards, many journeymen (including surprising numbers of Europeans) still found it difficult to establish themselves in their own shops as independent masters.

The Solvent of Race

The shoemakers finally renewed their organizational effort in 1788. Fifty-four "maestros de obra prima de zapatería" met on October 15 and empowered Nicolás Riguy, José Luis de los Santos, and Juan José Romero to lead the effort.[52] It is clear that the decision of Governor Intendant Paula Sanz to permit the silversmiths to operate as a guild and cofradía had energized the shoemakers. It is also clear from the origins of the three apoderados that immigrant master shoemakers still dominated the craft and provided much of its leadership. Juan José Romero, from Andalucia, and José Luis de los Santos, from Portugal, had signed the 1779 letter that initiated the original guild effort, while Nicolás Riguy was a more recent immigrant from Cataluña. Within a month of the general meeting the apoderados asked Nicolás del Campo, the Marquis of Loreto (viceroy, 1784–1789), to permit the creation of a guild. "Upon reflection," they wrote, "we fear that our profession will soon enter a level of decadence that will be greatly prejudicial to the public welfare because of the disturbed condition with which our occupation has developed without rules or ordinances for controlling apprentices, journeymen, or masters."[53]

The narrative presented to authorities made no reference to the 1779 guild effort or to the draft constitution produced by Regidor Gregorio Ramos Mexía. Nevertheless, the argument they now made for creating a guild was identical to the first petition. Without a guild, they claimed, legitimate masters were unable to maintain discipline or standards. Journeymen and even apprentices opened public shops and sold their products to the public before completing their instruction. Since these "false" masters were unable to produce high quality shoes and boots, they had to cut prices to survive, leaving everyone impoverished.[54] The picture painted by the craft leadership was certainly bleak, but the shoemakers had made these same claims before and now, almost a decade later, there were scores of additional journeymen and apprentices employed in Buenos Aires. Given that the apoderados presented this dire picture in a period of labor scarcity and generally upward-trending wages in the city, it might be wise to treat their claims as political packaging rather than substantive analysis. Since there had never been a guild of shoemakers in Buenos Aires, there is a high probability that a significant proportion of the local-born masters at any given time had spurious credentials.

The shoemakers, following the successful path of the silversmiths, proposed a two-stage process for establishing their guild. They sought the immediate implementation of a mandatory examination process for the rank of master with a prerequisite of four years of experience as an apprentice and two additional years as a journeyman. Once this essential prop for guild authority was in place, they promised to write a constitution that would provide for guild administration that would include "examinadores, veedores, fiscal, y alcalde." [55] Unlike the Ramos Mexía draft which had effectively placed guild governance in the hands of the cabildo, the apoderados in 1788 proposed that masters elect guild officers. They did not seek the imposition of ethnic, racial, or legal restrictions on recruitment or advancement within the occupation, but they did suggest that guild offices be reserved for Spaniards born in Spain or America.

Viceroy Loreto sent the petition to the fiscal of the audiencia, José Marquéz de la Plata, who imitated the earlier behavior of Regidor Ramos Mexía by both supporting the creation of a guild and ignoring the proposals of the shoemakers. He granted permission to hold meetings and draft ordinances, borrowing the now well-worn language used by the craftsmen themselves, agreeing that "the absence of this guild has permitted many abuses in prejudice to the public good." The viceroy authorized the master shoemakers to begin framing regulations, based on those of the Madrid guild of shoemakers, and ordered the alcalde of the second vote to preside at their meetings. [56]

On April 27, 1789, twenty-three master shoemakers met in the home of Alcalde Miguel de Azcuénaga, one of the city's wealthiest merchants and most important political figures, to draft a guild constitution. [57] Although Juan José Romero, one of the original apoderados, dissented from the group's decisions, the masters had quickly produced draft regulations without using any Spanish guild constitution as a model. [58] Their draft provided for the annual election of an alcalde, a *veedor*, a fiscal, and twelve *vocales* and permitted all master shoemakers, without ethnic or racial requirement, to vote and serve in guild offices. The guild, they pledged, would use fines and a portion of the three peso fee paid during visitas to compensate elected officers. Given the very modest incomes of masters in this craft, the fees and fines likely to flow to guild officers must have seemed choice plums.[59]

Because of the repeated assertion that there were large numbers of "false" masters practicing in the city, the enforcement of guild standards was an inherently dangerous business. As a result, the masters believed they could finesse this threat by accepting the credentials of all shoemakers with existing shops without challenge. Improved quality would come gradually as the imposition of rigorous examination standards on new masters lifted the performance of the trade. Master shoemakers who were slaves were the only group of practicing masters that the proposed regulations would force to surrender their existing craft rank.

In this draft the masters also sought to establish more control over the journeymen and apprentices they depended on. In a tight labor market with high wages, masters had little leverage over their dependents. In the unregulated conditions that existed in the city, journeymen had the ability to walk away from demanding masters without significant penalty, and even apprentices enjoyed substantial freedom to negotiate better circumstances for themselves. Without guild regulations, masters were often compelled to accept apprentices for indeterminate terms without enforceable contracts. As a remedy, the drafted constitution proposed a formal regime of written contracts recorded by notaries.[60] While the document offered some protections for apprentices, including an escape clause that permitted breaking a contract in cases of physical abuse or a master's incompetence, it also obligated parents, guardians, or slave owners to reimburse masters for expenses if an apprentice proved recalcitrant, lazy, or ran away.

The controls proposed for journeymen were more revolutionary. Because the city's unskilled laborers routinely earned the same wages paid journeymen shoemakers, there was little reason for a disaffected journeyman to endure a harsh or difficult master. Even if another position was not available in the shop of a master shoemaker, a journeyman could easily find temporary work at similar wages as a laborer. As a result, the draft constitution sought to enforce discipline among the craft's journeymen by requiring them to give eight days notice before quitting a master's shop. Some masters had tried to retain skilled journeymen by advancing wages, but it was common for journeymen to take off without repaying their debts. The proposed constitution stipulated that journeymen would have to liquidate unpaid debts before moving to a new employer. While these provisions provided some protection to the lower echelons of the trade, the document focused unambiguously on guaranteeing master craftsmen a disciplined and reliable workforce.

The ink had hardly dried on this draft constitution when the first signs of serious conflict arose. Juan José Romero, active since the first organizational effort in 1779 and one of the three masters selected as apoderados in 1788, announced his opposition to the central provisions of the constitution in a letter to the fiscal of the audiencia. His objective was nothing less than the comprehensive exclusion of foreign-born masters from guild offices. This, he argued, was the explicit policy found "in all of the cities of Spain where there are guilds." The other apoderados, José Luis de los Santos and Nicolás Riguy, disagreed with Romero immediately, arguing that excluding foreign masters from guild offices would inhibit immigration and retard the development of the profession, "one of the principal objectives of good government." Romero refused to back down and revealed his central concern in a new letter, "there are too many public shops for the market." This glut, he claimed, was the result of an increase in the number of "false masters many of whom were foreigners."[61]

The fiscal, Marquéz de la Plata, sent the protest to the cabildo's *síndico procurador*, Estansilao Zamudio, who flatly rejected Romero's position. The cabildo then asserted that under Spanish law foreigners married to Spaniards were not subject to expulsion from the city and, therefore, were naturalized and eligible for guild office. Seeking a compromise, the cabildo agreed that the guild could bar foreigners not married to Spanish citizens from guild offices. They also suggested rotating offices among Spaniards and foreigners as a compromise solution.[62] The cabildo, now engaged in imagining an ideal guild structure, proposing additional changes that held explosive potential given the racial mix within the trade. The cabildo ordered the shoemakers to remove from the constitution the proposed exclusion of slaves from the rank of master.[63] The cabildo stated forcefully, "this chapter is prejudicial to the Republic, it being apparent that there are many widows and families in this city that sustain themselves with the daily wages of their slaves."[64]

This proposal formally acknowledged that a slave trained in a skilled craft provided a form of economic security for Spanish families or, more likely, for widows or unmarried daughters who were thus protected against loss of social status if forced to work. The cabildo rejected the exclusion of slaves from the rank of master unambiguously because it attacked the economic self-interest of a powerful and influential constituency. Every other provision in the proposed regulations was economic in nature, focused narrowly on control of labor and market. The suggestion to bar slaves from the rank of master was in fact the only provision intended to enhance the shaky social status of the craft by establishing a clear boundary between its masters, as freemen, and the slaves increasingly visible in this and other skilled trades.

The shoemakers, responding to the realities of colonial porteño society, proposed restrictions on advancement based on legal condition, not race. The cabildo, responsive to the needs of slave owners, urged the craft to instead implement a broad policy of racial segregation in the guild. The cabildo explained that the mechanical arts in Buenos Aires had "suffered since the families of poor Spaniards hesitate placing their sons in the artisan crafts because they do not wish them to mingle or mix with the sons of the other castes."[65] While cabildo officials as well as essayists in local periodicals had made this argument previously, it is clear from the census of 1778 and *matrícula* of 1780 that nearly every shoemaker shop was already integrated by race and legal status.[66] Nevertheless, the cabildo pushed the shoemakers to install a clumsy mechanism for separating white apprentices from blacks and castas by identifying four Spanish masters who would accept only boys of pure European lineage. All other masters would be able to accept apprentices without concern for race. The proposed separation would not be mandatory and parents who were unaffected by these assumed social and racial scruples could place their sons with any master "if for them the union and mixing with those other boys of a distinct class was not objectionable." Once in receipt of the favorable opinion of the fiscal, the new viceroy, Nicolás de Arredondo, ordered the cabildo to again supervise the drafting of the constitution and the election of guild officers.[67] The cabildo gave this responsibility to the alcalde of the second vote, José Martínez de Hoz, who on January 20, 1791, offered his home for the guild's first election of officers.

The electoral meeting held on March 14, 1791, relied on the now revised constitution that permitted foreigners married to Spanish citizens or resident in Buenos Aires for ten years to participate in the guild without restriction. The document also accepted that all individuals with shops were legitimate masters eligible to vote in guild office elections. The shoemakers had surrendered completely to the opinions of the cabildo and revised their constitution to bar all pardos and morenos from guild office, stating that this would "give the guild an improved public image since individuals would hesitate to join a guild directed by castas."[68] Given the large number of blacks and castas in the trade, it is perhaps surprising that the master shoemakers had accepted these discriminatory provisions unanimously.

While the new constitution stipulated the powers of guild officials, it failed to provide electoral rules. As a result, the alcalde, Martínez de Hoz, and the guild apoderados invented procedures on the fly. They decided that the six masters with the most seniority in the profession should stand for the office of alcalde. Included in this group were Juan Esteban Caro, Juan José Romero, Manuel Antonio Sustaeta, Agustín Marín, José Farías, and Félix Sánchez. Romero, the most vocal opponent of the foreign masters, received the most votes, fifty, and became guild alcalde. Martínez de Hoz, after consulting with the shoemakers, then assigned the offices of veedor and fiscal to the second and third highest vote getters. Sustaeta became veedor, and Marín assumed the role of fiscal. The apoderados then proposed twenty-six individuals for the twelve positions of vocal. After the balloting, Joaquín Alvarez, who had received the most votes among the twelve, was denied office by Romero because he was a foreigner.[69]

Alvarez, a Portuguese immigrant married to a local woman, protested his exclusion from office and claimed there had been numerous voting irregularities. Alvarez asked that the election be overturned, claiming that Martínez de Hoz had allowed Romero to manipulate both the guild regulations and the Laws of the Indies to the detriment of the craft's foreign masters. He alleged that the alcalde had also allowed a large number of black and mulatto craftsmen to participate in debates and vote for guild officers, despite the clear prohibition found in the guild regulations. Not only was the meeting disorderly, he claimed, but black and mulatto masters had played a decisive role in excluding him from office, "by having raised a tumultuous voice" and demanding that foreigners be excluded from office.[70]

Alvarez also took Martínez de Hoz to task for having used the vote for guild alcalde to also determine who would serve as veedor and fiscal. These offices, he claimed, "ought to be separated in accordance with the electoral laws. Since each office has distinct functions, it is only reasonable that the examination and vote for each office evaluate the qualities and circumstances of those nominated separately." The most objectionable aspect of the procedure, according to Alvarez, was that this decision facilitated Romero's efforts to exclude foreigners.[71]

Despite their comprehensive victory in the election, Romero's partisans also requested the audiencia overturn the results because the Italian-born José Canepa had been elected vocal.[72] They stated, "we resist his election because it does not appear just to us because there are a considerable number of European and American Spaniards among whom it would be proper to select a vocal in place of this foreigner."[73] Martínez de Hoz, now completely out of patience with this contentious craft, replied that this protest was "contemptible," because it only represented the protestors' "passions and not reason." He went on to remind the protestors that the guild ordinances that had recently received the unanimous endorsement of the master shoemakers explicitly permitted the election of foreigners. All six candidates for the "three primary offices," he stated, had been Spanish citizens, and the names of only two foreigners were included on the list of sixteen candidates for the twelve positions of guild vocal.[74]

Juan José Romero, now the newly elected guild alcalde, appealed independently to the fiscal, Marquéz de la Plata, to complain about the alcalde's refusal to expel foreigners from guild office. Romero radically shifted ground by alleging that the foreign masters and cabildo officials had conspired to thwart both Spanish law and the legitimate constitution. According to Romero, the alcalde had read the constitution to the master shoemakers in the presence of Pedro Nuñez, the escribano of the cabildo, prior to the vote. But, he stated, "now it has come to the attention of the guild membership that this document is very different from the original and contains clauses that are much more favorable to the foreigners."[75]

Both the content and the tone of these protests reveal the tenuous presence of the culture of deference in late colonial Buenos Aires. Not only had the shoemakers refused Alcalde Martínez de Hoz's repeated efforts to quiet the meeting, but both Alvarez and Romero had alleged that the alcalde and the cabildo's escribano were complicit in violating the recently accepted guild constitution.[76] Romero had previously challenged the decisions of the cabildo and audiencia to permit the participation of foreign masters in guild affairs, dismissing their judgment as contrary to Spanish law. He now publicly claimed that the alcalde and escribano had behaved dishonestly. These claims liquidated whatever official goodwill for Romero's faction remained. Marquéz de la Plata replied to Romero on May 24, 1791, affirming the electoral procedures and ignoring Romero's allegations of tampering.[77] The accommodating tone and narrow focus of the fiscal's reply indicated his desire to avoid renewed conflict. The authorities wanted to move beyond the electoral conflict, but they would be disappointed.

It is clear that the majority of masters who self-identified as criollos in the 1780 matriculation of shoemakers supported Romero, but the foreign masters directed their increasingly angry protests at another segment of the craft. They complained bitterly that a significant number of black and casta masters were present at the electoral meeting and had actively participated in debates. Many, the immigrants alleged, had actually voted.[78] Joaquín Alvarez, the Portuguese master shoemaker denied guild office by Romero, claimed that nonwhite masters had actively intervened in the electoral process, despite their exclusion in the guild constitution. The foreign masters, he asserted, had been frightened and physically intimidated by the castas who supported Romero and by the other partisans of exclusion. Given that the constitution barred nonwhite masters from *active* participation in guild affairs, what was their objective at the electoral meeting?

The master shoemakers had unanimously accepted these discriminatory provisions at an open meeting with all the craft's black and mulatto masters in attendance. There were neither protests against these discriminatory provisions at the meeting nor subsequent appeals to authorities. Why had these black and casta master shoemakers so unambiguously committed themselves to denying office to foreign masters, rather than organize to protest their own exclusion from office when the new constitution was debated? While Spanish laws as well as local regulations — like the new regulations of the shoemakers — mandated racial discrimination, enforcement, the actual application of racial labels, always had a plastic and fluid quality in Spanish colonies. The assertion of broad categories of racial discrimination by political authorities, therefore, never produced uniform results.

Black and casta master shoemakers could only discover the meaning of the discriminatory provisions written into the guild ordinances with their implementation. Elected guild leaders would control and direct implementation. The guild election would therefore move the guild from its debate over abstract ideas of racial hierarchy and racial privilege to the practical business of assigning racial labels. This is why debate over provisions of the guild constitution that allocated opportunity and advantage by race produced so little heat and why the effort to elect guild officers blew up. Nonwhite masters were now compelled to organize and assert themselves since the assignment of racial labels to individual craftsmen was so much more important than the assignment of guild status to racial and ethnic groups.

Forced from cover by the election, black and casta masters supported the white faction that seemed least likely to enforce the racial provisions of the new constitution rigorously. In this context, Romero's faction represented the best of bad alternatives. Although Romero was born in Seville, he had been a resident of Buenos Aires for twenty-four years.[79] Nearly all the craft's criollos and those Spanish-born masters with the longest residency in the city supported his faction. The nonwhite masters correctly assumed that these groups were much more likely to implement the discriminatory provisions of the constitution using the relaxed and flexible racial designations that were the established norms in Buenos Aires, than were recent immigrants from Europe. The dispute over the election was not simply a struggle between Spaniards and foreigners; it was a confrontation between entrenched porteño masters, a handful of long-established Spanish immigrants, like Romero, and their black and casta allies, and the most recent immigrants from Europe.

The decisions of Fiscal Marquéz de la Plata and Alcalde Martínez de Hoz could not resolve this conflict. Instead, colonial authorities, exhausted by the contentiousness of the shoemakers, scrapped the disputed guild constitution and ordered the guild leadership led by Romero to produce a new constitution based on those of Madrid's guild of shoemakers.[80] The Madrid ordinances contained restrictions far beyond anything previously proposed in Buenos Aires, limiting, for example, apprenticeship to "old Christians."[81] It also barred guild members from introducing new styles of shoes and boots or novel production techniques not specifically sanctioned by the ordinances, a provision common in Spain and France.[82] The Madrid document also included provisions establishing a cofradía.[83]

The revised constitution presented to the master shoemakers on July 28, 1791, relied heavily on the Madrid ordinances, providing for the first time provisions for a cofradía devoted to craft patrons Saint Crispin and Saint Crispiniano. This body would collect dues separately to provide a minimal array of social benefits for masters and their families, including "a doctor and medicines in their sickness, candles and burial after their death." All masters, the draft stated, "without making distinction in this of nation, quality, and condition," would have a voice, a vote, and eligibility for office in the lay brotherhood.[84] The apparent liberality of these provisions disguised Romero's exclusion of foreigners from the more important and financially remunerative offices of the guild proper.

Chapter 2 of the proposed regulations stated the "duties, obligations and selection procedures of guild officers." These officials were to be elected annually and "in these elections only Spanish masters born in Spain and America [are eligible] with an absolute exclusion from these offices of those not known to be Spanish." Only Spanish masters would receive an "active voice" in guild proceedings. All other masters, foreigners from Europe, as well as blacks and castas were granted only a "passive voice."[85] Chapter 3 articulated a program designed to effectively eliminate foreign-born masters from the trade:

> That being one of the principal objectives of the guild that the Spaniards flourish with all possible comfort as is right and proper and is sanctioned by the laws old and new . . . the foreigners are prevented not only from obtaining the offices of the guild, but also the active voice at its meetings, moreover, in the future they will not be received as masters until, in the interim, the number of foreign masters with public shops is reduced to six.[86]

Despite their vocal support for Romero at the disputed electoral meeting, black and mulatto masters received the same rough treatment as foreigners in chapter 4, which limited them to a "passive" role in guild meetings and barred them from guild offices.[87] The highly visible cooperation between black and casta masters and Romero clearly did not mean the Romero faction favored a color-blind governance system or the full inclusion of pardo and moreno masters in the guild. These two factions had acted in concert to achieve an immediate, shared objective, the exclusion of foreigners. Romero and the members of his faction did not regard casta masters as equals; this was unimaginable in the colonial setting. Instead, Romero's decision to include this discriminatory provision was consistent with the previous draft constitution and consistent with the racial prejudices of his time and place.

Unfortunately for Romero colonial authorities were now universally alienated, the fiscal of the audiencia, José Martínez de Hoz, as well as the alcalde, who had presided at the violent electoral meeting, lodged immediate protests with the viceroy. Marquéz de la Plata dismissed the proceedings that had produced the new draft constitution as little more than a rubber stamp for Romero's discredited opinion, "it does not appear that this meeting did anything more than pass the twenty-five chapters read out of Juan Romero's notebook."[88] Predictably, Viceroy Arredondo, an early champion of the guild, responded to these protests by suspending enforcement of the disputed constitution.

The inability of the shoemakers to resolve their differences independently led the viceroy to commission a lawyer to draft an acceptable guild constitution.[89] Dr. Vicente García Grande y Cárdenas completed his task in March 1792 and sent it to the fiscal for his approval without seeking consent from the bickering shoemakers.[90] The lawyer's primary task was to solve the factionalism that had defeated the two prior constitutions. He began with the now well-established concession that everyone who claimed to be a master shoemaker and who currently maintained an independent shop in Buenos Aires would be regarded as a master.[91] He then went about the more difficult business of defining the status of the craft's constituent ethnic and racial groups. Included in the guild without obstacle were "all Spaniards, Europeans and Americans, who have a public shop and . . . the sons of foreigners known to have been born in Spain or America of Spanish mothers . . . and also the slaves of Spaniards [and naturalized foreigners] whose owners have provided the means for opening a public shop."[92]

To conciliate Spaniards and foreigners, he gave Spaniards a largely symbolic precedence at public and private functions of the corporation but stripped the constitution of Romero's guileless assertions of Spanish dominance. Instead, he partitioned guild offices between the contending factions.[93] While his draft permitted foreign-born masters and journeymen who could provide documents of religious regularity and were willing to swear formal allegiance to the Spanish Crown to join the guild, it denied young foreign nationals the chance to become apprentices. The lawyer's careful effort to distribute advantages and reconcile existing factions visible in the sections of the constitution devoted to foreign-born masters were absent from the sections that laid out the status of pardos, morenos, and other castas. Cárdenas's draft retained the prior draft's exclusion of black and casta masters from guild offices, but he went on to impose a humiliating policy of mandatory racial segregation at all meetings of the guild and cofradía.[94] Chapter 5, for example, created precise and prejudicial distinctions based on race for corporate meetings. The guild, Cárdenas wrote, "would establish a decorous distinction between masters who are white and freeborn on one side and on the other those who are Negro and either slave or free." Included in the first class were Spaniards, European or American born; Indians; and also foreigners who have met the requirements for residency and guild membership; and in the second class were "all those who are Negroes, both slave and free and those known generally to be mulattoes free or slave, although their color be much lighter." [95]

In the proposed constitution, these racial distinctions would then serve as the basis for a broad range of institutionalized discrimination aimed at nonwhite members of the trade. Cárdenas relegated black and casta shoemakers to a position of symbolic inferiority in all of the corporation's social and ceremonial functions. The masters of this second class were "to have in [guild] meetings and in church functions a place and order of seats inferior and separated from those of the masters of the first class." The white and Indian masters, who made up the first class were to be assigned their own "place and seating order in all meetings of the guild and functions of the cofradía and only they would have the active and passive vote in elections and in matters of guild government, that is, only they could vote for or be elected to guild offices." [96] Cárdenas's draft placed all nonwhite craftsmen at the mercy of white masters who would perpetually control the substantial powers of the guild administration. Blacks and castas would have no control over examinations for master, inspection visits, standards for materials and workmanship, or the levying of fines, duties, and dues. The alternative to this proposed separation, according to Cárdenas, would be "the drunken confusion that would be felt by freeborn, white men when mixed with Negroes who were either slave or free, and even subordinated to them in some cases. This, truthfully, would be something very strange and indecent." [97]

Within a month the fiscal of the royal audiencia approved the document and sent it to the master shoemakers for their assent. Following the guidelines set out by Cárdenas, the masters of the first class met in the presence of the alcalde of the second vote, voted to accept the document, and elected officers to govern the new corporation. These newly minted guild officers then asked the viceroy to establish the guild as a fully functioning body ad referendum, while awaiting final approval from Spain. Both the fiscal and the viceroy agreed, publishing the guild constitution on June 9, 1792.[98]

Different Paths and Similar Destinations

The leadership of the silversmiths, operating as a guild since 1788, began to face organized opposition for the first time as the shoemakers initiated their preparations to elect officers and enforce their new constitution.[99] In the case of the silversmiths, the implementation of craft standards through visitas and an attempt to conduct a new guild election provoked an open confrontation. Like the shoemakers, the silversmiths had agreed to accept every artisan with an independent shop in 1788 as a master in an effort to avoid disputes. This decision meant that a small number of established master silversmiths temporarily away from Buenos Aires had to present credentials to guild officers when they returned to the city or retake the examination for master.[100] Those who had previously practiced as masters resented this requirement and appealed to municipal authorities for relief.[101] Guild officers, jealous of their fragile authority, were quick to take offense when municipal authorities agreed to hear these complaints. Similarly, when some journeymen applied directly to the cabildo, rather than to guild officers, to set dates for examinations for master, guild officers complained bitterly of government interference.[102] Because enforcement of all decisions by guild officers ultimately required the support of the city's judicial and administrative institutions, these disputes held the potential to undermine the previously reliable goodwill of authorities.[103] The leadership's intemperate language in a succession of cases provided an opportunity for the alcalde of the first vote to remind them where the real power lay, dismissing the leadership's "frivolous pretexts" for refusing to comply with decisions by the cabildo.[104]

More consequential problems followed the guild's first visita in 1791. The guild's maestro mayor, Juan Antonio Callejas y Sandoval, notified the cabildo of his intention to inspect the shops of all master silversmiths because, he claimed, "many masters are mixing silver with base metals in order to defraud the public." The cabildo quickly approved the visita, but a small group of guild dissenters appealed to the viceroy to stop the inspection. Viceroy Arredondo dismissed the protest and permitted the inspection during which guild officials found five masters had violated guild statutes. The guild inspectors seized the goods and tools of the offenders and then closed their shops. Guild officers conducted a second visita six months later in March 1792, seizing the goods and tools of four masters, including three of those punished during the earlier visita.[105]

The two visitas bracketed a confrontation between the same guild officials and thirteen silversmiths who resisted their effort to conduct an election at the end of 1791. The master silversmith Salvador Grande refused to attend the electoral meeting. A guild officer went to Grande's shop to complain but was physically pushed into the street and called an "impostor and fraud" by Grande.[106] Following this direct challenge to the legitimacy of a guild officer, Grande filed a protest with the viceroy signed by twelve other silversmiths. The dissenters demanded that the viceroy reject the results of this disputed election because of "numerous irregularities." While the protest focused on the guild election, the signatories included every master punished for adulterated goods in the two guild visitas as well as four craft members who had other confrontations with guild officials over examinations or credentials.[107] In the exchange of charges and countercharges that followed the protest, the dissidents informed authorities that they would no longer pay dues or comply with the orders of guild officers.

The guild officers, all Spanish immigrants, exposed the previously hidden content of guild dissension in their reply to the viceroy. Predictably they dismissed the dissidents for their lax standards and fraudulent practices, but then they went on to reveal that these disputes were rooted in the city's contested racial hierarchy. The dissidents, the guild leadership complained, included "four mulattos and a chino," suggesting that their inferior status disarmed their complaints about electoral practice and guild regulation. Once provided with this convenient context, the difficulty of imposing discipline on subordinated castes, the viceroy ordered the dissident silversmiths to "observe punctually" the payment of dues and other obligations under threat of arrest.[108] Confident of their authority, the guild leadership attempted to crush their opponents with an unannounced inspection of the shop of dissident leader Salvador Grande, where they predictably discovered "numerous irregularities" and then seized his inventory and tools.[109]

The cycle of protests now afflicting the silversmiths revealed more completely than had the 1778 census the racial and ethnic makeup of the craft. While a majority of the masters were born in the Americas, 44 percent were European immigrants. Among the European masters, there were nearly three times as many Portuguese masters (thirteen) as Spanish (five), but Spaniards controlled the guild offices. We know from the protests that reached the viceroy that at least five of the seven American-born dissidents were castas. Once the internal debate about rights and privileges in this craft took on a racial character, no single decision from a colonial official, even the viceroy, could quiet the increasingly angry voices of the disenfranchised.

Enforcing the Racial Boundaries

In chapter 6 of *Through the Looking Glass*, Lewis Carroll stages a conversation between Alice and Humpty Dumpty that can serve as a useful point of access to the emerging racial contest within the crafts of Buenos Aires:

> "When *I* use a word," Humpty Dumpty said, in a rather scornful tone, "it means just what I choose it to mean—neither more nor less."
>
> "The question is," said Alice, "whether you *can* make words mean so many different things."
>
> "The question is," said Humpty Dumpty, "which is to be master—that's all."[110]

Complex racial nomenclature was an essential prop of the Spanish colonial social order, present in formal bureaucratic and judicial usage as well as in the more casual forms of everyday life. For the artisans of late-colonial Buenos Aires the effort to establish guilds forced these plastic and comfortable understandings of identity into venues where inelastic bureaucratic and judicial meanings pertained, meanings that could directly affect employment prospects and income.[111] Once this contest over racial identity was fully engaged, nominal disputes over training, craft standards, credentials, or access to guild office were predictably freighted with great consequence for both the shoemakers and silversmiths. It was inevitable in late-colonial Buenos Aires that collective corporate aspiration would prove unstable once European immigrants asserted the right to assign racial identity and therefore determine the life prospects of the local born. What marks this historical moment is the refusal of black and casta artisans to accept the claims of the Europeans.

Before 1791 no silversmith had referred to the race of another master in any official communication, even in the midst of disputes. After the bando of Paulo Sanz in 1788 allowed guild officials to actively enforce dues, inspection visits, and participation in guild elections, the resulting disputes spilled into the courts, and the racial identities of the dissenting faction became the fulcrum for these contests. When guild officers dismissed their opponents as "four mulattos and a chino," they presumed that colonial officials would instinctively assign the prejudicial synonyms that underpinned these labels in the colonial social setting — ill-disciplined, poorly trained, corrupt, and potentially violent.

The shoemakers' more formal effort to organize a guild foundered on these same shoals. Black and casta masters were a much more visible and important faction within this trade and had organized early to deny European immigrants full political rights in the first two draft constitutions. Their alliance with the criollo-dominated Romero faction controlled both the initial drafting process and the first two guild elections, but Spanish and other European immigrants persisted until the 1792 draft constitution effectively closed the door on this strategy. While this constitution placed some limits of foreign participation, it gave cabildo officials and white guild officers the ability to deny black and casta masters any power in the guild.

Who is Who and What is What?
Counting the Shoemakers in 1792

The cabildo's decision to conduct a new census of shoemakers in 1792 proved to be the lit match tossed into the powder magazine. Unlike previous counts, the alcalde of the second vote, Antonio García López, and the escribano of the cabildo, Pedro Nuñez, personally conducted this census in order to reliably fix the "correct" ethnic and racial identity of guild members thereby avoiding new disputes over voting rights and access to guild office. This census would not imitate patterns of self-identification. While we now routinely dismiss race as a fixed, biological reality and emphasize the term's historical role in allocating wealth and power, these Spanish colonial officials were convinced that the boundaries of these categories could be established and enforced. In 1792 the alcalde and escribano together interviewed each shoemaker and assigned racial labels.[112] We must assume that even in these circumstances, some casta shoemakers found room to maneuver, claiming, for example, a proximate or other plausible label that would provide some

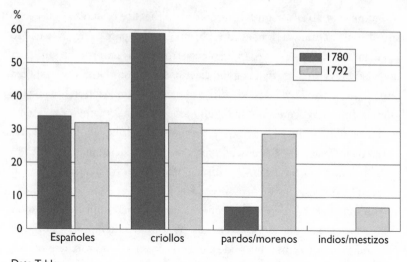

Data Table

	Españoles	Criollos	Pardos/ morenos	Indios/ mestizos
1780 (N = 130)	34% (44)	59% (77)	7% (9)	
1792 (N = 172)	32% (55)	32% (55)	29% (49)	7% (13)

FIGURE 13 **Master shoemakers by race, 1780 and 1792.** Source: The 1780 matriculation of zapateros is found in AGN, Interior, leg. 9, exp. 5. The 1792 guild census is found in AGN, Tribunales, leg. Z4, exp. 7.

small advantage within the racial constraints of the new guild constitution. Later events make it clear that a small number of mestizos and pardos asserted the status of indio to avoid being disenfranchised. Nevertheless, the conflicts among shoemakers and between shoemakers and authorities that led to the 1792 enumeration must have emboldened the alcalde and escribano to challenge some claims.

The results sent to the viceroy on July 24, 1792, confirm this.[113] Figure 13 compares the racial distribution of master shoemakers in 1780 and 1792 and indicates a significant change in the application of racial labels. While the percentage of Europeans in the craft was almost unchanged over the twelve-year period, falling slightly from 34 percent to 32 percent, every other category registered dramatic change. With closer official scrutiny of calidad, the percentage of criollo masters fell precipitously from 59 percent to 32 percent, a change matched by a reciprocal increase in the pardo and moreno category, which rose from 7 percent to 29 percent. Similarly, there was an increase in masters identified as indios or mestizos, from zero masters to 7 percent. A close examination of the two lists suggests that altered methods used to register shoemakers and assign racial labels, not changes in craft recruitment, produced the changes. That is, the increased number of casta and black masters in 1792 resulted from the relabeling of many masters who had self-identified as criollos in 1780.

Conclusion

It took thirteen years for the shoemakers to put in place the ambitions of the seventy-one masters who had met in 1779. After the failure of their initial effort and after the city's silversmiths had demonstrated that colonial authorities supported this form of corporate organization, the shoemakers reorganized and again took up their effort to create a guild. Leaders in both crafts persisted in their efforts to organize guilds because they understood that without the coercive capabilities of a formal guild they could not control quality, price, or access to the market. Even the routine business of collecting dues to support participation in civic celebrations like the coronation of the monarch or religious festivals like Corpus Christi had become the source of contention and division.

Larger forces were at work as well. Buenos Aires was one of the preeminent Atlantic cities of the late eighteenth century. Europe, Africa, and the vast South American interior all contributed to its rapid population growth, and all were connected to the rapidly expanding regional economy. Its merchants facilitated the profitable exchange of goods from the plantations of the Caribbean, the factories and workshops of Europe, and the mines, farms, and grazing lands of the South American interior. In this churning, unstable economic and demographic environment institutions of every sort were tested, forced to change, or overturned. These powerful forces did not exempt the traditional institutions of the skilled laboring class or traditional Spanish colonial understandings of race and identity. The racial and ethnic makeup of the city's plebe changed rapidly with the city's deeper integration in the Atlantic Basin and its growing influence over regional networks of commerce and migration. While the numbers of skilled European artisans increased, the migration of free castas from interior provinces and the importation of slaves from Africa and Brazil grew more rapidly still. Few skilled laborers or members of the governing class questioned the utility of guilds, but the essential question of how guilds, once created, would allocate opportunity across ethnic and racial boundaries proved nearly impossible to negotiate. Emerging ethnic and racial factions in the skilled crafts would soon test solutions to foundational questions of mobility and market access installed from above by colonial authorities.

4 | Collective Obligations, Self-Interest, and Race
The Guilds of Silversmiths and Shoemakers Fail

At nightfall on January 8, 1793, forty-eight black and casta master shoemakers gathered in the open courtyard of a sprawling two-story building near the Merced Convent. The building housed numerous poor families in its small apartments as well as a score of single men who paid a few reales a month to sleep along the interior walls of the building's two patios. Among the residents were five free pardo master shoemakers and three of their apprentices who together shared two rooms at the back of the structure. These black and casta shoemakers had come together to organize a collective response to recent developments in their craft, only a handful had been present in 1779 when shoemakers decided to create a guild. They were not eloquent men trained in debate; they spoke plainly and often with passion. At the end of a long work day they were tired and easily frustrated. By midnight they could argue no more. Following the lead of the meeting organizers, they unanimously decided to petition Viceroy Nicolás de Arredondo for permission to separate from the recently created Guild of Shoemakers and constitute a segregated Guild of Pardo and Moreno Shoemakers. They then chose Francisco Baquero, among the most visible allies of Juan José Romero in the long fight with the European immigrants who now controlled the guild of shoemakers, to represent them as *apoderado*. As the meeting broke up and the exhausted masters walked into the humid summer night, few anticipated the consequences of this decision.[1]

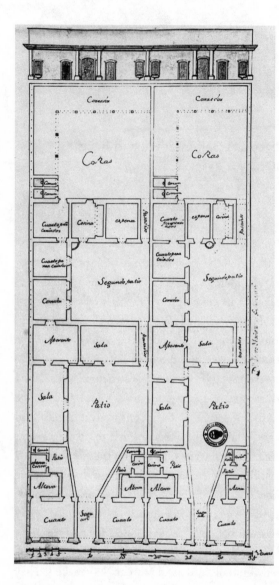

FIGURE 14 Architectural drawing of a large duplex, each unit with two patios and multiple rooms. By the 1790s some of these dwellings originally built to house the affluent families of merchants and officials had become subdivided and rented to groups of single laborers and artisans or shared among laboring families. A building like this hosted the meeting of pardo and moreno shoemakers. Published with the permission of the AGN, Buenos Aires, Argentina.

The False Dawn of the European Guild System in Buenos Aires

In March 1792 the master shoemakers had accepted the guild constitution drafted by the lawyer Dr. Vicente García Grande y Cárdenas. This was the third constitution unanimously accepted by master shoemakers. Cárdenas sought to end the electoral disputes that derailed the last constitution by excluding black and casta masters from guild offices and by narrowly limiting their participation in guild functions.[2] Once in possession of the new document, Viceroy Nicolás Arredondo decided to push forward with implementation and the election of guild officers without waiting for formal approval from the king. As a result, the cabildo's alcalde of the second vote, Antonio García López, and the *escribano*, Pedro Núñez, completed the new census of shoemakers focused on the application of racial labels as a preliminary to holding a guild election in July.

This constitution had required an enormous effort from the shoemakers as growing factionalism in the craft and conflicts with local and viceregal authorities proliferated.[3] From 1791 conflict within the trade played out along the fault line that separated immigrants from Spain and other European nations and an alliance of criollo masters, a small number of Spanish immigrants well established in Buenos Aires, like Romero, and black and casta masters led by Francisco Baquero. The next guild election would determine control of remunerative guild offices and subsequently the assignment of racial labels. This division had overwhelmed the craft's first two draft constitutions and led to angry confrontations and legal challenges that had frustrated every previous effort to elect guild officers. Despite this volatile and untidy process, Viceroy Arredondo and the *fiscal* of the *audiencia* now deepened their support for the guild and, implicitly, for the European faction.[4]

Master shoemakers had repeatedly asserted the ideal of corporate organization and unanimously accepted the previous draft guild constitution only to divide bitterly over implementation and the election of guild officers. In fact, no faction among the shoemakers had ever opposed guild organization; the issue roiling the craft was whether a guild, once it was formed, would reflect the social and racial norms of the colonial city of Buenos Aires or those of Europe's mature guild system. The stakes were high and all factions realized that control of the guild organization was the only effective way to protect themselves against the loss of social status and economic security.

The Final Battles

With the new guild census in hand, the cabildo called the shoemakers together to elect guild officers. Given the heated nature of earlier attempts, this meeting would test the success of the government's efforts to control the craft's "troublesome and divisive" faction. On July 30, 1792, Alcalde Antonio García López conducted the election in his home. In his subsequent report to the cabildo he gave no suggestion of problems, stating that he "explained [the constitution to the shoemakers] individually in the meeting . . . so that no one would be ignorant of the procedures and, being well instructed, they could elect the subjects who would exercise the offices with the most honor, integrity, and honesty." [5] He reported that the Spaniard, Antonio Porra, had been elected president and treasurer, and another Spaniard, Juan José Romero, the leader of the antiforeign faction, had been elected guild alcalde. As required by the constitution, a criollo, José Farias, and an Italian, Pedro Albansini, were elected as *veedores*. The constitution divided the guild's eight *vocales* among the craft's ethnic groups. The Spaniards elected Juan Saldeta and Juan Cara, while the criollos elected Manuel Antonio Sustaeta and Agustín Marín. The foreigners chose the Italian José Canepa and the Portuguese Manuel González Silba. Francisco Baquero and Juan de Díos Campuzano were elected vocales for the Indians, even though Díos Campuzano had been identified as a mestizo and Baquero as a criollo in the recently completed 1792 census. Finally, the Spaniards Nicolás Riguy and Martín Porra were unanimously elected to govern the *cofradía*.[6]

Antonio Porra, Martín Porra, Nicolás Riguy, José Labrador, and José Canepa immediately attacked these results in a protest to the viceroy, even though four of the signatories had been elected to guild office. The protestors cited a "large number of disorders and outrages that characterized the meeting" and called for the "immediate nullification of the results due to the well known evils with which the [elections] were practiced." [7] Fifteen additional masters, six Spaniards, five Buenos Aires criollos, and four Italians, wrote separately to the audiencia to complain about the complexities of the guild ordinances and the "confusion and disorder" of the meeting. Of the six Spaniards, five were very recent arrivals from Catalonia.[8]

The central problem they identified was the predictable result of Dr. Cárdenas's effort to avoid factionalism by partitioning guild offices among Spaniards, criollos, foreigners, and Indians while simultaneously excluding blacks and castas from participation. A successful implementation proved impossible, the protestors argued, because the constitution had provided no process for settling disputes over the assignment of ethnic and racial categories. Efforts to resolve these disputes at the meeting, they alleged, proved impossible because "all the craft's mestizos, pardos, and morenos were present during the election even though the constitution barred them from voting or holding office." The election results, the dissenters stated, "had been distorted by intimidation and the threat of violence." The balloting occurred, they stated, "but tumultuously and separated completely from the spirit of the ordinances."[9]

The protestors singled out the behavior of Juan José Romero, the leader of the antiforeign faction of masters, for their harshest criticism. As the fifteen dissenters put it, "Romero was the leader of all the disorders and confusions . . . [giving] repeated shouts and cries to the masters of the second class [blacks and castas] even though they did not have voice or vote." According to this testimony, pardo and moreno masters had been on their feet shouting challenges to the decisions of the alcalde and physically threatening their enemies. In this chaos, the dissenters said, the efforts of the masters of the first class to nominate and vote in accordance with the new constitution broke down. They illustrated their allegations by providing a telling detail that the alcalde had kept from his colleagues. Romero, they claimed, had caused such massive abuses of the ordinances and violations of decorum that the alcalde, Antonio García López, had been forced to call for an armed military patrol to establish order. Even the presence of these armed auxiliaries failed to quell Romero's loud and impassioned interventions. Finally, they recounted, the alcalde, exasperated beyond endurance, had the soldiers drag Romero from the meeting.[10]

The character of the meeting, as described by the European masters, suggests just how important the election was to Romero and his supporters. Their summary also makes clear that Romero and his black and casta allies were certainly not intimidated by the electoral setting, the home of one of the city's wealthiest and most powerful men, by the threats of the alcalde as their protests mounted, or, ultimately, by the presence of an armed military patrol. The fifteen protestors urged the viceroy to overturn the results and ban Romero from all future participation in guild affairs, "separate this Romero from the guild for his excesses and deprive him of both voice and vote perpetually." Given his outrageous behavior, they demanded that Romero should be "placed in jail for a period of time." Romero was a congenital malcontent and a manipulator, they alleged, "who had previously been ejected from the alcalde's home during a function to celebrate the coronation of our invincible and Catholic monarch."[11]

While the protestors focused on the need to overturn the election results, they pulled the curtain back on their larger purpose at the same time by claiming that "the very presence of masters of the second class created a violent and threatening situation." They described a tumultuous gathering where "the meeting place and nearby rooms were poorly lighted and the darkness combined with the noise and tumult around the patio created confusion that led to the mixing of masters of the second class with those of the first." As a result, "various masters of the second class, who had neither voice nor vote, voted, participated in the debates, and one was even elected to a guild office." The election of Francisco Baquero as one of the two Indian vocales served for the protestors as proof of the corrupt manipulation of the guild ordinances. "Baquero," they stated, "is a mestizo who is married to a free zamba and is so classified in the guild census."[12] They did not protest, on the other hand, the election of Juan de Díos Campuzano as the other Indian vocal even though the same census listed him as a criollo.

Four masters who the alcalde had denied the right to vote for officers at the meeting sent a separate complaint to the fiscal that illuminates the useful confusion that surrounded application of the term *indio* in the dynamic social and political settings of late colonial Buenos Aires. While the recently completed guild census identified two of these protestors as free morenos and the other two as free pardos, all four were officers in the Militia of Indians and one was that unit's commander. Their complaint, rooted in the everyday, deep-seated understandings of identity in the city, was that an officer in a militia unit of Indians was an Indian himself. The fiscal soon dismissed their request for the right to vote in future guild elections, a request they had carefully disguised as a question about contradictory usage in military and craft settings.[13]

The disappointed European faction claimed, in new protests, that Romero and his faction had "subverted both the letter and spirit of the recently accepted ordinances" by stirring the castas to action. According to them, Romero and his supporters had aggressively checked every effort by the alcalde to control the meeting, refusing even to obey the orders of the armed patrol. To drive home their point, the dissenting shoemakers did not hesitate to parade the alcalde's failure and incompetence in their complaint to the fiscal of the audiencia. In a parting salvo they claimed that the alcalde and escribano, bullied and intimidated by the actions of the black and casta masters, had decided "to continue the balloting and certify the results simply to prevent further outbursts and tumults."[14]

The fiscal asked Antonio García López to respond to these charges, and the alcalde confirmed the criticisms, noting "that five free mulattoes and two mestizos, all of whom were enrolled in the second class by the census, voted in the elections despite the direct prohibitions of the ordinances." And "contrary to the guild's electoral regulations," Francisco Baquero won election to guild office. Because of these irregularities, the alcalde admitted that a new election ought to be held and that only masters of the first class be allowed to attend. He reiterated the protestors' claims "that the very presence of the castas precipitated the confusion and clamor at the initial meeting." He further recommended that the fiscal bar Romero from the next electoral assembly as punishment for his transgressions.[15]

The newly elected *procurador general* of the guild, Nicolás Cabral, wrote separately to the fiscal to ask that the election be accepted despite, he admitted, the "many disorders and violations of ordinances." He sought to neutralize the protests of the foreign faction since they were, "foreigners and enemies of those elected."[16] The remaining seven officers elected in the disputed ballot also wrote to the fiscal to demand that he support the election results. The signatories included Juan José Romero and the now visible leader of the black and casta faction, Francisco Baquero.[17] In addition to these signatories, three Spaniards, two from Seville and one from Cádiz, two criollos, and the other man elected as an "Indian" vocal, Juan Díos de Campuzano, signed the letter. These prominent members of the craft dismissed their enemies as "foreigners or their lackeys" and claimed that overturning the election would undermine this guild, "so important to the public well-being," and ultimately lead to more "confusion and hostilities." Finally, they claimed that the nullification of the election would "blemish the reputation and honor of the master shoemakers."[18]

By the time Romero and his allies got around to defending their behavior against the allegations of the foreign faction, however, the fiscal had already signed an order to overturn the contested results and hold new elections. Undaunted by this apparent fait accompli, Baquero wrote again to the fiscal to defend the election results by disputing the evidence presented by the foreign faction. He pointed out that because the alcalde had ejected Romero from his home prior to the balloting and had the armed patrol at his disposal once the vote began, the claims of intimidation and bullying were obvious fabrications. In language strikingly similar to that used by his enemies, Baquero also placed the blame for the chaos on the alcalde. He claimed that García López had allowed the foreigners to introduce and utilize an adulterated census of the guild membership that unfairly relegated a number of masters to the second class, effectively denying them their rights. "The result," claimed Baquero, "was the mixing of the two classes and disorders." He asserted that only individuals listed in the first class on the "true census" had participated in the voting and therefore the results were valid. That is, Baquero claimed that the "five free mulattoes and two mestizos" who the alcalde claimed voted fraudulently were, in fact, "Españoles." He went on to dismiss the allegation that poor lighting and a crowded room made it impossible for the authorities to distinguish castas from masters of the first class. He asked the fiscal, "can you be persuaded that in a well-illuminated room the alcalde could not distinguish Negroes, mulattoes, Spaniards, and Indians? This doesn't seem believable because only one light and a short glance is enough to indicate the notable differences of colors . . . and castes." [19] According to Baquero, there was no "confusion" of the two classes. Instead, there was a deliberate attempt to disenfranchise some masters legitimately included in the first class.

Romero may have overstepped the bounds of propriety, Baquero conceded, but this was because of "his lack of culture and because of the injustice of the attempts to keep him from informing the masters of the fraud [use of an adulterated census]." If the fiscal decided to ban Romero from subsequent meetings, Baquero claimed, he would simply reinforce the position of the foreigners since Romero was "the individual that firmly demands the enforcement of the ordinances." Without Romero those supporting his position would be defeated, and "the offices of the guild will be left in the hands of foreigners." [20] In effect, Baquero was claiming that recent immigrants from Spain were "foreigners" who sought to colonize this craft. The real fraud, he claimed, was the foreigners' efforts to unjustly classify some master shoemakers as castas, not the fact that a small number of castas had voted.

The complexity of racial politics within the craft is suggested by Baquero's letter as well as by Romero's simultaneous dismissal of an unsolicited letter signed by thirteen self-identified "pardo and moreno master shoemakers" who sought to support Romero's position by asking the fiscal to stay his order nullifying the election. Among the signatories was "José García, captain and commander of the militia of Indians and master shoemaker." Three other signatories also identified themselves as officers of this same militia unit. Juan José Romero, the elected guild officer they had written to support, immediately wrote to the fiscal to dismiss the opinion of these nonwhite craftsmen because they were "not among the masters of the first class, and if of the second without either active or passive voice and vote in the elections . . . without the right to elect or be elected for the offices of the guild, [without] a legitimate right to give an opinion concerning the issue of nullifying the elections of July thirtieth.[21] Since the unsanctioned participation of nonwhite shoemakers in the election was the central issue in the debate over nullification, Romero was in no position to encourage or accept the active participation of self-identified pardos and morenos in support of his position. This battle was not over the justice of denying pardos and morenos and other castas full rights in this guild; it was instead about who *were* pardos and morenos.

The decision of the fiscal, Marquéz de la Plata, on November 16, 1792, swept aside the arguments of Baquero and Romero and ordered a new election where black and casta masters would be barred from attendance.[22] Events then moved swiftly with the new election held a month later. The newly elected guild officers sent the results to the audiencia nearly three weeks after the event. They informed authorities that Dr. Cárdenas had attended the meeting on December 18, 1792, and his presence helped assure "a precise compliance with the stipulated procedures of the guild regulations." They gleefully reported that the meeting had been held, "during the afternoon and evening and [had occurred] in terms so disciplined and peaceful that not a single individual voted without full liberty or without full instructions as was correct and just." Proof of the regularity and correctness of the proceedings, they smugly asserted, was "that until the present, a period of twenty days, no one has appeared to question or dispute the results of this second and correctly celebrated election."[23] Predictably, the group of masters opposed by Romero and Baquero as "foreigners and their allies" won a comprehensive victory. Among those elected were the Catalan Antonio Porra as treasurer and president, Nicolás Riquy, also a Catalan, as alcalde, José Labrador, another Catalan, and José Canepa, an Italian, as veedores, and Martín Porra, brother of the treasurer, and a Catalan, as procurador general.[24]

Activation of the guild constitution and the subsequent election of officers for the guild and cofradía had proceeded on a provisional basis and was sanctioned by the viceroy. Permanent institutionalization awaited formal approval by the king and his Council of the Indies, but the new guild leadership, long-thwarted in its determination to crack down on "false masters," mobilized to conduct its first inspection of the members' shops.[25] Before this could happen, however, Viceroy Arredondo received a copy of a royal decree, signed November 6, 1793, refusing the petition to recognize the guild of the shoemakers and ordering the suspension of all activities of the guild and cofradía. The king and council cited the absence of a preliminary royal license that, according to law, was required prior to the submission of applications for the erection of guilds and *cofradías*.[26]

Despite the clear intention of the king's decision, Nicolas Riquy, procurador general of the guild, appealed to the viceroy to "permit the economic and administrative functions of the guild to continue," claiming that the decree only suspended the cofradía, not the guild itself. The guild leadership, he promised, would comply with the cited law and apply for the necessary license for the erection of the cofradía "at an opportune moment for compliance." Remarkably, the fiscal of the audiencia upheld Riquy's interpretation on May 24, and Viceroy Arredondo then published a *bando* suspending the cofradía but permitting the guild to function because "they are so interested in the public well-being."[27] This decision followed in broad outline the earlier decision to permit the silversmiths to function as guild without formal license from Spain.

The Pardo and Moreno Shoemakers Change the Game

Following the decision by the colonial government to overturn the disputed guild election of July 1792, black and casta shoemakers pulled loose from their alliance with Romero and explored alternative ways to protect their interests. This process ultimately led to the meeting on January 8, 1793, and the decision to create a segregated guild summarized earlier. The guild census that had preceded the election confirmed their worst fears as the alcalde and escribano identified more than a score of masters enumerated as criollos in 1780 as pardos or mestizos. With the comprehensive victory of the foreign masters in the election that followed, black and casta shoemakers realized that they would now be subject to decisions made by an unsympathetic guild leadership while being forced to carry the full burden of guild dues and financial obligations.

Why did it take the black and casta shoemakers eight months and two guild elections to decide to directly oppose the new constitution, given its blatantly discriminatory provisions? Clearly, it was the cascading string of events that included the electoral victory of the "foreign masters," the marginalization of Romero, the removal of Baquero from the office of vocal, and the decision to categorically bar blacks and castas from future electoral meetings that finally precipitated their action. The essential question was not whether the guild ordinances were discriminatory but whether these men, personally and individually, would be subject to discriminatory provisions.

The role of Francisco Baquero in these events suggests the potential leverage present in the everyday workings of the *régimen de castas* in late colonial Buenos Aires. The master shoemakers elected Baquero as one of two Indian vocales in the disputed election of 1792. Census takers in 1778 had identified him as a mestizo as did the alcalde who conducted the 1792 guild census. His enemies suggested to the fiscal that this racial identification plus his marriage to "a zamba" fixed his status as a master of the second class. Baquero was careful in applying racial terms to himself in his correspondence with authorities. In letters to the viceroy, Baquero asserted other components of his *calidad*, identifying himself as a master shoemaker and a captain of the Militia of Indians rather than using a term like mestizo or pardo. In correspondence with local authorities he never claimed to be an indio, even though the master shoemakers had elected him to serve as one of the two "Indian" officers in the guild. He did, however, claim to be an indio in a letter to the king. The location of his identity in this difficult to define interstice of the régimen de castas did not prove an obstacle to his leadership of the pardo-dominated shoemaker faction seeking separation from the white guild. Perhaps reflecting on his new role, Baquero had altered his self-identification after 1795 and now consistently self-identified as a pardo in his correspondence with local authorities.[28]

Given the public nature of Baquero's fierce campaign to defeat the "foreign" faction, we know something of his courage and political skill. He serially confronted the elected leaders of his craft, the alcalde of the cabildo, the fiscal of the audiencia, and eventually the viceroy to defeat the full implementation of the discriminatory guild ordinances drafted by Dr. Vicente García Grande y Cárdenas. Why had Baquero and his closest supporters never protested the incremental construction of racial discrimination across multiple drafts of the guild constitution? Why had he failed to act when the final draft included the imposition of humiliating provisions for "the comprehensive separation of masters of the second class" in all guild meetings? What finally moved Baquero away from his alliance with Romero and into open opposition to the guild leadership and ultimately to demanding the formation of a separate black guild? The timing suggests that it was the audiencia's decision to overturn the electoral victory of the Romero faction in 1792 and to hold a new electoral meeting closed to masters of the second class that signaled future exclusion from guild office to Baquero and his followers. As the victorious guild leadership marginalized Romero's allies, the blacks and castas, as a guarantee that Romero would never recover from his defeat, Baquero prepared his allies for the next round. The January 8, 1793, meeting and the selection of Baquero to seek a separate guild "in all inferior and superior tribunals" was the outward manifestation of this new consciousness and commitment.[29]

Pardo and Moreno Shoemakers Organize

Baquero moved quickly to establish the case for racial separation in a letter addressed to Viceroy Nicolás de Arredondo. He reminded the viceroy that the foreign officers of the guild now barred "pardos and morenos, both free and slave, and other castas" from assuming any role in the election of officers or other craft governance because (quoting from the guild constitution) this "would cause the drunken confusion that is felt by free whites when they are mixed with blacks, either slave or free. And, if subordinated to the latter in some cases, it would be a strange and indecent matter for the whites."[30] Separating the shoemakers into separate, racially distinct guilds would, he cleverly argued, more perfectly realize the very objective sought by the foreign masters.

Baquero went on to remind Viceroy Arredondo that Spanish law as well as ample precedent in the Spanish colonies sanctioned the creation of segregated guilds and cofradías, citing the segregated militia units and cofradías of Buenos Aires as proof that racially organized corporations functioned responsibly. These nonwhite organizations, he claimed, run "without scandals or disorders and with a financial regularity that is exemplary." In the case of the shoemakers, Baquero asserted that the pardos and morenos "were as useful to society and the public as Spaniards and Indians."[31] He cited the racially segregated guilds of Lima, Havana, and Cartagena as additional precedents, an array of distant examples that suggests that Baquero and his supporters had harvested information about the experiences and achievements of similar communities in other colonies. Among the masters of the second class in Buenos Aires, he confidently asserted, "there are many with proven ability, good conduct, and prudent habits to undertake the offices of alcalde and veedor," within the proposed guild of pardo and morenos.

Baquero requested that the viceroy suspend all financial fees and penalties assessed by the leadership of the white guild since the 1792 election and prevent the officers of the guild from undertaking "an [inspection] visit of the shops, as provided for by the ordinances and [collecting] two pesos in dues from each master enrolled in the census of shoemakers for the benefit of the guild." When notified of Baquero's requests, Martín Porra, newly confirmed procurador general of the guild, responded on January 30, 1793, by bitterly attacking Baquero's request for a separated black and casta guild, prefacing his substantive arguments with a lengthy rehearsal of contemporary beliefs (legal, theological, and popular) that buttressed the discrimination and prejudice written into the guild ordinances. There were, Porra asserted, "hierarchies in nature that distinguished individuals and groups one from another." Societies separated noble and common orders and then divided these two categories by wealth, power, and prestige. The institutionalized racial hierarchy of the guild was, Porra claimed, "the replication of the hierarchies found in nature and throughout the Christian world." The guild ordinances were written to avoid imposing "an artificial and unnatural equality on the guild." The current guild leadership, with the support of the alcalde and fiscal, had finally defeated the efforts of the Romero faction to subvert "the natural order and structure of all social organizations" by permitting pardos and other castas to vote and hold office in violation of both guild rules and law. Even if free, he reminded the authorities, blacks and castas "ought to live subject to the control of whites."[32]

The intent of Baquero's petition, Porra claimed, was a blatant attempt to escape the rigorous application of the guild's racial requirements. Picking up the argument recently made by the leadership of the silversmiths, he argued this petition was an effort by masters with "dubious credentials and poor training" to escape the guild officers' commitment to quality and craftsmanship. If Baquero accomplished his ends, Porra suggested, the nonwhite guild "would become an intolerable and insufferable burden" to society because of "the inevitable frauds and irregularities" that would occur.[33] If unconstrained by white master artisans, he complained, black and casta shoemakers would be overtaken by their natural sloth and criminality.

Porra attempted to disarm Baquero's use of the success of racially separated guilds in other cities of Spanish America as precedent by noting that the guilds of mulattoes and blacks established in Lima and other cities had resulted from the "pity of the King" and that "those [mulattoes and blacks] of this city do not yet have that privilege." He also speculated that segregated guilds had only succeeded in other cities because there were larger numbers of black and casta craftsmen. Buenos Aires, he claimed, was a distinctly different situation. In his only prediction that would prove prophetic, Porra argued that there were not enough free mulatto and black masters to financially sustain a separate guild administration. He held that "a guild should be composed only of master craftsmen, because, although journeymen may have aptitude and receive good training, they are legally restricted from exercising the offices of a guild." The petitioners were, he acknowledged, worthy and able men, but they would be bound to fail, "even though they are now filled with fervor and are willing to make sacrifices; they will soon arrive at their ultimate ruin." [34]

In an opinion dated February 8, 1793, the fiscal dismissed the petition of the nonwhite shoemakers as "unfounded and, moreover, contemptible because it will lead to further discords and dissensions which will frustrate the end and objective that has motivated the very founding of this guild." Acting upon the advice of the fiscal, Viceroy Arredondo rejected Baquero's petition the next day. Undeterred, Baquero appealed the decision on February 25, but the fiscal again decided against Baquero, noting with an economy of language that "there is no place for [Baquero's] petition." [35]

Notified of the fiscal's opinion, Baquero informed the viceroy and audiencia on July 12 that "in these circumstances [he had] no further recourse with this level of government," stating that as "apoderado of the pardo and moreno shoemakers" he intended to carry his appeal to the royal court, "as is the right of all Spanish vassals." Black and casta craftsmen had come to this decision because, "the justification for [their] petition in every aspect is well known." [36] Baquero soon located and retained an apoderado in Madrid who addressed an appeal to the king and Council of Indies on January 17, 1794, seeking the establishment of a segregated guild of pardo and moreno shoemakers. [37] This communication introduced "Francisco Baquero, Indian and captain of militia" (his first direct claim to this calidad), as leader of the black and casta faction and reviewed the events that led to the appeal. The central grievance placed before the king was the exclusion of nonwhite masters from any active participation in the administration of the guild. "The Spaniards, foreigners, and Indians," had arbitrarily denied "those who are pardo or moreno" from active and passive roles in the guild, "while subjecting them fully to the financial obligations of the white members." It was this attempt to relegate black and casta shoemakers to a position of inferiority solely because of their race that had caused dissension and discord.[38] Left unresolved in this letter was why the victorious faction would have excluded Baquero, "Indian, and captain of the militia."

As he had already demonstrated, Baquero did not hesitate to criticize the most powerful representatives of imperial power in the Viceroyalty of Río de la Plata as he pressed his case before the Spanish court. Despite the provisions of Spanish law and the existence of ample precedent, he noted that colonial authorities in Buenos Aires had been consistently hostile to his petition to separate from the white guild. Any further appeal to those authorities, he told the king, would be useless. In fact, Baquero asserted, "the viceroy and his fiscal were so supportive of the white guild leadership that they knowingly violated legal procedures by allowing the shoemakers to hold meetings and draft ordinances without prior receipt of the required royal license." Saving the best for last, Baquero reported that even after receipt of the king's decision to suspend the guild, Viceroy Arredondo and the fiscal had decided to sanction the enforcement of the administrative and economic provisions of the guild charter.[39] The highest levels of the colonial establishment in Buenos Aires, according to Baquero, had subverted the royal will and were directly responsible for the guild's continued operation. The reason for this, stated Baquero, was "that the viceroy and the fiscal shared with the foreign leadership of the united guild . . . a repugnance for the black and casta masters."[40]

Baquero requested the necessary royal license to hold meetings and form ordinances for a separate guild of pardo and moreno shoemakers, noting as he had in Buenos Aires the ample precedent found in racially segregated militia units and cofradías. These bodies were sanctioned, Baquero stated to the king with eloquence, "by your Majesty's pity and operate with an efficiency and effectiveness that could well be emulated by Spaniards and other vassals of your Majesty with a more privileged color."[41] Despite Baquero's aggressiveness in condemning the actions of the viceroy and audiencia, the king and his Council of the Indies decided to sustain the appeal of the pardo and moreno shoemakers, granting Baquero's petition for a separate guild on January 29, 1795.[42]

At the same time the king and Council of the Indies responded to the "official" guild's request for "permission to found a guild and cofradía" filed in the wake of the king's November 1793 order to suspend all guild and cofradía functions.[43] Although the immigrant-led guild had received de facto authority by Viceroy Arredondo to hold meetings, conduct examinations, and regulate shops, the "official" faction had judiciously petitioned the king for a formal license.[44] While the king's favorable response to the request of the white guild was expected, the decision to simultaneously sanction the black and casta guild arrived like a thunderbolt, sweeping aside the official guild's claims to control and regulate all shoemakers in the city.

In effect, every decision taken by the "foreign" guild leadership since their electoral victory, every fine and fee assessed over the previous two years, was now in question. Baquero's success had deeply complicated the viability of the official guild. The king and council recommended that both guilds use the existing ordinances and avoid any major or new expenditures of time and effort. The decree also recommended that both groups suspend their efforts to found cofradías until the separate guilds received final royal approval, thus creating a simplified trajectory through the bureaucracy.[45]

Crisis Overtakes the Silversmiths and Shoemakers

While the shoemakers staggered from crisis to crisis, the silversmiths had continued to operate as a guild despite the absence of a formal constitution. The craft's elected leadership routinely carried out *visitas* of shops, conducted examinations, and collected dues and fees from members. Periodic, but unpredictable, eruptions of ethnic and racial conflict punctuated these basic corporate functions, shadowing the dangerous trajectory of the shoemakers. After 1792 a dissident faction operated among the silversmiths that included the masters most often discovered with adulterated goods and punished during visitas or fined for failure to pay guild dues and fees. Nearly all were blacks or castas who saw themselves as victims of racial animus. For them the guild leadership's discourse of quality, skill, and probity was self-serving cant. As a result, their appeals of specific decisions and penalties to the cabildo and fiscal increasingly challenged the very legitimacy of the guild. In less than a year the guild of silversmiths exploded in conflict when nine dissidents began a campaign of noncompliance, refusing to participate in guild elections or pay dues. They also requested the colonial government grant them permission to "separate from the guild of silversmiths" because it was based on "ordinances and statutes that do not have the approval and sanction of the Royal Council of the Indies."[46] Their language and tactics signaled that black and casta silversmiths and shoemakers followed events in each other's craft closely and suggested the likelihood that plebeians across the city tracked these conflicts through conversations in *pulperías*, taverns, and residences.

The death of Juan Antonio Callejas y Sandoval, who led the guild of silversmiths for more than a decade and maintained good relations with colonial authorities, gravely weakened the official faction. His replacement, Jorge Troncoso, proved to be a fierce defender of guild prerogatives, but he demonstrated little diplomatic skill in his dealings with the cabildo, fiscal, and viceroy once under attack from the craft's dissident faction.[47] Closely tracking the argument made earlier by the official shoemakers' guild, Troncoso claimed in a letter to the viceroy that while cofradías needed royal approval guilds required only acceptance by local authorities. His letter revealed at the same time that the guild leadership had responded to the noncompliance and disruptions of the dissidents by denying them the right to participate in guild affairs because "those who are not Spaniards or Indians" should not have the right to vote or hold office.[48]

Regardless of the specific complaints of the dissident silversmiths and shoemakers, Viceroy Nicolás de Arredondo remained a reliable ally of guild leaders in both crafts. The new round of complaints from the dissident silversmiths and their petition to separate and create a new guild filed in 1792 coincided with efforts by the viceroy and cabildo to impose order on the increasingly factionalized shoemakers by insisting on a new guild constitution based on a Spanish model and adapted by Dr. Vincente García Grande y Cárdenas. Seeking to force the two contentious trades into a single pathway, Arredondo now ordered the silversmiths to seek a royal license and employ Cárdenas to "formulate complete ordinances."[49]

As this process moved slowly forward, a new conflict undermined the tone-deaf guild leadership's relationship with the cabildo, which it increasingly depended on for the enforcement of its orders. When the cabildo ordered the craft leadership to examine Juan Antonio Domínguez for master in 1794, Troncoso, displaying the assertiveness that would serve him so poorly, responded by dismissing the cabildo's role and demanding Domínguez apply directly to guild officers.[50] He then went on to suggest the inappropriateness of Domínguez's petition since he was "unable to demonstrate *limpieza de sangre*." The alcalde impatiently swept aside Troncoso's pretensions, stating that the cabildo would only enforce guild provisions that were "adaptable to this country." The alcalde's meaning was clear: limpieza de sangre was not realistic in "this country."[51]

By the end of 1795 Domínguez had appealed to the viceroy since the silversmiths continued to refuse to conduct his examination despite the cabildo's order to proceed.[52] He told the viceroy that he had been a "master silversmith" with his own shop since the late 1770s. Forced to leave the city by his poverty, he returned to find his status denied by guild officers who questioned his calidad. He sought to brush aside the guild complaint that he could not prove limpieza de sangre by noting that "there are among the master silversmiths many who are publicly known as mulattoes and other various castas who cannot substantiate their good birth." Domínguez took the occasion to take a direct swipe at the *maestro mayor*, stating that "the apoderado Jorge Troncoso . . . is among the master silversmiths publicly known to be a mulatto." It is worth noting that Troncoso did not reply to this allegation.[53]

In the midst of this dispute, the leaders of the silversmiths finally applied for a royal license, arguing that a guild would end the "numerous frauds that afflict the city" by imposing effective controls on "the pardo and casta masters who perpetrate them."[54] The king replied on May 13, 1796, granting the request for a license with the specific purpose of ending the "many adulterations of goods of gold and silver produced by some artisans of that capital."[55] Ramón Xímenez y Navia, *síndico procurador* of the cabildo, now ordered Troncoso, apoderado and maestro mayor, to begin the drafting process. In response the predictably overreaching Troncoso took the opportunity to tell Xímenez y Navia that the guild leaders would no longer tolerate the insubordination and disorders of the dissenting faction.[56]

While the silversmiths and shoemakers had followed very different paths they were in 1796 forced by bureaucratic decisions to begin framing constitutions, despite more than two decades of false starts and disappointments. By the time the king had ordered colonial authorities to facilitate the formation of two guilds of shoemakers and a guild of silversmiths, Pedro Melo de Portugal y Villena had succeeded Nicolás de Arredondo as viceroy. The new viceroy, unburdened by the bitter legacy of years of internecine conflicts that had attached to his predecessor's relationship with the crafts, presided over a meeting of the audiencia on July 18, 1796, that resolved the formation of "guilds that will totally separate the Spaniards from the mulattoes, Negroes, and other castes." He also allowed the shoemakers to hold meetings, formulate ordinances, and enroll their members subject to final approval by local and royal authorities. In response the cabildo ordered its alcalde of the second vote to supervise the formation of the guild of black and casta shoemakers and undertake a census of the nonwhite shoemakers.[57]

The Guild of Pardo and Moreno Shoemakers

The escribano of the cabildo finished the census of black and casta shoemakers on August 18, 1796, "aided by the free mulattoes Francisco Baquero, Pedro Rivas, Celestino Molina, and Alberto Pérez."[58] This census like all its predecessors produced its own controversies. On August 16, Baquero had informed authorities that he was "adding the Indians who were previously in the guild of Spanish masters" to his membership, and indeed, the completed census reflected this decision.[59] The viceroy and audiencia later rejected this presumption, "since according to . . . laws, they [Indians] are expressly included with and added to the Spaniards in various chapters of similar ordinances that have been adopted in other times, and as the Tribunal of Indians of this jurisdiction has always understood."[60]

Baquero's request that the *alquacil* forcibly enroll Bartolo Catana in the guild of pardos and morenos "under threat of arrest to prevent further resistance" further illuminates the complicated assignment of racial identity in this trade. Those conducting the guild censuses of 1780 and 1792 had not enrolled Bartolo Catana. He was probably a recent arrival in Buenos Aires, and his calidad had not been vetted in the crucible of racial confrontation and litigation that afflicted the shoemakers for more than five years. The "foreign" leadership of the white guild had not identified him as a pardo or casta as they purged their enemies from active participation in the guild, and he had not signed the documents that set in motion the effort to create a segregated black and casta guild. Catana's circumstances were like those of Baquero and his closest supporters before 1792. There is some irony therefore in Baquero's demand that he be compelled to enroll as a pardo. Although Catana finally accepted the imposition of this label, the incident indicates clearly that not all nonwhite shoemakers, especially those not yet excluded from the white guild, shared Baquero's enthusiasm for the creation of a black guild.

The census identified fifty-nine black and casta master shoemakers who supervised the work of seventy-nine journeymen and forty-four apprentices (figure 15).[61] Only six of the masters were slaves. Even though the census included only black, casta, and Indian shoemakers, there were numerous novelties in the application of racial terms. The escribano assigned the labels *naturales*, *moreno libres*, *moreno esclavos*, *pardos libres*, and *pardos esclavos*. In another seventeen cases he applied the term *pardo* without assigning legal status. Many of these were probably free. The guild census of 1792 indicated that six of those identified as pardos without clear stipulation of legal status were free. A seventh had been identified as mestizo in 1792 and was free as well. Only two of the remaining ten cases were listed as slaves in 1792. Given the high incidence of manumissions among black and mulatto artisans, it is certainly possible that at least some of the remaining eight ambivalent cases were free in 1796, but we cannot be sure.

A close comparison of the 1796 census of pardo and moreno masters with the 1792 guild census illustrates the slippery nature of racial nomenclature. In 1792 the alcalde and escribano undertook the guild census with the intention of establishing who was *really* white (Español) or Indian (indio). In 1796 the census was conducted to determine who was black or casta. Unsurprisingly, a comparison of the two documents provides some anomalies. Twenty-three of black and casta masters enrolled in 1796, or 39 percent, were not present in the 1792 count. Among the thirty-seven men recorded in both counts, sixteen masters (44 percent) were assigned the same calidad in both documents. In twenty cases (56 percent of the masters found in both counts) the escribano assigned different labels from those applied just four years earlier. Most of these discrepancies are easily anticipated given the imprecise application of adjacent terms like moreno and pardo or indio and mestizo. Some of the others suggest the underlying unreliability of racial terminology more generally. For example, two masters identified as mestizos in 1792 were labeled free mulattoes in 1796, and one master identified as a mulatto in 1792 was identified as an indio four years later. Finally, in an equally wonderful transformation, a master shoemaker enrolled in 1792 as a Spaniard was identified as an Indian in this matriculation. Given that Baquero himself was called at various times indio, pardo, and mestizo, we should be prepared for these ambiguities. What is undeniable, however, from the 1796 census is that the effort to create a separate guild was overwhelmingly a pardo enterprise.

Given the labor-intensive nature of artisanal shoe manufacturing, we can use the distribution of journeymen and apprentices in the workshops of masters as a proxy for representing the volume of business and, with less

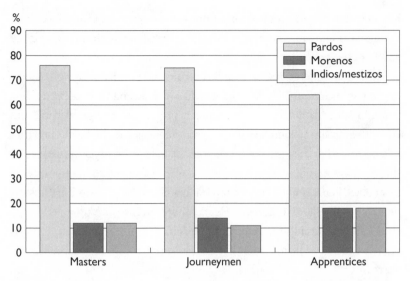

	Masters (N = 59)	Journeymen (N = 79)	Apprentices (N = 44)
Pardos	76% (45)	75% (59)	64% (28)
Morenos	12% (7)	14% (11)	18% (8)
Indios/mestizos	12% (7)	11% (9)	18% (8)

FIGURE 15 Black and casta shoemakers by rank (1796). Source: The 1796 census of pardo and moreno *zapateros* is found in AGN, División Colonia, Sección Gobierno, Interior, leg. 41, exp. 14, 9 vta.

confidence, business income among shoemakers, assuming that the more prosperous shops employed the largest number of apprentices and journeymen. Did black and casta parents and guardians display race consciousness as they placed their sons as apprentices? Alternatively, did they place their dependents with white masters to enhance later economic prospects? The answer to both questions may be yes. The 1796 census of black and casta shoemakers reveals that European immigrant and black master shoemakers both attracted larger numbers of black and casta journeymen and apprentices than did criollo masters. Only nine of seventy-nine pardo and moreno journeymen worked for criollo masters, and four of this nine were in the shop of a single successful criollo master with an elite clientele, Rafael de la Rosa. Seventeen worked for Spanish and other immigrant European masters. The rest, fifty-five pardo and moreno journeymen or 70 percent, worked in the shops of black or casta masters. The dispersal of apprentices imitated this pattern: 66 percent of nonwhite apprentices were located in the shops of nonwhite masters, while Indian and mestizo masters employed another five apprentices.

Having completed the census, Baquero turned to the pressing business of funding the guild. He asked the alcalde of the second vote for permission to require dues from all potential members of the nonwhite guild in order to cover the rapidly accumulating costs of the census and the heavy expenses related to earlier protests and legal appeals. While the royal order permitting a separate guild had ordered the return of all dues and fees collected from black and casta masters by the leadership of the white guild, "this has not occurred" Baquero noted.[62] He had more success forging a guild constitution than forcing the return of theses funds. A draft constitution was ready by July 6, 1798, and soon after it was sent to the fiscal of the audiencia for review.[63]

The royal decree had ordered the two contending groups of shoemakers to utilize the ordinances of Cárdenas. Nevertheless, the draft hammered out by the nonwhite shoemakers eliminated virtually all allusions to moral or spiritual matters and abandoned the troublesome cofradía completely. It pared the administration of the proposed guild to four offices (an alcalde, a veedor, a fiscal, and a procurador) and created a novel means for filling them. As a response to their experience of chaotic and divisive elections in the united guild, the black and casta masters proposed to select their officers in a lottery where "a young boy" would draw names from an urn. Once selected these guild officers would be compensated from the fines and fees levied on the membership, but as was predictable among men of very modest resources the fines and fees the nonwhite masters sought to establish were less than those in use in the united guild.[64]

The draft constitution took aim at those black and casta journeymen and apprentices who worked in the shops of criollo and immigrant masters, requiring them to relocate with one of the masters "of their own class." This, claimed Baquero, was necessary to permit the effective policing and supervision of training by guild officers.[65] Unspoken, but obvious, was this provision's potential to punish white shoemakers by withdrawing scores of nonwhite laborers from their shops. Given that the pool of apprentices and journeymen in Buenos Aires was overwhelmingly nonwhite, the prejudice and discrimination that had led to Baquero's initiative would carry a steep price if this draft was implemented.

Perhaps as compensation to the scores of black and casta apprentices and journeymen who would be forced to relocate with implementation, Baquero and his allies proposed a fundamentally different environment for the trade's journeymen and apprentices. Their draft constitution removed many of the obstacles to advancement previously faced by journeymen and apprentices under the constitution of the united guild. They reduced the required apprenticeship term from four years to three years, leaving in place the two-year minimum term journeymen had traditionally served before becoming eligible to take the examination for master. Similarly, they required that slaves who sought the rank of master present the written authorization of their owner as a prerequisite for the exam. On the other hand, they simplified the examination and made it less expensive than the united guild's exam, only sixteen pesos, requiring that candidates only produce one pair of men's and one pair of women's shoes that met the guild's standards for quality.[66] Once in place the altered selection process for guild office, essentially a form of lottery, would have combined with the streamlined probationary term and less expensive exams to speed shoemakers through guild ranks and offer the likely prospect of enjoying the remuneration due guild officers.

More revolutionary was the proposal to permit black and casta journeymen to have limited access to the city's growing market in ready-to-wear shoes. From 1779 the most visible leaders of the guild movement had railed against "false masters" and journeymen who opened shops and sold directly to customers, routinely condemning this trade in their communications with the cabildo and with the colonial government as a source of "frauds" and as an obstacle to public order. During the two decades consumed in the pursuit of a united guild of shoemakers, the number of journeymen working outside the supervision of masters and selling directly into the market had grown exponentially. Central to this process was the willingness of *pulperos* to buy shoes in volume from journeymen on speculation and then sell these less-expensive, ready-to-wear shoes to customers. The threat was no longer the limited competition of "false masters" but rather the maturation of an alternative form of production connected to mass consumption by the mounting willingness of small shopkeepers to buy shoes in wholesale volumes.[67] The constitution of the united guild had outlawed this trade completely, and the cabildo at the urging of guild officers enforced the prohibition by seizing all ready-to-wear shoes from the city's pulperías.[68] The pulperos went to court, defending their practice as a service to "the poor" because they did not "require full and immediate payment [from customers]." So, at the same time the united guild faced the growing threat posed by Baquero's separatist faction, it was drawn into an expensive and ultimately hopeless litigation with the pulperos.[69]

The black and casta shoemakers proved more permissive than their immigrant rivals. Article sixteen of their proposed ordinances dealt with the growing trade in cheap ready-to-wear shoes carried on by the pulperos. The regulations authored by Cárdenas and put in place by the white guild had uncompromisingly banned the sale of locally produced shoes by those not established as master shoemakers. While the ordinances of the nonwhite shoemakers asserted that "it is well known that many injustices result from the sale of shoes in the various pulperías and shops of this city and as a result the guild prohibits all of its journeymen members from producing shoes for this type of sale under the threat of confiscation of the shoes produced."[70] But this apparent prohibition was liberally offset in succeeding articles of the ordinances.

Article seventeen authorized the guild leadership to select "eight or more" pulperías or shops in various parts of the city to serve as licensed outlets for "all types of shoes." The guild would permit its black and casta journeymen to sell ready-made shoes to these designated middlemen "at a price adjusted to the quality of the material and workmanship" with one-fourth of the price set aside for the guild treasury. By way of explanation, Baquero and his allies cited the potentially destructive effects a complete ban would have on journeymen and the inconveniences that an absolute prohibition would have on poor consumers. The draft constitution also gave black and casta journeymen the right to accept work outside the shop of an accredited master "whenever they find themselves unoccupied." In fact the ordinance directly permitted journeymen to work on ready-to-wear shoes while employed in the shops of masters as long as they gave priority to the work assigned by the master and "completed it punctually."[71]

Decades earlier when the guild effort began, every individual who entered the trade as an apprentice succeeded or failed within a narrowly defined and rigorously enforced vocational curriculum. Journeymen who failed to reach the status of master for lack of sufficient technical skill or for lack of the necessary capital were forced to leave the trade or accept a perpetual position of dependency in the shop of a master.[72] The system that pertained in 1798, when Baquero submitted his ordinances to vice-regal authorities, had been substantially altered by the development of the ready-to-wear trade. Master shoemakers now produced more expensive custom-made boots and shoes for the city's *gente decente*. Journeymen and apprentices aided in this production and also handled the bulk of repairs and alterations. This was not unlike the system that had previously characterized the entire profession. An alternate system, however, had grown up alongside this conservative model. The growth of the ready-to-wear trade provided journeymen shoemakers with an alternative to the expensive and time-consuming process of becoming a master, effectively improving their income and enhancing independence. While most journeymen continued to be associated with a master, they earned additional income by making repairs or producing ready-mades on their own time and selling wholesale to pulperos. One indication of this is the presence of five black journeymen in the 1796 census of nonwhite shoemakers who worked independent of any affiliation with a master. The apparent toleration of this trend evidenced in the ordinances of the nonwhite guild suggests that the trade in ready-to-wear shoes did not directly compete with the limited traditional custom trade of the masters. Rather, the ready-to-wear shoes marketed by pulperos represented an expansion of the shoe market to include portions of the urban lower classes that had previously worn sandals and other alternatives to professionally produced shoes.[73]

As the silversmiths undertook drafting a constitution for their trade, the shoemakers now proceeded tentatively to achieve an unlikely goal for the poorest craft in a second-tier colonial capital city, the creation of two guilds of shoemakers. Viceroy Melo de Portugal y Villena, upon receipt of the royal order permitting the formation of racially separated guilds of shoemakers, had ordered the cabildo of the city to cooperate with the leadership of both groups in formulating ordinances and compiling membership lists, but it was only in 1799 that both sets of guild regulations were submitted to the cabildo of Buenos Aires by the two groups of shoemakers.[74]

Disappointment, Challenge, and Conflict

The silversmiths pursued the creation of a guild in an ad hoc manner until dissension caused by the implementation of production standards, the collection of dues and fees, and a clumsy effort to exclude black and casta masters from guild office led to division and appeals to authorities.[75] The desire of the craft leadership to escape these constraints led it to petition the king for a license to create a formal guild. When the king and council granted permission in 1796, guild officers led by Jorge Troncoso drafted a constitution.[76] Ominously trailing along behind the effort to formalize the guild was a slow-moving legal protest filed before the audiencia in 1791 by the craft's dissident faction of black and casta masters.[77] These craftsmen continued to refuse to pay guild dues or pay fines assessed by guild officers for adulterated goods. In response, the craft leadership singled out the shops of the dissidents for intense scrutiny and unannounced inspections that led to the repeated seizures of goods and tools, incrementally beggaring the dissidents. Then, on December 23, 1797, the fiscal of the audiencia, Dr. Julián de Leyba (sometimes written "Leiva"), finally published his opinion on the 1791 protest, stating that that the collection of all dues and fines by the "guild" leadership since 1769 had been illegal in the absence of a guild constitution sanctioned by royal approval. He then went on to suggest that the dissidents return to court to demand the return of all fines and dues assessed by guild officials.[78]

While the fiscal's decision left open the possibility of completing the draft constitution and submitting it for royal approval, it was a heavy blow to the guild officers.[79] The decision would effectively bankrupt the guild that had few resources and threaten its officers directly with financial ruin if the fiscal found them personally accountable. Worse still, there would be no opportunity to replenish depleted coffers since the dissident faction, nearly half the membership, was no longer obligated to pay dues and fees. Viceroy Melo de Portugal y Villena delivered the deathblow when in 1798 he declared that "no guild exists" in response to additional appeals.[80] Troncoso and the other officers had tried and failed to crush their opponents, and now they lacked the resources to even pay the legal fees accumulated in their effort to win vindication from the colonial authorities.[81]

The shoemakers had pursued the same objective, the creation of a guild, in a more deliberate and traditional way.[82] Years of conflict and legal appeals led to the unlikely 1795 decision of the Spanish king to permit the creation of two racially segregated guilds of shoemakers in Buenos Aires.[83] Viceroy Melo de Portugal y Villena, having replaced Nicolás de Arredondo, ordered the cabildo to cooperate with the leadership of both shoemaker factions in formulating ordinances and compiling membership lists upon receiving the royal order.[84] Two years passed before black and white shoemakers submitted their separate ordinances to the cabildo for approval.[85] These submissions coincided with the decisions of the fiscal and viceroy that effectively destroyed the guild of silversmiths.[86]

On May 20, 1799, Cornelio Saavedra, síndico procurador of the cabildo, announced the results of his review of the two proposed guild constitutions. This opinion has been long-recognized by historians as an early and unambiguous assertion of Enlightenment era political economy.[87] Saavedra urged his colleagues on the cabildo to reject both constitutions. While conceding that the cabildo had previously sanctioned and encouraged the formation of a guild of shoemakers, he pointed out that the shoemakers had generated "an infinity of complaints and court cases, first between nationals and foreigners, then between [themselves] and the pardos and morenos." Saavedra expressed some sympathy for the injustices that had propelled the city's black and casta masters to appeal to the king, acknowledging that white shoemakers had sought nothing less than the subordination and impoverishment of this group through the imposition of high fees and race-based exclusion from guild offices. Nevertheless, he dismissed both guild constitutions to avoid creating "the monstrosity of a body with two heads."[88]

After summarizing the strife-ridden history of the shoemakers' guild, Saavedra directed his attention to the larger topic of the guild system itself.[89] He summarily dismissed guilds as contrary to public well-being and regional economic development.[90] Guilds, he asserted, subverted the basic rights of man, increased the misery of the poor, placed obstacles in the path of industry, and hindered the growth of the population.[91] While colonial officials had until this moment uniformly asserted the usefulness of guilds in eliminating the vagrancy and laziness that afflicted the Buenos Aires plebe, Saavedra turned these assumptions on their head. He urged the cabildo "to protect the natural right of every man to work to [achieve] the limit his industry will permit," stating that:

> We all know that Nature's Author obligated man to live by the sweat of his brow. Because of this the right to work is the most sacred privilege conferred on the human race. It is delirious to persuade yourself that someone needs the permission of a guild in order to not be a burden to society, not to be lazy or to earn one's bread. To say that the Supreme Power, that the Prince, is someone who can sell the right to work is a monstrosity.[92]

Turning from this general attack on guilds as a restraint on liberty and individual ambition, Saavedra argued that the elaborate supervisory structures proposed by the guilds along with their related fines, dues, and contributions would "end by depriving [the shoemakers] of the just fruits of their labors." He asked rhetorically, "How many journeymen languish for want of the twenty-five or fifty pesos necessary to pay for the examination as a master? How many apprentices are forced to wait four years even though by virtue of their industry and talent they would make good journeymen [immediately]?" Saavedra believed that the costs for examinations and other impediments would predictably force too many talented and industrious apprentices and journeymen to put off advancement and financial independence. Guilds, he argued, functioned to benefit a small number of masters who profited from the artificially depressed market competition and from the salaries they earned from guild offices. "Isn't it a paradox," asked the procurador, "that it takes the space of six years to learn how to make a pair of shoes?" By forcing journeymen and apprentices into a prolonged period of economic dependency, Saavedra asserted that guilds discouraged marriage and a beneficial increase in the population. Because journeymen and apprentices were unable to provide for wives or children due to their penury, he asked, "how many have abandoned their country to seek their fortunes elsewhere?"[93]

From the beginning of the organizational process in 1779, municipal and colonial authorities supported the efforts of both shoemakers and silversmiths as essential to public welfare. Saavedra would have none of this, naively claiming that since the suspension of the unified guild in 1793 the quality of locally produced shoes had actually improved as demonstrated by a decline in consumer complaints. This, he asserted, meant that consumers acting independently were the best defense against frauds and poor quality goods. If a consumer was dissatisfied, he could return the article and demand satisfaction or refuse to do business with the offending artisan in the future. In Saavedra's idealized expression of market behavior, honest and competent producers would always drive out competitors who sold shoddy and defective goods.[94] The invisible hand of Adam Smith was visible in every word of Saavedra's opinion, and the role of good government, he claimed, was to oppose monopoly and special privilege, not supervise and control markets.[95]

The full cabildo supported its procurador and refused both guild constitutions. It claimed that "the continuous complaints and the disturbances of the peace" caused by the shoemakers were, by themselves, sufficient reason for refusing the petition of a group with "such a well-known spirit." The source for this angry statement was likely the *regidor*, Gregorio Ramos Mexía, who had first lost patience with the shoemakers twenty years earlier when he sought to draft the craft's first guild constitution, ultimately dismissing them as "a craft in which drunkenness and other vices are so deeply rooted."[96] According to the cabildo he again served on, guilds were "unjust monopolies."[97]

For precedent, the Buenos Aires cabildo relied heavily on the abolition of French guilds carried out by Louis XVI's minister, Turgot. The cabildo quoted favorably from the French decree, including the opinion that guilds were characterized "by a general desire that consists of reducing, as far as possible, the number of masters, and making the acquisition of master's status difficult if not impossible for all except the sons of existing masters." Permitting the formation of these two guilds would, according the cabildo, lead necessarily to a "plague of guilds."[98] The cabildo even suggested that the viceroy urge Charles IV to emulate the unfortunate Louis XVI, a bizarre idea given that the French king had recently been beheaded during the social and political upheavals that followed in the years since Turgot's 1776 decree. Despite the prominent place of the French Revolution and the regicide as symbols of a world turned on its head and a collapsed natural order, the cabildo of Buenos Aires hardly paused to catch its collective breath in 1799 as it urged the viceroy and king to embrace the reform ideology of the Enlightenment.

The shocked leadership of the white shoemakers asked the fiscal and the viceroy to reverse the decision of the cabildo. Nicolás Cabral, guild procurador, delivered a heated rebuttal of the decision and the ideological assumptions employed by the cabildo. "We do not live in France," noted Cabral. The authors of the cabildo's decision, he argued, had read too many false authors and sought "to introduce in our monarchy a type of liberty that is foreign to it and is opposed entirely to the best interest of its government." Cabral held that the opinion of Saavedra and the decision of the cabildo were "useless and vicious" since both had exceeded the limits of their legal authority. The only issue legitimately within the competence of the cabildo was "whether or not it would be convenient to form separate guilds of shoemakers."[99] Cabral argued that guilds were an essential and necessary component of Spanish society and noted that the recent creation of a *consulado* and the continued functioning of the "guild" of silversmiths were adequate precedent for favorable action on the petition by the shoemakers.

These protests found no traction with colonial authorities, forcing the European immigrant faction to recognize their vulnerability and now seek compromise with the black and casta faction they had wanted to exclude from guild governance. Cabral offered to reestablish the de facto racial arrangements that pertained in 1791 before his faction's electoral victory, telling the cabildo that the white masters would concede "some administrative offices in the guild to the free mulattoes and Negroes" if it allowed the creation of a single guild of shoemakers.[100] While this proposal offered broader access to guild office than Baquero and his allies had achieved by obfuscating the application of racial labels in the guild election of 1791, too much time had been lost and the authorities were no longer sympathetic to the larger objective of creating traditional corporate organization.[101]

The cabildo and the colonial bureaucracy adamantly refused to entertain further discussion of the guild question.[102] These same authorities insisted that both groups of shoemakers pay the entire cost associated with thirteen years of disputes and appeals even though most of those practicing this trade in 1800 had not played any role in the legal challenges that led to the debts.[103] Frustration with these costs led one group of younger pardo masters, now burdened by an assessment of fifteen pesos each, to petition the fiscal to bar Baquero from acting on behalf of the black and casta shoemakers by holding meetings or addressing authorities.[104]

Conclusion

Both the shoemakers and silversmiths had been repeatedly frustrated in their efforts to create formal guilds modeled on European practices that the many immigrants among them had known first hand. Their initial efforts coincided with the creation of the Viceroyalty of Río de la Plata and had received enthusiastic support from colonial authorities from 1780 into the 1790s. The silversmiths began their efforts in 1769 and the shoemakers a decade later in 1779, but the two crafts traveled very different paths. The silversmiths forged an ad hoc structure that depended on the willingness of colonial authorities to legitimize their actions ex post facto, while the shoemakers pursued a formal guild constitution from the outset.

Although their paths were different, both crafts had received dependable support from local authorities. Viceroy Nicolás Arredondo, in particular, had lent his prestige and authority to every effort to recreate traditional craft organizations in Buenos Aires, even in the face of growing racial and ethnic conflict within these trades. Both organizational efforts led inexorably to growing levels of racial and ethnic animosity within the crafts in large measure because of the prominent leadership role played by European immigrants. Elections of guild officers, the determination and enforcement of production standards, and other issues routinely took on racial and ethnic character because the enforcement of standards was at root a device for allocating income. Each new contest led both groups of craftsmen into the courts, undermining local political support and, over time, drawing the colonial judicial and political establishments into these contests on the side of European-born masters. These contests and their ultimate resolution illuminate the colonial character of this society.

The political elevation of Buenos Aires by the creation of the Viceroyalty of Río de la Plata in 1776, its dramatic demographic and commercial growth, and the accumulated wealth that resulted from expansion inevitably fueled the large ambitions of the political establishment. For Bourbon bureaucrats guilds, like paved and illuminated streets, theaters, bullrings, and improved hygiene and medical services, signaled progress and civilization. Viceroy Vértiz gave the guild movement its first push in 1780, but every viceroy until 1804 publicly supported this corporate ideal as did the fiscales of the audiencia and a succession of municipal alcaldes. European immigrant artisans saw in this enthusiasm the opportunity to enhance the prestige of their occupations while creating a vehicle for subordinating and controlling local black and casta competitors. As these objectives became visible during the effort to write craft constitutions or implement inspections, black and casta artisans found numerous ways to thwart their rivals and compete for power. They used the courts; they forged alliances with sympathetic colleagues; and, when pressed, they used intimidation. Once these battles began, we see the willingness of black and casta artisans to contest the authority of powerful officials in face-to-face confrontations as well as in colonial courts. There was little deference expressed and little fear of consequences. The documents speak eloquently to the frustration and anger that this assertiveness produced among the colonial governing class of Buenos Aires.

By the end of the 1790s the political and economic contexts for these struggles had been transformed by the slave trade and shaken by the geo-political events in France and in Saint-Domingue. The failures of both the silversmith and shoemaker guilds were highly public events that developed episodically over more than a decade. The central issue raised by the waves of internal racial conflict and judicial appeals was the very endurance of colonial social and racial hierarchies. How reliable were these presumptions about order and deference when black and casta artisans could physically threaten European masters and even intimidate the cabildo's alcades with-out punitive consequences? What did it mean when a casta shoemaker re-jected a decision of the viceroy and carried his protest to the royal court? The effect of this cycle of protest and confrontation was multiplied as news of each conflict spread through the city's markets, pulperías, taverns, and *canchas de bolos*, contributing to growing disquiet in Buenos Aires. These highly public conflicts proliferated along the foundational colonial fault line of race and were infused with urgency by a rising tide of slave imports and public fear of slave restiveness.

Disappointment and frustration were the chief legacies inherited by the city's artisans. European-born craftsmen had sought to establish the tradi-tional guild regime they had experienced before emigration while insisting on a more perfect enjoyment of colonial racial advantages. Their unantici-pated achievement was the creation of a self-conscious and confident casta opposition. As this long struggle developed, black and casta artisans had gained practical experience with the colonial bureaucracy and with Span-ish law; they had also learned to push back when authorities disappointed them. By the end of 1799 the hope of recreating a *porteño* artisan community in imitation of the historic institutions and social arrangements that existed in Europe had comprehensively failed as the local political class embraced the ascendant, new political economy of Liberalism. In place of the now de-bilitated ideal of corporate identity, Buenos Aires hosted a more assertive, if racially factionalized, artisan class that was both disappointed in the local political class and more willing to flex its muscles.

5 | The "French Conspiracy" of 1795

On April 13, 1795, two jailers took the Italian clockmaker Santiago
Antonini from his cell in the municipal jail located behind the cabildo. Shaking with fear, he needed the support of his jailers as he
climbed the rough wooden staircase to the second floor. Antonini
and the moreno laborer José Díaz had both experienced the use of
torture in their interrogations by the *alcalde de primer voto*, Martín
de Álzaga, thirteen days earlier. The alcalde again met Antonini at
the top of the steps and displayed for a second time the instruments
of torture. Álzaga warned the terrified prisoner that unless he answered every question fully he would bear full responsibility for the
torment that followed.

With rumors of a planned slave insurrection gathering strength
in early 1795, Viceroy Nicolás de Arredondo had appointed Álzaga
to lead an inquiry. By the end of March police agents had interrogated hundreds and arrested more than thirty, the majority of the
prisoners were foreign-born artisans and shopkeepers, but Álzaga
feared that the full conspiracy was not yet visible. As a result, he
had asked the audiencia's permission to use torture when interro-
gating two of the prisoners he regarded as most dangerous, Antonini and Díaz, the latter a man who bundled hides for export and
sometimes worked for a livery stable. Álzaga had questioned the
two under torture on March 31 without producing new leads for the
inquiry. Convinced that he was dealing with hardened revolutionaries, the alcalde returned to the audiencia and received permission
to torture the two a second time unless they now fully disclosed the
conspiracy.[1]

Antonini was a poor artisan who lived near the Plaza Mayor in a rented room he shared with two other artisans. Born in Saluzzo in the Piedmont region of the Kingdom of Sardinia, Antonini had immigrated to Buenos Aires without the appropriate license, leaving behind in Spain his Spanish wife and son. While a resident in Buenos Aires he lived in obscurity until implicated in the purported conspiracy to raise a slave rebellion. Nearly all those arrested in 1795 were either single or married men who had migrated from Europe or from the interior provinces without their wives. A smaller number were local-born criollos or castas, including the native-born master shoemaker Manuel Antonio Sustaeta, who had been a close ally of Juan José Romero and Francico Baquero during the guild controversies of 1792 and 1793.[2] While Álzaga ordered the arrest of only two slaves, his agents had found many useful informants about the conspiracy among the city's slaves.[3] In fact, slaves had identified both Antonini and Díaz as leading conspirators. In a city roiled by both xenophobia and racism, the mounting fear of a slave rebellion had confounded logic by leading to the arrest of scores of free European immigrants.[4]

A confluence of powerful destabilizing agents, including rising prices, a spike in the mortality rate, disruptions to Atlantic trade, and the rising volume of the slave trade, had unsettled previously reliable social and economic conventions during the 1790s.[5] Colonial Buenos Aires had reached an inflection point. From the late 1770s the city had benefited from a broad economic expansion.[6] The free artisans and laborers of Buenos Aires enjoyed nearly full employment and high wages until the middle of the 1790s. They then faced falling real wages for the next two years and the competition of a fast-growing slave population.[7] In the outdoor trades, like carpentry and bricklaying, as well as in factories and bakeries, slaves began to displace apprentices and journeymen from traditional positions by the end of the decade.

Between 1791 and 1795, the organizational efforts of both silversmiths and shoemakers entered a period of crisis after years of fractiousness and angry public confrontations between European immigrant masters and their black and casta rivals. As dissident factions in both crafts carried their protests through the colonial bureaucracy and in some cases into the streets, these disputes had become public and notorious. Every laborer and artisan in Buenos Aires would have been aware of these conflicts and the issues that fed them. We must assume as well that when a group of angry casta shoemakers prevented the election of guild officers and forced an alcalde to call for armed assistance to maintain order in his private residence the event became a popular topic of conversation, if not humor, across the city.

As threats and challenges accumulated in Buenos Aires, two distant events, the French and Haitian revolutions, attached new and unsettling meanings to the city's contentious and unstable social and economic realities. By 1795 colonial authorities perceived an angry plebe predisposed to confrontation and potentially susceptible to the seductive arguments of revolutionary agents. The intensifying commercial rhythms that linked Buenos Aires to Spain, Cuba, and other sugar islands of the Caribbean meant a parallel intensification in the flow of news and ideas. Every ship returning to the estuary from Cuba brought news of the slave insurrection in Saint-Domingue, and every ship arriving from Spain brought news of the French Revolution and the course of Spain's war with revolutionary France. Pamphlets and books, both contraband and legal, supplemented these informal communications for the city's literate minority.

A Disorderly and Ill-disciplined City

Greed and fear intersected in unpredictable ways in the thriving slave markets of Buenos Aires. In these venues the city's growing wealth helped float a nearly insatiable demand for slave labor. Late colonial prosperity financed the city's direct participation in both the rapidly expanding, direct slave trade with Africa and in the still important slave trade with Brazil.[8] By 1795 slave ownership was distributed across nearly the whole of society. Hundreds of the city's slave owners were men and women of very modest resources who lived lives that were materially indistinguishable from those lived by their slaves. Many had purchased their slaves on credit. As one visitor to the city put it in 1794, "there are an increased number of slaves in the city and many families have no property other than their slaves . . . these the law obligates to provide their owners with a daily payment."[9] In practice thousands of slaves sought their daily wage with little or no direct supervision in the streets of Buenos Aires.

The integration of so many slaves in the wage economy and the necessary independence with which these slaves looked for work created a general sense that the deference and discipline expected of slaves was being sacrificed for the masters' profits. As a result, urban residents increasingly viewed slaves as confrontational, willful, and lawless. Public officials seldom complained about the productivity of slaves, but complaints about the lack of deference, "the obedience and respect due a master," were legion. Spanish law allowed slaves to take masters to court to dispute legal status, demand the right to purchase freedom or the freedom of family members, or demand the right to seek a new master (*papel de venta*) because of abuse or mistreatment. In most instances, weeks or even months of confrontations and beatings with a public character preceded a slave's recourse to the courts. While the conflicts were intensely personal, neighbors and more casual witnesses disseminated details across the city in ways that increased the general concern that slave discipline and public order were at risk. This cycle of legal confrontations culminated in the 1790s, when 51 of the total of 133 legal cases brought by slaves between 1776 and 1810 occurred.[10]

As the African component in the servile population increased, slaves came to be seen as more foreign and more threatening to the city's social and cultural order. While Buenos Aires now depended on slave labor and most members of the *gente decente* owned slaves, there was a rising tide of complaints directed to both municipal and colonial authorities that slaves were ill disciplined, aggressive, and disrespectful toward property and the racial hierarchy. When propertied residents of the city complained to the cabildo or to colonial authorities about criminal activity and violence or the lack of public order, they routinely attached these fears to slaves and, to a lesser degree, free blacks. As early as 1787 a *bando* issued by Viceroy Loreto sought to tame the streets by ordering the arrest of "anybody not known to the neighborhood or who provokes suspicion because of the way [they speak] or the clothes [they wear]."[11]

This punitive measure had limited success, and in 1794 Viceroy Arredondo ordered the recruitment of twenty *alcaldes de barrio* to help maintain public order due to the city's rising number of "robberies, homicides, and other excesses."[12] The immediate failure of alcaldes de barrio to control the streets of their districts led the cabildo to create an "auxiliary force" recruited from neighborhood property owners to patrol streets and plazas after dark.[13] In the poorest suburban precincts this force of unpaid auxiliaries failed to even protect the alcaldes de barrio from insults as they made their rounds. In desperation the alcaldes de barrio, including Manuel Ruíz Obregon, Anselmo Cárdenas, and Thadeo Torres, wrote to inform Alcalde Martín de Álzaga that the "vagrants and thieves" of their districts had completely overwhelmed their resources and that they urgently needed the assistance of armed military patrols.[14]

The cabildo and upper levels of colonial government repeatedly, if ineffectively, engaged the problem of slave discipline.[15] African dances organized by slaves and free blacks had been banned without apparent effect.[16] Juan José de Vértiz y Salcedo, who later served as viceroy, first banned African dances in the city as "indecent" when serving as governor in 1770.[17] Despite the ban, the blacks Agustin Borja and Sebastian Pellizar, "in the name of the natives of the nation Cambunda," sought an exemption to the general prohibition of dances in 1789. In response, the cabildo restated its objection, dismissing the "obscene dances of blacks and the pernicious consequences that follow." Despite bans, however, the slave community continued to find the means to continue this practice, even embedding traditional dances and traditional religious beliefs in the celebrations organized by black *cofradías* or, as time passed, by unofficial organizations of African nations.[18] In October 1795, for example, Domingo de Sena and Alfonso Calacete, "blacks of the Conga nation in this capital city," wrote to the cabildo to propose their participation in celebrations of the arrival of the new viceroy, Pedro de Melo Portugal y Villena. They intended "to organize street dances following the practice of their nations" on the day of the arrival as well as the following day. They then boldly reminded the cabildo that these dances followed the "useful" practice of African dances on Sundays and feast days (despites the bans) "when each nation organizes dances following their custom and with the discretion that these diversions ought to have."[19]

Throughout this same period the cabildo tried to restrict gaming and drinking, diseases, its members believed, that infected both slaves and the free plebe. *Pulperos* were the focus of this attempt at moral prophylaxis. Cabildo members believed, with some reason, that pulperos acted as fences for silver and other goods stolen by slaves while simultaneously serving as sources of criminal intelligence, promoting robberies and crimes of violence. In the 1790s the cabildo increasingly justified its expanded supervision of the city's *pulperías* and gaming places because, as they asserted, gaming and drink encouraged "slaves to rob their masters and commit other outrages."[20] Gaming, especially the debts that accumulated from betting, was a particular threat. The cabildo and the viceroy routinely ordered slaves and free laborers away from card tables and games of skill with little success, culminating in 1804 with the futile effort to ban all *canchas de bolos* because of the "vagrants, bums, and criminals" and "slaves" that congregated there to gamble.[21]

A Geopolitics of Fear

One of the props of the city's commercial expansion in the era of neutral trade was its export of hides, tallow, and, especially, dried and salted beef to Cuba and other plantation colonies. The ships that carried the dried beef and other products of the viceroyalty to Brazil and the Caribbean depended on mixed crews of slave and free seamen. As these crews distributed the products of the Río de la Plata and gathered tropical produce, especially sugar and tobacco, they informally collected news about revolutionary events in Saint-Domingue as well as evidence of mounting fears of slave insurrections elsewhere. On returning to the Río de la Plata, common seamen, ship officers, and passengers disseminated this intelligence through the plazas, cafes, taverns, pulperías, and other public places of Buenos Aires. Given the rhythm of maritime arrivals in the estuary, hardly a week went by without news of insurrection or slave unrest.[22]

News of the French Revolution and later insurrection in Saint-Domingue arrived in Buenos Aires in unpredictable and incremental ways. Buenos Aires was separated from Cádiz by 6,235 miles (10,035 kilometers) and from Havana by 4,263 miles (6,861 kilometers). Even without the disruptions and uncertainties associated with wartime depredations, it routinely took goods and communications three to four months to reach the estuary from Spain and more than two months from Cuba. Nevertheless, images of the French regicide and anticlerical attacks on the Catholic Church were discussed everywhere in the city. While news from Saint-Domingue increased local fears of slave violence, the French Revolution also provided a dramatic imaginary of the era's revolutionary content for the residents of Buenos Aires.[23] Viceroy Arredondo would refer to France and the enthusiasts of revolution as "the seductor nation and its proselytes."[24]

Because Spain was at war with France, many in Buenos Aires saw the French Revolution as an attack on civilization itself. Robespierre, even more than Toussaint L'Ouverture, was popularly viewed as the demonic embodiment of the Atlantic's revolutionary age. He was the subject of angry dismissals and vilifications from the city's pulpits as well as a target of vituperation or, sometimes, admiration in conversations in barbershops, pulperías, and cafes. Few knew in detail the events in France or the role of Robespierre in these events, but he was widely seen as the "evil motor" and "bloody tyrant" of the revolution. The potency of Robespierre as a symbol of revolution meant that when someone said, for example, "Robespierre was talented enough to be master of the globe" or "the French had opened the eyes of other nations to the progress of liberty," these statements implicitly carried in their wake a well-understood inventory of images and meanings.[25]

Even before the beginning of the war with France, Spain had sought to prevent the introduction of books and pamphlets with revolutionary content in its American colonies. When the Spanish government informed the viceroy of impending war with France on January 25, 1793, these efforts were intensified, but enforcement proved difficult in the Río de la Plata where trade in contraband was deeply rooted and customs officials corrupted. In a colonial world habituated to the importation of contraband products from slaves to cloth, political contraband slid along well-worn paths and into common consumption. Even before war with France, revolutionary propaganda had found its way to the Río de la Plata. On June 19, 1789, for example, customs agents in Montevideo confiscated a shipment of ornamental medals engraved with the motto "Libertas Americana." More inflammatory still were colored prints depicting the execution of Louis XVI that had not only evaded customs authorities in Montevideo but reached Salta on the frontier with Alto Perú.[26]

Urged on by the Spanish government and supported by local fears, Viceroy Nicolás de Arredondo ordered customs officials to impound any French ship found in viceregal ports. The first French ship seized in the viceroyalty's waters was the French privateer El Dragón that had docked in Montevideo shortly after news of the declaration of war. When searched by customs agents, the ship yielded a rich store of banned books, including many works by Rousseau and Voltaire.[27] As tensions on both sides of the estuary mounted in the final months of 1794, the viceroy ordered an increased level of military patrolling in Buenos Aires.

Popular fears mounted when one or more unknown culprits pasted hand-written *pasquines* (pasquinade or lampoon in English) attacking local authorities on the walls around the city's central plaza. Pasquines had long been a part of Spanish colonial political life, and officials in Buenos Aires had found it difficult to identify authors and prosecute them. In the most common forms, pasquines attacked officials or other prominent residents in insulting terms for their private scandals or unpopular political decisions. Despite the anger that these scurrilous or sometimes humorous documents produced among those targeted, authorities grudgingly tolerated them in most cases.

In late 1794 a series of inflammatory pasquines warned of a planned insurrection and condemned Viceroy Nicolás de Arredondo for his failure to protect the public.[28] The anonymous authors claimed that a vast conspiracy of unnamed foreigners sought to incite a slave rebellion. These incitements to political action and the public fears that gave them urgency coincided with the racial conflicts that overtook the guilds of silversmiths and shoemakers as well as with rising consumer prices.[29] News that the king had overturned the decisions of Viceroy Arredondo and the audiencia and granted the city's black shoemakers permission to create a separate guild shocked the city's elite, given the black and casta shoemakers' aggressive challenge to the decisions of the colony's highest authorities. When small slips of paper, each with the era's revolutionary ideology reduced to its essential core, "¡Viva la Libertad! ¡Viva la Libertad! ¡Viva la Libertad!," appeared on the walls of buildings around the central plaza, *porteños* predictably invested this political incitement with meanings derived from distant revolutionary threats.[30] This provocative and economic expression of revolutionary intent initiated a new round of reactionary pasquines that excoriated Arredondo and other officials for their inactivity and complicity in the face of revolutionary threats.[31]

While the military inadequacies of Spain were clear by 1794, the military reach of the French Revolution was at best an indirect and distant threat to the Río de la Plata.[32] The French Navy and French privateers were incapable of comprehensively blockading the ports of Buenos Aires or Montevideo or delivering a military force capable of dislodging Spanish power. These French naval assets did, however, dramatically increase the risks of shipping the region's exports across the Atlantic to Europe or north to the Caribbean.[33] The depredations of French vessels did not close regional ports or effectively blockade Buenos Aires, but this local effect of a distant war did provide a threatening geopolitical gloss to every deprivation, every price increase, and every rumor of conspiracy. Unrelated price increases for local staples, like wheat, moved popular opinion in Buenos Aires toward the idea that greedy "French" bakers were hoarding wheat and driving up the price of bread.[34] In May 1795 the *fiel ejecutor*, Don Francisco Velaustigui, informed the cabildo that "the clamor of the people" had forced him to arrest a number of bakers.[35]

The fact that the city's bakers relied on slave labor served to reinforce the appearance of a single, integrated threat: slave insurrection connected to local agents of foreign aggression. While France provided powerful images of a world turned on its head, an executed king and priests driven from their churches, it was the slave rebellion in Saint-Domingue that provided the Buenos Aires elite with a revolutionary narrative that seemed to best fit local facts. Did the masters of Buenos Aires more effectively control their slaves than had the slave masters of Saint-Domingue in 1791? No one believed this. The absence of supervision and discipline were the nearly universally understood signature of the Buenos Aires slave regime.

The Investigation Begins

In a context where many feared the city was slipping into chaos, Viceroy Nicolás de Arredondo appointed Don Martín de Álzaga the cabildo's *alcalde ordinario* to investigate rumors of a planned insurrection in Buenos Aires, noting specifically reports that "private individuals" had made "considerable purchases of ammunition."[36] Álzaga quickly formed a team of agents and began to track down the rumors.[37]

Álzaga's powerful personality and deep prejudices would give the inquiry a relentless and xenophobic character. He had emigrated from the Basque region of northern Spain as a youngster and gained crucial experience in the shop of the successful and influential merchant Gaspar Santa Coloma. He was hostile to the relaxed commercial rules put in place during the war with France and persistently condemned those suspected of contraband. By 1795 Álzaga was connected to the wealthiest merchant families in Buenos Aires by kinship and commercial dealings and had become the most powerful member of the cabildo. He also had a well-deserved reputation as a difficult and over-bearing man.

Many slave owners sought out Álzaga to report what they saw as a new belligerence and aggressiveness among their slaves. Some claimed that slaves no longer demonstrated the deference expected of them, failing to give way when passing in the street or when entering a public shop. One elderly woman told Álzaga that her female slave, when corrected for poor work habits, angrily stated, "soon I will hold the power." Another informant, Don Juan Angel Freire, told authorities that his elderly mother's slave, Pasquala, had said that she "would soon be dressed better than the most important people of the city." [38] Don Francisco de Quebedo passed on the secondhand story of a Franciscan priest who had overheard two pardos talking about a planned insurrection in a pulpería near Plaza Monserrat. Among the telling details enriching this story was the priest's claim that one of the slaves had used the word *libertad*.[39] More to the point, a nervous owner of a slave employed in the city's shipyard informed Álzaga that his slave had threatened his free workmates, saying that "on Good Friday we will all be French." [40]

The slave population was also on edge as a result of the rumors circulating across the city. Antonio, the slave of Don Francisco Yzarzabal, told an alcalde de barrio that he had gone to a "baile de tamba" (the word spoken was likely *tambo*, the place where African societies met for dancing) where he heard "various blacks say they would rise up to escape the power of the Spanish." [41] While most of the testimony provided to Álzaga's agents was secondhand or worse, authorities also found informants who could provide the solid details that gave real urgency and direction to the investigation. The discussion of a planned insurrection was so widely circulated in Buenos Aires that the master carpenter Lazaro Ferri felt comfortable asking two slaves, owned by others but employed on one of his projects, if they were "implicated in the uprising." They told him, with a similar absence of inhibition, that they were not involved but admitted that other slaves had asked them to join the conspiracy.[42]

This gathering cloud of rumor and fear suggests that news from Saint-Domingue increasingly framed the already contentious relationship between slaves and masters in Buenos Aires, providing slaves with an ominous new narrative of resistance and autonomy that had a predictably unsettling effect on the masters who sought to direct them. As authorities in Buenos Aires collected testimony about a new aggressiveness in the slave community, it became abundantly clear that many of the propertied men and women of Buenos Aires had been frightened by news from Saint-Domingue and that their slaves knew it. While war with France created the immediate context for political action, it was the potent images of slave insurrection that would dominate the events of 1795, ensnaring Antonini, Díaz, and others.

This was the context in which public attention began to focus on the city's small population of French residents, most of them located in shops and residences near the Plaza Mayor.[43] The group included a single French noble family, the Liniers, and a handful of wholesale merchants involved in the Atlantic trade, among them Juan Barbarín (also known as Jean Cap-depón or, alternatively, Jean Cap de Pon). There were larger numbers of French artisans, including some French-speaking Italians and Spaniards from Navarre. Among the most visible were the bakers Juan Luis Dumont and Juan Antonio Grimau, both of whom had had recent run-ins with the cabildo's fiel ejecutor over hording wheat and selling poor quality bread.[44]

The Web of Conspiracy

The thirty-eight-year-old French merchant Don Juan Barbarín was the first person arrested by Álzaga on February 26, 1795. Pedro Muñoz de Olaso, Álzaga's chief agent (*teniente de alguacil mayor*), reported testimony about a heated discussion of the events in France that transpired in the barbershop of the Spanish immigrant Juan Martín Carreto in November 1794.[45] According-ing to Muñoz de Olaso, witnesses claimed that Carreto permitted "free and confidential conversations" that had finally led to a violent argument about revolutionary France. Discussion of the war among the barber's clients led to a series of angry denunciations of everything French. One of the cus-tomers in the shop, the French merchant Juan Barbarín, had remained quiet as these xenophobic condemnations escalated, but he finally objected, pro-vocatively proclaiming that the French people "had good reasons to im-prison and execute Louis XVI."

Alone in defending the French and apparently provoked beyond endur-ance, Barbarín went on to suggest that "Spanish people might have good reasons to imitate the French." Don Baltasar García, present during the argument, claimed that Barbarín had also said, "it is unfortunate that the Spaniards had not done the same thing."[46] Frustratingly, other witnesses to the confrontation in the barbershop lacked the detailed memories of Muñoz de Olaso's most helpful informants. The barber Don Juan Martín Carreto remembered only that "someone" (*un fulano*) had attempted to justify the regicide. Don Fernando Díaz de la Ribera was equally vague but added the tantalizing detail that a "Frenchman" had said that Robespierre "was capable of being the owner [*dueno*] of the world." Díaz de la Ribera also claimed that he had challenged this remarkable belief by asking, "What did this capacity consist of given the atrocities, the abandonment of religion, and the murder of the king?" Barbarín, according to Díaz de la Ribera, answered by saying, "if Robespierre had caused many deaths he must have had motive to do so." One of those present in the barbershop during the argument, Baltasar García, became so agitated he attempted to strike Barbarín with a chair. When thwarted, he went outdoors and threw the chair at Barbarín's nearby retail shop. Cooler heads soon intervened, preventing bloodshed.

The barber Juan Martín Carreto asserted in his testimony that before the war Barbarín had claimed to be from Valencia in Spain and that all his friends in Buenos Aires had been Spaniards. After news of Spain's declaration of war against France, Barbarín had dramatically changed his patterns and habits, seeking the friendship of other French residents and asserting his French origins. Other informants claimed that Barbarín now ignored the Spaniards he had previously socialized with. Among these new acquaintances, Carreto noted that Barbarín now spent a great deal of time with the young French immigrant Pablo Mayllos y Marcana (rendered in other documents as Mallos). Barbarín's every action would now be subject to intense scrutiny by Álzaga and his agents.

Some of the testimonies collected by Álzaga and Muñoz de Olaso suggested that Barbarín maintained potentially subversive associations, thus placing his apparently spontaneous effort to defend the French regicide in a darker political context.[47] Muñoz de Olaso informed Álzaga that Barbarín "maintained a *tertulio*" frequented by French immigrants and other foreigners in his home. According to other witnesses, Barbarín had also "purchased gazettes with news of France" and then shared these periodicals promiscuously with others. For Álzaga the elements of formal conspiracy that had eluded him as he had tracked down rumors and dead ends in the first weeks of the investigation were now visible for the first time.

The alcalde and his assistants now fanned out to interview Barbarín's neighbors and business associates. Many of those questioned spoke respectfully of the suspect, noting his honesty and good habits. Some informants, however, wondered about his very public interactions with the city's slave community. Barbarín had drawn the attention of many neighbors and customers by allowing slaves to visit him in his home and by treating his own slave, Manuel, with surprising affection and generosity. More damning still, witnesses asserted that Barbarín regularly permitted slaves from the *hermandad* (brotherhood) of San Benito to enter his home.[48] Many of Barbarín's neighbors remarked on the merchant's intimacy with members of this slave hermandad, an intimacy he had apparently maintained during his nearly ten-year residence in Buenos Aires.

News of the alcalde's intense inquiry into the affairs of the French merchant attracted a new wave of testimony. A sergeant attached to the local military garrison informed Álzaga that on numerous occasions he had witnessed Barbarín and his slave Manuel walking along the riverfront during the hours of siesta. This informant pointed out that the timing of these walks, a period when few pedestrians would be in the streets to overhear, and the pair's apparent disregard for the local siesta custom appeared suspicious. What could the subject of these secretive conversations between master and slave have been, he asked. Once asked, the question seemed to produce its own answer.

By the time Álzaga questioned Barbarín face to face, the Frenchman had been in jail for weeks and was shaken to his core. When asked by the alcalde to explain his apparent intimacy with the slave community, Barbarín testified that he had served as treasurer of the black religious organization the Archicofradía de San Benito (also called Hermandad de San Benito) until recently, when he had decided to resign. When asked to explain this resignation, Barbarín claimed that his barber Juan Martín Carreto had warned him that rumors had linked his service to this black hermandad to the feared slave uprising. He had immediately resigned to allay suspicion. Barbarín went on to remind Álzaga that his service with the black hermandad was not remarkable. Many other men of substantial means, he noted, had served in similar capacities with segregated organizations of slaves and free blacks in Buenos Aires.

This was undeniably true. It was the custom throughout the Spanish Empire to require the appointment of white officials to supervise the fiscal affairs and the public behavior of elected black officers, black lay brotherhoods, and black guilds. White officers also routinely commanded segregated black militia units. The Hermandad de San Benito was only one of many black organizations in Buenos Aires where white officials supervised black members. Members of the hermandad paid dues and collected alms in the city's streets to help pay for members' burial costs and for special masses for the souls of deceased members. These funds were also used to help pay for the hermandad's celebrations associated with San Benito's feast day. It was Barbarín's practice of receiving these alms in his home that would capture Álzaga's attention.

According to testimony gathered from his neighbors and associates, Barbarín's welcoming behavior toward the slaves he supervised as an officer of the confraternity fell outside the boundaries expected of a man of property. A number of witnesses, including Francisco Tellechea, confirmed that Barbarín often allowed members of the hermandad to enter his home when delivering the alms they solicited in the city's streets and markets.[49] Although no one had felt it necessary to report these practices to authorities earlier, these actions now appeared ominous, even dangerous, in light of fears of a slave uprising. That someone of Barbarín's status encouraged this type of casual association with slaves seemed dangerously egalitarian to Álzaga. In an era when revolutionary events in Saint-Domingue dominated conversation, any intimacy with slaves seemed inherently subversive.

The unusual familiarity that Barbarín maintained with members of the black hermandad of San Benito led inevitably to questions about his apparently warm relationship with his slave, Manuel, whom he had owned for three years. Numerous informants from the neighborhood suggested to Álzaga that the Frenchman treated his slave "with great demonstrations of affection and love." Barbarín's neighbors corroborated the earlier testimony of the patrol sergeant who had observed the master and slave taking afternoon walks along the banks of the Río de la Plata. These informants also told Álzaga that Barbarín seemed to treat the slave more like a friend than a servant. One informant commented in detail on the "intimacy and affection" that characterized the conversations between this master and slave. Another reported that the slave Manuel had boasted to other slaves that his owner had recently promised him his freedom. Álzaga wondered what Barbarín expected in return for this promised freedom? Could he have used the promise of freedom to recruit Manuel into the conspiracy?

In the eyes of the alcalde, Barbarín's decision to hire a young French immigrant, Pablo Mayllos y Marcana, to teach Manuel to read and write was perhaps the most suspicious and damming aspect of this unusual and complex relationship between a slave and his master. It only took a few days for Álzaga to discover the background and habits of Manuel's twenty-eight-year-old tutor. After arriving in Buenos Aires, Mayllos had struggled to support himself as a private tutor and "letter writer." In addition to the income he received from a small number of private students, he often set up a small table in the Plaza Mayor near the cabildo where he wrote letters for clients found among the city's largely illiterate, urban underclass. For a

FIGURE 16 The Plaza Mayor with the cabildo at the center in the background. The municipal jail was located directly behind the cabildo and the offices used by *alcaldes de barrios* were located next door. Source: C. E. Pellegrini, *Recuerdos del Río de la Plata* (Buenos Aires: Libreria L'Amateur, 1969). Published with the permission of the publisher, Libraría L'Amateur, Buenos Aires.

small fee he composed letters to distant kin or, in some cases, to employers or public authorities in other cities. He took his meager meals at pulperías and shared a rented room with another single man, Fermín Sotes. When questioned, Sotes, rather too eagerly, volunteered to Álzaga that Mayllos often returned to the room very late at night.[50]

A French immigrant who knew of the merchant's desire to locate a tutor for Manuel had introduced the nearly destitute Mayllos to Barbarín. Mayllos had eagerly forfeited his unpredictable earnings as a letter writer to accept Barbarín's generous wage of four pesos a month to provide private instruction for the slave Manuel. As this relationship deepened, Mayllos had at times stayed in Barbarín's home as a guest and had entered into the merchant's social circle. Almost from the moment Mayllos was brought to the attention of the investigators, they wondered if he could be the author of the revolutionary pasquines. Álzaga noted in a report that Mayllos's hand seemed very similar to the hand that had written the word *liberty* on the small papers scattered around the Plaza Mayor. Mayllos and the slave Manuel soon joined Barbarín in jail.

Barbarín's warm relations with Manuel seemed to suggest a quiet challenge to what Àlzaga and other slave owners held to be an essential prop of the colonial social order, the power of master over slave. The deeply conservative alcalde saw the bloody excesses of the French and Haitian revolutions as predictable outcomes that inevitably followed the questioning of religion and monarchy and, more specifically, the authority of master over slave. The bloodshed, property destruction, and sacrilege unleashed by both revolutions had their roots, for Àlzaga, in the secularizing passions of the era and the dangerous erosion of a divinely inspired social order.

Álzaga finally turned his full attention to the slave Manuel. Under questioning, Manuel freely admitted that he and his master had occasionally taken walks together. He agreed that he was treated "with love and dressed well," but he claimed that his master never talked about the revolutions in France or Saint-Domingue. He admitted that Barbarín had promised him his freedom but stated that would only occur if his master returned to Spain or postmortem if he died in Buenos Aires. Álzaga then asked Manuel about his tutor Mayllos. Why had his master paid a tutor to teach him to read and write? Manuel replied that his master wanted his help in managing the shop's accounts. If he learned to read and write then Barbarín would be free to leave the shop when business demanded. What, the alcalde inquired, was Manuel reading? Manuel replied that he generally only read accounts and letters relative to his master's business, but Barbarín was willing to read "any book" to him to advance his instruction. Despite the explanations offered by Barbarín and Manuel, Álzaga clearly thought this relationship between slave and master revealed dangerous egalitarian leanings.[51]

A Slave's Angry Voice

Almost at the same time that Álzaga began his pursuit of Juan Barbarín, his investigators uncovered a new lead, the unambiguous articulation of a direct threat to the colonial order. Don Miguel García de Bustamante provided the crucial testimony. He reported that while visiting in the home of Doña Cecilia (Zezilia in document) Soliban they had begun to talk about "the conspiracy that everyone thinks threatens the capital."[52] Doña Cecilia passed on to Bustamante that her moreno slave, José Albariño, knew details of the plot. Her husband, Don Jacinto Albariño, *maestro mayor* of the ship carpenters, profitably employed José as a cook for the caulkers and ship carpenters who worked at the local shipyard. Recently, José's supervisor had complained to her that José had stated to the workers during a break that "on Good Friday they [the city's slaves] would adjust accounts." Later testimony indicated that José made this inflammatory threat after enduring a series of taunts and insults from his coworkers. Unaware of this background, Doña Cecelia confronted José who tried to pass his statement off as a joke. When informed of these inflammatory statements, her husband, Don Jacinto, loaded his shotgun, and pointed it at José's heart, telling him that death "was what a slave willing to conspire against his owner's life deserved." Desperate to placate his master and save his life, José promised to tell everything he knew about the planned Good Friday uprising.

With the shotgun no longer pointed at this heart, José told his masters that his participation in the uprising had been solicited by "a criollo without office or employment but decent in his appearance." While this description would eventually prove misleading, José's claim that this revolutionary recruiter assured him that "decent citizens" were committed to the conspiracy raised alarms. Once contacted by Don Jacinto Albariño, the alcalde subjected José to a comprehensive and focused interrogation that led quickly to José Díaz, a married sixty-two-year-old migrant from Corrientes who had lived in Buenos Aires for over a decade. In the numerous documents generated by the judicial process, Díaz was variously identified as a mestizo, pardo, and moreno. In his testimony to Álzaga, Díaz referred to himself as a moreno. Díaz, José testified, had told him "the French would unite with the blacks of Buenos Aires in a rebellion that would offer liberty to everyone." Hoping to illuminate the full plot, Álzaga urged Don Jacinto Albariño, to have his slave seek out Díaz to discover the names of his coconspirators. Álzaga's first priority was the location of the arms and ammunition accumulated by the conspirators and the discovery of the plot's leaders. Approached again by José, Díaz told him "that six thousand armed men are waiting for orders in Buenos Aires and more in Paraguay, Corrientes, and Santa Fe."

José now recalled another damning incident for Álzaga. When he had complained about his master's treatment to Díaz, he had replied that "masters forced their slaves to work too hard," and it was this mistreatment that led them to "plan a rebellion." According to the now talkative José, Díaz had also stated "the uprising would unite the French, Indians, mulattos, and blacks to achieve freedom for all." Díaz, José claimed, had warned him to be ready so that "when the shouts [announcing the uprising] are heard, slaves should be prepared to kill their masters and their families and then go to the plaza with all the money and firearms they found in their masters' homes." Unwilling to rely on José's amateur sleuthing and the often-conflicting testimonies passed on by the slave's master, Don Jacinto Albariño, Álzaga's agents now questioned Díaz directly under oath on March 1, 1795, hoping he would reveal details about the conspiracy. Following this interrogation, they arrested Díaz and conducted him to the city jail where he was placed in leg irons. A week later, as the investigation of Díaz moved forward, Álzaga's investigators unearthed another promising lead as they interviewed slaves working in the bakery of the French immigrant Juan Luis Dumont. This investigative thread would eventually lead to the arrest of the clockmaker, Santiago Antonini, and others.

As the investigation gathered speed, Álzaga questioned Díaz directly for the first time. The prisoner admitted knowing José but denied knowing Juan Barbarín or his slave Manuel, now both in jail. When pressed for details, Díaz claimed to know nothing of the "planned uprising of the French." He tried to put as much distance as possible between himself and José Albariño, at first denying he knew the slave by name. Unable to sustain this fiction, he then admitted having had various conversations with José, including a conversation where José had told him that his master owned "seven or eight firearms" in good condition.[53] Álzaga then questioned María Ignacia, the second wife of the once widowed José Díaz, focusing immediately on who frequented their home. Rather than a collection of potential revolutionaries, she provided Álzaga with a thin list of impoverished relatives and neighbors, "my sister Beata, two poor boys, and my uncle Jacinto who sometimes visits from his farm." Did her husband have firearms? He had a "knife and a small shotgun." When asked if "a Negro" (the slave José) had come to the house looking for her husband, María Ignacia denied the visits, thus putting all of José's most damning testimony at risk. Her story, corroborating that of her husband, was that at the time José claimed he had met with Díaz to discuss the planned uprising she and her husband had been in the cathedral to hear the sermon at noon and then retuned home for *maté*. According to María Ignacia, she and her husband later attended a second sermon delivered at the chapel of the Royal Hospital. While José's testimony had offered up Díaz as a fire-breathing revolutionary who urged slaves to murder their masters in their beds, María Ignacia's testimony portrayed Díaz as a religiously observant family man whose life was dominated by homely routines. Had José, reported to authorities by his master for his incendiary remarks, merely sought to deflect attention to Díaz to save himself?

While Álzaga focused on Díaz, Don Jacinto Albariño continued to press his slave José for more details. After one session that mixed threats and promises of rewards, Don Jacinto Albariño reported to one of Álzaga's agents that José had now exposed additional details about the planned attack on Good Friday. José remembered that Díaz had told him that once the rebels had taken the fortress and killed the garrison "the viceroy will be beheaded because he is a thieving dog who is sending all our silver to Spain."[54] Álzaga quickly found others to verify the outline of José's damning testimony. Don Diego Alvarez remembered a conversation with Díaz in the home of Pedro Carrasco "more or less three months ago." Díaz, he claimed, said with "too much pride" that soon the "Spaniards would yield to the points of the lances and knives of the blacks and Indians." Díaz then went on to say that after the revolt "all the property of the Spaniards would be given to the Indians and blacks." Carrasco, whose home served as the site for this outburst, and María Lorenza, who was also present, confirmed this damaging testimony. Despite his belligerent language and confrontational stance confirmed by many witnesses, a thorough search of the Díaz home on March 22 produced only a single knife and an old shotgun. More frustrating still to Álzaga was the absence of revolutionary documents in this humble *rancho*, no lists of conspirators, no manifestos, and no plans of military fortifications. The leader of a slower-moving inquiry might have paused to wonder how close to the center of a conspiracy this nearly illiterate, unskilled laborer might be.

When Álzaga returned to the jail to question Díaz, he had received new testimony that the prisoner had scandalized his neighbors a decade earlier by praising the Andean revolutionary Tupac Amaru. Convinced that Díaz was dangerous, Álzaga pressed him for the names of everyone with whom he had talked about the "French insurrection." Díaz continued to deny everything, claiming he had never talked about an insurrection with anyone, but he admitted that a slave, whose name he did not know, had told him that his master had stored "machetes" (*macanas*) near the Church of San Nicolás. Using the sworn testimony gathered from others, Álzaga forced the prisoner to admit a series of small lies in his earlier testimony. He had in fact spoken to the slave José on a number of occasions; he had been jailed previously for a number of small crimes, including assault; and he had passed on rumors about the "uprising of the French and blacks" in his conversations with others. But he continued to assert that he was "innocent of the planned insurrection."

Álzaga was convinced of Díaz's involvement in a conspiracy, but he had reached a dead end. While it appeared clear to Álzaga that he had recruited José for the conspiracy and spoken to others of this insurrectionary plan, the alcalde still knew nothing of the conspiracy's organization, leadership, or membership. It was at this point Álzaga summarized his findings to the fiscal of the audiencia, noting that multiple witnesses testified that Díaz had talked about the insurrections over months and had threatened others with violence based on the conspiracy. He also noted that Díaz had claimed in conversation with José to be one of the leaders of the conspiracy, although there was no corroboration for this. While the fiscal reminded Álzaga that alcaldes de primer voto were not permitted the use of torture, the full audiencia nevertheless authorized the questioning of both Díaz and Antonini under torture on March 30, 1795.[55]

The next day at eight o'clock at night jailers brought Díaz from his cell to a second-story room in the cabildo building where instruments of torture were stored. Waiting for Díaz were Álzaga, the surgeon Bernardo Nogué, and a Franciscan priest.[56] Álzaga now read the standard judicial proclamation to Díaz, warning him that he must reveal the "principal authors of the conspiracy" or suffer terrible consequences. When Díaz again insisted that he knew nothing more, the jailers led him to the "lugar de tormento." Álzaga now informed Díaz that "whatever injury or mutilation of [his] body, even [his] death, would not be caused by the acts of the torturer because [he had] not confessed the truth." The jailers then forced Díaz into a chair, fastened knotted cords to the large muscles of his arms and legs, and began to tighten them one after another with a winch. Despite Díaz's cries for mercy, "Jesus, Mary, and Joseph help me please," he screamed, Álzaga pressed on until the surgeon intervened, reporting later to the fiscal that Díaz had lost circulation in one leg and his left arm had been dislocated.

Given that the jail was located only fifty steps from the place of torture, Díaz's screams surely penetrated the cells housing Juan Barbarín, his slave Manuel, and Antonini terrifying them as well as the other prisoners. The Plaza Mayor with its markets and food stalls were only a few yards from this scene of brutality and, even though only a few score were present in the plaza in the early evening, they all must have heard the screams. How long did it take for the story to spread across the city, entering every home and shop? In a city already on edge because of late-night police searches, increased military patrols, and mounting arrests, the torture of Díaz created a sense of imminent threat and impending violence.

The first torment of Díaz had produced no new information, neither the name of a single conspirator nor the location of a hidden arms cache. For Álzaga his failure to break Díaz confirmed the prisoner's perverse and criminal attachment to the conspiracy, rather than his innocence. Now completely out of patience, Álzaga returned to the audiencia and sought permission to torture Díaz a second time using more severe methods. The first torment had failed, he argued, because the prisoner was a hardened and committed revolutionary. Without hesitation the audiencia granted the alcalde's request. Thirteen days after the first torment jailers returned Díaz to the second-floor room.

The jailers placed José Díaz in a chair with broad arms and again secured his legs and arms with straps, but this time they forced his hands into heavy leather gloves fastened to the arms of the chair, leaving the tips of his fingers exposed. Then, at Álzaga's command, the torturer slowly forced a steel blade underneath the nail of each finger on Díaz's right hand. The torturer began turning and twisting the blade while Díaz begged for mercy and cried out to God for mercy. The torment lasted twenty-eight minutes without producing a single new revelation. Unable to continue with the left hand because of the injuries caused by the previous torture, Álzaga suspended Díaz's interrogation and returned to the audiencia to request permission for a third torture. With the city now on edge and with so little benefit extracted from the first two tortures, the fiscal refused this request, noting the two "cruel" tortures already inflicted on Díaz.

The Slave Juan Pedro's Story

While the investigation was still focused on Díaz, Álzaga sent agents to the bakery of the French immigrant Juan Luis Dumont (sometimes written *Dumonte*) to begin interviewing his laborers, slave and free, on March 8, 1795.[57] Juan Pedro, an African-born slave purchased in Rio de Janeiro by a Spanish artillery officer and later sold to Dumont, was among the first they interviewed. Juan Pedro's testimony had an electric effect on the inquiry.[58] He told his interrogator, and later repeated to Álzaga, that his master regularly held "meetings of Frenchmen" in his home that lasted all afternoon. According to the slave, Dumont's guests always toasted "liberty" after eating and drinking their fill and before leaving for their homes around six o'clock at night.[59] While Álzaga's investigation had led already to the arrest of Juan Barbarín and José Díaz, he had not convincingly tied either prisoner to a group of coconspirators. Given Díaz's bombastic narrative of planned attacks on the city's military garrison and the execution of the viceroy, Álzaga believed that there had to be large numbers of conspirators backed by significant resources. Now, with the testimony of Juan Pedro, Álzaga had what he believed was a first glimpse of this formidable conspiracy.

Álzaga pressed Juan Pedro for details. Who attended these revolutionary meetings? Who was the leader? Where were the documents and arms? Juan Pedro was immediately helpful. He named Dumont's foreman the criollo Antonio Gallardo, Don Antonio "el relojero" (this was Santiago Antonini, also called "el relojero gordo"), Don Andres "the tailor who lives near the sergeant major," Don Juan "el cojo" (the cripple), the pulpero who lives near the Church of the Conception, the shoemaker Manuel (Sustaeta one of Francisco Baquero's allies), and a "tall Frenchman" who worked for Don Santiago de Liniers. Just as a locomotive slowly gathers momentum to set a chain of freight cars in motion, Juan Pedro slowly and convincingly provided the alcalde with the compelling details that would focus the investigation on his master, Juan Luis Dumont.[60]

Few of the alcalde's previous informants, despite an apparent universal eagerness to be useful, had offered any details. Witnesses and informants seldom identified suspected conspirators by name, they were "tall" or "fat," they dressed "decently" or not. Witnesses told police agents that arms were collected "near Plaza Monserrat" or at an unnamed pulpería. The ever cooperative Juan Pedro, when pushed for information, was almost always able to remember a telling detail. He recalled, for example, that in late 1794 Dumont's group had quickly abandoned their meal when a military patrol passed by. According to Juan Pedro, the threatening presence of the soldiers led Dumont's group to relocate their meetings to a farm (*quinta*) in the nearby countryside. With little effort Álzaga discovered that the farm belonged to a member of a French noble family, the Conde de Liniers, and was managed by the Conde's younger brother Santiago.[61] The Conde, well-connected at the Spanish court, held a royal license to produce dried beef for the Spanish fleet but was seldom directly involved in the business. His brother Santiago held the rank of captain in the Spanish Navy and managed the Conde's assets in Buenos Aires. With these discoveries Álzaga could see, for the first time, figures of a stature that might threaten the colonial regime, figures influential enough to serve as conduits for the venomous content of the French and Haitian revolutions.

When asked about arms, Juan Pedro's testimony suggested that his master owned what seemed an inexplicable armory for a baker, "two carbines, three shotguns, a sword, and a wide-bladed lance as well as four pistols." He also claimed that Dumont had tried to recruit him into the conspiracy. Juan Pedro recalled that Dumont had sent him to the Liniers estate with food in anticipation of a meeting of the conspirators. Once there Juan Pedro alleged he had seen arms hidden behind barrels of lard in a storehouse. He also remembered that the estate manager (later revealed to be the French national Carlos Josef Bloud) had closely questioned him about his background and knowledge of weapons. Juan Pedro proudly repeated to Álzaga what he claimed to have told the foreman: He had served as a soldier in Guinea and had used firearms before his transportation as a captive to Brazil. Once in Brazil he claimed that he had had additional experience with firearms and swords. Juan Pedro testified that Bloud sent him back to Dumont after this conversation with a note. After reading what Bloud had written, Juan Pedro claimed that Dumont had said, "I purchased you for evil and, if you serve me as I command on a Thursday or Friday . . . I will set you free." Two days later Juan Pedro presented additional details of the planned uprising to Álzaga, confirming the Maundy Thursday or Good Friday date for the attack on the garrison and the planned execution of the viceroy.

Álzaga reacted quickly, sweeping up every member of the Dumont circle and searching their homes and businesses. The only person to escape arrest was Santiago de Liniers, who oversaw management of the rural estate which Juan Pedro claimed was the conspiracy's organizing center.[62] Liniers would prove too connected and too powerful to arrest without enormous effort and very convincing evidence. When Álzaga demanded the keys to his estate and to the strong boxes he kept there, Liniers waited days before answering and then wrote directly to the viceroy rather than to Álzaga. He complained to Viceroy Arredondo that Álzaga had ignored the protocols required when treating a person of his rank and position.[63] Álzaga heatedly dismissed the claimed exemption and the viceroy informed Liniers that he would have to grant full access to the estate. In the end Álzaga's agents searched the quinta three times and had every letter and copybook written in French translated and closely examined without discovering damning evidence. Nevertheless, the bitter recriminations and accusations exchanged by the two powerful men would fester for over a decade. While Liniers escaped arrest in the dragnet, the alcalde ordered the arrest of his two employees as well as a female cook at the quinta.

With thirty men and one woman now in the city jail Álzaga collected testimony that seemed to confirm many of Juan Pedro's claims. Dumont certainly was at the center of a large group of mostly unmarried artisans and petty retailers. Also prominent in the group were immigrants like Antonini who had left their families behind in Europe. The majority of Dumont's friends were foreign born, most French speakers or French nationals. They met three or more times a week to share meals in private homes or, sometimes, in taverns or cafes near the Plaza Mayor.[64] While the alcalde's agents found no arms cache at the Liniers estate, the search of Dumont's home yielded the weapons reported earlier by Juan Pedro. A small number of firearms were then uncovered at the homes of the other members of the Dumont circle. Additional witnesses confirmed Juan Pedro's damning testimony of group toasts to liberty. Álzaga was even able to establish a tenuous connection between the Dumont group and Juan Barbarín, the first suspect arrested in the inquiry. Pablo Mayllos, whom Barbarín hired to teach the slave Manuel to read, shared a room with the twenty-seven-year-old clockmaker Santiago Antonini. Antonini had been illegally residing in Buenos Aires since 1792 and was among Dumont's closest friends.[65]

A late-night search of Antonini's room by Álzaga's agents, who were accompanied by a military patrol, provided another link to the broad conspiracy. Hidden in Antonini's bedclothes agents discovered a small *pasquín* where a bold hand had written "¡Viva la Liverta!" (a misspelling of the Spanish word *libertad* or, given Antonini's origin, perhaps the Italian version of the word). Antonini was present during the search and defended himself by claiming that the soldiers or police agents who conducted the search had planted the pasquín. Arrested immediately by Álzaga's agents, Antonini clumsily attempted to bribe Pedro Muñoz de Olaso, the teniente de alguacil mayor, with "an ounce of gold" as the patrol marched him to the jail.[66] For Álzaga, the attempt to brazenly bribe his subordinate in front of witnesses confirmed that Antonini was a ringleader. Álzaga later came to

FIGURE 17 The document that delivered Santiago Antonini into the hands of the torturer. Published with the permission of the AGN, Buenos Aires, Argentina.

believe that the pasquín found among Antonini's possessions had been produced by Mayllos, Antonini's roommate and the slave Manuel's tutor.

Having decided to secure permission to question Díaz under torture, Álzaga asked the audiencia to also permit the use of torture with Antonini, Dumont, Gallardo (Dumont's foreman), and Juan Polovio (a Sardinian-born pulpero and friend of Dumont) as well.[67] The court responded quickly with permission to proceed with José Díaz and Antonini, the individual from Dumont's circle in possession of the damning invocation to liberty.[68] Díaz and the Italian clockmaker suffered their first torments on March 31. Both faced the *tormento de cordeles*. Once finished with Díaz, Álzaga showed the instruments of torture to Antonini and then had him secured in a chair. As the torturer tightened the thick knotted cords attached to Antonini's arms and legs, his cries could be heard across the city. The effect on his friends in the nearby cells, many under threat of torture, must have been terrifying, but the alcalde learned nothing new. He now returned to the fiscal of the audiencia, claiming that the tormento de cordeles was useless when applied to hardened revolutionists and committed conspirators like Antonini or Díaz. The fiscal granted permission to subject both Díaz and Antonini to a second torture, on April 13.[69]

This time jailers had to carry the terrified prisoner up the steps to face the alcalde. As Antonini was being warned that he would be responsible for any injuries, or even death, suffered as a result of the torments, he broke. He admitted to Álzaga that he had participated in the conspiracy, naming Dumont as a prime organizer and his roommates and friends as co-conspirators. Now Álzaga finally had the confession that had eluded him in the preceding weeks. He pressed Antonini to connect the Dumont group to Liniers as well as to Díaz and Barbarín and demanded the location of the conspiracy's arms caches. As Álzaga pushed for the details that would condemn Antonini's friends to the torment that now threatened him, the clockmaker recovered his strength and disavowed his earlier testimony. With these words he knowingly condemned himself to the awaiting torture. Dragged into the chamber and strapped into the chair, Antonini suffered fifty minutes of horror as the torturer forced his steel blade beneath each fingernail. Writhing in pain, Antonini begged God and the saints to save him but offered no new information. Again Álzaga had failed to gain new leads or conclusive evidence, even as Antonini's cries again punctured the city's sleep.

This terrible event effectively ended the practice of judicial torture in colonial Buenos Aires. When Álzaga returned to the audiencia to ask for permission to torture Antonini a third time, the judges immediately refused. They then went on to turn down Álzaga's request to question Dumont, Polovio, and Gallardo under torture. Santiago de Liniers never faced arrest and was not forced to answer Álzaga's questions directly. Nevertheless, the judicial case proceeded.[70] On May 3, 1795, the fiscal announced he would seek the death penalty for Antonini and the others implicated with Dumont, but this threat would have little traction with the now disaffected audiencia.

With Álzaga's inquiry exhausted and the audiencia embarrassed, the lawyers appointed to defend the accused provided the coup de grâce. One after another they pointed out the absurdities in Álzaga's allegations: Could anyone imagine that the little educated and often-drunk José Díaz threatened the colonial order? Where was the arms cache collected by Dumont and his friends? Who were the leaders of the planned insurrection? How had the alcalde constructed this case? Was it based entirely on the testimony of two angry slaves, José the shipyard cook, and Juan Pedro the disgruntled slave of Dumont?

Don Pedro Medrano, appointed as Dumont's lawyer, effectively deconstructed Martín de Álzaga's case for the audiencia. He produced testimony that showed that Juan Pedro was notorious for his rebelliousness and violent temper. His first master in Buenos Aires, Colonel Don Josef García Martinez de Caceres y Garre, had failed comprehensively in his efforts to control him. Juan Pedro was, according to Medrano, a chronic runaway and known thief who had actually faced down a military patrol sent to return him to the colonel after an escape. Frustrated by his slave's willful and relentless refusal to accept his authority, the colonel had decided to "sell" Juan Pedro to Juan Luis Dumont rather than send him to a frontier presidio. The cost to Dumont was one loaf of bread a day delivered to the former master. This made clear, claimed Medrano, that Juan Pedro was so difficult and rebellious that his first owner had effectively given him away.

Medrano went on to describe the events that had precipitated what he called Juan Pedro's false testimony. Transferred to the authority of Dumont and employed in his bakery, Juan Pedro had continued to run away. Desperate to assert his authority, Dumont purchased iron cuffs and had a cell constructed in the bakery to control Juan Pedro and his other slaves. Unsubdued, Juan Pedro robbed the bakery's cashbox and fled to the arms of his lover. When an alcalde de barrio captured and returned him to Dumont, the baker ordered a heavy iron collar riveted around his neck. Why, Medrano asked the audiencia, would Álzaga believe this undisciplined and vengeful slave's testimony? [71]

Medrano went on to explain the arms found in the bakery. There were "many weapons," he admitted, but bakers "were forced to work with the people most vile, abusive, and disposed to conspiracy against their owners." He claimed that every baker in Buenos Aires feared for his life and took measures to protect himself from his slaves, "if you examined every bakery and similar shops you would encounter the same or greater numbers of arms," he asserted. [72]

Having already received word that peace negotiations had ended the war with France, the audiencia announced its decisions in these related cases on September 10, 1795. The audiencia sentenced Barbarín and all the foreign nationals in Dumont's circle to exile in Spain and confiscated their property, although all ultimately escaped deportation. The shoemaker Juan Antonio Sustaeta and the other criollos endured months of jail before their final release. José Díaz, the sixty-two-year-old free moreno already tortured twice, received the harshest sentence: ten years in prison on the desolate Malvinas Islands. It is impossible to fix precisely the origins of these odd decisions by the audiencia. Had the court responded to calls for mercy or been moved by political expediency or embarrassment?[73] What is clear is that by late 1795 Martín de Álzaga was the only official in Buenos Aires still willing to hold thirty prisoners, arrested on mostly uncorroborated evidence and subjected to brutal conditions, in the public jail located only a short distance from the Plaza Mayor and most important civil and ecclesiastical authorities.

In the end all of the prisoners sentenced to exile by the audiencia, except Díaz, would gain their freedom and remain in Buenos Aires. The audiencia made no effort to enforce its decision to exile most of the prisoners to Spain. Antonini remained in the city and became a client of Santiago de Liniers. Juan Barbarín began a business with Carlos Josef Bloud, Liniers's ranch foreman, while his slave Manuel eventually gained his freedom. José Díaz, the poorest and most vulnerable of all those arrested, remained in prison as authorities released the others one after another. In the end his wife died heartbroken and impoverished while he remained incarcerated in the Malvinas. After numerous failed appeals for mercy addressed to the viceroy, his sister wrote to his warden on the queen's birthday to beg once more to have his imprisonment relocated from the Malvinas to Buenos Aires. On August 25, 1796, José Díaz was finally granted this "grace" requested by his sister and was returned to the city to serve his full sentence of ten years in the city jail.[74]

In their efforts to disarm the evidence arrayed against their clients, the lawyers for Antonini, Dumont, and Barbarín had all attacked Álzaga's conduct. They questioned his motives and his methods and damned his decision to use torture. With the advent of peace with France, the French ambassador to Spain, Dominique-Catherine Perignon, addressed Spanish Prime Minister Manuel Francisco Domingo de Godoy y Álvarez de Faria, the Prince of the Peace, to demand justice for the "French citizens arrested and imprisoned in Buenos Aires and Montevideo." He also condemned Martín de Álzaga as a "petty magistrate" and a "rich and superstitious, ambitious and vindictive man." Intent on injuring Álzaga's reputation, the French ambassador claimed the alcalde had sought to profit from his persecution of French citizens by seizing their property.[75] These charges as well as the criticisms of the local lawyers must have been nearly unendurable to a prickly and proud man like Álzaga and help explain his later pursuit of a vendetta against Liniers, who he regarded as the protector and patron of the Dumont group.

Conclusion

The preceding period of racial conflict within the city's artisan community, the startling willingness of nonwhite artisans to confront colonial authorities, and the news of distant revolutionary events gave urgency to the prosecution of this so-called French conspiracy by colonial authorities. The inquiry, arrests, and tortures also coincided with a period of rising prices and import shortages that roiled labor relations and shocked an urban population complacent after nearly twenty years of growth and prosperity. While distant revolutionary events in France and Saint-Domingue agitated the city and provided disturbing imagery of hierarchy overthrown, porteños also connected these events and images to the already existing anxiety promoted by a fast-growing slave population whose presence was made clear by African drumming and dances and, in the minds of many residents, by rising crime rates. While the catalysts for Álzaga's inquiry were external, the French and Haitian revolutions and Spain's war with France, it was the local experiences of artisanal conflicts among shoemakers and silversmiths, market manipulations by bakers, and the mounting numbers of African slaves that gave these external threats real traction in Buenos Aires.[76]

There is little evidence that any of those arrested in 1795 were actively involved in a political conspiracy. Authorities discovered no arms cache, propaganda, or organized leadership. Yet, the meaning of these distant revolutions for the Buenos Aires plebe and for the city's slave population is clear. As Álzaga's investigation gathered momentum, slaves routinely rehearsed the images and words that frightened masters and rulers alike. When a slave said "on Good Friday we will all be French," we must presume that he signaled with this one word, *French*, the full meaning of contemporary revolution.[77] Or, when a female slave disciplined by her mistress said, "soon I will hold the power," she intuited that in this moment of uncertainty and fear her mistress understood her threat.

José Díaz, an impoverished migrant from Corrientes barely able to write his name, was certainly not a conspirator, but he had at his disposal a broad vocabulary of revolutionary images and terms as well as a strong sense of the experience of injustice. When Díaz evoked an image of the bloody rising that would set things right for the slave José Albariño, he said "the French would unite with the blacks of Buenos Aires in a rebellion that would offer liberty to everyone," clearly identifying the chief agent of revolutionary change, France, and the chief revolutionary objective of the era, liberty. He also offered a telling evocation of one broadly felt, local grievance and his own bold remedy, "the viceroy will be beheaded because he is a thieving dog who is sending all our silver to Spain."[78]

Tamer complaints and proposed remedies circulated in the marginally more affluent circle that surrounded Dumont and Barbarín. "The French had good reason to execute their king," Barbarín said. He also said "Robespierre was capable of being the owner [dueno] of the world."[79] Dumont and Antonini and their friends routinely raised their glasses to toast liberty, and Pablo Mayllos y Marcana, or someone like him, wrote the word *liberty* on slips of papers and pasted them on public buildings at great personal risk. Events in France and Saint-Domingue were clearly known in surprising detail in the precincts that hosted the city's artisans and laborers. It is clear that, once disseminated, this powerful subversive language and inventory of symbols as well as the notorious actions of revolutionaries were now available as vectors for the expression of local grievance and dissatisfaction.

By the time Álzaga's inquiry had run its course, the colonial government's uneven and heavy-handed reaction to the immediate threat posed by war with France as well as the reaction to the threat of slave insurrection demonstrated in Saint-Domingue shook the city and cowed a restive plebe. Long-established rhythms, rituals, and the steadying force of habit and conformity that had previously given shape to plebeian participation in colonial civic life were gravely weakened by the end of the decade. While there were few potential revolutionaries in Buenos Aires at the end of the 1790s, the vulnerability of Spain and the weakness of local Spanish institutions were placed in bold relief by the political passions, moral temporizing, and incompetence that had swept Álzaga, the audiencia, and the viceroy into a cycle of arrests, torture, and judicial failures that dominated Buenos Aires in 1795.

6 The Reproduction of Working-Class Life

Needing, Wanting, Having, and Saving

Fearing that his death was near, the immigrant silversmith Juan Antonio Callejas y Sandoval prepared his will in 1787. After surviving his grave illness, Callejas y Sandoval died in 1793, leaving his wife and two sons an estate of nearly sixteen thousand pesos. This was an enormous accumulation for an artisan in late colonial Buenos Aires. The achievement is more impressive given the fact that Callejas y Sandoval had arrived from Spain as a young man without any capital other than his skills and a few tools of his trade. He quickly established himself as an honest and skillful silversmith in a city where silversmiths were notorious for fraud and sharp practices. Once married, Callejas y Sandoval became a man of property and a leader of his craft's efforts to create a guild.

Producer goods (tools, an inventory of finished goods, and silver plate) made up approximately 25 percent of the value of Callejas y Sandoval's estate. The value of his nine slaves represented another 10 percent according to court-appointed appraisers. Among the adult slaves were four journeymen silversmiths who worked in their master's shop. Callejas y Sandoval also owned three male slaves who he rented out as day laborers and two female slaves who served his wife in the family home. At the time of probate the court acknowledged that three of the four slaves who worked as journeyman silversmiths were runaways and their whereabouts unknown. Unlike most artisans, Callejas y Sandoval owned his family residence. In addition to the living area, the building included an *esquina*, a corner room with a doorway and counter turned to face the intersection of two streets, where he conducted his business. This prosperous artisan also owned a second house that produced a steady stream of rental income in the superheated Buenos Aires real estate market. With their furnishings these properties were worth approximately seven thousand pesos or about 40 percent of his estate.

His probate also revealed a large and complicated web of debts and credits. While his customers owed him nearly three thousand pesos for goods purchased on credit, he in turn owed more than eight thousand pesos to merchants for the materials used in his trade and for loans that financed the purchase of his slaves.[1] The estate of Callejas y Sandoval, an estate similar in size to those of many upper-level bureaucrats and professionals, was not representative of the general experience of artisans in late colonial Buenos Aires, but it does illuminate the potential rewards available to a minority of this class during the late colonial economic expansion.

More typical of the city's master artisans was the shoemaker Juan Felix Duarte. The *porteño* Duarte was married to a local woman, Juana Francisca Labao Recio, and they had two daughters, aged thirteen and seven, at the time the testament recorded in 1793. Although he had accumulated only a modest fortune, Duarte, like Callejas y Sandoval, owned his family home, estimated to be worth three hundred pesos. This house also included an esquina where he sold shoes and serviced customers. Duarte claimed in his testament that his inventory of finished shoes, tools, and materials was worth less than a hundred pesos. Although his household furnishings included two silver candlesticks, signaling the family's social aspirations, the total value of his furniture and clothes was less than seventy pesos. In addition to these meager assets, Duarte left his wife a debt of forty-two pesos offset, on paper, by more than three hundred pesos owed to him by his customers. In the end these debts proved uncollectible.

The will makes it clear that Duarte's house and shop, the largest portion of his estate, had been purchased by Duarte's wife from her assets, rather than from his income as a shoemaker. Although Juana had received no dowry from her parents at the time of her marriage, she later inherited a female slave from her mother's estate. Juana sold this slave and used the funds to buy a younger slave. Her acuity was demonstrated when she later sold the second slave with enough profit to purchase the family home and another female slave.[2] Material success, even on the modest scale of Juan Felix Duarte and his wife, typically depended on investing scarce capital in real estate, the houses and shops that framed these working lives, or in

FIGURE 18 One of the few remaining examples of a late-colonial era *esquina*. The door pitched kitty-corner to the intersection, which maximized an artisan's access to customers. Photograph by author.

slaves, slaves either trained in artisan crafts or rented out as day laborers. The income and financial acumen of wives and the impact of even small inheritances, dowries, or gifts from parents often proved more important to the acquisition of wealth than did wages.

Neither the affluence of Callejas y Sandoval nor Duarte's tenuous claim to respectability was truly representative of plebeian experience. Most of the city's artisans and laborers died without accumulating possessions beyond the clothes they wore, a few tools, and, perhaps, the utensils used to prepare and eat their meals. Only a minority married or lived independently because the costly burden of daily subsistence left them without the funds needed to pay for a rented room or feed a family. The material circumstances of the free black shoemaker Pascual Braga are much more representative of plebeian experience. His estate included a small house in poor condition that he had inherited from his mother, his clothes (two shirts, a pair of pants, and one pair of worn shoes), and the tools of his trade. At the time of his death his tools were being "held as collateral" for an overdue advance on wages he had received from the master shoemaker Francisco Albarado. Braga's estate was further encumbered by an additional twenty-eight pesos in debt owed to other creditors, including ten pesos owed to the neighborhood baker for bread.[3] These debts along with Braga's expressed desire for a "decent" burial left his widow with no inheritance at all.[4]

Most male plebeians were unlikely to either accumulate property or marry during their working lives. As a result, they lived in an intensely masculine environment. They shared meals and housing at the end of the day with workmates from the shop, small factory, or construction site. They also spent their leisure time with workmates or neighbors. If these micro-environments became intolerable because of violence, bullying, or mounting debts or because of unemployment, men from this humble strata picked up and moved. They moved within the city or to cities elsewhere in the viceroyalty, like Montevideo or Córdoba. Some returned to Europe or to provincial cities of the interior. Their possessions, packed in a small chest or rolled in a blanket, were no impediment to mobility. Poverty forced the poorest to rent or borrow the tools of their trade, a cost docked from their future wages. Because employers routinely docked the costs of mistakes from wages as well, a run of bad luck or the effects of illness could precipitate a financial catastrophe for an individual or family.

The Struggle for Daily Bread

Any effort to illuminate the lives and explain the actions of plebeians must begin by placing those lives in a context framed by consumption and income. Fortunately, the surviving documents permit the reconstruction of a reliable price history for late colonial Buenos Aires.[5] By tracing eight of the most important comestibles through the records of religious establishments as well as government records, I constructed a time series. In addition, I estimated a rental series from surviving religious and governmental records. While some components of basic consumption were absent in these records, the commodities included in the series can usefully serve as proxies for other products.[6] For example, a major source of protein in the porteño diet, beef, is missing, but the records of the local military garrison provide a price series for salted beef. It is included here as a useful proxy, capturing as a composite the cost of fresh beef and salt (a dietary foundation) as well as labor costs associated with production.

A basket of dietary staples, rather than a single staple of mass consumption like corn, must serve as the basis of our effort to measure changes in the cost of living.[7] Table 4 provides price series for wheat, rice, garbanzos, yerba, sugar, beans, wine, and salted beef that indicates a clear pattern of cyclical and secular price increases.[8] Changes in the price of wheat had the greatest impact on the lives of plebeians. Economic historians of eighteenth-century Europe have demonstrated the central importance of bread prices to the lives of the urban poor.[9] E. P. Thompson focused on the centrality of this basic food when he stated, "throughout the Industrial Revolution the price of bread (and of oatmeal) was the first index of living standards, in the estimation of the people."[10] As a result, substantial increases in the price of bread propelled much of the violent popular protest in preindustrial European cities, humbling many officials who failed to effectively control the price and availability of this essential product.[11] Historians of colonial New Spain have similarly demonstrated the close relationship between rising maize prices and violence.[12]

We know little about diet in colonial Buenos Aires, and what is known is focused on the consumption patterns of elite and middle groups.[13] Nevertheless, it is clear that the diet of plebeians in late colonial Buenos Aires was closer in content to that of the popular classes of contemporary Europe than to the diets of either Mexico or Alto Peru where maize commonly retained pride of place.[14] In Buenos Aires cuisine retained a Spanish character, although the abundance of cheap beef meant there was more protein in the plebeian diet. The cabildo granted a monopoly for the city's meat provisions and established an *arancel* (list of controlled prices) for fresh beef. Prices for this food therefore moved within tight margins and were among the most stable food prices.[15] Although poverty was common, the abundance of cheap meat meant that starvation was virtually unknown, although there were periods when meat was scarce.[16] In July 1802 during a region-wide drought, for example, the cabildo signaled the crucial importance of abundant beef supplies when it stated its fear that "a single day without this staple in the plaza would produce the most fatal consequences because this is the universal and common food for every class of people."[17]

Because bread, not cheap meat, was the basic staple of the Buenos Aires plebe, municipal authorities also strove to prevent price increases that might trigger violent protest.[18] As was common in Spanish colonies, the cabildo of Buenos Aires controlled the price of bread through the imposition of an arancel that adjusted the weight of a one peso loaf of bread to reflect changes in the market price of a *fanega* of wheat.[19] That is, a loaf of bread always cost one peso but the weight of the loaf was reduced as the market price of wheat rose. Because the typical plebeian consumer attempted to

TABLE 4 Changes in prices, in reales, of selected commodities, 1775–1812

Year	Wheat/ fanega	Rice/ arroba	Garbanzos/ arroba	Yerba/ arroba	Sugar/ arroba	Porotos/ arroba	Wine/ botija	Salted beef/ quintal
1775				12	44		15.5	
1776	16	27	19	12	53	31	14.3	32
1777	29	24		15	57		12.2	33
1778	27	17		15	68	27	14.9	28
1779	28	18	18	16	45	36	15	
1780					63	40	16	
1781	40	25	27			36	15	
1782		25	21	22	56		14.9	25
1783		16	22	22	44	28	12	24
1784		24	20	20	44	28	11.8	
1785	40		21	18	40	43	12.5	
1786	40	21	21	23	48	32	12.7	24
1787		17	17	23	49	32	13.3	24
1788	14	20	16	24	64		11.5	20
1789	14.5		15	22	72		8.7	20
1790	15		18	22	48	32	8.5	20
1791	15	24	20	17			12	20
1792	15	10	15	17	36	32	9.4	20
1793	16	13	13	14			8.8	20
1794	12	22		18	32		9	
1795	22	14	15	16	40	32	12.1	32
1796	28	25	15	18	51	32	12.3	20
1797	25	29	16	16	56	36	15.5	25
1798	21	23	14	18	50	48		24
1799	21	15	15	18	52		14.8	
1800	28	17	11	18	48		14.5	25
1801	34	34	18	19	29		15	25
1802	26	31	25	18	36	64	14	25
1803	72	23	29	19	29	54	13.7	
1804	71	18	34	20	33	40	11.1	
1805	70		31	19	33	31	14.7	
1806	71	20	25	18	33		16	64
1807		16		23	40		18	62
1808		18	28	24	40		19.5	64
1809	34	24		22	72	35	20	62
1810	43	27	26	22	31	37	18.2	
1811	42	26	23	40	38	44	13	
1812				32			13.1	

maintain a consistent level of bread consumption, we can only discover the effects of rising prices on the quality of life by closely tracking the price of wheat rather than the price of bread.

The price of wheat in Buenos Aires fluctuated broadly as was common in most eighteenth-century societies.[20] There was a powerful upward movement in the price of wheat in the last decades of the colonial era that must have had a strong impact on the lives of the working poor. The first increase began in 1780 and lasted nearly to 1787. Wheat prices then fluctuated between fourteen and twenty-eight reales per fanega until a second period of dramatic price increases occurred due to a drought in 1802–1804.[21] During this time of famine and epidemic in most of the viceroyalty new highs of seventy-one and seventy-two reales per fanega eclipsed the previous high of forty reales per fanega. In the midst of this shock, officials noted that the cost of a pound of bread would buy six to eight pounds of meat in the city market.[22]

The fluctuation of wheat prices displayed in table 4 was similar to price histories elsewhere. Economic historians have demonstrated similar volatility for contemporary Spain. One investigator summarized the upward movement of Spanish wheat prices in the period 1779–1783 as "one of the most spectacular trends registered in world economic history" and then identified numerous cyclical fluctuations of up to 100 percent in urban bread prices during the eighteenth century.[23] A general similarity with the Spanish case does not substantiate the specifics of the Buenos Aires wheat series of course, but it does suggest that the range of price fluctuations found for Buenos Aires fell well within the experience of the late-eighteenth-century Spanish world.

The other foods included in table 4 were also important components of the porteño diet in the late colonial era as indicated in convent and hospital accounts. Both criollo and Spanish-born members of religious communities used rice as an accompaniment for beef, chicken, and fish and as a sweetened pudding. We may assume that rice was also common on the tables of propertied members of the plebeian class, especially European immigrants and better off criollos. It was not as important to the diets of single men who often lived together in back rooms and patios where cooking facilities were limited. The place of sugar in the local diet, on the other hand, was clearly important.[24] Virtually all urban groups in America and Europe increased their consumption of sugar during the eighteenth century.[25] Although not a dietary staple, sugar was a highly desired discretionary purchase, a penny luxury. The availability and price of products like sugar, tobacco, and yerba determined in large part the working class's definition of good or bad times.

Prices for tobacco were set by a state monopoly. Yerba, however, was traded in the marketplace. Travelers often noted the nearly ubiquitous consumption of yerba among native-born working men and women.[26] Artisans working in shops and bakeries as well as the laborers paving streets, mending the seawall, or moving heavy carts through the city all took morning and afternoon breaks to share yerba.[27] The custom of drinking yerba played a central role in establishing social relations and transmitting cultural values in a city characterized by short-term employment and high levels of immigration. The etiquette of sharing yerba when taking a break from work or when relaxing after work helped establish sociability and comradeship.

The late colonial working class consumed large quantities of wine and brandy.[28] Consumption was partially the result of the deprivations experienced by almost all plebeians; hard work, lack of privacy, and limited prospects all propelled men toward the induced camaraderie of alcohol.[29] There were few solitary drinkers among urban artisans and day laborers. Young men commonly took their first drinks in the company of workmates, and drinking rituals and customs helped forge personal and corporate bonds throughout life.[30] But alcohol provided cheap calories as well. Municipal authorities attempted to control alcohol sales in the city's pulperías, which offered food, drink, and dry goods as well as diversions and companionship.[31] One common complaint was that pulperías offered *aguardiente*, brandy, in lieu of coins as change for small purchases thus seducing slaves and the free poor to theft or worse. Although it is impossible to stipulate actual levels of alcohol consumption, we can assume levels in Buenos Aires were similar to those of contemporary Europe. If this was the case, the average adult worker in the city consumed between one and one-and-a-half liters of wine per day.[32] Brandy was even more popular among porteño plebeians with consumption as high as a half liter per day, a pattern that connected predictably to violence, accidents, and absenteeism.[33]

We cannot generalize from the pattern of price inflation found for wheat in the last decades of the colonial period to other basic commodities. We can best explain variations in the prices paid for basic foods by examining the conditions that affected supplies of each commodity at their points of origin, with imports and locally produced goods often moving in different directions.[34] Garbanzos, beans, and salted beef originated on local and regional farms and ranches. Yerba, wine, and sugar were produced in the interior of the viceroyalty, especially Paraguay, Mendoza, and Tucumán, but considerable quantities of wine and sugar were imported as well.[35] Wine was a common import from Spain while quantities of sugar were imported from Brazil and Cuba in exchange for dried and salted beef exports.[36] Finally, Brazil was the primary source of rice consumed in Buenos Aires.

FIGURE 19 An encampment of carts used in the trade between Buenos Aires and the towns and cities of the viceroyalty's interior provinces. Source: C. E. Pellegrini, *Recuerdos del Río de la Plata* (Buenos Aires: Libreria L'Amateur, 1969). Published with the permission of the publisher, Librería L'Amateur, Buenos Aires.

It is clear that from the mid-1790s Buenos Aires experienced rising prices across the board with the steepest increases registered by wheat and meat. Plebeians must have adjusted their diets to compensate for price increases of preferred foods, but these adjustments were appreciated through the lens of cultural expectations.[37] Reduced consumption of preferred foods negatively affected popular understandings of well-being and social justice.

Shelter from the Storm

Housing was an extremely important and very expensive component of the cost of living. Members of the plebe lived in a wide range of housing situations. A minority owned homes and a smaller number owned multiple family housing. The vast majority rented rooms or, in many cases, paid a small amount for a place to sleep at the back of a shop or even in a hallway. By the 1790s merchants looking for a dependable rental income to offset the unpredictable cyclical profits of wholesale trade began to construct large multiunit buildings in Buenos Aires.[38] In these apartment blocks families typically shared access to a rough kitchen, seldom more than an open cooking fire or outdoor adobe oven located at the back of the building, with neighbors. Single men or married immigrants living away from their families commonly shared a single room with workmates or friends; censuses demonstrate that as many as five to ten single men often shared a single room. Some master artisans and owners of brickyards and bakeries offered minimal housing to their apprentices or journeymen as part of their compensation.[39] In these crowded, uncomfortable circumstances slaves and freemen, the native and foreign born, whites, castas, and blacks all lived together in rough material equality.[40]

Both the cabildo of Buenos Aires and the Convent of San Ramón owned rental apartments and these records provide the basis for the rent series presented in table 5. This series is a composite of rents collected for three separate groups of one-room apartments located in the city center.[41] As indicated in the table, rental costs rose following the creation of the Viceroyalty of Río de la Plata as the urban population grew more rapidly than the housing stock. Rents moderated early in the 1790s. As the independence era began rents pushed upward again. This pattern suggests that housing construction begun during the 1780s and 1790s in response to high rents gradually caught up with population growth caused by transatlantic and internal migrations. The decision of the patriot government to tax or, in some cases, expropriate the wealth of Spanish merchants and bureaucrats, groups that had previously invested in the construction of housing, slowed new construction after 1810. At the same time the redeployment of rural and provincial militia units to help defend the city after 1807 put new pressure on already scarce housing.[42]

At first glance it might appear that petty retailers, artisans, and laborers would improve their housing as incomes increased, since average rental costs remained more stable than basic food prices. However, the reality was far different. Throughout the period the average cost of a small apartment in Buenos Aires remained beyond the reach of many if not most urban wage earners. If we use the median wage paid to laborers as a proxy for the incomes of most plebeians, two reales per day until 1801, we see that the three to four pesos per month charged for decrepit apartments near the city's economic center were beyond the reach of many.[43] Even less skilled laborers earning four reales a day in 1804 would have found the eight pesos per month for a median, one-room apartment owned by the Convent of San Ramón nearly impossible to afford, especially during times of under-

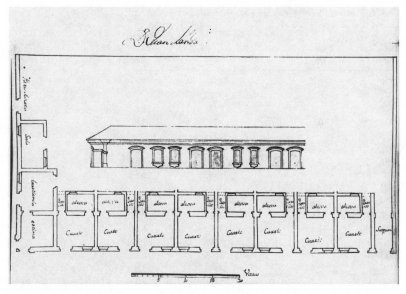

FIGURE 20 A block of small apartments built in 1780s that included an *esquina* at the left corner. Published with the permission of the AGN, Buenos Aires, Argentina.

employment in winter months. Even better paid journeymen bricklayers and carpenters, men who earned twice the wage of laborers, would have found the rents of modest apartments impossible if they temporarily lost employment or suffered injury.[44] Scarce housing stock and high rental costs also depressed marriage rates since men of this class traditionally sought independent housing when they married. This prolonged the dependency of young adult workers forcing them to remain in the homes of parents or employers. One British resident said in 1807 that "the poor are compelled to remain single from the very bare resources on which they depend for subsistence, and are accustomed to consider the married state as fraught with heavy burdens and inevitable misfortunes."[45]

Probate records suggest that many plebeians lived on the city periphery on unclaimed or unoccupied property in *ranchos*, rough adobe buildings constructed in the style commonly found in more rural areas.[46] These suburban districts appear to have had the form and character of the *villas miserias* that provide shelter to the working poor of modern Buenos Aires.[47] John Constanse Davie visited the city in 1796 and remarked upon the "wretched little hovels" of the poor, especially in "the suburbs, inhabited principally by

TABLE 5 Average monthly rent for a single-room apartment in central Buenos Aires, 1770–1812

Year	Monthly rent	Year	Monthly rent in pesos
1770	5.8	1792	
1771	6	1793	
1772	7.3	1794	8.8
1773	8.5	1795	8.9
1774		1796	
1775	7.9	1797	9
1776	9	1798	9
1777		1799	9
1778	10	1800	8.9
1779	10.3	1801	9
1780	10.8	1802	9
1781	11.4	1803	8.6
1782	10.8	1804	8.4
1783		1805	8.8
1784	10.8	1805	8.8
1785	10.7	1806	8.3
1786		1807	9
1787	10.8	1808	8.3
1788		1809	9
1789	9.7	1810	9.3
1790	9.8	1811	10.2
1791	9.7	1812	11.3

mestizos and blacks," where the huts "present a similar aspect to [the poorest parts of London] but are a hundred times dirtier and more miserable."[48] Since the residents of these suburban precincts were undercounted in colonial censuses, we cannot discuss with confidence what part of the working class resided in these districts, but we can assume that housing costs were substantially less than those presented in the urban rental series.[49]

High rents also impeded the advancement of journeymen. Master artisans, particularly in the indoor trades needed to purchase or rent a business location, since it was generally understood that a master was an independent craftsman who dealt directly with the public. Master artisans generally rented two-room corner apartments as close to the central plaza as possible, using the esquina as their shop while their families lived behind a curtain in the second room. Since the rental costs for these larger, better located apartments were substantially higher than the average presented in table 5, we should presume that many artisans in indoor trades were forced to remain journeymen because their incomes did not permit this investment.[50]

Table 6 presents a weighted consumer price index for the period 1776–1811. It indicates three periods of significant upward price pressure, first in the 1780s, again in the 1790s, and finally reaching period highs after 1803. It is not an accident that this cycle coincided with a period of massive wealth transfers from Potosí and other interior provinces to Buenos Aires through the workings of the colonial fiscal system.[51] The food and rent prices presented earlier were adjusted with statistical weights to reflect consumption patterns.[52] The weights used here were assigned to both establish the relative importance of each article for which prices were available and to serve as proxies for other imported and domestically produced foods. Despite the problems inherent in any effort at price history in the prestatistical era, the composite series for Buenos Aires represents an unusually detailed and reliable basis for the analysis of changes in the cost of living in comparison with other studies of Spanish America in the eighteenth century.

Commissary records as well as municipal employment records provide a coherent and uniform record of food purchases over long periods. Soldiers and Spanish naval crews while in port received one or two meals a day paid for by the colonial treasury. Similarly, the municipality employed scores of prisoners and free laborers in street paving and construction work throughout the late colonial period, using public funds to pay for one meal a day. The diets of these groups are not perfect proxies for plebeian diet, but they can serve as a starting place. The diet provided to the crew of the *Nuestra Señora del Rosario*, a Spanish naval vessel, in 1806 offers a representative example.[53] The diet was both boring and nutritionally inadequate. Bread (hardtack) composed 55 percent of the total food expenditure. The remainder was allocated in the following manner: meat, 25 percent; yerba, 10 percent; and onions, salt, and other condiments, 10 percent.[54] Free laborers and prisoners employed by the cabildo to pave the Calle de la Aduana in 1805 received a similar diet (bread, meat, condiments, and yerba) with the cost distributed in similar proportions.[55]

Fortunately, a surviving record from 1783 allows us to produce a more confident representation of plebeian diet, one that reflects consumer preferences. The Buenos Aires cabildo received a continuous steam of income from rental properties seized after the Jesuit expulsion in 1767. To maintain this stream of rental income the municipal government periodically initiated maintenance and renovation projects. In 1783 scores of carpenters, masons, and laborers worked for 106 days to remodel the largest of the former Jesuit properties.[56] Following completion of the project, city officials accused the project supervisor, Lorenzo Cavenagoy, of misappropriating funds. In the inquiry that followed he produced a comprehensive accounting of all job-related expenditures, including daily expenditures for food. Cavenagoy claimed that he had been able to attract and retain this work force at wages lower than those typically paid in the city by offering high-quality food as partial compensation. As a result, we can assume that the diet provided to skilled and unskilled laborers on this project much more closely replicated seasonal variety and plebeian preferences than did the diets provided to soldiers and prisoners.[57]

There are a number of surprises in this detailed record of food expenditures, among them are that fish, rather than beef, was the main course on 54 of the 106 working days, reflecting in part the dietary requirements of the religious calendar.[58] Although some salted fish was consumed (mostly imported cod) in Buenos Aires, the consumption of fish caught in the nearby estuary was more common.[59] Fresh beef, roasted on a spit, provided the main course for the remaining 52 working days. The meals provided to this mixed crew of artisans and laborers also included squash, onions, garlic, tomatoes, lard, salt, green peppers, and bread. The amount spent on bread was significant. While 252 pesos were spent on meat and fish during the 106 days, 214 pesos (40 percent of total expenditures) were spent on bread. This percentage was similar to that found for the local garrison and for municipal construction gangs. It was also similar to the level of expenditures for bread and other grains found for contemporary European urban workers.[60] Yerba was the only beverage provided to workers at this construction site, although we may assume wine and brandy were routinely consumed after hours.

Rations, like wages, reflected the essential hierarchies that defined nearly every work site and housing arrangement. The perceived prestige of a craft as well as differences in skill and seniority levels among workers determined the quality of the diet. On this project skilled craftsmen were provided white bread while laborers and slaves received cheaper dark bread, a common feature of local custom.[61] Despite the now well-known nutritional benefits found in dark bread, the skilled and lesser skilled understood this distinction as a clear marker of status and income. E. P. Thompson remarked on this distinction in the case of contemporary English artisans, noting that

FIGURE 21 The artisans and laborers of Buenos Aires consumed large quantities of wine produced in the interior of the viceroyalty. This early-nineteenth-century watercolor depicts a muleteer delivering casks of wine. Source: Emeric Essex Vidal, *Picturesque Illustrations of Buenos Ayres and Monte Video, Consisting of Twenty-four Views* (London: R. Ackermann, 1820).

"the white loaf was regarded jealously as a symbol of their status."[62] But there was no difference in the quantity of bread served the two groups, a daily ration was one *quartillo* or one quarter of a one peso loaf, exactly nineteen ounces of bread in 1783.

Skilled craftsmen enjoyed other dietary advantages in addition to white bread. Masters and journeymen received double rations at noon. Since the daily ration cost the cabildo slightly more than one-half a real on average, the double ration represented an additional two and one-half reales of income per week for skilled workers in addition to the wage differential. Put another way, the weekly premium represented by this extra ration was slightly more than what a laborer earned for a day's work. It is unclear from the surviving record whether this second ration was ordinarily consumed by the worker himself or was shared with members of his family. Regardless of how this benefit was consumed the double food ration remained an important benefit, reducing both individual and family food costs to the skilled.

Although the city enjoyed access to abundant and therefore cheap beef, fuel for cooking fires was always relatively expensive due to the near absence of nearby forests. In this case the city government purchased twelve cartloads of wood at six pesos per cart to provide cooked beef or fish with every meal. This means that the cost of firewood was roughly 35 percent of the total cost for food and drink over 106 days. Many visitors to the city, including the Yankee merchant David Deforest and the English officer Alexander Gillespie remarked on the high cost of fuel. In fact many of the city's bakeries and brick manufacturers fired their ovens with dried bones discarded by the local abattoirs to reduce costs.[63] As a result, many single men ate most cooked meals at midday at work where they pooled fuel costs with workmates. Evening meals seldom included more than bread and cheese and, sometimes, fruit.[64]

The detailed records of this project serve as the basis for calculating the weights used to construct table 6. A weight of 40 was assigned to wheat. This may understate actual proportions in plebeian diets. While wine was not served with the noon meal at this project, we know it was an important part of the local diet, indeed of diets throughout the Spanish world.[65] In this index, wine is assigned a weight of 7.5, a weight justified by contemporary indications of consumption by the popular classes. A weight of 20 is assigned for rent, a compromise figure lower than indicated by our rent index of city-center apartments and somewhat more than the minimal costs paid for ranchos on the city's periphery or for shared space in backrooms and patios. The other assigned weights are as follows: rice, 10; garbanzos, 2.5; yerba, 7.5; sugar, 5; beans, 2.5; and salted beef, 5.[66]

It proved impossible to construct a reliable price series for clothing. Nevertheless, it is possible to explore clothing costs anecdotally. Three court cases from the early 1780s provide evidence for plebeian clothing expenditures. A civil suit brought by a shoemaker seeking payment for shoes sold on credit included testimony about standard shoe prices. According to witnesses, shoes for an adult male sold for two pesos while women's shoes cost one peso, six reales, and shoes for an adolescent male cost one and a half pesos. Children's shoes cost five reales.[67] Evidence suggests that laborers in Buenos Aires often went barefoot or fashioned rough sandals or shoes from untanned leather in response to these relatively high prices.

The cost of a typical plebeian wardrobe seldom exceeded twenty-five pesos.[68] A representative wardrobe of a journeyman valued at seventeen and a half pesos included one pair of used shoes (worth twelve reales), one

FIGURE 22 Fishermen land their catch for delivery to Buenos Aires. Source: Emeric Essex Vidal, *Picturesque Illustrations of Buenos Ayres and Monte Video, Consisting of Twenty-four Views* (London: R. Ackermann, 1820).

sombrero (sixteen reales), one poncho (thirteen reales), one pair of wool socks (thirteen reales), two shirts (sixteen and eighteen reales), one vest (twenty-seven reales), one pair of pants (twenty reales), and a cloth cap (six reales).[69] To acquire this meager wardrobe a journeyman bricklayer earning the average daily wage in his trade needed to work eighteen days while an urban laborer needed to work seventy days. Many probate records noted that a decedent's clothing had no value, since working men and women wore their clothing until reduced to rags. The problems of hygiene and cleanliness are obvious. Alexander Gillespie, a British officer captured in 1806 but allowed to roam the city, noted in his memoir that "the poverty of the lower classes is always apparent in their garments, and their filth."[70] All contemporary evidence seems to corroborate this harsh judgment. In 1792 when a thief robbed a master hatter of "all his possessions," his cash, clothes, and tools, the court stipulated they were worth only thirty pesos.[71]

All economic historians concede that any cost of living index constructed for a historical population is necessarily an imperfect representation of the quality of material life. Nevertheless, an index of the cost of living remains

TABLE 6 Weighted cost of living index (1776 = 100)

Year	Index number	Year	Index number
1776	100	1794	85.2
1777	133.2	1795	109.5
1778	128.6	1796	129.3
1779	131.1	1797	125.4
1780	153	1798	114.4
1781	171	1799	112
1782	169.4	1800	129.4
1783	163	1801	153.8
1784	164.8	1802	130.8
1785	163.7	1803	240.6
1786	165.8	1804	240.9
1787	131.4	1805	224.3
1788	100.9	1806	205.4
1789	98.6	1807	189.2
1790	97.5	1808	173
1791	97.1	1809	157
1792	88.7	1810	173.7
1793	89	1811	190.1

Note: The following weights were assigned to the commodities found in table 4 and the rents found in table 5: wheat, 40; rice, 10; garbanzos, 2.5; yerba, 7.5; sugar, 5; porotos, 2.5; salted beef, 5; wine, 7.5; and rent, 20.

a valuable interpretive asset, since it provides the most reliable guide to how price changes impacted the lives of average people. As table 6 shows, the creation of the viceroyalty initiated a dramatic period of price inflation that peaked in 1781 with an index number of 171. The index then fell back gradually, returning in 1787 to approximately the level of 1777. Between 1788 and 1794 the index fell to its lowest levels in the late colonial period with 1794 providing the lowest index number. The remaining years of the colonial period experienced higher prices. Beginning in 1803, cost of living rose steeply in a period of brutal price inflation. Recovery from this event was inhibited by political and military crises initiated by the first British invasion and persisting through the wars of the independence era. Although this index ends with a decline from these unprecedented levels of high prices, the period-ending index numbers remained between 50 and 70 percent above the base year. These price increases powerfully affected plebeians, who were forced to adjust their diets.[72] Since traditional foods culturally identified as necessities provided a basic marker for quality of life, the upward inflection of prices was experienced as impoverishment as artisans and laborers liquidated scarce savings or resorted to loans to cover the shortfall.[73]

Changes in the crude death rate, or number of deaths per one thousand inhabitants, can suggest the social cost of high prices. When not distorted by epidemics, this statistic tends to directly reflect changes in the quality and availability of food supply. To limit the effects of epidemics, two eight-year cohorts were created to measure the impact of changes in the cost of living on mortality in Buenos Aires. I compared the 1788–1795 cohort, a period when the cost of living index was lowest, to the 1803–1810 cohort, when the index peaked. During the era of low prices the city's average crude death rate was 24.1 deaths per one thousand inhabitants per year. In the period of highest prices (an era of drought, monopolistic market practices, and political instability) the rate rose 43 percent to 34.4 deaths per one thousand inhabitants.[74]

Admissions to the Casa de Niños Expositos, the city's foundling hospital, corroborate the relationship between high prices and heavy social costs. In the period of low prices, 1788–1795, the hospital admitted an average of 85 abandoned children per year. During 1803–1810, when the cost of living index reached its highest levels, the admission of abandoned children leapt to 110 per year, an increase of 23 percent per year. During 1804 when the index reached its highest point the Casa de Niños Expositos admitted 120 abandoned children, leading the cabildo to condemn the increasingly common practice of abandoning children in the streets and other public places of the city.

Wealth, Material Culture, and the Colonial Economy

Low wages, unpredictable employment, and high prices ensnared the lives of most plebeians. Yet, while the struggle for food and shelter dominated the lives of so many, a minority of artisans and small-scale retailers were able to open shops or factories, purchase homes, and even accumulate silver plate, jewelry, and rich furnishing. What explains the different life trajectories of these plebeians? If we cannot track the material conditions experienced by the urban masses with complete confidence, we can illuminate the outlines of those lives elevated beyond mere necessity by an examination of surviving testaments and probate inventories.[75] These records necessarily serve as a more reliable guide to the lives of master artisans and the owners of bakeries and brickyards than to the lives of laborers. Although our analy-

sis must proceed with caution, these are very rich records that provide a remarkably detailed record of plebeian wealth holding and material culture
while at the same time providing access to details of the life cycle and economic decision making by both individuals and families.[76]

Average total physical wealth for this group, the combined value of all
assets except financial assets and obligations (credit and debt), was a surprisingly high 4,106 pesos. This average was influenced by the estates of a
small number of wealthy owners of factories. Median wealth, in this case a
better reflection of average experience, was a still substantial 1,907 pesos,
roughly four times the annual wage of a skilled journeyman carpenter or
stone mason in Buenos Aires. Since a well-paid carpenter could earn 420
pesos a year in late colonial Buenos Aires, a median estate value of 1,907
pesos suggests that we can confidently use this source to represent broad
experience. Table 7 displays the composition of the wealth of artisans and
small manufacturers, presenting mean values, high values, and the percentage of decedents without inventoried wealth. The table presents five
broad categories that are in turn broken down into narrower, more specific
subcategories. The table, for example, subdivides the category of producer
goods into tools, inventory, slaves, and livestock.

Putting aside for now a discussion of slave ownership, the most striking characteristic of table 7 is the low average values found for producer
goods. Given that master artisans and the owners of small manufacturing
enterprises were over represented in testaments and probate inventories and
given that the decedent population was older and therefore wealthier than
the general plebeian population, we must assume that the average value of
tools, inventory, and livestock represented in the table was actually lower
in the general plebeian population. The fact that 23 percent of the plebeians
found in these two sources did not own the tools they used in their trades
is remarkable. The average value of the tools owned by all decedents was
259 pesos, an amount that suggests the city's meager potential for economic
development in the late colonial period. Among those with tools, the vast
majority had only simple hand tools. Table 7 overstates the average value of
tools owned by artisans and other skilled manual laborers since the handful of relatively costly mills, ovens, and related equipment used by millers,
bakers, and brick and adobe makers elevated the average. Among artisans in skilled indoor trades (tailors, shoemakers, and silversmiths among
others) the average value of tools and equipment was less than 70 pesos. The

TABLE 7 Composition of private wealth: artisans of Buenos Aires (values in pesos of eight reales)

		Mean	High value	Percentage with zero
I	Producer goods	1,039	8,184	9
	(a+b+c+d)			
a.	Tools	259	5,000	23
b.	Inventory	238	2,468	63
c.	Slaves	505	2,755	36
d.	Livestock	18	730	89
II	Real estate	2,852	22,442	38
	(e+f+g+h)			
e.	Residence	2,310	17,773	38
f.	Business	168	3,450	88
g.	Rental property	327	12,856	91
h.	Rural property	48	1,356	91
III	Consumer goods	215	1,779	34
	(i+j+k+l)			
i	Household goods	120	1,179	42
j	Clothing	34	451	58
k	Jewelry	20	726	92
l	Silverware	40	963	75
IV	Financial assets	694	18,332	79
	(m+n)			
m	Cash	323	17,362	82
n	Claims	371	5,931	74
V	Financial liabilities	705	24,100	69

Total physical wealth (I+ II+ III): mean = 4,106 pesos and median = 1,907 pesos

*If the high value of 17,362 pesos is removed the average value for cash in the estates of decedent artisans falls to 140 pesos, a more representative estimation.
**If the high value of 24,100 pesos is removed, the average financial liability of decedent artisans is reduced to 487 pesos.

technological primitiveness and small scale of manufacturing for colonial Buenos Aires is clear.

Inventory, the combined value of finished goods and raw materials, averaged 238 pesos, and the individual high value was 2,468 pesos. Both the low average value and the relatively small high value were predictable given the low levels of investment in tools and equipment. More startling is that 63 percent of all master artisans and manufacturers had no inventory, no raw materials or finished goods, on hand at the time of their deaths. This is the very definition of hand-to-mouth production. The general poverty of this class of small manufacturers and skilled wage earners and the low levels of consumer demand noted earlier all help to explain the small amount of capital invested in inventory, but the more important explanation is found in the structural marginality and unpredictability of local and regional markets that discouraged any accumulation of inventory or raw materials.[77]

The low average value for livestock and the absence of any livestock in the inventories of 89 percent of working-class decedents are predictable in a city with no heavy industry.[78] With the exception of the grinding wheels used by millers there was no need for animal traction. Most porteño artisans and small manufacturers only used livestock to transport themselves or their goods. As a result, the only large investments in livestock were found in the estates of those involved in milling, brick and adobe making, and cartage. In fact, very few urban manufacturers produced goods on a scale that made the ownership of wagons and animals practical. When animals (and carts) were needed to move goods, they could be rented at low cost.[79]

The sources indicate that 20 percent of all artisans and small manufacturers had neither tools nor inventory or livestock and only 18 percent of all artisans had tools and inventory appraised in excess of five hundred pesos. It might be argued that the accumulation of five hundred pesos or more of producer goods represented a substantial amount in a city where few skilled wage earners had annual earnings of more than two hundred pesos. Yet we must recognize the extremely limited production potential represented by an average investment of this scale in manufacturing. The structural problem imposed on the economy by this level of investment in producer goods is obvious. Even if consumer demand for local manufactures increased as a result of increases in average earnings, rising population, or through a disruption in the supply of imported goods due to blockades or other external forces, the city's artisan and manufacturing sectors would have been unable to respond effectively with increased production. This was a city that relied on hand tools, a city that multiplied its production through the slow and costly process of purchasing and training slaves or, less typically, by adding apprentices to the artisan workforce.

There was a complex relationship between the financial resources of this class and its willingness to invest in increased production. It is clear that investment in producer goods did not increase proportionally as the capital resources of plebeians grew. In fact, 30 percent of artisans and manufacturers with estates worth ten thousand pesos or more owned less than two hundred pesos in producer goods. Put another way, decedents whose total estates were valued at less than one thousand pesos had 67 percent of their estates invested in tools, inventory, and raw materials, while those with estates worth more than five thousand pesos averaged only 25 percent. This suggests that as the wealth of the most-skilled plebeians increased, they diverted capital away from tools, machinery, and inventory and toward consumption or investments in other physical assets. Their most likely purchases were slaves and real estate.

Among the most prosperous plebeians, master artisans and owners of bakeries, brickyards, and small foundries, the ownership of slaves was very common. The average value of slave property owned by this group was slightly more than five hundred pesos, twice the amount invested in tools. Representing 48 percent of the total value of producer goods, slaves made up the second largest component of wealth, only surpassed in value by real estate. While slaves were found in at least 20 percent of the inventories for artisans in indoor and outdoor trades, every baker and every owner of a factory or brickyard owned slaves. Among the members of this wealthy strata an average of 25 percent of all wealth, or approximately one thousand pesos, was invested in slave property.

In fact ownership of two or more slaves was more common than the ownership of a single slave. While 36 percent of slave owners owned a single slave, 43 percent owned between two and five slaves, and 21 percent owned between six and twelve slaves. Even among relatively poor artisans, the ownership of two or more slaves was not uncommon. The master carpenter Isidro Gonzales, for example, owned three slaves valued at 770 pesos, a sum that accounted for nearly 80 percent of his total estate at the time of his death.[80] Andres Vibas, the native-born owner of a brickyard, had the largest slave holding among probated artisans, twelve slaves valued at 2,690 pesos.[81]

One of the few heavy industries in colonial Buenos Aires, a bronze foundry owned by the merchant Estevan Villanueva, illustrates clearly the deep interconnection between slavery and industry. On the eve of his marriage to the widow Dionicia López in 1788, his factory and other possessions were inventoried and appraised. It is clear both from the long list of Villanueva's customers and his wealthy and powerful creditors that this foundry was a substantial enterprise. Goods produced by Villanueva in Buenos Aires were wholesaled to merchants in the interior cities of Córdoba, Tucumán, and Salta as well as distant Peru. The volume of sales outside Buenos Aires is suggested by the debt of nearly three thousand pesos owed to Villanueva by customers in these distant markets. Although Villanueva was not a typical manufacturer, we can see in his enterprise the benefits and the limits imposed by dependence on slaves.

Although primarily a bronze foundry, the factory also produced iron, brass, tin, and lead products. Among the many goods inventoried were products for the rural market (stirrups, spurs, bells for oxen, shovels, and pitch forks) and for urban consumers (cooking grills, chocolate makers, metal buttons, and tools like mason's plumbs and hammers). The inventory, both raw materials and finished goods, and all the tools and equipment had a combined value of 3,503 pesos, a sum that would have placed Villanueva's factory among the most heavily capitalized manufacturers found in Buenos Aires.

Villanueva had no training in metallurgy and exercised no direct supervision of the factory. From the least-skilled laborer to the factory supervisor the entire workforce was made up of slaves. Effective control was exercised by two slaves that were master artisans, Domingo, who made molds and supervised the preparation of the metal, and Estevan, who supervised the finishing process, including soldering, filing, and polishing. These skilled slaves directed the labor of eight additional slaves who worked in the factory. Another slave, the mulatto Juan Blas, traveled on his own to interior cities selling the factory's products. At the time of the inventory Blas was absent in Lima representing Villanueva. Among the eight slaves employed in the foundry were six journeymen (one lame), two laborers, and a cook. The total workforce was valued at 2,895 pesos, or 45 percent of the total value of the foundry business.[82] Both the size of Villanueva's slave workforce and its focused specialization were unusual but not unique. Earlier in the viceregal period the Catalonian immigrant Tomás Batlla had also built a successful bronze foundry. When he died his will provided that his slaves continue to operate the foundry until his eldest son gained his majority.[83]

It was more common for artisans and small manufacturers to purchase slaves to achieve a complex matrix of business and personal objectives. As noted above, the silversmith Juan Antonio Callejas y Sandoval owned nine slaves. Four of the slaves he owned were trained as journeymen silversmiths and worked at his side, and two others worked as laborers in construction.

This mix of skilled artisans, unskilled laborers, and household slaves was fairly common among the slave owners of this class.[84] One of the city's wealthiest and most respected barber surgeons Tiburcio López de Heredia, for example, owned six slaves, including two journeymen who worked in his shop, two adult males without clear occupations, and an adult female and her young child.[85] Female household slaves were even common in the estates of Spanish immigrants who owned little real property. This suggests that slave ownership was also a type of conspicuous consumption; the maintenance of a "decent" household signaled to neighbors by the presence of servants often proved more attractive than did investments in real estate or producer goods. Many slave owners, in fact, were only able to purchase slaves by borrowing the purchase price, a sometimes dangerous expedient. José Yanes, a modestly successful baker, employed four male slaves in his business. All these slaves had been purchased with money borrowed from a local merchant at 5 percent. When he died unexpectedly in 1800, his wife was left encumbered with substantial debt and few prospects.[86]

Without modern social guarantees such as life insurance and social assistance programs, better-off plebeians sought to provide for their family's future by purchasing and training male slaves who could provide heirs with a dependable source of income. The candlemaker José Melendez, for example, owned little more than his tools, clothing, and a few chairs, an estate worth less than 100 pesos. Yet, he also owned a slave, a twenty-year-old journeyman candlemaker. Melendez's will required this slave to maintain the business and complete the training of a free apprentice who was in the second year of a four year contract. In his testament Melendez promised the slave future manumission if he provided ten additional years of faithful service to his widow and children.[87] Poorer artisans sometimes purchased a slave or slaves in partnership with workmates or local merchants. The master armorer Francisco Ibárzabal purchased the slave Pablo in equal partnership with the merchant Manuel Rivera for 325 pesos. Once trained as an apprentice in Ibárzabal's trade, Pablo's future wages were divided between the two investors with a larger share granted the armorer in recognition of the cost of training.[88]

Real estate absorbed a substantial portion of the capital accumulated by the city's artisans and manufacturers. Among those probated, 62 percent owned real estate with an average value of nearly three thousand pesos. Real estate was the most important wealth component for members of the skilled working class, greater by a factor of ten than investment in tools and equipment and nearly three times larger than the investment in all producer goods (tools, inventory, slaves, and livestock). Examined as an aggregate component, real estate represented 60 percent of total wealth.[89] Among decedents who owned some real estate, 44 percent owned real estate valued at less than two thousand pesos. Less than 10 percent owned real estate worth more then ten thousand pesos. The five wealthiest members of this group had accumulated real estate holdings worth fifteen thousand pesos or more, a very substantial amount, similar in scale to the property owned by colonial bureaucrats and military officers. The importance of real estate was closely associated with net worth, with 76 percent of those with net worth in excess of five thousand pesos having 60 percent of their assets in real estate.

The baker Pedro Palavecino, one of the richest artisans in colonial Buenos Aires, left an estate appraised at 44,109 pesos in 1799. His wealth compared favorably with the estates of high-level colonial officials and all but the richest export merchants. Real estate represented 50 percent of his total wealth. At the time of his death Palavecino no longer owned a bakery, having retired from active business. However, he continued to earn substantial rental income from two large apartment houses appraised at 5,435 pesos and 7,421 pesos. Court-appointed appraisers valued his personal residence at 8,586 pesos.[90] Although the value of Palavecino's real estate investments was unusually large, the proportional significance of real estate in his holdings was common among members of the skilled working class. The criollo brickmaker Ramón Saran, for example, owned real estate that included a residence (4,448 pesos), a rental property (2,394 pesos), and his brickyard (1,955 pesos).[91] In this case, 88 percent of net worth was accounted for by real estate holdings. The purchase of a private residence was the most common form of real estate investment. Among decedents, 62 percent owned their residence, making this the third most common form of property after tools and slaves. The mean value of plebeian residences was 2,310 pesos. The median value of 672 pesos was closer to common experience where humble adobe ranchos on the periphery far outnumbered brick residences near the city center. In 1779, the shoemaker Antonio Rodríguez left an estate appraised at 1,713 pesos, a few hundred pesos more than the median value of an estate for the men and women of this class. His home, a straw-roofed adobe rancho built on the edge of the city was worth only 104 pesos.[92] By way of contrast, the most expensive private residence, valued at 17,773 pesos, was owned by the carpenter Joaquin Estevez de la Cruz, a Portuguese immigrant.[93]

The material poverty of the plebe is best illustrated by the low average value of consumer goods found in their probate inventories. More than half of probated plebeians (56 percent) owned less than a hundred pesos in clothing and household possessions at the time of their deaths. Despite the fact that some members of the working class had accumulated estates of considerable value, only 19 percent of all decedents had accumulated consumer goods worth four hundred pesos or more. Even among the wealthiest artisans and manufacturers, those with a net worth of more than one thousand pesos, 36 percent had consumer goods worth less than one hundred pesos. Sometimes appraisers specifically stated that the decedent's clothing had no monetary value because it was so old or in such poor condition that it could not be sold.

Few owned basic household goods like furniture, cooking utensils, and crockery, and only a minority of these owned trunks and boxes to store their clothes and other personal goods. The average probate value for household goods was 120 pesos and the median value 45 pesos. The furniture of the bricklayer Manuel Ortega was appraised at 50 pesos. It included a trunk, two rough tables, six painted chairs, six unfinished chairs, four small benches, three old shelves, a large ceramic pot, two wooden barrels, and a handful of kitchen utensils.[94] Even fairly affluent artisans seldom owned more than a handful of household goods. The silversmith Manuel Antonio Pimienta, for example, left a substantial estate that included six slaves, but his furniture was appraised at less than 100 pesos. He owned a round table, eight chairs, a cedar chest, a leather trunk, a jewelry box, and three religious objects.[95]

A web of debts and loans bound plebeians together and in turn connected them to other sectors of the urban community. A surprisingly large group of decedents, 82 percent, had no cash at the time of their deaths, and only 26 percent of decedents were owed money by others. Most lived close to the economic margin, compelled to spend nearly all of their earnings to cover immediate needs.[96] Few had savings other than the equity accumulated in real estate or slaves. A single wealthy artisan who had been liquidating assets as he prepared to return to Europe died with 17,000 pesos in cash, inflating the average cash for the entire group to 323 pesos.[97] By removing this exceptional case, the average cash reserves for all plebeians fell to 140 pesos, a figure more in agreement with the other measures of economic well-being found in our analysis.

Although petty debts were a common feature of everyday life, 70 percent of those probated died without outstanding debts. This may be because members of this class attempted to reduce debt as the end of life approached or because heirs of the very poor disposed of possessions and debts outside the probate process. Through most of their lives plebeians were enmeshed in complex webs of petty financial obligations. Many customers bought the products of shoemakers, silversmiths, tailors, and other artisans on credit. Artisans then carried these small debts for terms of days, weeks, or even months. Master artisans often advanced wages to their journeymen or even to apprentices as they neared the end of their probationary terms. Laborers in small factories, cart drivers, and unskilled construction workers routinely borrowed from their employers against future earnings whenever they confronted some extraordinary financial obligation like the cost of medicine, baptism, or burial costs or the need to recover from a period of unemployment. In a city with a tight labor supply employers saw these small loans as a means for attracting and keeping workers. Workmates and neighbors could often be counted on to cover the cost of food or drink with a small loan. When unable to repay a loan secured by his tools, an artisan could face lost employment opportunities or the need to rent tools and thus diminished wages.[98] In the case of a master artisan the loss of tools could lead to employment as a journeyman, a humiliating loss of status and income.

In 1790 Francisco Baquero, the casta master shoemaker who would become leader of the pardo and moreno guild effort, was arrested and jailed for an unpaid debt of eighty-one pesos and four reales owed to his former journeyman Mariano López. After seven days in jail Baquero gained his release by citing a *cédula* of 1786 that prohibited authorities from arresting artisans or seizing their tools for debts. This proved only a temporary victory, and Baquero was eventually required to repay the full amount plus court costs. Testimony made Baquero's obligation clear, and the ultimate legal victory of the creditor was never in doubt. But the highly personal confrontation between this master and journeyman usefully reminds us that debt held the potential to overturn colonial expectations of deference and subordination associated with craft rank.

Mariano López had recently left the Spanish Navy in Buenos Aires with the eighty-one pesos and four reales in previously unpaid wages. Already working for Baquero and living in his home, López agreed to loan this windfall for a term of four months to the master he so completely depended upon. Baquero failed to repay on time, attempting to deflect López's entreaties by questioning the terms of the agreement and claiming that the cost of the journeyman's room and board as well as a charge for using borrowed tools should be deducted from the debt total. That is, Baquero attempted to thwart López's demand for repayment by reminding him of his dependence and inferiority. López responded as a creditor, not as a journeyman shoemaker, and changed the nature of the conflict, using a campaign of shame and intimidation to force payment of the debt. He used the court to compel the testimony of a series of master shoemakers who would disseminate news of Baquero's embarrassing circumstances to others in the trade. He simultaneously sought to force repayment by a series of carefully staged face-to-face confrontations calculated to humiliate Baquero in front of his family and neighbors, even flashing a knife in the street in front of Baquero's shop. In the end, the courts accommodated López, but along the way he had taken every opportunity to mobilize public opinion to his benefit, making clear the potential costs to reputation and community status of ill-considered debts.[99]

Nevertheless, access to credit eased the flow of daily life and carried plebeians through periods of unemployment or other difficulties. The account books of *pulperos* always carried scores of small debts that facilitated the purchases of the urban poor. In many ways these obligations sorted out and organized the social fabric of the plebeian world. As a result, it is not surprising that the more affluent members of this class, master artisans, petty shopkeepers, and owners of bakeries were owed 371 pesos on average at the time of death. Most of these debts were for less than 5 pesos. Although most plebeians received and offered credit in small amounts and for short terms, some master artisans and small manufacturers required significant credit. The average debt found for the men and women in the probate records was 705 pesos, but the debt of a single baker who had borrowed 24,100 pesos inflated this average.[100] If we remove this exceptional case, average debt was a still-substantial 487 pesos. Access to credit was one of the most important predictors of material success, as nearly every estate appraised at 1,000 pesos or more included significant debt.

Immigrants generally had greater access to credit then did the native born as is indicated in the probates. Immigrants were also wealthier on average than the native born, and we must assume that their enhanced ability to borrow helped fuel the relative success of immigrants. Although the native-born members of this class could rely on family and friends, probate records suggest that large loans were more readily available to immigrants. While only 13 percent of native-born artisans had outstanding loans of more than two thousand pesos, nearly 28 percent of immigrants had borrowed similar amounts. In fact, many of the loans of one thousand pesos or more were contracted in Europe prior to emigration.[101] Preferential access to the substantial credit needed to open a bakery and acquire the slave workforce common to this industry explains better than any other factor the rapid takeover of the local baking industry by Spanish immigrants in the 1790s. This advantage also benefited immigrants in other plebeian industries where borrowed capital could provide a clear competitive edge, like the Villanueva bronze foundry. As a result, the net wealth of Spanish immigrants, indeed European immigrants generally, was approximately 40 percent greater than that of the native born.

The Social Determinants of Success

Estimates of average wealth for a series of social, occupational, and demographic categories are provided in table 8. As we can see there was little difference in wealth between the indoor trades (like shoemakers, silversmiths, tailors, and sailmakers) and the outdoor trades (like carpenters, blacksmiths, and bricklayers).[102] Manufacturers (owners of bakeries, brickyards, and foundries), few of whom were trained as artisans, enjoyed a demonstrated advantage relative to both traditionally skilled artisan groups. Entrepreneurial skills, not craft skill, supported the upper ends of this class. In fact many of the most successful, wealthiest artisans in Buenos Aires had left their crafts behind through investment in a completely new field.

Very few of the working-class testators with estates worth more than a thousand pesos remained within the narrow boundaries of their crafts throughout their working lives. The pursuit of traditional artisan career objectives, the perfection of specialized manual skills and promotion within the craft hierarchy, were not objectives likely to produce substantial material rewards in colonial Buenos Aires. A minority of men and women in the class of skilled manual workers did acquire substantial wealth by turning away from artisan manufacture. Many abandoned their trades completely in order to pursue more profitable enterprises. Jacobo Padín, an immigrant

FIGURE 23 A cart from the city's slaughter yard location on the outskirts of the city delivers beef to the butchers in the Plaza Mayor. Source: Gregorio Ibarra, *Trajes y Costumbres de la Provincia de Buenos Aires* (Buenos Aires: César Hippolyte Bacle y compania, 1833).

combmaker from Galicia, noted in his will that he no longer owned the tools of his trade and had not maintained a shop since he purchased a small fruit farm owned previously by the Jesuits. He then expanded his agricultural pursuits by acquiring a large farm where he grew peaches for the urban market.[103] More typically, however, artisans and other skilled workers maintained some connection with their crafts while pursuing new interests in agriculture or commerce. The blacksmith Juan Ygnacio de Echeberria, a Basque immigrant, retained a substantial involvement in his trade, maintaining a shop that employed two slaves trained as journeymen, but he also earned income from a ship employed in the profitable grain trade with interior provinces.[104]

Although this form of career crossover was common, there were some artisans who entered a new skilled trade, most commonly through the purchase of a skilled slave or the hiring of free craftsmen to run the new business. For example, the Galician immigrant Joseph Gómez Belmundes owned one of the city's most successful brick factories.[105] In his testament he indicated that he was also the owner of a silversmith's shop run by a slave who was a master silversmith. The specialized tools and inventory of this second undertaking were worth six hundred pesos. This process of diversification was not limited to the wealthiest members of the working class. Roque Antonio Angelino, an impoverished criollo blacksmith, described in his testament a pathetic personal estate that he estimated at less than a hundred pesos. It included a "few tools" embargoed by the local court in an unsettled civil suit and a small stock of dry goods worth a few pesos that he traded in the outlying hamlets of the region in partnership with a mulatto woman.[106] It is among the wealthiest members of this class that entrepreneurial diversification is clearest. The criollo blacksmith Francisco Abrego, for example, accumulated a substantial rural estate that included more than six thousand head of cattle and seventy oxen. Remaining involved on a daily basis in his original occupation, Abrego left his profitable rural enterprise in the hands of three slaves.[107]

Among plebeians found in probate records, women had a slight wealth advantage over men, but this advantage resulted from the statistical impact of two large estates. The fact that there was no clear disadvantage in average wealth found among women resulted from the common practice of widows running shops and factories after the deaths of husbands or fathers. Basilia Antonia Pinto, the widow of Miguel Alcaraz, continued to run the family carpentry business after her husband's death. When she died in 1785 she left a substantial estate worth 8,751 pesos that included a home worth 6,656 pesos and tools and inventory worth another 235 pesos. Her enterprise depended in large measure on the skills of four male slaves trained as carpenters by her husband before his death.[108] The more modest circumstances of Francisca Salinas provide a better guide to the place of women in this largely masculine corner of the colonial economy. Francisca had inherited a brickyard upon her husband's death a decade earlier, and she left behind an estate of 1,409 pesos after her own death in 1808. More than half of this total was inventory and the value of an elderly slave, appraised at 95 pesos, who made the bricks.[109]

As indicated in table 8, family transfers of wealth (dowries, inheritances, and gifts) exercised a powerful influence on the ways that the colonial economy allocated opportunity and success to plebeians. These transfers came in many forms: cash, goods, and property among others. The most important forms of property redistributed among family members were real estate and slaves. Both of these assets had the potential to multiply in value and effi-

TABLE 8 Average wealth of artisans by occupation, birthplace, age, sex, and family wealth transfers

Occupation	N	Average wealth
Indoor trades	26	3,810
Outdoor trades	42	3,849
Manufacturers	17	5,498
Birthplace		
Native born	46	3,223
Spainish	22	5,448
Other immigrants	17	5,064
Age		
20 and under	24	1,154
21 to 50	27	6,542
Over 50	34	4,408
Sex		
Male	75	4,141
Female	10	4,365
Family transfer		
None	69	3,602
Up to 2,000 pesos	12	4,091
More than 2,000	4	14,144

Note: Total wealth does not include cash, credits, or debt.

cacy over time. Among plebeians probated, transfers of up to two thousand pesos produced on average a wealth premium of roughly 12 percent relative to those plebeians who had received no help from their families. Transfers of more than two thousand pesos, on the other hand, produced the remarkable wealth premium of 70 percent, lifting this privileged group of plebeians above their peers. For example, Rafael Salomón, a very successful baker who made his fortune in Buenos Aires after emigrating from Cádiz, used his native-born wife's substantial inheritance of four thousand pesos to begin his business.[110] Francisco Ibárzabal, an illiterate journeyman armorer employed by the local Spanish garrison, had arrived in Buenos Aires penniless and without the tools of his trade. Forced to work as a laborer, he had improved his circumstances when he married Catalina, the widow of another armorer who had inherited her husband's tools. This small inheritance lifted the two from penury and gave Ibárzabal the chance to open his independent shop where he employed his slave also trained in this craft.[111] Thomas Batlla had emigrated from Cataluña while his wife Raimunda Maléz remained in Spain. He used her modest inheritance of one hundred Catalan *libras* to establish a small bronze foundry that would serve as the basis of his fortune.[112] In his will he asked his executors to keep the foundry open by using four skilled slaves he had trained to sustain his family.

Real estate was one of the most common forms of parental inheritance, typically the inheritance of the family residence or some portion of its value, if executors sold the property to satisfy the claims of creditors or to divide among heirs. The brickmaker Juan Verois benefited twice from this form of intergenerational transfer. His wife inherited a small house from her parent's estate, selling it later and using the capital to expand her husband's brickyard. Verois himself then inherited a small fruit farm on the outskirts of the city from his mother's estate.[113] The combination of these two inheritances propelled the couple into competition for the leadership of their industry. Antonio de Costa, a carpenter born in Lisbon, made a similarly fortunate match with the creole daughter of a colonial official, Francisca Gutierrez. She entered their marriage with more than a thousand pesos in goods and cash and then inherited five hundred pesos in back salary owed to her father by the Royal Treasury.[114]

Conclusion

The research presented here illuminates the material context of plebeian life in late colonial Buenos Aires. The prices of fundamental staples experienced both short-term cyclical changes and a powerful long-term upward trend, especially in the last decade of colonial period. The small enterprises that employed most plebeians were dependent on limited credit mechanisms dominated by merchants and, on a smaller scale, by family. While credit was available to the poor as well as to the rich, it is clear that the limited nature and relatively high cost of credit, especially for loans of five hundred pesos or more, limited the ability of artisans and small-scale manufacturers to purchase the equipment, raw materials, and, in the case of slaves, labor necessary to increase production or achieve greater productivity and efficiency.

The analysis of wealth holding reveals the complex ways that the wage labor and petty entrepreneurial activity of plebeians interacted with this colonial economy, which was increasingly integrated in the Atlantic market. The importance of inheritance, investment in real estate and slaves, as well as the apparently negligible influence of occupational identity and ethnicity on material success suggests important differences between this viceregal capital and the longer established capitals of Lima and Mexico City. Buenos Aires was not only a newer capital but, in the terms of the late eighteenth century, it was a more modern city as well. The absence of guilds left artisans with few protections but allowed the more entrepreneurial members of this class to enter the market at the wholesale level. This minority, in trades as diverse as baking and shoemaking, increased production by purchasing slaves or hiring more journeymen and then sold their products at a discount to retailers. Credit made expansion possible and the most successful artisans had become very rich relative to their class.

7 | Working-Class Wages, Earnings, and the Organization of Urban Work

On Monday February 15, 1787, the journeyman bricklayer Josef Silva awakened before dawn with the stirring of workmates with whom he shared a room behind the stables near Plaza Nueva. The city government temporarily employed Silva and his two roommates to make repairs on a decrepit apartment block seized from the Jesuits twenty years earlier when that Catholic order was expelled from the city.[1] Like most laboring men, Silva and his roommates started the workday at sunrise, but this week they would not begin work until Wednesday morning. This was not an unusual pattern in late-colonial Buenos Aires.

We do not know what these three men did during their two-day hiatus from the cabildo's employment records, but contemporary records suggest that they likely had accumulated enough money to pass a few days of leisure rather than return to work. For most single, laboring men, leisure meant time spent at a neighborhood *pulpería* or tavern drinking and gambling. These venues of masculine sociability offered *canchas de bolos*, card tables, and cheap drink.[2] Once savings were exhausted, Silva and his roommates would return to work almost certain of finding employment.

This case provides a useful reminder of how a competitive labor market could create a space within which workingmen and women might occasionally assert autonomy, taking pleasure from their ability to hold the demands of employers at arm's length. Silva and other single journeymen typically shared housing with other laborers and lived from day to day on their wages. Their combined property seldom exceeded a few shirts and the wooden utensils they used for cooking and eating. Yet many felt they could afford to stay away from work, drinking and gaming without serious consequence. Strong labor demand and rising wages in late colonial Buenos Aires meant that Silva and others could exercise considerable independence. In a hierarchical society that was predictably dismissive of plebeian culture and increasingly willing to use force to compel regular employment and a reliable labor supply, the decision to stay in bed or to walk away from an abusive employer could be a liberating exercise in autonomy.[3]

Although there are some exceptions, few historians of colonial Spanish America have engaged the plebeian masses in ways that effectively illuminate the daily lives of laboring men like Silva.[4] As a result the dense matrix of distinctions and classifications that arranged the lives of the plebe, guiding marriage choices, family and household organizations, and employment patterns, are lost. These distinctions were not mere artifacts of decisions made by colonial bureaucrats or elite prejudices; in essential ways plebeians created these distinctions and fiercely defended them when the workings of the colonial economy or the enthusiasms or prejudices of elite reformers threatened to alter or eliminate them. Despite the rich literature produced over the last three decades by historians of the Spanish colonies, we know surprisingly little about the ways in which plebeians interacted with the economic forces that affected Spanish America's late colonial era.[5]

My assumption is that daily labor (the search for work, the mastery of tools and the acquisition of skills, the daily rhythm of the workplace, and wages as well as the networks of sociability established through work) provided the essential context within which the urban masses of Spanish America lived their lives. If we reveal this world, we will restore in some measure the full complexity of these lives.[6] In pursuit of these objectives I reconstruct the history of wages, earnings, and employment patterns for late colonial Buenos Aires. This effort culminates with an examination of real wages that suggests that the economic and political crises of the last decades of the colonial era had a powerful effect on the plebeians of Buenos Aires, disturbing or subverting long-established hierarchies and forcing a broad experimentation in economic and political behavior.

Wages, Occupations, and Skills

In colonial Buenos Aires important differences in levels of income and quality of material life not only distinguished trades from one another but

FIGURE 24 An early-nineteenth-century watercolor of the Plaza Mayor. The Recova bisected the plaza and provided numerous locations for artisan shops and small retail establishments.
Source: C. E. Pellegrini, *Recuerdos del Río de la Plata* (Buenos Aires: Libreria L'Amateur, 1969). Published with the permission of the publisher, Libraría L'Amateur, Buenos Aires.

also distinguished the capacities and experiences of individuals employed in the same trade. These consequential differences were clearly visible within every shop or work site. Historians have sensibly presumed that the employment histories and income levels of master artisans were distinct from those of apprentices and journeymen, but the actual scale of these differences has never been examined systematically. Across occupational lines the pattern of these differences is less clear. Could journeymen in some crafts earn more than masters in others? Did changes in the demand for specialized skills produce steady employment in some crafts while artisans and laborers in other crafts experienced unemployment or underemployment? Were trends in the wages of the skilled and unskilled similar? Were the profits of master artisans who sold directly to clients or to wholesalers similar to the earnings of masters who worked for wages in the public sector?

Students of colonial Spanish America have generally ignored this intersection of social and economic history or treated it anecdotally.[7] In fact, the importance of free labor in the economy of colonial Spanish America remains largely unexplored. Complex and persistent mechanisms of discrimination and the expanding use of slave labor framed the experience of the Buenos Aires plebe, but market forces were often as influential in constructing the complex social stratification of this class. Historians have not adequately acknowledged the importance of the economy in forming colonial, social relations at the level of the plebe.[8] One result is that historians have often corroborated rather than challenged the presumed social potency of racial hierarchies asserted in the *régimen de castas* or used in the workings of the colonial bureaucracy. The most common interpretive models incline historians toward either an undifferentiated subaltern reality based on economic exploitation or a differentiated subaltern hierarchy based on color and ethnicity.

In Buenos Aires the Spanish colonial government was the most important employer of artisans and laborers in the building trades. The account books of the Royal Treasury offer comprehensive and uniform accounts of wages for skilled artisans as well as laborers in the building trades throughout the late colonial period.[9] These same records also include wage and employment records for other skilled crafts like caulkers, ship carpenters, armorers, and sailmakers, as well as for less skilled groups like common seamen and laborers. The cabildo and the city's many religious establishments also hired large numbers of artisans and laborers for shorter periods of time for street paving or for construction projects. The wage series analyzed here derive from all three sources.[10]

Table 9 displays the median wages (midpoint in the distribution of wages) for ten plebeian occupations for the period 1770–1815.[11] Eight occupations received daily wages while two occupations, seamen and rural laborers, generally received a monthly wage. In addition to cash wages, some workers received food, drink, and housing as partial compensation. For example, in 1805 fourteen men employed by the municipality to haul stone to build a wharf received approximately seven reales a month in food in addition to their wages.[12] Alternatively, a smaller number of colonial artisans and laborers received cash supplements to help pay for food. After 1781 sailors employed by the Spanish Crown received a food stipend of three pesos per month in addition to cash wages. In table 9 and in subsequent calculations these sums are simply added to the cash wage figure, since workers could spend them at their discretion.

The table provides strong evidence that wages in the late colonial period fluctuated in predictable ways with changes in supply and demand. Demo-

TABLE 9 Median wages of urban workers in selected occupations, 1770–1815

Year	Carpenters	Brick-layers	Black-smiths	Caulkers	Ship carpenters	Sailmakers	Armorers	Sailors	Urban laborers	Rural laborers
	reales per day	reales per day	reales per day	reales per day	reales per day	reales per day	reales per day	pesos per month	reales per day	pesos per month
1770	10	8	6	18	18	8	7	8	4	6
1771	10	8	6	18	18	8		8	4	6
1772	10	8	6	18	18	8		8	4	6
1773	10	4	6	18	18	8		8	4	6
1774	10	4	6	18	18	8		8	4	6
1775	8	4	6	18	18	10	3	8	2	6
1776	8	4	6	18	18	8	3	8	2	6
1777	8	4	6	18	18	8	3	8	2	6
1778	8	4	6	18	18	8	3	8	2	6
1779	8	4	6	18	18	8		8	2	6
1780	8	6	6	18	18	8	3	11*	2	6
1781	8	4		18	18	8	3	11	2	6
1782	8	4		18	18	8		11	2	6
1783	8	4		18	18	8		11	2	6
1784	8	4		18	18			11	2	7
1785	8	4	8	18	18	8		11	2	6
1786	8	4	8	18	18			11	2	6
1787	8	4	8	18	18	8		11	2	6
1788	8	4	8	18	18	8		11	2	6
1789	8	4	8	18	18	8		11	2	7
1790	8	4	8	18	18	8		11	2	6
1791	8	4	8	18	18				2	7
1792	8	4	8	18	18				2	7
1793	8	4	8	18	18			11	2	7
1794	8	4	8	18	18	8		11	2	7
1795	8	4	8	18	18			11	2	7
1796	8	4	8	18	18	8	5	11	2	7
1797	8	4	8	18	18	8	5	11	2	7.5
1798	8	4	8	18	18	8	5	11	2.5	7.5
1799	8	4	8	18	18		5	11	3	7
1800	8	4	8	18	18	8	5	11	2.5	7
1801	8	4	8	18	18	8	5	11	3	7
1802	8		8	18	18	8		11	3	7
1803	8	4	8	18	18	8		13	3	7
1804	8	4	8	18	18	8	5	13	3	7
1805		4	8	18	18	8		13	4	7
1806	10	5	8	18	18	8	8	13	4	8
1807		5	8	18	16		8	13	4	8
1808		5	8	16	16	8	10	13	4	8
1809	10	5	8				10		4	8
1810	10	5	8		16	8	10	13	5	8
1811	10	5	8	16	16	8	10	13	5	12
1812	10	5	8	16	16	8	10	13	5	12
1813	10	5	8	16	16		10		5	
1814	10	5	8	16		8	10	13	5	
1815	10	5	8	16	16		10	13	5	10

*Eight pesos per month plus three additional pesos for food.

graphic forces, changes in port activity, altered commercial relations with the interior, and political and military events all influenced the local labor market. These large forces affected each occupation differently, producing a series of distinct wage histories. Skilled workers in the outdoor trades (carpenters, bricklayers, masons, and blacksmiths) experienced less wage volatility than did less skilled urban and rural laborers, *jornaleros* or *peones*. During the last decade of the colonial period, however, laborers enjoyed the upside of this volatility, gaining higher percentage wage increases than did those in more prestigious skilled occupations.

Unlike other occupations, the three port-related trades found in these records, caulkers, ship carpenters, and sailmakers, remained nearly immune from the effects of these economic and political forces. Throughout this period they remained the best-paid wage workers in the city. When Spanish authorities created the new viceroyalty to thwart Portuguese ambitions in the region they needed to develop port services capable of sustaining a larger naval presence. The imperial government therefore recruited nearly all members of these trades in Spain, inducing them to emigrate by wage premiums and long-term contracts. As a result, the wage levels of the caulkers and ship carpenters were equal to or higher than the salaries of most lower-level colonial bureaucrats and junior level officers in the Spanish army.[13] A journeyman caulker who worked 245 days in 1787, for example, earned more than a doctor of canon law employed by the Cathedral Chapter of Buenos Aires and most of the officials employed by the Royal Treasury.[14] This pattern stood Spanish social presumptions on their head and must have produced deep resentments.

If combined, the experiences of these skilled and less skilled trades permit a general periodization of the city's wage history. There was a general decline in local wages following the arrival of the military expedition led by Pedro de Cevallos and the subsequent creation of the Viceroyalty of Río de la Plata in 1776. The wages of sailors and blacksmiths then began to rise during the 1780s. This tentative increase anticipated a more general upward movement of wages that would lift the incomes of nearly all of the city's artisans and laborers in the 1790s. Finally, there was an even more dramatic series of wage increases beginning in 1806 that lasted to the end of the colonial period.[15]

The most surprising aspect of this wage history was not the broad expansion in wage levels during the military emergency of the last years of the colonial period; it was the general decline in wages that coincided with the Cevallos expedition. We might expect that the burst of economic activity tied to this expedition and the establishment of the viceroyalty would have propelled wages upward.[16] Unfortunately, there have been no efforts to measure precisely the short- and long-term economic effects of the military campaign against the Portuguese at Colonia and the creation of the new viceroyalty, but it is clear that the effort to provision and house the officers, enlisted men, and ship crews of the Cevallos expedition promoted local agriculture, manufacturing, and construction. Local prices, especially for staples and housing, certainly increased in the wake of the expedition as demand quickly outpaced traditional supplies of goods and services.

But why did wages fail to move upward with prices? The payroll practices of the Spanish military offer the best explanation. Enlisted ranks were uniformly paid low wages. In the case of Spanish garrisons in the New World, the effects of low wages were compounded by the irregular and unpredictable manner in which they were paid. As a result, off-duty soldiers from Spanish garrisons and common seamen in port sought and held jobs in the civilian economy.[17] Although most of these temporary job seekers found employment in less skilled job categories, such as stevedores and laborers, some enlisted men had civilian training and experience in skilled artisan trades like baking, shoemaking, and carpentry. The size of the Cevallos expedition, 116 ships and nearly 19,000 men, produced a substantial short-term distortion of the city's labor market and led to a general decline in wages, despite the dynamic expansion of the regional economy and resulting price inflation.

Once lowered by military wage seekers, the recovery of the city's wage rates was slowed by the expanded garrison left in place after the expedition, by the effects of expanded immigration from Europe and interior provinces, and by the growing slave trade. After 1790 the accumulated effects of increased commercial activity, rising population, and, after 1806, a series of military events that pulled large numbers of wage earners into military service finally pushed wages up dramatically. The expansion of imports and exports and the city's long construction boom were financed in large part by the expanding resources of the public sector. During the last two decades of the colonial period, the colonial and municipal governments had become the city's largest employers, powerfully affecting the demand for both skilled and unskilled labor. Nearly every category of wage earner enjoyed the dramatic upward adjustment in wages after 1806 when a rolling succession of military emergencies, including two British invasions and the military campaigns of the early independence period, pulled thousands out of the labor supply.[18] As large numbers of urban and rural workers entered the militia and regular army the city and surrounding agricultural and grazing areas were left desperately short of labor.[19] As noted in table 9, wage increases of 20 percent or more were not uncommon in both urban and rural occupations during the last decade of the colonial period.

Tulio Halperín Donghi produced a very useful estimate of the colonial government's civilian wage bill.[20] He presents government expenditures as five-year aggregates, and the government wage disbursements shown in table 10 reflect his organization. The total wage bill for four categories of civilian wage earners fell from a high of 112,133 pesos during 1791–1796 to a low of 50,431 in 1796–1800. After this plunge, total civilian wage expenditures rose gradually to the end of the colonial period. Still, at the end of the colonial period the total civilian wage bill was only 56 percent that of the 1791–1796 period.

In addition to changes in total public-sector wage expenditures, there were also important changes in the distribution of wage payments among the four occupational categories used by Halperín. Total wage payments to two groups, sailors (3) and skilled laborers (2 and 4), declined 77 percent and 46 percent respectively from the first five-year period to the last. By the end of this period only the wage bill for unskilled labor was larger than in 1791–96. Halperín's study indicates that during the final two decades of the colonial period, wages paid to unskilled workers increased to consume a larger share of the government budget than wages paid to skilled workers. This change in public-sector employment coincided with the beginning of the upward surge in unskilled wages illustrated in table 9.

The wage totals presented in table 10 represent only a fragment of public-sector employment however.[21] The cabildo's wage payments are not included in Halperín's figures and were often on a similar scale. In fact, they may have been greater during periods of peak construction in Buenos Aires. The undeniable effect of total public-sector employment was to bid up wages and aggravate the city's chronic labor shortage. This meant that the cabildo was periodically forced to suspend street paving and other construction projects to force unskilled labor into the countryside during the harvest season. When this measure failed to provide the necessary labor in

TABLE 10 Total wages paid by the colonial government

Skilled	1791–96	1796–1800	1801–1805	1806–1810
1. Laborers	19,271	14,010	10,619	25,691
2. Artisans	30,506	17,257	11,028	9,046
3. Sailors	53,578	10,350	29,301	28,820
4. Other urban- skilled labor	8,778	8,814	5,758	—
TOTAL	112,133 pesos	50,431 pesos	56,706 pesos	63,557 pesos

Source: Tulio Halperín Donghi, *Guerra y finanzas en los orígenes del estado Argentino 1791–1850* (Buenos Aires, 1982), 64–65, and 126.

1782, the cabildo ordered the city's brickyards to suspend work in order to compel more laborers into harvest employment.[22]

The records used to construct table 9 also indicate a persistent pattern of wage differentials within crafts and skill levels. Journeyman artisans had the broadest range of wage rates. I examined closely the distinctions among artisan ranks and among occupations and calculated medians for each category. A representative sample of cases can be used to illustrate the complex intersection of skill, experience, and opportunity. Typically, historians and economists have ignored wage differentials within occupations and have calculated average wages (means or medians) for entire occupations.[23] While useful, this form of statistical presentation eliminates important differences in wages and earnings within occupations, disguising the impact of economic performance and technological change on discreet skill levels. Because I am interested in social and cultural issues as well as economic behavior, I preserved the most important ranks and job classifications. Two skilled occupations, carpenters and bricklayers, and one unskilled category, urban laborers, conveniently represent these broad patterns.

Carpentry was the largest of the city's construction trades with well over four hundred operatives in 1810. As noted in table 9 the median wage for carpenters fell from ten reales to eight reales in 1775 and remained at this level until 1806 when it returned again to ten reales. The gently undulating wage pattern represented by the median wage disguises, rather than illuminates, the wage experience of carpenters employed in work sites of various sizes across the city. Closer examination suggests not only that carpenters on the same job received a broad range of wages but that an individual carpenter might receive a different wage from day to day and from job to job.

With the exception of 1805–1810 the colonial government employed large numbers of carpenters. The wages paid to these carpenters reflected differences in skills and seniority as well as changes in labor demand. The colonial government employed a *maestro mayor* to supervise its carpenters. He received a substantial annual salary of 300 pesos per year plus a daily food supplement of four reales. In 1781 the government increased this salary to 400 pesos despite the fact that journeymen and laborers in this trade received no wage increase. During the period 1799–1802 when the government increased the number of carpenters on its payroll, it hired a second maestro mayor to help supervise but paid each of these two supervisors one half the salary previously paid to a single incumbent. After 1806, in the period of greatest distortion of the labor market, the government returned to the previous model, employing a single maestro mayor at the very substantial salary of 720 pesos plus a food supplement.

It is the wage experience of journeymen that offers the best vista from which to view how alterations in economic conditions affected the incomes of plebeians. At this intermediate level of the skilled trades the documents illuminate a range of skill and seniority levels. Wages reflected these differences closely, ranging along a broad scale from four to twelve reales per day. That is, the best-paid journeymen earned as much as three times the wages paid to less skilled journeymen, while both worked side by side on the same jobs. Municipal and colonial governments also employed common laborers who were paid two reales per day as helpers. These laborers carried and prepared raw materials and cleaned up. Neither journeymen nor laborers received a food ration from the colonial government, although private-sector employers often offered this benefit to carpenters in Buenos Aires.

In 1792 the wages paid to the most-skilled journeyman carpenters fell to ten reales from twelve reales, but their wages later returned to the higher rate in 1796 when the labor market tightened. As the daily wages of the most-skilled carpenters rose, wages paid to the least-skilled journeymen increased as well, rising 50 percent to six reales, roughly three times the daily wage paid unskilled laborers in Buenos Aires. During the era of war emergency, the wages of the most-skilled journeyman carpenters increased again, reaching fourteen reales in 1807 and then sixteen reales in 1810, a level 25 percent greater than the previous high. Although there was great variety in the wages paid, more than half of the journeymen carpenters employed by the colonial government received at least eight reales or more per day from 1770 to 1815, a very substantial daily rate. Nevertheless, through-out the colonial period it was always the most senior supervisory carpenters who experienced the largest wage increases. While the salary of the maestro mayor increased 80 percent between 1770 and 1810, the wages of senior journeymen in this trade increased only 25 percent, making this a better representation of the general experience in this trade.

In addition to higher wages, the most-skilled journeymen carpenters also experienced more secure employment than did less skilled and younger members of this trade, although few men worked anything like a full, twelve-month year. Almost all of the lowest paid journeymen, those earning four or five reales per day as well as laborers hired as helpers, worked less than six consecutive months for the colonial state in any given year. In many cases, the government employed a single individual two or three different times during the year, and these periods of employment varied in length between weeks and months, reflecting the rhythms of the job and weather conditions. Although most of those dropped from the government's payroll surely found other work quickly, many carpenters, especially the youngest, least-skilled workers, must have experienced significant periods of unemployment every year.

The colonial government also employed large numbers of masons and bricklayers (*albañiles*).[24] Unlike the maestro mayor carpenter, the supervising master artisan in this trade received neither an annual salary nor a cash supplement for food. Instead, the government paid various incumbents a daily wage of sixteen reales, only four reales more than the best wage paid to a journeyman carpenter. While supervisory responsibilities were concentrated in the hands of a single carpenter, it was not uncommon to find two or more master albañiles employed at the same time by the colonial government.[25] As was true for carpenters, median wages paid to journeymen masons fluctuated little from 1770–1815; the wage was ten reales at the beginning of the period, falling briefly to nine reales in 1800, and returning to ten reales after 1805. However, wages paid to journeymen on the same construction site routinely ranged from six reales to twelve reales per day. After the British invasions, when militia service pulled thousands out of the labor pool, the wages of the most-skilled journeymen albañiles rose first to fourteen reales and then sixteen reales a day.

In this trade, laborers, rather than journeymen, numerically dominated work sites. The median wage for bricklayers was therefore determined by the wages paid to lesser-skilled laborers rather than journeymen, as was the case with carpenters. As can be seen in table 9, the median wage for brick-layers was eight reales in 1770, declined to four reales in 1775, and increased only to five reales in 1807 in the midst of city-wide wage inflation. This distinct trajectory resulted from a decline in the number of journeymen relative to lower wage laborers. Laborers in this trade, however, received one or two reales more per day than laborers hired in other trades in Buenos Aires after 1805. This small skill premium diminished at the end of the colonial period as the wages paid to all laborers rose.

Government employment records suggest that laborers hired as helpers in the bricklaying trade enjoyed greater employment security than did laborers hired by other employers for other purposes. This small benefit tied to specialized work experience actually signaled the weakening of traditional guild organization as formal apprenticeships declined in late colonial Buenos Aires. This was strikingly clear in this trade where not a single apprentice was employed by the colonial government during the period 1775–1810. The wage premium enjoyed by journeymen relative to laborers was offset by the substantial cost borne by young men forced to enter the occupation as laborers rather than as apprentices. Traditionally trained artisans regarded laborers as an inferior skill category, and they were permanently barred from rising within the traditional artisan hierarchy or earning the higher wages reserved for journeymen and masters. However, these public-sector employment records clearly show that the city's maestros mayores relied more and more on these less skilled workers as apprenticeship, the traditional route to gain access to skills, improved income, and status, declined.

As the percentage of journeymen masons and bricklayers on each job declined, median wages tended downward as well. Not only did the government move to substitute lower paid laborers for higher paid journeymen, it also experimented with new supervisory positions and a new craft nomenclature after 1800. New supervisors called *sobrestantes* replaced the maestros mayores, and the sobrestantes were paid eight reales, not the sixteen reales previously paid to the maestros mayores. If the daily wage can serve as a proxy for skill level, then the government was now supervising the bricklayers and masons on its jobsites with a journeyman rather than with a master albañil. The government simultaneously discarded the distinction between laborers and journeymen, calling all masons and bricklayers work-ing under the supervision of its sobrestantes, *operarios*. Wages were still ar-rayed along a broad scale with the highest-paid operario actually receiving twice the daily rate paid the supervising sobrestante, sixteen reales. With the exception a very small number of the most skilled receiving this sub-stantial wage, the government paid nearly all other operarios the traditional laborer's wage of four or five reales per day. Although the position of sobre-stante survived to 1815, the government dropped the term operario in 1801, reestablishing the distinction between journeymen and laborers in response to the complaints of journeymen.[26]

While the wage experiences of these skilled trades helps to illuminate the complexity of wage custom, wages paid to the city's mass of unskilled laborers offer the most useful measure of broad plebeian experience. These urban and rural laborers were not insulated from market forces by craft-related recruitment, training, and employment practices or by the habitu-ated practice of those who employed the skilled trades. Habit slowed the impact of altered market forces in these cases. While master carpenters, for example, had good reasons to both insist on the hiring of journeymen and the maintenance of traditional wage rates, no one had a similar interest in protecting the wage custom of unskilled workers. Without specialized skills to differentiate among the mass of laborers, wages move in close synchro-nization with changing labor demands. As a result, the wages of laborers have a pattern distinct from the wages paid the more skilled and better-organized craftsmen.

Before 1776 urban laborers received four reales per day. It was these least-skilled urban workers who suffered most from the subsidized compe-tition of off-duty military personnel after the arrival of Cevallos's expedi-tion, and, as a result, their wages fell to two reales and remained at this de-pressed level for twenty years. Even during periods of peak labor demand, such as the harvest season, they found themselves competing with prisoners and other involuntary laborers, including Indians sent from the Paraguayan missions. These forces combined to retard wage increases until the second half of the 1790s.[27] From then to 1803 wages fluctuated between two and three reales per day. After 1804 the wages of laborers rose to an average of four reales, although some employed by the cabildo in the construction of a new seawall earned as much as six reales per day at this time.[28] After 1810 the median wage rose again to five reales, propelled by military recruitment. In this final period, laborers working for the city earned wages traditionally available to only the most-skilled artisans in the building trades.

Rural laborers in the province of Buenos Aires received monthly wages. From 1770–1784 their median wage held steady at six pesos per month and then trended upward. After 1789 the monthly wage of seven pesos appeared for the first time, becoming the median rate in 1794. The period of labor dislocation that started in 1806 pushed the monthly wage of rural laborers to eight pesos in 1807 and then to twelve pesos in 1811. As the military emergency abated after 1815, monthly wages retreated to ten pesos.[29] Most rural workers received food and housing in addition to money wages, but we have no way at this time to assign a monetary value to this supplement.[30]

Were public-sector wages, represented in table 9, indicative of wages paid to private-sector workers in these or related occupations? Wage records found in surviving notary copybooks suggest that the periodization and the direction of changes in wages paid to less skilled laborers in both the city and surrounding rural areas were similar in public and private sectors. However, these sources also indicate that public-sector wages for laborers were always marginally higher than those paid in the private sector.

There were, however, more significant differences between public- and private-sector wage levels among artisans. Because the private-sector record is fragmentary and because we cannot control for differences in workforce size, individual skill levels, and other determinants of wages, it is impossible to create a reliable wage series that we could compare with the public-sector series presented in table 9. Nevertheless, it is clear that master artisans and skilled journeymen in the public sector consistently earned higher wages than similarly skilled craftsmen in the private sector. The wages of master masons and bricklayers in the private sector, for example, fluctuated between six and nine reales per day until 1803 when ten reales became the standard wage paid by private employers. That is, the private-sector wage for a master in this trade was slightly less than the median wage paid to skilled journeymen by the government. Journeyman masons in the private sector earned only slightly less than did masters, with the difference between these two artisan ranks never more than two reales per day. This was a very narrow skill premium indeed given the extra time and investment necessary to gain the rank of master. A similar wage pattern existed among carpenters, although private-sector wages in this trade were one or two reales higher per day at all skill levels than those earned by masons and bricklayers. Yet wages from private employers for both skilled trades were inferior to those paid by the government.[31]

In the private sector many journeymen in the construction trades independently contracted for work without the intervention or supervision of masters. As a result, journeymen were often able to earn wages that were similar, if not the same, as those paid to masters.[32] Except for masters employed in the public sector and a small number of masters whose reputations gave them a near monopoly of large projects, few masters in the colonial construction trades were able to consistently earn a wage more than 10 percent higher than that paid to journeymen. Journeymen in the construction trades, however, earned substantially more than common laborers who worked alongside them, receiving wage premiums of 40 percent to 50 percent relative to laborers from both public and private-sector employers.

Wage records of similar quality have not survived for the city's indoor trades. In nearly every case, artisans in these skilled occupations maintained small shops employing a few apprentices and journeymen. Wage records have not survived for the small number of *porteño* enterprises where masters employed substantial numbers of journeymen and less skilled laborers. Instead, we have scattered records of wages for some indoor trades found in judicial records, the accounts of ecclesiastical establishments, or in probate inventories. Because we cannot combine these fragmented wage records to produce a reliable wage series, they must be discussed anecdotally to suggest possible comparisons with the much more reliable outdoor series presented in table 9. In general, journeymen and laborers in the indoor trades of late colonial Buenos Aires received lower daily wages than workers in construction and metal trades with similar skill and seniority levels.

Some evidence of wage custom among shoemakers is provided by testimony in a 1790 civil suit brought by a journeyman to recover a loan given to the master who employed him. Because this was the largest of the city's crafts and because shoemakers were contemporaneously involved in a series of political conflicts and lawsuits over the organization of a guild, it is important to examine their economic circumstances in some detail. According to the testimony of five master shoemakers, journeymen in their trade received two reales per day plus a noon meal and minimal lodging, commonly a straw mattress in the master's home or shop. During the late eighteenth century the most important meal of the day was consumed at noon, and for most plebeians this was likely to be the only meal that included meat and vegetables. When masters did not provide food and housing, journeymen received between three-and-a-half and four reales per day in wages.[33]

Some pay records for journeymen shoemakers are found in the payroll accounts of the Mercedarian Convent of San Ramón for 1802 and 1806. In these cases journeymen received six reales per day without the provision of food or lodging.[34] Compared with the earlier record, this may suggest that there had been a gradual upward trend in wages in this trade, although this increase was less substantial than that gained by the city's common laborers or the least-skilled journeymen in the city's construction trades. If compared with the median wages paid to journeymen bricklayers and carpenters employed by the same Mercedarian convent, we see that shoemakers with similar training and skill earned 40 percent to 50 percent less than their contemporaries in the construction trades.

In response to a civil suit in 1793 one of the city's *regidors* interviewed two master silversmiths about their earnings. They testified that they took a profit of between five and six pesos on the standard goods they produced such as a candelabra or silver platters and expected larger profits on special orders for luxury goods. They also testified about the wages they paid to their journeymen, claiming that a "competent" journeyman earned eight reales per day, but an "old journeyman with failing sight" could earn no more than four reales. These skilled and experienced witnesses informed the regidor that the need to purchase tools and raw materials routinely reduced the income of members of this skilled trade.[35]

Tailors, the city's second largest artisan trade, appear to have been even more disadvantaged. The absence of even a minimal guild structure in this trade meant that neither prices nor quality controls were enforceable. At ground level this was a struggle between traditionally trained artisans, almost all men, and scores, perhaps hundreds, of women desperate to provide for their families by selling homemade clothing at lower prices. Few women sewed full time or produced goods in quantity, but they did produce enough to satisfy much of the market for low cost clothing. One British soldier who had been a prisoner of war in 1806 remembered this trade as being "chiefly females."[36] Despite this testimony, however, no women were identified as tailors in any surviving employment records or contracts. This suggests that there were, in effect, two parallel trade structures, one male and one female, with vestigial guild terminology (master, journeyman, and apprentice) still in use among the men. The scant surviving evidence suggests that traditional artisans had lost control of the market by the last decade of the colonial period.

We have a dependable wage record for nine "master tailors" employed by two different ecclesiastical establishments in 1796.[37] Eight masters received four pesos per month, while the ninth earned only three pesos per month. The record does not indicate that these master tailors received housing or food, although this seems likely since their cash wages were so low. By comparison unskilled laborers who worked on farms and ranches owned by these same religious institutions earned seven pesos per month plus food and housing. Even common seamen employed by the colonial government earned on average eleven pesos per month in 1796. If these wages were representative, a master tailor's investment in his skills—the unpaid period of apprenticeship, the payment of examination fees, and the purchase of tools, if he followed the traditional forms—produced pitiful earnings inferior to those paid to the least-skilled laborers in Buenos Aires. This humiliating monetary devaluation of skills could not have been lost on contemporaries and must have been one of the factors that influenced a decline in apprenticeships in the late colonial period.[38]

Master bakers, on the other hand, were compensated at levels comparable to those paid masters in outdoor trades. However, there is some evidence suggesting that earnings declined for this trade at the end of the colonial period. The accounts of both the Mercedarian and Bethlemite monasteries provide monthly wages for master bakers from 1775 to 1802.[39] Until 1799 master bakers earned thirty pesos per month, something like nine times the wages paid to master tailors. Wages for master bakers then fell to eighteen pesos through the period of the British invasions. Unfortunately, these records provide no explanation for this loss in earning power. Since there was a general upward trend in the wages of other groups during the same period, some special characteristic of or evolution in the urban economy must be sought as an explanation for the falling wages. The development of large-scale, more efficient bakeries that were increasingly able to meet the needs of both individual and institutional consumers must have contributed to decline in wages for master bakers.[40] Also, the increased capacity of these more efficient bakeries that used slave labor allowed institutions that had previously produced their own bread to cut costs through the elimination of labor and related obligations. As small institutions turned from producing their own bread to consuming the commercial, mass-produced product, employment opportunities for individual master bakers declined.

These records and fragmentary wage agreements for painters, furniture makers, candle makers, and musicians suggest that wages in the city's indoor trades moved in a parallel fashion to the public-sector wages represented in table 9. However, wage levels and rates of increase were consistently inferior to those paid in outdoor trades. Market demand for the labor and products of these artisans grew more slowly than was the case in construction trades and port-related trades, and, as a result, even the city's least-skilled laborers benefited more from the transformation of the local economy than did these highly skilled artisans.

Slavery and Free Labor

The expanding flow of migrants after 1776 from the interior provinces of the viceroyalty and from Europe augmented the Buenos Aires plebe. These two migratory streams integrated into the urban labor force in distinct patterns. Internal migrants distributed across the workforce with the majority finding work as laborers and a minority entering the skilled trades. The flow of European immigrants contained a larger percentage of masters and journeymen in the skilled trades as well as street-level merchants like *pulperos* and *mercachifles*. Artisans migrating from the internal provinces were more likely than Europeans to have training in low-prestige trades like shoemaking or bricklaying. These generalizations disguise a richly complex world that included Spanish-born beggars and successful native-born master silversmiths and bakers. Despite these anomalies of social position and income, it is clear that the economic expansion that followed the creation of the viceroyalty served as a powerful magnet, drawing thousands of free migrants from the interior provinces and Europe. While these very substantial migratory flows augmented labor supply, they failed to stall the upward movement of wages.

Between 1790 and 1810 Buenos Aires legally imported something like 20,000 slaves, and thousands of additional slaves likely entered the city illegally.[41] That is, by the last decade of the colonial period the volume of slave imports had more than overtaken free migration.[42] Unlike earlier decades when the majority of slaves were sent to interior cities, the majority of those imported after 1790 were integrated into the urban labor market. Most slaves worked for wages, hiring their time with little or no direct supervision from their owners. The fact that wages rose steeply, despite rising slave imports, suggests both the potency of the local economic expansion and the labor cost of militarization after 1806.

Most of the city's slave owners regarded their slaves as investments that they expected to produce dependable dividends.[43] The purchase and training of slaves, not the purchase of tools or machines, was the most important and most predictable way that artisans and other skilled workers sought to profit from the rising demand for goods and services in Buenos Aires.[44] Although few members of the skilled working class owned more than one or two slaves, artisans owned more slaves than any other class except wholesale merchants by 1810.[45] At a time when untrained slaves imported from Africa or Brazil cost two hundred pesos on average, trained slave journeymen were valued between four hundred and six hundred pesos.

The period of highest wages in colonial Buenos Aires coincided with the greatest volume of African slaves present in the labor market, distinguishing this case from Brazil and Cuba where rising rates of slave participation in skilled and unskilled occupations tended to slow or retard the rate of wage increase.[46] In Buenos Aires during the late colonial period, a dynamic labor market allowed both the free labor majority and a large slave minority to react to changes in supply and demand. In fact, the ascending wage curve in the city and its hinterland facilitated a deep integration of slave and free labor regimes after 1778.[47] Because slaves in Buenos Aires commonly had significant discretion in contracting for employment and retained portions of their income, this urban labor force remained flexible and responsive to changing labor demand unlike other slave regimes, even as the numbers of slaves increased.

Earnings

Students of economic history must constantly remind themselves of the substantial difference between daily wage rates and earnings.[48] Table 9 presented average daily compensation for a range of occupations. Without an analysis of actual employment experience, we cannot assume that weekly, monthly, or annual earnings were no more than multiples of these daily wages. Was continuous employment at a constant wage the common experience for the artisans and laborers in colonial Buenos Aires? Our discussion to this point makes it clear that this was not the case.

Treasury accounts demonstrate the complexity of jobsite organization

FIGURE 25 Slave women clean clothes at the riverbank behind the fort. In the background men and women bathe in the river. Source: Emeric Essex Vidal, *Picturesque Illustrations of Buenos Ayres and Monte Video, Consisting of Twenty-four Views* (London: R. Ackermann, 1820).

and the fluidity of working-class employment.[49] In September 1785 a master bricklayer earning two pesos per day supervised a large crew of journeymen and laborers. The ten journeymen under his command received either ten or twelve reales a day, while the forty-one laborers or helpers earned four reales a day.[50] As was typical across the city, the skilled journeymen set the foundation and built the walls while laborers prepared mortar and carried stones and bricks. Although the Royal Treasury paid the wages of the laborers, they worked in effect for the journeymen who exercised de facto control of the work site, set standards, enforced the pace of work, and determined who was hired. All these workingmen were part of the same class, but we must not ignore the very real differences in wages, status, authority, and actual work experiences among them.

Similarly, there was great variability in continuity of employment. During a seven-month period in 1780, the colonial government employed twenty-five different journeymen bricklayers to repair a wall. Only one man worked all seven months while the majority, fifteen, worked only a single month on this project.[51] We must assume that most of the bricklayers who disappeared from government pay records found alternative employment during the rest of the year. It would be a mistake, however, to assume that they all worked a complete fifty-two week year or that they always earned the wage they had earned while working on the government project.

In 1785 the colonial government employed a crew of bricklayers for a project that lasted eleven months. Of the forty-six journeymen hired during this term, twenty-six worked only a single month while only seven worked six months or more. The wages of the bricklayers on this job fluctuated in response to local labor supply. Juan Sánchez, for example, earned a common laborer's rate of four reales per day from February to May, then earned the median journeyman's wage of ten reales per day through November, and finally ended the year earning nine reales a day. Andres Ysla, a journeyman employed for two months, began at the highest wage, fourteen reales per day, in June but earned only ten reales per day in July. One final example from this job helps to illustrate the fluidity of wage custom in the late colonial period. The journeyman bricklayer Bautista Rodríguez earned seven reales per day when first employed in April 1800. The following month he received six reales a day. Then, between June and August, Rodríguez's daily wage returned to seven reales.[52] He then left government employment for two months, returning in November and December to earn eight reales a day.[53]

Carpenters experienced similar wage patterns to masons. In 1775 the colonial government employed 109 journeymen carpenters who earned between five and twelve reales per day. Fewer than 50 percent of these men worked six continuous months or more. In fact, 30 of the 109 journeymen worked less than two months for the government. For example, the journeyman carpenter Vicente Marques was first employed in February 1775 at eight reales per day. During March and April he earned ten reales but experienced many days of unemployment. He was not employed by the government in May, and when reemployed in June he was paid his original wage of eight reales per day.[54] What should we estimate were his annual earnings or the earnings of his workmates?

Local market conditions largely determined wage levels in colonial Buenos Aires. Increased demand for labor provoked by the government-led building boom following the creation of the viceroyalty or the constriction of the labor supply that resulted from the impact of military recruitment after 1806, for example, exercised powerful influence over wages. In this colonial economy the decisions of the colonial state or the municipal government also exercised a powerful effect. The city council's commitment to pave city-center streets, for example, tended to bid up laborers' wages. Similarly, the colonial military's purchase of boots for the infantry garrison pushed up the wages of journeyman shoemakers, while the civilian government's decision to construct new offices for the tobacco monopoly or build a seawall pushed up wages in the construction trades.

We also find clear evidence of seasonality in wages in nearly every urban trade. During the winter months when the working day was shortened by darkness (usually the loss of two or more hours) all of the city's artisans and laborers earned a lower daily rate. Where this pattern can be viewed most clearly, in the construction trades, the seasonal wage decline was on the order of 10 percent. A chronic problem for the working class was that reduced income always coincided with seasonal increases in food costs. Given the difficulty of accumulating savings for the members of the urban skilled working class, the winter months must have been very difficult indeed.

Did the employment patterns of less skilled workers imitate the rhythms of artisan employment? The pay records of the municipal slaughter yard for April 25, 1787, to the end of October 1787 illuminate the wage experience of the city's least-skilled workers.[55] During this time one hundred laborers were employed in a range of tasks from butchering animals to repairing a small boat. The two individuals who serially held the position of *capataz* or foreman earned ten pesos a month. The two most experienced laborers under their supervision received nine pesos per month, and one of these received an additional six reales per month for guarding the cashbox at night. All other employees were common laborers with limited skills who were paid eight pesos per month, two pesos more than the median monthly wage paid to laborers in nearby rural districts. Although wages were noted at a monthly rate, eighty-two of the one hundred employees actually worked less than a month and were compensated for odd days at a lower wage.

The forty-nine men who worked less than two weeks in the slaughter yard received a daily wage of two reales, the city-wide median wage for common laborers. This suggests that laborers who worked a full month, in effect, received compensation calculated on a month with thirty-two working days. Since the maximum workweek was no more than six days, this meant a small premium was paid to longer-term employees. Temporary laborers employed for a specific task (two laborers hired to repair a launch

FIGURE 26 Laborers slaughtering cattle for the Buenos Aires markets. Source: Emeric Essex Vidal, *Picturesque Illustrations of Buenos Ayres and Monte Video, Consisting of Twenty-four Views* (London: R. Ackermann, 1820).

and one laborer hired to cut wooden stakes) also received two reales per day. All employees, regardless of task or skill level, received a food ration in addition to cash wages. This ration included meat, yerba, salt, lard, bread, and, less regularly, vegetables, sugar, sausages, and wine. Among common laborers, at least those in this brutal and filthy business, there was very little employment continuity. Employment was typically for periods of days or weeks, not months or years. Only ten of the one hundred employees hired during this period worked the entire four months, while sixty-nine worked less than a month. We must assume that many of the individuals who left this job passed quickly to alternative employment. However, it is clear that few, if any, common laborers in colonial Buenos Aires worked six day weeks, fifty-two weeks per year.

Temporalidades, the colonial account that managed former Jesuit properties, provided one of the best records of daily employment for this period. It covers a fifteen-week period (from November 15, 1786, to February 24, 1787) when a group of bricklayers and their helpers constructed a two-story house in central Buenos Aires.[56] Seven journeymen worked on this project and one of them, Joseph Ferreyra, acted as the capataz. It is important to reiterate again the widespread practice in Buenos Aires of using a senior journeyman in place of a master artisan to supervise construction jobs. Only Ferreyra worked the entire fifteen weeks, but two other journeymen worked ten or more weeks. Four journeymen worked seven weeks or less. Wages reflected the recognition of differing skill levels and experience: Ferreyra earned twelve reales per day; two journeymen earned eleven reales; two others earned ten reales; and one received nine reales.

All thirty-nine laborers who worked with these journeymen bricklayers were paid four reales per day. Nine laborers worked thirteen weeks or more, while twenty laborers worked six weeks or less. Both journeymen and laborers averaged five days of work a week during the project. Scheduled days off or mandatory half days were concentrated on Fridays. Absenteeism predictably occurred on Saturdays and Mondays (the porteño equivalent, perhaps, of the contemporary British and North American laborer's blue Monday).[57] Since the average workweek was five days, laborers on this job earned an average of twenty reales per week or, potentially, 130 pesos per year. At the median journeyman's rate, eleven reales per day, weekly earnings were between fifty-five and sixty-six reales. Annual income, assuming fifty-two weeks with five days of employment, was 357 pesos. But can we use these short-term projects to estimate the average number of working days or annual earnings?

There is little agreement among scholars on the length of the colonial work year. The eighteenth-century Spanish intellectual Pedro Rodríguez, Conde de Campomanes, estimated that manual workers worked between 270 and 280 days per year.[58] The Argentine historian José M. Mariluz Urquijo suggested that workers in Buenos Aires during the 1820s worked approximately 290 days per year.[59] Both estimates of average working days per year were derived in similar fashion by subtracting Sundays as well as secular and religious holidays from 365.[60] Both authors presume, therefore, that continuous employment was the norm. These calculations fail to account for days of unemployment imposed by market conditions or the weather. They also fail to account for voluntary unemployment, the discretionary substitution of leisure for income, illustrated by the decision of the journeyman Josef Silva to stay away from work that opened this chapter.

Daily employment records indicate that plebeians (artisans and laborers) in late colonial Buenos Aires worked an average of 245 days per year.

There are compelling reasons to accept this lower estimate. As is still true, workers in construction and other outdoor trades lost working days due to inclement weather. They also experienced periods of short-term unemployment during winter months when construction starts traditionally fell off. More broadly, artisans in indoor and outdoor trades as well as the larger class of less skilled laborers worked generally for short periods, hired for a day, week, or occasionally a month. At the end of each project, individual workers were forced to search again for employment. So, how many days or portions of days were consumed by this intermittent cycle of employment and job search?

During periods of full employment and high wages when savings were possible some members of this class chose leisure rather than additional income by taking days off.[61] Police and judicial records document clearly that pulperías hosted a large and loyal clientele of artisans and day laborers who enjoyed strong drink and games of skill and chance more than work. The cabildo's repeated recourse to ineffective vagrancy codes and attempts to outlaw gaming document the persistent and largely successful efforts of workingmen to maintain their independence and autonomy.[62] The relationship between the cost of subsistence and housing on one hand and available wage levels on the other helped established the everyday understanding of the working year. Marital status and family size as well as individual ambition also helped to determine work rhythms.

Table 11 provides estimated annual earnings for four broad categories of wage laborers. The four arbitrary categories range from twelve reales per day (the wage earned by skilled journeymen in the construction trades and by masters in many indoor artisan occupations) to two reales per day (the city-wide median wage for common laborers). Two estimates of annual earnings were calculated for each category using working years of 280 days (the Campomanes estimate) and 245 days (derived from actual colonial pay records). Since the most-skilled, highest paid plebeians experienced the greatest continuity of employment, it is likely that the best paid journeymen also worked more days than did common laborers, but this distinction is not represented in the table.

Significant differences in wages and earnings were present horizontally across the occupational boundaries as represented in table 9 and vertically within each working-class occupation and within each job party and work site. Viewed from this perspective we see clearly the fundamentally hierar-

TABLE 11 Estimated annual earnings for skilled and unskilled workers

Number of Days	Daily Wage			
	Skilled		Unskilled	
	12 reales	10 reales	4 reales	2 reales
245	368 pesos	306 pesos	123 pesos	61 pesos
280	420 pesos	350 pesos	140 pesos	70 pesos

Sources: Average wages are derived from sources from table 9. Campomanes's estimate is in Juan Plaza Prieto, *Estructura economica de Espana en el siglo XVIII* (Madrid: Confereración Española de Cajas de Ahorros, 1975), 694. Jose M. Mariluz Urquijo, "La mano de obra en la industria portena," 616. Religious holidays were identified in *Almanak y kalendario general diario de quartos de Luna, segun el Meridiano de Buenos Ayres para el año del señor de 1797* (Buenos Aires: Real Imprenta de Niños Expósitos, 1797); and *Almanak o calendario y diario de quarto de Luna, segun Meridiano de Buenos Ayres para el año de 1809* (Buenos Aires: Real Imprenta de Niños Expósitos, 1809).

chical character of the colonial working class, a class often represented as a series of homogeneous occupational groupings by historians who rely on colonial census records.[63] Some historians of this class have emphasized the hierarchy of guild ranks (master, journeyman, and apprentice), others have concentrated on hierarchies of race and ethnicity, but none have captured the rich diversity and complexity of this class suggested by differences in income and wages.[64] As a result, some social histories of the colonial working class presume that individuals with the same craft rank in different occupations enjoyed similar levels of income. For Buenos Aires it is clear that, with a handful of exceptions, the income levels of masters in the indoor trades placed them in inferior circumstances to the least-skilled workers in the construction industry.

Many members of the colonial working class had earnings other than cash wages. As mentioned earlier, artisans and laborers commonly received food and, much less frequently, housing as compensation. Master carpenters and bricklayers working for the colonial government, for example, received between two and four reales per day for food in addition to an annual salary. Journeymen and laborers also commonly received food, usually the noon meal valued at roughly one and one-and-a-half reales per day.[65] For a worker employed 245 days, this represented approximately fifteen pesos per year in additional compensation.[66]

Many masters and journeymen were not simply wage earners; they were also small businessmen and manufacturers who earned income from employing labor and supplying raw materials. Some members of this class even derived additional income from agricultural activities. Clearly our discussion of changes in the living conditions experienced by this class cannot be based solely on wage income. Independent masters in nearly all the city's artisan trades were customarily paid for specific tasks rather than for a day's work. In this kind of arrangement master artisans provided both materials and labor. Earnings therefore included the markup on materials as well as labor. Painters and gilders employed in the decoration of the Mercedarian chapel in 1790 and 1791, for example, received 270 pesos for "gilding and painting the altar," and 32 pesos for producing "two paintings of saints." In 1783 the Mercedarians paid the cooper Juan Jose Bermudez 2 pesos and 6 reales for a water barrel and the carpenter Ygnacio Echeberria 8 pesos for constructing four wheelbarrows.[67] In these cases the master artisan was in effect an independent jobber who profited from employing labor, often using his own slaves, and supplying raw materials. It is impossible to fix a clear relationship between changes in wage levels and the income of artisans operating as independent businessmen. We can presume that the upward trend in wages paid to skilled workers reflected a general increase in the demand for specialized skills that would have driven up the incomes of most independent jobbing artisans as well.

Artisans, particularly master artisans in the building trades, also profited from the sale of raw materials and semifinished products to customers. Carpenters and bricklayers commonly acted as material wholesalers selling wood, brick, tile, and adobe to smaller contractors or individual consumers.[68] They produced and sold products such as doors, window frames, shutters, and exterior gates. Millers and bakers actively operated in the wholesale grain business. The largest speculators invested in what were, in effect, wheat futures, purchasing unharvested grain from farmers or the state (grain tithes or *diezmos*). They then held supplies until prices rose in the late fall and winter months. Although we cannot view the profits of these independent producers and speculators as typical forms of plebeian income, recognition of the diversity of income flows to this class reminds us of the limitations inherent in using wages to represent income.

Nevertheless, cash wages provided the primary, if not the sole, source of income for the majority of plebeian households. Few laborers or journeymen were able to accumulate adequate savings or find sufficient credit to enter the market as independent masters. The dire poverty of many journeymen compelled them to rent tools from their employers. Minus the cost of

TABLE 12 Weighted index of wages (1776 = 100)

1775	100.3	1796	108.4
1776	100	1797	117.1
1777	100	1798	124.6
1778	100	1799	115.9
1779	100	1800	123.4
1780	107.5	1801	123.4
1781	101.9	1802	124.6
1782	101.9	1803	139.6
1783	101.9	1804	139.6
1784	107.7	1805	139.6
1785	107.1	1806	148.1
1786	105.2	1807	151.7
1787	105.2	1808	152.4
1788	105.2	1809	152.3
1789	107.7	1810	177.3
1790	105.2	1811	177.3
1791	107.7	1812	177.3
1792	107.7	1813	177.3
1793	105.2	1814	172.3
1794	107.7	1815	172.3

Note: Weights were assigned to the wage histories of individual occupations based on their proportional importance in contemporary census records of 1778 and 1810. This index includes the wages of carpenters (20), bricklayers (15), iron workers (10), caulkers (2), ship carpenters (1), sailmakers (1), armsmakers (1), sailors (5), urban laborers (30), and rural laborers (15).

using their master's tools, the daily wages of these journeymen seldom surpassed those of unskilled laborers. Only a small number of craftsmen, men with access to high wages, an inheritance, a dowry, or credit, were able to become petty capitalists as owners of bakeries, brickyards, or foundries and escape dependence on daily wages. Outside the experience of this fortunate cohort, wage income largely determined the quality of material life.

By calculating a broadly conceived wage index we can best represent the broad experience of this large class in late colonial Buenos Aires. Table 12 provides a single index number weighted to reflect changes in the median wages paid the ten occupations found in table 9 as well as changes in the relative size of each occupation across the period 1775–1815. This index provides a broad representation of how changes in the colonial economy affected the lives of the city's plebeian class, but it is important to recall the variety of wage experience demonstrated earlier as well as earlier discussions of employment patterns and earnings. As can be seen in table 12 there was little improvement in wages until 1797 when the index began to move steadily upward, and in 1803 the index stabilized for three years. Wages then moved dramatically upward again as the colonial government militarized the labor force in the face of two British invasions, and by 1815 the index had increased 28 percent from 1800.

The weights used in this wage index emphasize the proportional importance of laborers among the plebe of Buenos Aires relative to the most-skilled groups of artisans. The weights also reflect the proportional importance of artisan crafts as indicated by colonial censuses and the craft matriculations of 1780. That is, the median wages paid to the members of the largest crafts have been given greater weight than median wages paid to operatives in the smaller crafts. Because the most dramatic wage increases were enjoyed by the most-skilled artisans, the proportional weight of laborers in this weighting scheme acted to retard the rate of increase in the wage index relative to prices, just as increases in the price of wheat, the most important dietary commodity, influenced the movement of the cost-of-living index. Following the well-known argument of John Rawls that social welfare changes are best evaluated from the perspective of the least advantaged, the wages of laborers are offered as both an indication of changes in wages and as a measure of social justice.[69]

Real Wages in an Era of Drought and War

While Buenos Aires remained a city of high wages to the end of the colonial period, the city's artisans and laborers faced a succession of daunting economic challenges after 1795. Colonial job seekers focused the negotiation of daily or long-term employment on wage rates, and there was, no doubt, a presumption that rising wages signaled improved material conditions. But it was the translation of wages into consumption, leisure, and savings through the mediation of markets that determined the ways that colonial-era artisans, laborers, and their families understood their circumstances. In late colonial Buenos Aires prices increasingly moved in perverse ways that frustrated the ambitions and plans of artisans, small manufacturers, and laborers despite rising average wages.

During the last two decades of the colonial era prices for basic consumption goods proved more volatile than wages as we can see by comparing the price index from table 6 with the wage index found in table 12. The index number for wages (1776 = 100) in table 12 remained relatively stable from 1790 to 1796 (increasing less then 2.5 percent to 108) and then moved higher in stages. It reached 124 in 1798, 150 in 1806 and 177 in 1810. The price index

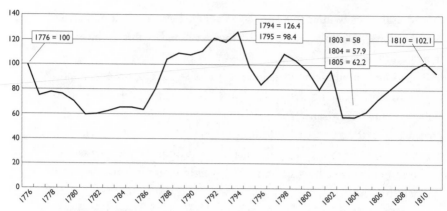

FIGURE 27 **Changes in real wages, 1775–1811.** Source: Commodity prices are derived from AGN, División Colonia, Sección Contaduria, Culto de Buenso Aires, Mercedarios, hospicio de San Ramón de las Conchas, libros 1, 3, and 5; Culto de Buenos Aires, Bethlemitas, Convento y hospital de Santa Catalina, Culto de Buenos Aires, Mercedarios, Convento Grande de San Ramón, Libro de Gastos, 1775–1815. Rent series were found in AGN, División Colonia, Sección Gobierno, Cabildo de Buenos Aires, Propios, 1770–1806; AGN, División Colonia, Sección Contaduria, Convento y iglesia de San Ramón de Buenos Aires, Inventorio de los bienes, muebles y inmuebles, 1788–1792; and AGN, División Colonia, Sección Gobierno, Cabildo de Buenos Aires, Propios, 1808–1812. Urban wages were found in AGN, División Colonia, Sección Gobierno, Archivo del Cabildo, 1770–1815; Obras Publicas, Canal de San Fernando, 1770–1808; Cabildo de Buenos Aires, Obras, 1805–1806. AGN, División Colonia, Sección Contaduria, Culto de Buenos Aires, Mercedarios, hospicio de San Ramón de las Conchas, libros 1, 3, and 5; Culto de Buenos Aires, Mercedariosconvento, gastos, libros 1, 2, and 3; Culto de Buenos Aires, Bethlemitas, Convento hospital de Santa Catalina; Culto de Buenos Aires, Mercedarios, Convento Grande de San Ramón, Libro de Gastos, 1775–1815.

(1776 = 100) in table 6 remained under 100 from 1789 to 1794. It increased to 129.3 in 1796 and then fluctuated in a narrow band until 1803 when it spiked to 240.6. Prices then moved downward in 1806, reaching 173.7 in 1810.[70] As the cabildo candidly summarized on August 7, 1804, "the last ten years have witnessed a high percentage increase in the prices of clothes, rents, food, and other articles indispensable for a decent subsistence."[71]

The best way to represent the intersection of wages and prices in the lives of the plebe is to calculate real wages, the urban wage index adjusted for changes in consumer prices. Figure 27 displays the movement of real wages for Buenos Aires between 1776 and 1811. As the figure demonstrates, rising prices muted or reversed the effects of rising wages over much of this period. In fact, during these three decades of political and economic transformation characterized by a growing urban population and by deeper integration in the expanding Atlantic economy, real wages did not permanently improve in Buenos Aires. While nominal wages had increased impressively,

FIGURE 28 Most residents of Buenos Aires depended on the delivery of potable water.
Source: Gregorio Ibarra, *Trajes y Costumbres de la Provincia de Buenos Aires* (Buenos Aires: César Hippolyte Bacle y compania, 1833).

real wages on the eve of the *cabildo abierto* of May 1810 were once again at the levels of 1776.

Real wages fell immediately after the creation of the viceroyalty as the city digested a larger workforce produced by immigration and then remained at this lower level until 1787. Real wages then took a strong, if undulating, upward track until 1794 when the highest real wages of the colonial period were recorded. A devastating region-wide drought blew the top off of food prices after 1802 and knocked real wages down. Even meat prices rose, causing Viceroy Joaquín del Pino y Rozas to tell the cabildo in 1802 of his fear that shortages would lead to political unrest. Three years later Viceroy Rafael de Sobremonte reiterated this concern, noting the "clamores de los habitantes de esta numerosa Ciudad."[72] In the face of these punishing blows, the real wage index hit bottom at 60 in 1804 and 1805 on the eve of the first British invasion.

Real wages recovered after 1806 but failed to surpass the levels of 1776. While rising prices propelled the steep decline of real wages in 1802, the recovery after 1806 resulted from rising wages occasioned by the military emergency and by moderating staple prices, rather than by increased economic activity. The militarization of the city after the first British invasion in 1806 artificially exacerbated the city's chronic labor scarcity even while blockades pinched commercial volume. Nevertheless, few plebeians enjoyed the full benefit of the late colonial era's high wages, which were offset by rising rents. What is clear is that after 1795 continuing increases in wages in Buenos Aires were overtaken by more rapidly inflating prices of basic commodities until finally, a tsunami of high prices provoked by region-wide drought and disruptions to Atlantic trade swept aside the long-established balance of wages and prices in the first years of the nineteenth century. As the English visitor John Mawe summarized in 1807, "they work hard and receive great wages, [but] seldom realize [own] property."[73] This was the economic context in which the artisans and laborers of Buenos Aires experienced the dramatic events of foreign invasion and political crisis after 1806.

Disguised by the performance of the real wage index were significant differences in the wage experiences of laborers and skilled artisans. Research on the wage history of the United States suggests that the wages of less skilled workers generally respond more readily to economic changes than do wages in the skilled sector because the effects of craft organizations or traditional wage customs are not present.[74] For Buenos Aires, the late colonial expansion in commercial activity, the growth in urban construction, and labor competition from an invigorated agricultural sector propelled a strong upward movement in the wages of the urban unskilled, but it took time for the effects of these large changes to gather momentum. Skilled wages in the artisan crafts were less volatile with reduced potential on both the up and down sides. This was the case in large part because of the willingness of artisans to enforce wage customs, the accepted ideal of wage differentials among skill levels, and, in Buenos Aires, by an increased use of slaves and unskilled laborers in jobs traditionally reserved for trained craftsmen. Nevertheless, evidence suggests that skilled groups also enjoyed dramatic increases in wages, especially in the last fifteen years of the colonial period.

We can identify two distinct epochs in the wage history of the late-colonial laboring class. From the mid 1770s to 1796 we find that the city's skilled workers successfully demanded and consistently received a wage premium for their training and work experience. After this date, however, we find that the wages paid to the unskilled laborers surged relative to those paid artisans. After 1796 cheap skills and expensive raw labor characterized the city's labor market.[75] Researchers have found a strong correlation between changes in statistical measures of wealth inequality and changes in the ratio of skilled and unskilled wages in other economies.[76] If the porteño case was similar, then the period after 1796 was most likely a period when the distribution of wealth moved toward greater equality. In other words, this was a period when the skilled working class experienced a perceptible decline in its income advantage over the city's unskilled workers.[77]

Conclusion

The urban wage index represented in table 12 shows that Buenos Aires remained a high wage economy throughout the colonial period with wages increasing modestly between 1784 and 1790 and then more steeply after 1797. By 1800 the wage index stood at 123. The next fifteen years, years of military emergencies and political transformation, witnessed even more substantial wage increases. The wage index hit 140 in 1805, 150 in 1807, and 170 in 1810. These dramatic increases resulted from the militarization of Buenos Aires that diverted artisans and laborers from the economy to the new militia units formed in the wake of the two British invasions and then by the military demands of the early stages of the independence struggle.

In the decade after 1800 rapidly rising prices occasioned by a regional drought and war-time disruptions to imports effectively erased the potential benefits attached to wage increases. While artisans and laborers earned wages unimaginable a decade earlier, they continued to find it very difficult to improve their circumstances because of short supplies and high prices. This was the perfect environment for the cultivation of mass frustration. Not only were the anticipated effects of high wages constrained by cycles of price inflation across all groups of manual laborers, but the traditional premiums paid to artisans for their skills were threatened as well.

The interdiction of Atlantic commerce during wartime, the advent of neutral trade, new fiscal and commercial policies, and natural disaster (the drought) affected the compensation of skilled and unskilled workers in distinct and contradictory ways. As has been found in other places and times, the wages of the unskilled in late colonial Buenos Aires responded more readily to these substantial changes in the economy than did the wages of the most skilled. The city's most-skilled artisans as well as many small manufacturers were regulated by *aranceles* imposed by the city government and by deeply rooted wage customs associated with their craft traditions. The increased use of slave labor in artisan crafts also slowed the pace of wage increases. Less skilled labor adjusted more readily to the late colonial economic expansion of Buenos Aires, especially to the growth in urban construction, including public works like street paving, and to the rising labor needs of an expanding agricultural sector, and, as a result, less skilled laborers were rewarded by a substantial increase in average wages. There were some exceptions, like those trades that were especially useful to commerce or to the military after 1806. Put another way, as the colonial order was put under increasing pressure by geopolitical events, the two British invasions and the crisis in Spain occasioned by the French invasion of the Peninsula, the city's laboring elite, skilled artisans, faced growing pressures and more difficult circumstances. That is, the value of skills was declining as slave imports rose and the use of less skilled labor in positions previously reserved for journeymen increased.[78] The traditions and institutions that had long organized plebeian society in Buenos Aires were in crisis.

8 | An Empire Lost
The Plebe Transformed

On March 3, 1836, Lieutenant Colonel Manuel Macedonio Barbarín died at the age of fifty-five, leaving behind a widow and seven children.[1] Following his death the city's major periodical, *La Gaceta Mercantil*, memorialized his life and career. The article outlined his long military career that started in the colonial era and remembered in glowing terms the "talents, valor, and honor so necessary for a man of the *circumstances* [emphasis added] of Barbarín." The writer went on to assert that the "laurel of honor would decorate the tomb where his remains will rest." Barbarín's death, the author asserted, was a great loss to the "people" and to his family, "who cried inconsolably."[2]

Barbarín had risen through the provincial military ranks in the politically tumultuous 1820s, gaining his last promotion as a result of actions in defense of Juan Manuel de Rosas in 1834. He had earlier established his relationship with Rosas when he committed the militia unit he commanded to the caudillo's aggressive reassertion of personal authority in the province of Buenos Aires in 1831. The author of the obituary saw no need to linger on the most interesting biographical details of the heroic soldier's background, although he had hinted at them when he placed these substantial achievements in the intentionally obscure context suggested by the words "a man of the circumstances of Barbarín."

Because Barbarín was well known in Buenos Aires, these "circumstances" were public knowledge and well understood by readers of the obituary. Barbarín was a moreno who had witnessed the transformative events of the last years of the colonial era.[3] He had been born in 1781 in Angola and brought to Buenos Aires by the slave trade in the early 1790s. He was still a slave in 1807 when he took up arms and joined the popular resistance to the second British invasion. As the result of his heroic actions Barbarín was one of the hundreds of slaves singled out by the colonial government for their actions and entered into a lottery that would reward a lucky minority with manumission.[4] Freed by the lottery, Barbarín entered the military as a soldier in a segregated militia unit and slowly rose through the ranks. He was already a captain in 1810 at the advent of the independence struggle.[5]

Manuel Barbarín first entered our story in 1795 when Martín de Álzaga ordered his arrest along with that of his master, Juan Barbarín, during the investigation of the purported slave conspiracy. In the first decade of the nineteenth century Manuel and many of the other alleged conspirators of 1795, indeed the entire porteño plebe, experienced a period of rapid and chaotic political and social change, propelled forward by both the deterioration of the colonial order and by unforeseen geopolitical events. By the time the city took its first step towards independence on May 25, 1810, the laboring classes, both slave and free, had entered political life in ways that were unimaginable in 1795. Between 1806 and 1810 their massed physical presence, their demands, and the distribution of their anger and affection largely determined the fate of British ambitions and Spanish colonial institutions in the South Atlantic.

The City Humiliated

On the evening of June 24, 1806, Viceroy Marqués de Sobremonte celebrated the birthday of a young adjutant who would soon become his son-in-law, Don Juan Manuel de Marín. The evening began with a dinner at the viceregal residence. The party then moved to the Nuevo Coliseo, the city's modest theatrical venue, to see a performance of *El sí de las niñas*, a Spanish comedy then enjoying success with porteño audiences. Along with the viceregal party the audience included most of the city's elite. When the viceroy entered the audience rose and the theater's small orchestra of black freemen struck up a martial air. No one anticipated the events that would quickly follow.[6]

During the performance Viceroy Sobremonte was informed that British ships appeared to be disembarking less than a day's march from the capital. Although British warships had entered the estuary previously, no one suspected that Buenos Aires would be the target of a direct land attack.[7] In the days that followed, the viceroy made decisions that destroyed his reputation and authority. As British forces gathered near Quilmes, local militia units were called to arms by ringing church bells, but the hopelessness of the situation was soon evident.[8] Militia units were poorly armed and badly led, and Spanish regular units were little better. In the decisive actions on July 26 and 27, the local force broke ranks after a few volleys fired by a British force of fewer than 1,600 men.[9]

Before the first shots were fired, the viceroy had prepared his family and household to flee. With the decisive clash with the British imminent, Sobremonte retreated from the battlefield with key military units, leaving the militia to face certain defeat.[10] Back in the city, the viceroy ordered treasury funds loaded onto carts and then he retreated from the city, escorted by a large military force.[11] With the city now undefended, Spanish military and civilian authorities negotiated surrender with British representatives sent by General William Carr Beresford.[12]

All surviving sources agree that the city population was shocked and distraught by this humiliating defeat. It is not clear that a more determined political and military leadership could have defended the city, but many believed this to be the case. Martín de Álzaga, who when serving as alcalde had prosecuted the conspiracy charges of 1795, wrote to a commercial colleague in Montevideo on July 5, 1806, of the "terrible disgrace and detestable infamy that occurred with the surrender of this capital city to 1,500 inexperienced English [troops] incapable of defeating a third of this citizenry." Álzaga was more colorful in August when writing to another business associate. He described the surrender as being "delivered like sheep . . . to 1,500 or more British wolves."[13] Manuel Belgrano later remembered his "indignation" at the entrance of "the enemy troops in their unimpressive numbers."[14] Juan Manuel Beruti referred to "this fatal unforeseen disgrace." He went on to remember "a day and night without the flow of tears ceasing."[15] Mariano Moreno also said: "I have seen in the plaza many men cry because of the infamy with which we were delivered [to the British] and I have cried more than any other."[16] Mariquita Sánchez, like most contemporaries, found it impossible to describe the humiliation without focusing on the viceroy: "how can we paint the circumstance of this viceroy, whom we charge with all this confusion and with his [inappropriate] effort to save the treasury funds."[17]

Despite the comprehensive collapse of Spanish authority, Beresford held Buenos Aires only forty-five days. The British flag was hardly unfurled over the fortress walls before a small number of Spanish military leaders who had not surrendered and countless civilian volunteers began planning to retake the city. The key figure was Santiago de Liniers, the French nobleman serving in the Spanish Navy, who Martín de Álzaga had suspected of sedition in 1795. Despite his French nationality he was a highly visible member of the regional elite in 1806, his status due to his noble birth and to the wealth and social connections of his father-in-law, the merchant Martín de Sarratea. At the time of the capitulation Liniers commanded a small Spanish military and naval force in the Banda Oriental that was not subject to the surrender. Granted permission to enter Buenos Aires to see his family, Liniers made contact with local patriots and arranged for a small military force to cross from Montevideo to support the uprising.

Liniers and his subordinates organized enthusiastic volunteer units, most funded and led by the city's most successful merchants. While he managed to install some discipline in this popular force, it is clear that personal rivalries, ethnic friction, and the absence of a clear military chain of command created an environment where ambitious individuals and rival factions often pursued their own interests.[18] The British recognized this political complexity and sought, with very limited success, to find political allies, even discussing possible independence. As Liniers's forces gathered to attack the British garrison, Juan Martín Pueyrredón, a local-born son of a French merchant and a close associate of Liniers, initiated a last minute effort to draw Beresford into a focused discussion of independence, but it was frustrated by the first exchanges of gunfire.[19]

Once patriot forces were fully committed, Beresford was compelled to surrender after two hours of resistance.[20] An endless succession of public celebrations and nearly universal exultation now replaced the tears and humiliation of late June. Few in the city failed to recognize that neither the viceroy nor the upper tiers of the Spanish colonial administration played a significant role in this great victory gained in the king's name.

Finding New Leaders and Inventing New Forms

Despite the euphoria, nearly everyone realized that the threat was not over. British authorities initially reacted to the news of victory and the arrival in England of the captured Spanish treasury as an unanticipated windfall

FIGURE 29 An early-nineteenth-century view of the fort and viceroy's residence located on the bank of the Río de la Plata. Source: C. E. Pellegrini, *Recuerdos del Río de la Plata* (Buenos Aires: Libreria L'Amateur, 1969). Published with the permission of the publisher, Librería L'Amateur, Buenos Aires.

and immediately began organizing a large military force to reinforce Beresford's distant garrison.[21] Before this force could arrive in the South Atlantic, news of Beresford's surrender forced the British government to prepare a still larger military and naval force to reestablish control over the entire region.[22] As this force gathered, Santiago de Liniers and a volatile mix of Spanish career officers and local militia commanders recruited and trained new militia units.

This force was fundamentally different in character from the one swept aside by Beresford in June. While Spanish officers remained prominent, guiding drills and directing the tactical planning, militia commanders were increasingly assertive and confident in military councils. It was clear that the professional military had lost status. The new militia commanders were generally members of the local commercial elite, men like Pueyrredón and Cornelio Saavedra, who often viewed themselves as socially superior to regular officers.[23] These new commanders not only recruited the enlisted ranks but also paid for uniforms and arms. Enlisted men in these cases were clients and dependents in addition to being military subordinates.[24]

This was not the only novelty. Some militia units, most notably the Legión de Patricios Voluntarios Urbanos de Buenos Aires led by Cornelio Saavedra, introduced the practice of electing officers.[25] These innovations created new interdependencies that linked officers and enlisted ranks in ways that privileged personal charisma and private economic power.[26] It also created a new style of military leadership that relied in part on heightened visibility and a vocabulary of public gestures that suggested accessibility and patriotic passion to the plebeians who filled the enlisted ranks. As the threat of a second British invasion gathered in the distance, the city's military force had taken on a foundationally different character.

A larger and more consequential change affected the enlisted ranks.[27] In preparation for the uprising that forced Beresford's capitulation thousands of humble porteños had joined militia units or organized workmates and neighbors into nontraditional fighting forces, many armed only with homemade lances, knives, and shop tools.[28] The cabildo acknowledged the crucial role of unincorporated plebeians in the June 12, 1806, attack on British forces when it told the king that nearly all of the 180 dead and wounded were "citizens," not professional soldiers or militiamen.[29] In fact, the Reconquest had begun spontaneously without direct orders from Liniers.[30] Once engaged, the rage and energy of the lightly armed popular force preceded militia and regular army units through the streets toward the main British force.[31] Cries of "behead the infidels" and "knife them" suggest the social character and temperament of this force as it neared the plaza.[32] Even after surrender British officers were threatened and assaulted by gangs of plebeians.[33]

Nearly all the participants, from the city's wealthiest merchants to the unorganized crowd of slaves, apprentices, and journeymen who had thrown themselves on the British, saw this remarkable victory as confirming this city's unique military vocation. Individuals who had resisted every effort to expand the militia before 1806 now clamored to enlist. As a result, militia units organized by origin or race before August 12 faced a tidal wave of new recruits, many of whom had fought to take back the city.[34] By the end of the year a majority of the city's artisans and laborers had enlisted.[35] Despite the enthusiasm of the recruits, militia commanders were appalled at their lack of discipline and petitioned the cabildo to close all pulperías and gaming locations from six to eight in the morning to prevent what they saw as the drunkenness and disorder of the plebe from spilling onto the parade ground.[36]

These very consequential alterations in the size, recruitment, and leadership of the colonial military establishment occurred simultaneously with profound changes in political culture that, in the end, would prove a more potent threat to the colonial order than had British arms.[37] Two days after Beresford's surrender, the cabildo convoked a "Junta General," effectively a *cabildo abierto*, bringing together the most important ecclesiastical, civilian, and military officials as well as the city's wealthiest men.[38] After providing for public celebrations of the victory, the assembled dignitaries voted to remove all regional military units from the command of the viceroy, granting this authority to Liniers.[39] While the junta convened, Sobremonte was just across the estuary in the Banda Oriental, but neither the cabildo nor *audiencia* solicited his opinion.[40] In effect the cabildo had presumed the authority to strip the viceroy of his local military command without consultation with Spain.

This novel and highly public process, in effect the popular election of Liniers as chief military authority, made the judges of the audiencia so uneasy that they withdrew from the cabildo building. Nevertheless, the audiencia's regent accepted the duty of informing the viceroy of this controversial decision.[41] Sobremonte, finding it nearly impossible to retain even a simulacrum of authority, resisted for two weeks before acknowledging the appointment of Liniers.[42] The fact that this decision occurred with so little debate suggests the uncertainty that had overtaken colonial authorities at the highest level as well as the ambition and self-importance of the new political actors now fully visible in Buenos Aires in the wake of the city's brilliant military victory. If a new style of political leadership appeared on August 14, 1806, then a new assertiveness among the popular classes was now evident as well.[43]

As the Junta General met, a large and boisterous crowd gathered in the plaza in front of the cabildo building.[44] Junta participants later made it clear that all those assembled in the cabildo meeting room heard the crowd jeer and insult Viceroy Sobremonte as well as more distant targets like the court favorite Manuel Francisco Domingo de Godoy y Álvarez de Faria, Spain's "Prince of the Peace."[45] As the meeting proceeded, plebeians forced their way into the cabildo building, filling the stairwells and hallways. Those closest to the debate passed news to their friends outside. While the crowd outside shouted "Long Live the King!" and "Long Live Spain!" or, alternatively, threatened, "Death to the Traitors!" those in the stairwells chanted their support for Liniers and beat on the doors of the cabildo council room. One observer remembered this as the moment when "democratic enthusiasm made its first appearance face to face with the privileged classes."[46]

Sobremonte soon received news of this violent and threatening behavior by the crowd and protested to the cabildo and audiencia and then to Liniers directly. His letter to Liniers focused on the actions of the plebe. He complained to Liniers: "the people and enlisted troops" gathered in the plaza and "cheered you while insulting me." These violent public attacks had shaken the viceroy who alleged that Liniers had staged the spectacle.[47] The willingness of the authorities in Buenos Aires to permit his public vilification, including "threats against [his] life," was startling in this previously tame setting. The viceroy would now keep the estuary between himself and Buenos Aires.[48]

Some witnesses to the event claimed that Liniers and some of his closest allies, including the commanders of recently formed volunteer units like Juan Martín Pueyrredón, were in the plaza in front of the cabildo mingling with the assembled plebe as the junta met.[49] When informed, the viceroy called this behavior "insubordinate." Liniers, worried of possible disciplinary action, tried to distance himself from the plebe, claiming that both the vocal passion of the crowd and the junta's decision to grant him military authority had been a surprise. In his version of the story he claimed to have been on the outskirts of the city attending the burials of some captured British soldiers who had died of wounds received during the Reconquest when "a multitude of people" approached and proclaimed him as "their captain general." Liniers claimed that he told these noisy supporters that he did not want to be "the leader of a mob" and had even threatened "to return to Montevideo" unless they subsided. Instead the crowd followed him back to the city center chanting his name in the street as he sought advice from the bishop. Fearing the viceroy's wrath, or the judgment of authorities in Spain, Liniers claimed to Sobremonte that he had sought to reject the proffered military command.[50] Regardless of the merits of this story, it is undeniable that once notified of the decision to grant him extraordinary powers, Liniers, fully a man of his era, elected to accept this appointment from the open gallery of the cabildo building as the urban masses shouted his name.[51] In this moment Liniers became Argentina's first personalist leader, an exemplar of what we should see as a Romantic style of politics, or the public, highly theatrical melding of a leader's ambition and collective aspiration.

The Viceroy Deposed and the City Defended

Once the second British force had gathered in the estuary its commanders determined to take Montevideo before attempting a second attack on Buenos Aires. As the siege of Montevideo began, Sobremonte again demonstrated his incompetence, withdrawing from the defense without risking his troops.[52] He then refused to provide the horses and wagons necessary to support a relief force sent by the cabildo of Buenos Aires under the command of Liniers.[53] With the relief force stalled the garrison of Montevideo capitulated on February 3, 1806. The porteño force then retreated across the estuary.[54]

The loss of Montevideo destroyed what was left of Sobremonte's authority.[55] Public opinion in Buenos Aires was now universally hostile to the viceroy and even Spanish officials refused to defend him. Martín de Álzaga, again *alcalde de primer voto* of the cabildo of Buenos Aires, called another Junta General.[56] Because the audiencia had initially resisted the effort to strip the viceroy of his local military authority, the judges had become targets of popular anger in Buenos Aires. A series of pasquines appeared in the wake of Montevideo's capitulation, threatening "Death to the Viceroy and Judges!," "Down with the audiencia!," "Long Live Liberty!," and "Let's Raise the Republican Flag!"[57] After four days of popular demonstrations demanding the viceroy's removal, the junta stripped Sobremonte of his office and ordered his arrest on February 10.[58] Spain would never fully reassert its authority in Buenos Aires.

Politics and public administration now had a popular and unpredictable character. The legitimacy of local military, and increasingly civilian, authorities now effectively depended on the actions of emergency cabildo sessions where the presence of colonial officials, military officers, and royal judges gave a plausible appearance of representativeness and legitimacy.[59] This augmented cabildo, in turn, depended on and solicited the support of a mobilized, vocal plebe.[60]

The decision to remove Sobremonte from office followed the script from August 14, 1806. Once again, a crowd of many thousands gathered in the plaza and scores pressed against the cabildo doors or gathered in the stairwells. Some plebeians even mounted the cabildo tower to ring the bell, the traditional signal of an emergency. According to one witness the crowd shouted, "No Vice King, no Royal Audience, down with them, hang them!" They also shouted, "Death to the Viceroy," "Death to the judges," and "Long Live Liberty!"[61] Large crowds now gathered in front of the cabildo of Buenos Aires to shout the word that had justified the torture of Antonini and Díaz in 1795. In these circumstances the assembled delegates acted quickly to remove Sobremonte and order his arrest. The audiencia assumed the chore of formalizing these momentous decisions by informing the king.[62] As the British threat gathered in the estuary, the region's future was in the hands of the native-born militia officer corps and cabildo, not Spanish colonial authorities.[63]

By the time the British attacked on Buenos Aires, nearly the entire male population of the city had enlisted or joined informal groups of *guerrilleros*.[64] Some sources claimed that an implausible thirteen thousand men were under arms, including two thousand slaves.[65] The successful recruitment of the city's servile population was both an expression of the patriotic ardor of slaves and the calculated manipulation of the slave population's hope for freedom by military leaders.[66] In March 1807 José de María addressed the cabildo as "commander of the troop of slaves" to remind councilors that slaves "could find no better prize than liberty" for their future service in defending the city. Santiago de Liniers initially supported this request and the cabildo agreed in principle, but wrote to him privately to say that, "this prize [freedom] can only be granted if it did not prejudice the rights of slave owners and was based on verified actions in battle." Well aware that the arming of slaves in the French Caribbean had led quickly to the abolition of slavery, the cabildo warned Liniers that José de María held the "most delicate post that in this day might appear" and went on to order him replaced, noting this dangerous character "who is not capable to command [the slaves] . . . because of his notorious bad disposition."[67]

Filled with false confidence and impatient to engage the British, Liniers and his commanders decided to block the British advance on July 2, 1807. The result was a crushing defeat that sent this broken force of militia and regular troops fleeing back to Buenos Aires.[68] With the survivors disorganized and dispersed and with Liniers and many senior commanders out of contact with leaders in the city, Martín de Álzaga directed the city's defense.[69] In place of a set piece battle in the open he ordered the remaining forces and thousands of volunteers to take positions on rooftops and doorways and placed snipers in church towers. While the British paused on the outskirts, the porteño militia placed artillery to cover all of the streets leading to the Plaza Mayor as civilians built barricades and dug trenches.

Having swept aside resistance on the outskirts, General Whitelocke divided most of his force into three columns and sent them through the narrow streets toward the plaza on July 5. The city's defenders, cut off from their units and from the chain of command, created informal fighting units of ten to fifty men to disrupt British forward positions and ambush stragglers.[70] In the city center volunteers armed with grenades and discarded weapons joined the combat. As the British advanced, many civilians fought from the rooftops throwing rocks and bricks at the passing troops.[71] While the cabildo had initially armed slaves with short swords and knives, many picked up discarded rifles and pistols as the battle raged around them.[72]

The British enjoyed success on the periphery of the city where their massed strength could crush defensive efforts. But once the British force divided into columns and entered the city's grid pattern, it lost this advantage because the narrow streets prevented assembling a mass larger than fifteen or twenty riflemen at the point of attack. As the forward movement of the attacking force slowed, intense fire from rooftops and steeples proved devastating. Four blocks from the Plaza Mayor all of the British columns bogged down and took defensive positions as ever larger numbers of militiamen and civilians attacked. Unable to either move forward or retreat in order, one British column after another surrendered.[73] Militia officers now found themselves in the unanticipated role of protecting surrendering British soldiers from an enraged plebe crying out for blood. British officers later remembered "an immense armed and enraged population" that "threatened to massacre [Colonel Robert Crauford's force]" if it continued to resist.[74] Recognizing the hopelessness of his position Whitelocke accepted Liniers's humiliating conditions, agreeing to exit both Buenos Aires and Montevideo and order naval forces from the estuary as well.[75] One of the unanticipated results of the capitulation of thousands of British soldiers, many surrendering to small groups of civilians and slaves, was the mass appropriation of weaponry by what one witness dismissed as the "*chusma*" or rabble.[76]

The spontaneous popular reaction to Beresford's occupation and to the threat of a second British invasion created a large militia force that withdrew thousands of men from a tight labor market and initiated a period of

FIGURE 30 This cartoon published in a popular London periodical suggests that General Whitelocke had behaved in a cowardly manner when he surrendered to Liniers in 1807. The devil on the left asks if the general has the courage to regain his honor by using the pistol. Published with the permission of the John Hay Library, Brown University.

remarkable wage inflation.[77] The cabildo and military exacerbated this crisis by paying militiamen wages that in many cases were higher than those paid in the civilian economy.[78] Moving this militarized population back into the civilian economy would test the creativity and resolve of the government and ultimately bankrupt the colonial fiscal establishment.

This was the context in which the ambitions and rivalries of the major political actors and their allies gathered strength. No historian has successfully forced the events of 1808–1810 into a neat template of competing factions or parties. In addition to local conditions and the actions of local political actors, distant events helped overwhelm the colonial system's inherent entropy. In less than three years Spain negotiated peace with Great Britain, Charles IV and then Ferdinand abdicated the Spanish throne, Napoleon invaded Iberia and placed his brother Joseph on the Spanish throne, the Portuguese royal family arrived in Rio de Janeiro, and Spanish patriots created governing juntas to resist the French. In this fluid and unstable environment, factions and alliances were forged, nurtured, and then ruptured in ways that complicate every effort to explain the last years of Spanish colonial rule in Buenos Aires.

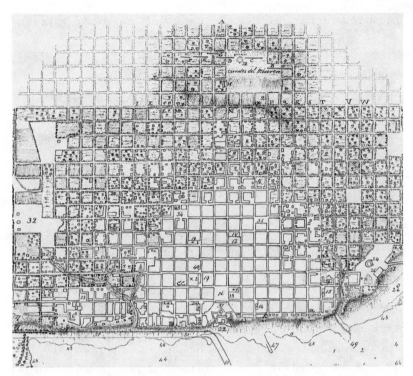

FIGURE 31 Map of Buenos Aires produced by British officers prior to 1807 attack. Published with the permission of the John Carter Brown Library, Providence, Rhode Island.

It is clear that the removal of Viceroy Sobremonte in 1807 shattered the institutional status quo established in 1776 with the creation of the Viceroyalty of the Río de la Plata. In the wake of this action neither Santiago de Liniers as interim viceroy (1808–1809) nor Baltasar Hidalgo de Cisneros as viceroy (1809–1810) would ever exercise the institutional power and personal authority that had been the norm previously. Simultaneously, the audiencia's tardy and grudging willingness to transfer the viceroy's military authority to Liniers in 1806 permanently compromised its own authority. Militarization further complicated the political environment. While the militia leadership, elevated by the two military victories, depended on the cabildo to legitimize its authority and pay its bills, neither the cabildo nor the Spanish administrative structure could control or direct this new, popular military force that had mobilized the city's free black and casta majority and the slave population.[79] Many pardos and morenos who had come to the attention of authorities in the cycles of protest and legal contests in the 1790s now reappeared on the civic stage, their status enhanced by heroic service against the British.[80]

Second Innings, Thwarted Ambitions, and Fiscal Emergency

Although the Spanish Court praised both Santiago de Liniers and Martín de Álzaga in the wake of these great victories, Liniers was the chief beneficiary of Spanish gratitude, named interim viceroy and granted the title Conde de Buenos Aires.[81] If his French nationality had put him at risk in 1795, Spain's alliance with Napoleon in opposition to the English-led Third Coalition in 1805 provided the platform for his meteoric rise to prominence during the two British attacks on Buenos Aires. With France as an ally and Britain as the enemy there were few obstacles in Buenos Aires or Spain to his rapid political ascent.[82] Filled with confidence, Liniers made a series of mistakes.

The two British attacks had disrupted commerce in the region for over a year. Merchants' shelves were empty and rural products remained stacked in warehouses or rotted in the Sun. Everyone knew that tons of British goods were available at fire sale prices in Montevideo and that British and American ships were poised to embark hides and other local products, but opposition from Álzaga and other Spanish merchants thwarted wholesale change. In response, Liniers winked at a rapidly evolved mix of legalization, secret deals, favoritism, and the long-established palm greasing that had always made the city's commerce work.[83] Liniers benefited indirectly from this new order as he and his allies directed foreign merchants to his French mistress, Ana Perichón de O'Gorman, and her relatives who extracted gifts and cash for facilitating transactions.[84] Liniers's enemies, Álzaga now chief among them, sent numerous denunciations to Spain complaining of his corruption. The corrosive affect on Liniers gained traction after the 1808 French invasion of Spain.[85] With France as Spain's enemy and Britain now an ally, Liniers's victories over Britain seemed smaller and his French nationality seemed more threatening to Spain.[86]

Negotiating with an Armed Plebe

The large and expensive militia force created during the emergency had become an insupportable fiscal burden by late 1808. All of the colony's responsible authorities, including Liniers whose personal authority depended on the loyalty of the militia, knew that the viceroyalty could not afford this force on a full-time basis.[87] These same political and fiscal authorities also knew that the city's militia would resist any pressure to disband or return to part-time service at reduced salaries.[88] The Patricios, the Cuerpo de Arribeños, and the Batallón de Naturales, Pardos y Morenos de Infantería resisted demobilization more than did units primarily recruited among Spanish immigrants since these artisans, laborers, and shop clerks were generally better off than the native born.[89] In a memoir written long after the events, Cornelio Saavedra remembered with some bitterness that the Spanish elite had pressed both Liniers and the Spanish Court to demobilize his unit because of the city's labor shortage and the treasury short fall.[90]

The mass of enlisted men were dependent on military wages, typically twelve pesos per month, an amount supplemented in many cases by housing and food allotments.[91] The *sargento mayor* of the Arribeños, Ildefonso Pasos, indicated the potentially destabilizing effects of demobilization in a letter to Liniers in July 1807. He baldly stated that his unit, recruited among casta laborers and journeymen from the interior provinces, must be kept on full military wages, noting that "the majority of the men would be indigent . . . [and] if deprived of this income would likely turn to robberies." He went on to state that his own experience had shown "that military service could be a way of life."[92] Poverty among the enlisted ranks of the Arribeños as well as the Pardos and Morenos was no surprise. The cabildo had acknowledged this in December 1806, well before the second invasion, when it provided five hundred pesos for the Arribeños and three thousand pesos for the Pardos and Morenos to pay for uniforms because of the "notorious poverty" of the former and the "misery and complete absence of resources" of the latter.[93] These were the defenders of Buenos Aires one British officer remembered as "a revengeful rabble, inflamed with superstitions, hatred, and religious bigotry."[94]

Even militia officers resisted demobilization. While Liniers's enemies falsely claimed that the militia force sustained a bloated officer corps of "one thousand eight hundred officers" to suggest the interim viceroy's corruption to Spanish authorities, the actual number was still an unsustainable twelve hundred including noncommissioned officers.[95] With the native-born militia units' resistance to demobilization clear, expressions of hostility towards the officer corps became more common. In 1809 the Spanish resident Diego Ponce de León, writing to José Moñino y Redondo, Count of Floridablanca, referred to the military officers associated with Liniers as "the scum of the earth."[96] Similarly, Manuel Beruti, writing in 1811, remembered twenty-four officers who "in the old Spanish government did not have anything and later [after entering the military] found their luck."[97] A British resident characterized Liniers's promotion practices as "raising to the rank of officers, the most abandoned members of society, and others whose want of honour assured him that they would act whatever part he assigned them."[98]

Forcing demobilization would be difficult since militia officers and enlisted ranks had also become more assertive and less deferential in the light of their victories. The fact that castas and blacks filled the enlisted ranks of the local-born units gave this assertiveness an edge.[99] In the week following Beresford's surrender, the cabildo began to complain of "outrages" and "scandals" in the streets and public places caused by armed militiamen. Only a minority of the militiamen called to full time service in 1807 lived in barracks subject to the discipline of officers. Most continued to live with their families or in the loose aggregations of single men found in the city's rooming houses while retaining their uniforms and weapons. As a result, armed militiamen circulated in the streets, taverns, and gaming establishments with no effective controls, each man seeing himself as a hero, regardless of former condition, and declaring his willingness to respond to any insult to his honor. An armed and confident plebe was the key to the defense of the city, but city leaders soon realized the explosive potential contained in this transformation.[100]

The mobilization and arming of slaves in 1807 raised even more fundamental fears of disorder and social conflict. Joaquín Guzman, a slave of the Domincan convent, led more than three hundred slaves organized in four companies and armed with machetes in 1807.[101] Many other slaves entered the combat spontaneously as British columns forced their way into the city, and some slave owners brought their slaves with them when they volunteered.[102] Following Whitelocke's defeat the cabildo in alliance with Liniers sought to quickly disarm the city's slaves. Slave volunteers had served with distinction in both the Reconquest and defense of the city, but authorities realized that there was a troubling downside to the experience of armed slaves fighting and killing European soldiers in the streets of Buenos Aires. While military commanders tried to prevent slaves from arming themselves with captured British firearms, the chaos of the streets during combat meant that hundreds of firearms were in the hands of slaves by the time a ceasefire was in place. Two days after the victory the cabildo asked slaves who had participated in the defense to register so that the city could acknowledge their "important services to the king and the nation," offering two pesos for each firearm and eight reales for each sword or bayonet turned over to authorities. While these small compensations reduced the weaponry present in the slave community, no one believed that this measure could fully contain the dangerous mix of collective self-confidence and political passion now loose in this population.

Thousands of slaves had participated in the military action and hundreds had distinguished themselves.[103] Everyone recognized that some grand gesture was necessary for those who survived.[104] The cabildo proclaimed that slaves had fought "with the fierceness of free men," but repeated the caution signaled to Liniers before the second attack that manumissions could not be granted without compensating owners even though "this was the reward granted to slaves in the past" when they defended the king.[105] Because the cabildo lacked the resources to compensate every master if all slaves who actively participated in the defense of the city were freed, it sought a way to trim the celebration of the slaves' heroism and selflessness to fit its tight budget.[106]

The cabildo first committed to freeing all slaves "mutilated and disabled" by wounds and then settled on a lottery to distribute twenty-five additional manumissions among deserving slaves.[107] It was immediately obvious that this shortsighted policy would push the slave community dangerously close to insurrection.[108] Representatives of other political institutions, the military, and the ecclesiastical establishment hustled to find funds to pay for additional manumissions. In the end 130 slaves gained freedom in a ceremony on November 12, 1807. The number included 60 slaves wounded in the battle and another 70 selected by lottery.[109] Despite these measures, slaves who had fought with distinction were still writing to the cabildo and to colonial authorities to seek manumission based on heroic actions two years after the surrender of Whitelocke. One advocate complained long after the lottery that "many [of the wounded] still shed tears over their cruel fate to continue in bondage."[110] Other frustrated slaves suggested that the government offer ten pesos to the slaves who were not freed.[111]

The Pardos and Morenos, free men all, were formed in ranks by their officers in front of the six hundred slaves entered in the lottery as a way to prevent the disappointment of those not emancipated in the lottery from igniting a demonstration.[112] In addition to participating in this ceremony, the Patricios published a long panegyric that urged "the valiant slaves" to accept "the expressions of gratitude of the patriotic people" as compensation for their heroism. Typical of the prevailing ideology this document went on to warn slaves freed by the lottery to avoid "vices and laziness."[113] After the lottery Liniers acknowledged the repressed anger and disappointment of the slave community when he explained his decision to suspend the death sentence of the slave Sebastian by telling the audiencia that, "it is necessary, taking into account the current situation, to manifest with concrete action [our] recognition for the good services of the lower classes. . . . I am waiting for a similar sentence passed upon a white defendant so that the blacks do not have any reason to think that they are the only ones suffering such harsh punishment."[114]

French Conspiracy Redux

In the unstable political context produced by the abdications of Charles IV and Ferdinand VII and the French invasion of Spain, the cabildo under Álzaga's guidance sought to turn the Spanish junta against Liniers. At a time when the junta was fighting for its life against French armies, the claims that the interim viceroy had elevated scores of French nationals to positions of influence in the military and bureaucracy of the viceroyalty proved devastating. In a colony with relatively few foreign residents, it is clear that a surprising number of French nationals held highly visible positions after 1807. Some were members of well-established mercantile families like the Pueyrredóns. Juan Martín de Pueyrredón was among the most prominent militia commanders in 1806. He became one of Liniers's closest advisors and was present in the Plaza Mayor on August 14, urging the plebe to demand the cabildo abierto grant military command to Liniers.[115] Pueyrredón also had close ties with the wealthy merchants that dominated the cabildo as was demonstrated by their decision to send him to Spain as their lobbyist after Beresford's surrender. A second, less well-established group included French nationals attached to the circle of Ana Perichón de O'Gorman, a French national who had emigrated with her parents and siblings from the French Indian Ocean colony of Mauritius in 1797. She was the wife of an Irish resident of Buenos Aires, Tomás O'Gorman, who Álzaga and others suspected of spying for the British. In 1806 she began a very public affair with Liniers, making her home a center of uninhibited political conversation and commercial deal making.[116] Her brother Juan Bautista

Perichón served as an officer in a militia unit created in 1806. Shortly after the surrender of Whitelocke, Liniers sent Perichón to France to give Napoleon the details of events in Buenos Aires.[117] This mission raised suspicions in both Buenos Aires and Spain and when Perichón crossed into Spain from France authorities ordered his arrest in Cádiz, but he later escaped from prison.

The cabildo's complaints about French influence in the government and military command under Liniers had both a xenophobic and a class character.[118] In a letter of October 15, 1808, the cabildo laid out its case. It claimed that many of the officers appointed by interim viceroy were "those whom a short time ago we saw as convicts, laboring in chains in public projects, those against whom charges are still pending as robbers, jailers, corporals and others dregs of society, today we see them wearing the badges of lieutenant colonels." They went on to complain that even though the emergency was over, Liniers was recruiting a new militia unit with a French officer corps "by birth or by character."[119]

Embedded in this characterization was an implicit backward reference to the events of 1795. Certainly among the most startling of these newly important men identified as French "by character" was Santiago Antonini, the Sardinian clockmaker arrested as a member of the Dumont group in 1795. In September 1806 as the city prepared for the second British invasion, Antonini, still a practicing clockmaker, wrote to the cabildo to propose the creation of a militia unit of "French, Italian and Maltese" volunteers. One week later "the senior military commander," Liniers, responded that the proposal "to form a unit of French and Italian artisans was not convenient although it merited gratitude" and suggested these artisans join existing units.[120] Still, within months, Liniers appointed Antonini to serve as commissary general, a position of significant responsibility and high visibility, since this official controlled the budget for provisioning and housing the greatly enlarged military. Liniers's decision to elevate Antonini suggests that his courage in the face of his torture and his refusal to implicate others (remember that two of Liniers's employees were in jail with him) had created a personal connection between the two. Once the second British invasion was defeated, Liniers sent Antonini to the United States to purchase weapons and then to Spain as his personal agent. This was a completely unanticipated trajectory for a man so notoriously identified in Buenos Aires with what Álzaga and others still believed was a conspiracy to raise a slave rebellion.

FIGURE 32 In anticipation of the second British invasion, Santiago Antonini wrote to Santiago de Liniers to request appointment as commissary general. He also asked that his son, Antonio, be appointed as his lieutenant. Liniers, chief military commander after the dismissal of Viceroy Sobremonte, confirmed the two appointments in the notation on the left. Published with the permission of the AGN, Buenos Aires, Argentina.

Cabildo members objected to another appointment as well. Alejandro Duclos Guyot was the captain of a French merchant ship detained in Montevideo during the war with France (1792–1795). He returned to the Río de la Plata in 1807 and volunteered for military service against the British. Duclos soon became one of Liniers's most visible aides along with Ana Perichón's brother Juan Bautista. In addition to his French nationality, Duclos drew the attention of critics because colonial authorities in 1795, Álzaga among them, had believed that he was associated with the Dumont and Antonini group.[121] The fact that Liniers elevated two men so visibly and publicly associated with the political hysteria and arrests of 1795 suggests that his enormous popularity encouraged him to take bold political risks.[122]

At least one contemporary remembered that the "mass of proletarians" had consecrated "a type of cult around the General Liniers."[123]

The Military "Election" of January I, 1809

The best measure of Álzaga's ascendancy within the tight circle of rich and powerful mercantile families that staffed the cabildo was his repeated selection as alcalde of the first vote during the crisis of 1806–1809.[124] By late 1808 a confident Álzaga and his chief supporters had determined to force the interim viceroy's removal. He forged an alliance with the governor of Montevideo, Francisco Javier de Elío, a difficult career officer who had served under Liniers without distinction during the second British invasion. Elío accomplished the first step of the conspiracy when he created a junta in Montevideo and then refused to accept Liniers's authority.[125]

On January 1, 1809, the outgoing cabildo reelected Álzaga for an unheard of third successive term as alcalde of the first vote.[126] The incendiary intention of this action was to provoke a confrontation that would lead to the viceroy's resignation.[127] Álzaga and his allies expected Liniers to reject the cabildo's election and intended to use his rejection to justify mobilizing Spanish-dominated militia units and a popular demonstration, the massed employees and other dependents of Spanish wholesale merchants and shopkeepers, who would reliably clamor for the creation of a local junta in imitation of Montevideo.[128] Unfortunately for the Álzaga faction, the supporters of the interim viceroy had been aware of this plan since November.[129]

On January 1 when Álzaga and his closest allies, including the future revolutionary Mariano Moreno then serving as cabildo secretary, crossed the plaza to the fortress to present the cabildo's election results to Liniers, they were confident they held all the cards.[130] Their military allies were mobilized to control the plaza where a loud crowd of civilian supporters were also gathered. Seeking to stir the anti-French passions of the plebe, an anti-Liniers poem was distributed that stated, "the people know he is French . . . and that he is without a doubt another Napoleon."[131] The conspirators were surprised when Liniers accepted the cabildo election results and then offered to comply with Álzaga's demand that he resign; the real test of strength was still to come.[132]

Cornelio Saavedra, commander of the city's largest militia unit, the Patricios, entered the viceregal apartment before Álzaga and his allies could announce Liniers's resignation.[133] He had previously prepared the Patricios and other loyal military units, including the Arribeños and Pardos and Morenos, for rapid deployment.[134] These units together represented the native-born porteño working class in arms. He had also readied civilian supporters loyal to Liniers to rush to the plaza to counter the pro-Álzaga demonstration. When Saavedra's larger force, supported by a large popular demonstration, assembled across the plaza from the Spanish immigrant militia units, the city reached a tipping point. In effect this armed assembly mimicked the divisions that had appeared among the city's artisans during the guild confrontations of the early 1790s, native-born units with their ranks largely filled by black and casta artisans and laborers faced the Spanish units loyal to Álzaga and the cabildo whose enlisted ranks included a majority of immigrant artisans and retail clerks. Again, numbers favored the native born. These units and their mobilized civilian supporters, the two manifestations of the city's popular masses, would now mediate and decide the struggle for political supremacy between the regions first two populist leaders, Liniers and Álzaga.[135] With the Patricios, Arribeños, and Pardos and Morenos commanding the plaza, Liniers accompanied by Saavedra showed himself to the crowd and was greeted by cheers of "Long Live Liniers."[136] Out manned and out gunned by the Liniers loyalists, Álzaga's military allies had no chance to tilt the balance.[137]

With the contest in the plaza settled by a limited exchange of threats and shots, it was time to sort out the perpetrators. Liniers disarmed and later disbanded the Spanish militia units and exiled Álzaga and the other cabildo members to Patagonia.[138] Yet, despite the apparent comprehensiveness of this victory, Liniers emerged weakened and now unambiguously dependent on the Patricios, Arribeños, and Pardos and Morenos. He would stand under the shadow of Saavedra and the criollo officer corps for the remainder of his term.[139] In their efforts to dismiss and insult their victorious enemies, Álzaga's allies in Montevideo focused predictably on the growing visibility of the plebe in Buenos Aires, deploring the role played by "low people" in the events of January 1 and characterizing the Patricios and Arribeños as "vagrants, adventurers, and plotters."[140]

Liniers rewarded his military supporters with promotions and plum assignments, a group that one local critic had categorized as "former prisoners and vagrants."[141] The Montevideo junta quickly extracted Álzaga and his allies from their Patagonian exile. Once relocated in Montevideo, the January 1 conspirators provided Spain's Junta Central with their version of the event that emphasized the racial and class basis of the armed confrontation in the plaza. They remembered that "the plaza and streets were occupied by the Patricios, without exclusion of the blacks, mulattos, and Indians . . . [and as a result] these castas, too numerous and as well instructed [as the Spanish militias] in military tactics, gained for the first time the full comprehension of their power." They went on to condemn the "willful pride, the arrogance, and ferocity" displayed by the "numerous armed and trained castas" toward the Spaniards in the plaza.[142] From their perspective, class and racial deference were as comprehensively defeated in 1809 as Whitelocke had been in 1807.

When the Spanish junta finally notified Liniers of the appointment of Baltasar Hidalgo de Cisneros to replace him, his allies urged him to resist the transfer of power.[143] Given that Governor Elío of Montevideo had already created a junta, denounced Liniers, and given refuge to Álzaga and the other plotters of January 1 without suffering any consequence, the interim viceroy's reticence must be taken as loyalty to Spain and, ultimately, to Ferdinand VII. If Liniers was the first populist political figure to take the stage in Buenos Aires, his populism, constrained by loyalty to the colonial order, was fundamentally different in character from the mature form that would soon appear.

The Beginning of the End

The Spanish Junta Central replaced Liniers in February 1809 before it had a full account of the failed January 1 *golpe de estado*. Inaccurate English accounts claiming Liniers had declared his allegiance to Napoleon had circulated in Cádiz, quickly liquidating any residual support he had in the junta. As a result, the new viceroy arrived in Montevideo fearful that he faced enemies on all sides, in Montevideo a junta of unknown loyalty headed by Elío and in Buenos Aires the possibility of a French secessionist conspiracy.[144] This explains Cisneros's timid approach to his capital city. Once assured that Elío was not a direct threat, Cisneros wrote to Liniers asking him to cross the estuary to Colonia to meet.[145] As this negotiation unfolded, Saavedra and other senior militia officers sought to win Liniers's commitment to create a junta and establish effective independence.[146] Liniers refused this suggestion, traveled to Colonia, and remained there while Cisneros embarked for Buenos Aires.

Cisneros was soon forced to recognize that many "maintained the spirit

FIGURE 33 Church of Santo Domingo, the scene of a key confrontation between militia and British forces. Cannon shot from the battle are still visible in bell tower on left. Photograph by author.

of party, this fatal ferment of dissension and rivalry," which was articulated in "cafes and other public places whose owners are responsible for permitting these behaviors."[147] Days after Cisneros took the reins of the viceroyalty, Santiago de Liniers returned from Colonia without official recognition or formal honors and moved quietly to a private residence. Within hours of his return Cornelio Saavedra and nearly every high-ranking criollo officer as well as a large crowd of more humble supporters arrived to welcome the return of their hero. The proximity of this event to the viceregal residence presented a clear message to Cisneros, the city's militia and plebeian masses remained loyal to Liniers.[148] While Liniers exercised great restraint and continued to treat the new viceroy with respect and deference, he refused to return to Spain, despite the orders of the Spanish junta. Instead he relocated to Córdoba as a private citizen.[149]

As military costs overwhelmed fiscal resources, Cisneros found himself in an impossible situation. Unless he cut military expenses his government would collapse, but any comprehensive demobilization could provoke the active opposition of the militia, now operating as an armed political party. Unwilling to try a test of wills, Cisneros attempted a desperate compromise in the face of "deficits that increased daily." He reduced the number of militia battalions receiving full salaries to five, but included in this number every unit that had supported Liniers on January 1. As a sop to the demobilized units he permitted their officers to retain their *fueros* while saving the wages previously paid both officer and enlisted ranks.[150]

Cisneros simultaneously attempted to win the support of the Spanish faction by suspending the judgments against Álzaga and his allies and allowing them to return to Buenos Aires.[151] This decision completed a remarkable and dangerous series of political decisions undertaken by authorities in Buenos Aires and Spain.[152] The cycle began with the August 14, 1806, Junta General that removed Sobremonte's military command and was followed by the February 10, 1807, decision by a second Junta General to strip Sobremonte of his office and order his arrest. In both cases the Spanish king confirmed these unusual and irregular decisions without imposing punishments or even reprimands on those responsible or complicit, including the audiencia, cabildo, and regular army officers. Instead he named Santiago de Liniers interim viceroy and Conde de Buenos Aires. Now Viceroy Cisneros suspended the judgments against Álzaga and his allies who had attempted to oust Liniers on January 1, 1809. The failure of weak Spanish governments and weak colonial institutions in Buenos Aires to impose consequences on any of those responsible for these challenges to traditional authority combined to create a dangerous moral hazard that encouraged the risk-taking behaviors that propelled the city towards May 25, 1810.

Cisneros also made an effort to more effectively control the plebe. Even before the new viceroy's arrival, Liniers had issued a *bando* that "urgently" provided military patrols to shore up the city's *alcaldes de barrio* who were losing control of the poorest neighborhoods.[153] Many British officers had commented on levels of violence and property crime in their memoirs following the events of 1806 and 1807. One claimed that "murders are constant among the rabble: no less than one hundred and six were committed in Buenos Aires between January and May last."[154] Cisneros was certainly convinced that the city's disorderly and assertive plebe was responsible for rising levels of violence and property crime.[155] Responding to complaints of the city elite in September 1809, he imposed new, harsher punishments for vagrancy. At the same time he banned the carrying of firearms and knives, established new controls on gaming places and pulperías, and imposed severe punishments for pasquines.[156] Simultaneously, Cisneros and the officer corps dealt with rising levels of desertions and a perceived loss of discipline in the mobilized militia units. One manifestation of this concern was the decision by the command staff to threaten grave punishments to the growing numbers of enlisted men who were pawning their uniforms to buy *aguardiente*.[157]

Tossed Aside by the Invisible Hand

The fiscal and commercial crisis forced Cisneros to invite interested parties to debate liberalized trade in 1809. The most effective advocate for change was Mariano Moreno, former secretary of the cabildo and closely associated with Álzaga in the January 1809 conspiracy. He argued for free trade as the best strategy to promote economic prosperity, regardless of the impact on local industry.[158] Miguel Fernández Agüero defended the traditional system and warned of the destructive impact of imports on local artisans, pointing out that there were 19,000 pairs of British factory-made shoes and other manufactured goods waiting in the harbor. He asked, "is it not the truth that this action will cause the shoemakers, blacksmiths, carpenters, and a multitude of artisans to close their shops and abandon the trades that sustain a multitude of families with honor?"[159] Moreno had no patience for this solicitous concern for plebeian well-being. Paraphrasing the dismissive arguments presented by Saavedra in 1799 when he dismissed the organizational aspirations of the shoemakers, Moreno asked, "is it not a scandal that a pair of well-made boots cost twenty pesos in Buenos Aires?" He continued: "if these [British] goods are inferior to those produced in the country, they will not cause any problems; if they are superior, they will promote emulation and force our artisans to improve the quality of their goods."[160]

Given that the fate of the city's shoemakers was so centrally featured in this debate and given the shoemakers' demonstrated willingness to challenge the opinions of colonial authorities during the hotly contested organizational effort, the absence of any organized effort to influence this debate is striking. Certainly, the prior accumulation of debilitating legal costs had intimidated both white and black and casta masters. Almost a decade earlier a group of young black and casta masters was in open rebellion against craft leaders, condemning Baquero for his "selfish and sinister" leadership that had accumulated large legal fees. By 1803 the collective debt of pardo and moreno shoemakers had risen to 1,037 pesos.[161] While not the only threat to this craft, this debt had helped push scores of shoemakers from their trade and into full-time military service after the British attacks.[162]

Given the scale of the commercial and fiscal crises facing the city, the outcome of this debate was inevitable: the opening of the port to British goods. While exporters enjoyed the benefits of expanded trade with foreign markets, the economy of Buenos Aires remained fragile and volatile. Prices fluctuated wildly, rising when goods were scarce and then plunging when foreign goods appeared in volume. Local artisans and small manufacturers in particular operated at great disadvantage in this environment, unable to anticipate what products the next ship would offload and fearful of maintaining inventory or purchasing raw materials on the expectation of future consumer demand. Moreno's victorious argument, like that articulated ten years earlier by Cornelio Saavedra, contemptuously dismissed the traditional protections of skilled trades in Spanish colonial cities.[163] After 1809 neither guilds nor colonial commercial policies would protect artisans in Buenos Aires from the powerful forces rapidly transforming the Atlantic market.

In this difficult and unpredictable period one institution proved a reliable bastion for a plebe battered by the rising volume of Atlantic trade, the urban militia. Free black, casta, and criollo artisans and laborers had not only entered the militia in large numbers but most had remained in full-time service earning twelve pesos per month long after Whitelocke's surrender. As the institutions and social arrangements that had organized and directed the plebe in the colonial period fell away — guilds, occupational recruitment and training standards, networks of credit, and neighborhood affinities — military units with their fluid hierarchies and strong institutional loyalties provided alternative rituals, hierarchies, training regimes, and, most importantly, incomes.[164]

The Cabildo Abierto of May 25, 1810

On May 18, 1810, Viceroy Cisneros informed the public that Seville had fallen to the French and that Spanish resistance was now led by a Regency relocated to Cádiz. Spanish control of Buenos Aires would last one more week.[165] With the Spanish government's survival unlikely, the viceroy sought the support of Saavedra and other local military commanders.[166] They told him in a face-to-face meeting that the Spanish government that had appointed him no longer existed.[167] Saavedra then asked the shaken viceroy if "this immense territory [the viceroyalty] should recognize the sovereignty of the merchants of Cádiz and the fishermen of León [the two parts of Spain still outside French control]."[168]

In the city's plazas and other public places, popular support for creating a junta grew. Cisneros reported later to the Spanish junta that on May 20 the alcalde Juan José de Lezica had pressured him to agree to a junta by reporting that "a convulsion was visible among the people."[169] On May 21 the cabildo, confronted by an increasingly organized and focused "public" mobilized in the Plaza Mayor, asked the viceroy to resign and called for a cabildo abierto to be held the next day.[170] Many witnesses claimed that the crowds pressing the cabildo to act on May 21 and 22 were both smaller and more organized than that dominating events in 1806 and 1807, and one witness claimed that the streets were filled with people who demonstrated the "serenity of a bullfight."[171] Although Saavedra later recalled the plaza was "full of people" crying "Down with Cisneros!" other observers disagreed, remembering smaller crowds and the appearance of a new "popular" leadership.[172] Antonio Luis Beruti and Domingo French were the two street-level leaders most obviously in control of the crowd now pressing the cabildo for action. According to witnesses they had recruited their partisans among "artisans."[173] Some remembered as well that many in the crowd were armed "with knives and pistols."[174]

Only 221 of the 450 *vecinos* invited to the May 22 cabildo abierto attended.[175] Evidence suggests that soldiers from the Patricios assigned to guard access to the plaza prevented many known Spanish loyalists from attending while permitting supporters of a junta to join the meeting without invitations. Cisneros affirmed this story when he wrote to the Spanish junta to claim that the militia "refused to let the honorable vecinos pass while allowing those allied with the conspiracy through." Moreover, he asserted, "some officers passed out invitations without names" to flood the meeting with allies.[176] With many loyalists excluded from the assembly and with the "Legión Infernal," the militants led by Beruti and French, pressing into the cabildo's chambers, the assembly determined to create a junta with little opposition and then delegated to the cabildo the selection of junta members.

Despite their effective efforts to gain acceptance of a junta, the faction favoring de facto independence or some form of autonomy stumbled by failing to stipulate the junta membership. This mistake was evident when the cabildo published the junta's composition on May 24. News that Viceroy Cisneros had been named president provoked an irresistible wave of protest. Civilian activists and militia officers met continuously in the barracks of the Patricios while larger, less formal groups with a strong plebeian character gathered near the cabildo.[177] Armed groups roamed the streets pulling down the printed notices that identified the members of junta.[178] The apparent victory of Viceroy Cisneros and those seeking to slow the pace of political change on May 22 was simply unsustainable in the heated climate of May 1810.[179]

Throughout this tight cycle of protest and argument native-born militias and plebeians controlled the plazas and streets of the city, demanding a new assembly. When a second cabildo abierto met on May 25, participants quickly set aside the first junta and dispossessed Cisneros of any residual political power. They then granted Saavedra the presidency of a new junta that also included Juan José Castelli, officer in the Patricios and long an active supporter of independence, Manuel Belgrano, previously attached to the Carlota faction, Manuel Alberti, a cleric, Miguel de Azcuenaga, militia officer and powerful landowner, two Spanish merchants, Juan Larrea and Domingo Matheu, and two nonvoting secretaries, Juan José Pasos and Mariano Moreno.[180]

At each stage of the city's rapid political evolution from 1806, the militias and the plebe had shared control of the Plaza Mayor, renamed Plaza Victoria to celebrate victory over the British, as well as the halls and galleries of the cabildo and used this strategic ground to push their collective objectives.[181] These groups had been present continuously in Plaza Victoria from May 17, when news of the fall of Seville arrived, through May 25. Contemporaries and most historians agree that the size and assertiveness of this popular force had peaked well before May 25. The historian Roberto Marfany concluded that generations of historians and nationalist politicians had invented the idea of broad popular enthusiasm for the decisions of May 25 for their own purposes. According to him, Domingo French and Antonio

Luis Beruti had manufactured and directed the "popular" demands for the second cabildo abierto and the removal of Cisneros.[182] He points out that some witnesses remembered that many present in the halls of the cabildo or in the plaza on the morning of May 25 actually went home for siestas as the assembly met, a detail suggesting that popular political passions were, at best, constrained.[183]

While the size of the crowd on May 25 may have been smaller than earlier political confrontations, one witness, Francisco Saguí, remembered a "multitude of people . . . all armed" in the plaza. He also suggested that military commanders made clear to the cabildo that they would not use their forces to keep the crowd from entering the cabildo's meeting rooms, leaving the invited representatives no alternative but to remove Cisneros and create a second junta.[184] An anonymous witness remembered a "multitud" in the plaza in addition to the organized demonstrators led by French and Beruti.[185] While it is also true that these "leaders" and "managers" were more obviously present in the crowd on May 25 than in earlier episodes of popular action, it is important to recognize that the repeated experience of popular protest in Buenos Aires had produced well-rehearsed routines and a common inventory of gestures and political language that had the effect of maintaining pressure on authorities while draining demonstrations of the spontaneity and passion present in earlier, "unscripted" demonstrations. That is, the smaller crowds of May 25 would have retained the potential to effectively signal the public mood by using a shorthand of words, gestures, and behaviors that were now well understood by the political class in a city habituated to popular demonstrations after more than four years of mass action. Nevertheless, one British witness to these events remembered it as a "unanimous proceeding of all the people, which had been long in preparation."[186]

The crowd pressing the invited delegates to act on May 25, like the demonstrators massed in front of the cabildo in 1806 and 1807, had been mobilized in large measure by the freewheeling political discussions now common in plebeian venues like taverns, gaming dens, markets, and workplaces of the city center and humble suburbs. At each stage of the slow-motion political crisis that led to May 25, plebeian opinions and grievances had helped to refine and polish the political representations of the city's new "public." Popular opinions performed in public places like the Plaza Victoria, as well as the stairwells and galleries of the cabildo, were rooted in more than a decade of plebeian experience in Buenos Aires, rather than mere spontaneous reactions to distant geopolitical events like the fall of Seville. The porteño plebe had been buffeted by a succession of heavy blows that included the debilitation of craft organizations, the growing competition of European manufactures, and the African slave trade. The accumulated experience of these challenges had given the popular demonstrations of the past four years their hard edge. The threats and insults directed at Viceroy Sobremonte, defeated British troops, and the followers of Álzaga by plebeian crowds reflected these shared experiences. At the same time, the intense cycle of mobilization had drained these performances of their energy. Just as voter passions cool and turnouts decline over time in long-functioning democracies, the Buenos Aires plebe would have been more confident of a favorable political outcome in 1810 with the commitment of fewer resources after five years of successful political practice.

More important still, the mostly militarized plebe of 1810 was necessarily less spontaneous and individualistic than earlier. The colonial plebe of the 1790s was transformed by 1810. The Spaniards and other European immigrants who had dominated crafts and trades in the 1790s had long lost their ability to direct events as a result of the failure of the guild effort and the failed coup of 1809 that marginalized European militia forces with their enlisted ranks filled by immigrant artisans. Free black and casta artisans and laborers, on the other hand, were now more fully integrated in civic culture and more assertive due to their full incorporation into the militia units that had dominated the events of January 1, 1809, and now continued to receive salaries.

This is not to suggest that the native-born propertied classes who assumed power on May 25 abandoned the view that the Buenos Aires plebe was volatile and dangerous. The emerging political class of the independence era, unlike the late colonial authorities whose power they inherited, saw this assertive and politically mobilized plebe as crucial to the realization of their ambitions and evolved the means to direct it on the fly. Yet they continued to fear the plebe as a threat to order and property. When Liniers acted to reinforce the alcaldes de barrio with military auxiliaries to contain the "revoltosos" and "vagos y ociosos" in early 1809, he signaled the essential content of the city's politics for the next two decades.[187]

Conclusion

The physicist Per Bak used the metaphor of a sandpile to describe the way that small events can transform large and apparently stable systems in a series of conceptually interesting publications. He asked, "what common features lead to interdependence and complexity?" And, "why can accidents occur that have dramatic global consequences?"[188] He suggested that if we slowly pour grains of sand on a cone-shaped sandpile, the structure will increase in size until it reaches a point, what he calls a "state of criticality," where it can grow no more and remain stable. Each grain of sand added from this point on sets off a landslide that reshapes the pile. His discussion usefully connects to the slow-motion, incremental transformation of the plebe and the local and international events that serially challenged Spanish rule in Buenos Aires. Between 1795 and 1810 the city's political and economic arrangements reached Bak's "state of criticality." In this process a plebe, cut loose from the institutions and customary practices that had attached it to the ancien régime, began to act in ways that challenged existing colonial social and political arrangements and influenced the new social and political structures of the post-1810 nation.

The series of decisions by municipal and colonial authorities that led to the destruction of the guilds of silversmiths and shoemakers was only the most visible component of a broader transformation of labor organization in Buenos Aires. By the end of the 1790s the city's skilled laborers no longer collectively controlled recruitment, training, or standards. Craft organizations in Buenos Aires survived into the last decade of the colonial period only as ceremonial and ritual forms. Even more consequential changes affected the ground-level experience of labor. By the end of the colonial period slavery had penetrated every occupation, every skill level, and nearly every jobsite. Many master artisans had facilitated and benefited from these changes by purchasing and employing slaves. What emerged across the last decades of the colonial era was a more entrepreneurial, less corporate, sense of self and community. Growing racial and ethnic diversity reinforced these new fault lines, undermining corporate identity and setting the plebe loose to find new forms of collective identity and new forms of civic participation.

When the geopolitical crises of the Atlantic world kicked the props out from under the colonial regime in the Río de la Plata the plebe embraced a new structure that could effectively organize their political and social aspirations and give purchase to their collective ambitions: the militia. This suggests why one of the junta's first initiatives after May 25 was to roll back the cuts to active duty salaries paid to the militia.[189] These large alterations in the social structure of the society had prepared the plebe to find and rely on leaders willing to address them directly in a vocabulary that gave voice to at least some of their ideals and grievances. It is surprising and yet predictable that the two most effective expressions of this new political style were Martín de Álzaga and Liniers, two key figures from 1795.

The period bracketed by the cabildo abierto of August 14, 1806, which replaced Viceroy Sobremonte as chief military commander with Liniers, and the cabildo abierto of May 25, 1810, marked the first appearance of personalist politics in Buenos Aires. We first see this Romantic style of political self-representation and careful staging in the events of August 14. While his closest allies worked the crowd in the Plaza Mayor to demand the destitution of the viceroy, Liniers was conveniently absent in the suburbs, an absence that forced the crowd to march en masse to return him in triumph to the city. Throughout the military threat leading ultimately to the defeat of the second British invasion, Liniers used the mounting power of his popularity to help mobilize and direct the new militia army through an array of staged appearances and personal interactions with the enlisted ranks. When Martin de Álzaga and the cabildo sought to depose Liniers on January 1, 1809, they appropriated the essential elements of this new political style, marching very publicly across the great open space of Plaza Victoria to the interim viceroy's residence to demand his resignation while having prepared a supportive "public" of Spanish militia units and a "popular" crowd of Spanish commercial employees to legitimize their coup. A parallel, mass organization of native-born militia and massed plebe saved Liniers and prepared the ground for the junta. Saavedra stayed close to this now well-rehearsed script on May 24, 1810, when he theatrically resisted the demands of his closest allies and supporters that he serve as president of the new junta, thus preparing an irresistible popular demand for his ascendency a day later.[190]

The city's artisans and laborers also collectively inserted themselves in the era's incipient forms of mass political expression. Their successful political interventions, to force the removal of Sobremonte and compel the elevation of Liniers, for example, like their experience of battle in 1806 and

1807, put in place new narratives and understandings that turned a colonial plebe previously organized to sustain long-existing Hispanic craft institutions into a "people" self-consciously invested in the invention of new political forms and the elevation of new leaders. Certainly the plebe drew on its customary values and vocabulary as it accompanied the dispossession of Sobremonte and the defeat of Álzaga with the insults and challenges so central to their traditional expressions of honor and shame. In the midst of these novel political inventions (including the election of militia officers and street demonstrations) elements of traditional plebeian identity reappeared, including the privileging of skills, the maintenance of hierarchies responsive to collective objectives, and elaborate public ritual. Leaders elevated by contested and irregular means, Liniers the prime case, would now legitimize their claims to power on the massed authority of the transformed porteño plebe.

Epilogue

Santiago de Liniers and four other Spanish loyalists were executed by firing squad on August 26, 1810, near Cabeza del Tigre, a poststation on the road between Córdoba and Buenos Aires. The Primera Junta that had come to power with broad support from the plebe in Buenos Aires on May 25 ordered the execution. In addition to Liniers, the junta sentenced to death the governor intendant of Córdoba, Juan Gutiérrez de la Concha, who had served with Liniers in 1807, the local bishop, Rodrigo Antonio de Orellano, and three lesser officials, including a militia commander. In the end the junta spared only the bishop.

With most of Spain occupied by French armies and with the legitimacy of the Spanish Regency's claims to rule the colonies disputed, the creation of a junta in Buenos Aires in May 1810 was in many ways inevitable. But a succession of economic shocks begun in the 1790s and the social changes they engendered after 1800 had also helped prepare the ground for this momentous event. A devastating region-wide drought forced a rise in food costs and a local market opened to more direct competition with European goods by the effects of war combined to lower real wages and reduce employment security for the porteño plebe even before the first British invasion. At the same time a booming slave trade increased pressure on the wages of free artisans and laborers while simultaneously devaluing skills and threatening the traditional social status of manual labor. The result was a plebe detached from the structures and habits of the old regime and politicized by decades of conflict within artisan trades and with colonial authorities. The popular militia force created in response to the two British invasions provided this stressed and transformed plebe with alternative collective identities, rituals, symbols, and loyalties. The militias also provided alternative sources of income competitive with current wages. As the imperial crisis developed, the officers of these popular military organizations, many elected by the ballots of the enlisted ranks, helped guide the demonstrations, popular assemblies, and political decisions that produced the *cabildo abierto* on May 25 and selected the membership of the junta. Despite the powerful energies driving the accommodations, alliances, and shared objectives ascendant in May, the cadre leading the junta would soon fracture, and in the wake of this calamity a second generation of political and military leaders found the means to more effectively discipline and control the revolutionary plebe.

Paying Debts and Unwinding Loyalties

When news of the momentous May events in Buenos Aires reached Santiago de Liniers, who was in retirement in Córdoba, the former viceroy joined with Juan Gutiérrez de la Concha and other Spanish loyalists to organize resistance to the Buenos Aires junta.[1] More than anything else, however, the junta's decision to exile Viceroy Cisneros and the members of the audiencia convinced Liniers to prepare for armed action.[2] He initially advocated that the leading loyalists of Córdoba withdraw with their military forces to Alto Peru to unite with Spanish forces there and in the viceroyalty of Peru. Misled by the vocal encouragement of Córdoba's cabildo and by a growing number of loyalist militia volunteers, he reluctantly accepted Gutiérrez de la Concha's recommendation to continue training local forces in preparation for an inevitable confrontation with forces sent from Buenos Aires. In the meantime, Liniers sought to coordinate with Spanish administrators in Peru and Montevideo.[3]

In the end none of this mattered. Desertions decimated the loyalist force of roughly one thousand as the military units sent by the Buenos Aires junta approached Córdoba.[4] Recognizing that they could not resist this larger force, Liniers and the other loyalist leaders fled towards Alto Peru, but they had tarried too long. As they struggled north, most of their military escort deserted, leaving Liniers and his chief allies with few resources and even fewer options. Desperate, Liniers, Gutiérrez de la Concha, and the bishop split up in the vain hope this would slow their pursuers. Despite this decision, troops loyal to the Buenos Aires junta captured them all within two

FIGURE 34 Home of Santiago de Liniers and his family at time of the British invasions. Photograph by author.

days. With his hands tightly bound behind his back, Liniers watched as his captors pillaged his baggage.[5]

The former viceroy and the others were already under a sentence of death pushed through the junta by Mariano Moreno, who served as one of its two secretaries.[6] Moreno and the other junta members had reacted quickly to organize and send a military force north once they had received news that Liniers was involved in the Córdoba loyalist opposition. They remembered well the events of 1806 and 1807 and feared that Liniers, the most universally respected and admired resident of the viceroyalty, could become the focus of popular opposition. Their fears were rooted in the well-established fact of Liniers's popularity. As one contemporary later recalled, "the mass of the proletarians" had "consecrated a form of cult around General Liniers."[7] Certainly they remembered that he had created and trained a large military force quickly in response to Beresford's attack in 1806, and they logically feared he might do it again in opposition to the junta. Underlying the death sentence for Liniers was the junta's belief that political control of the north and continued access to the silver of Potosí were crucial to the commerce of Buenos Aires and to the fiscal bottom line of the new government.

Cornelio Saavedra, who had commanded the Patricios in 1807 and then saved Liniers from the attempted coup of January 1, 1809, led by Martín de Álzaga, signed the death sentence as president of the junta. Moreno and Liniers had a back story as well. Moreno, the younger man, had served as secretary of the Buenos Aires cabildo in 1809 and had supported Martín de Álzaga's effort to force the interim viceroy to resign.[8] Many of those directly involved in the capture and execution of Liniers had powerful ties to him as well. Colonel Francisco Ortiz de Ocampo, leader of the forces sent by the junta to crush the Córdoba opposition, had had his first military experiences as commander of the Cuerpo de Arribeños, a unit composed of the poor castas employed as laborers in the slaughter yards, docks, and warehouses under the command of Liniers.[9] In fact the force commanded by Ocampo in 1810 included units from the Patricios, the Arribenos, and the Pardos and Morenos, three overwhelmingly plebeian units that won the day for Liniers in 1809. Even though Ocampo was aware of the death sentence before his force entered Córdoba, he decided to send Liniers and the other prisoners to Buenos Aires rather than carry out the execution, informing the junta that this would avoid disaffecting the region's population.[10]

Once aware of Ocampo's failure to immediately execute Liniers, Moreno spurred the junta to action, fearful that Liniers's presence as a prisoner in Buenos Aires could lead to popular revolt. They quickly organized a second, much smaller force, under the command of Juan José Castelli, a member of the junta, to carry out the death sentence. Both Castelli and Domingo French, his second in command, had served as officers under Liniers and Saavedra during the heroic resistance of 1807, and both had played prominent roles in the events of May 25, 1810—French as one of the organizers of plebeian demonstrations in the Plaza Victoria. Moreno made clear his fear that any new temporizing would lead to disastrous consequences in a letter he sent to his ally Feliciano Antonio Chiclana. Delay or hesitation, he claimed, put the junta's survival at risk.[11] Chiclana, like Castelli and French, had also served as an officer in the Patricios and, along with French, helped mobilize plebeian demonstrators to demand the creation of the junta. Moreno need not have worried; Castelli and French proved reliable instruments of revolutionary justice.

After making contact with the escort moving the prisoners toward Buenos Aires, Castelli assembled the prisoners and read the death sentence. He then permitted the condemned four hours to confess to the bishop and another loyalist priest and collect their wits. Castelli's command then quickly carried out the execution. Although not a firsthand witness, Juan Manuel Beruti, one of the era's most reliable memoirists, gathered information from those who were and provided posterity with a plausible and arresting account of the event. He claims that Liniers faced his death bravely but died in agony because the soldiers, many veterans of the events of 1806 and 1807, had aimed away from his head and heart. With Liniers in terrible pain, Domingo French dispatched him with a pistol shot.[12]

The pathos and sorrow that attended the execution of the single most remarkable and famous figure yet produced by this young region powerfully affected Beruti and, we must presume, many others. In summarizing the meaning of this execution, the chronicler noted the exact number of years, months, and days that separated the execution of this "great man" from the surrenders of Beresford and Whitelocke. Beruti also remembered Liniers for his "generous, disinterested, warm, and courageous" personality and noted that he "died but his memory will not die in the noble and generous hearts of the good patriots of Buenos Aires."[13]

Beruti's generous characterization of Liniers suggests the legitimacy of Moreno's judgment that the hero of 1807 remained dangerously popular in Buenos Aires, especially among the plebe and the military. Ortiz de Ocampo's decision to suspend the junta's death sentence and send Liniers and the other prisoners to Buenos Aires, a decision that cost this officer the junta's trust, also indicates the former viceroy's continued hold on the loyalty of the largely plebeian military units created in the wake of 1806, as does the unintended cruelty of firing squad members who tried to avoid inflicting a fatal wound and, as a result, caused Liniers great agony.[14] While news of this execution had had a powerful effect on Beruti and many others in Buenos Aires, it caused a near mutiny among some of the officers and enlisted ranks that had accompanied Ocampo north to defeat the loyalist resistance and carry out the death sentence.[15]

A Year of Living Dangerously

As Beruti suggested, the execution of Liniers seemed like the end of an era as well as the end of a life. This is why he took such care to date the execution with reference to the dates of the liberation of Buenos Aires from British control in 1806 and the surrender of Whitelocke in 1807.[16] This small temporal space encompassed the bright arc of Liniers's celebrity and the eclipse of Spanish authority in Buenos Aires. Compressed in the tight orbit of these eventful four years were two British invasions, the French invasion of Spain, the abdications of Charles IV and Ferdinand VII, the creation of patriotic juntas in Spain, the effective secession of Montevideo from the control of Buenos Aires, the failed Álzaga coup of 1809, and the creation of the Spanish Regency in the face of new French military successes in Iberia. If the full reestablishment of Spanish colonial government in Buenos Aires was unlikely given the metropole's debilitation, neither the ultimate form of any successor government nor the character of new political leadership was clear as Beruti memorialized Liniers in the wake of his execution.

The execution of Santiago de Liniers pushed to the surface the rivalries and animosities that had been held in check during the first months of the junta. Saavedra, former commander of the Patricios and president of the junta, and Mariano Moreno, one of two junta secretaries, now openly struggled to control decisions. Moreno, seventeen years younger than Saavedra, had been the strongest advocate for the execution of Liniers and his allies. Once Castelli enforced the death sentence Moreno seemed to hold the upper hand. Castelli, now in command of the junta's forces in Alto Peru, continued to enforce the uncompromising and sanguinary policies advocated by Moreno, ordering the execution of prominent Spanish captives, Vicente Nieto, José de Córdova, and the intendant of Potosí, Francisco de Paula Sanz, after gaining a victory over loyalist forces at Suipacha on November 7, 1810.[17]

News of the victory at Suipacha reached Buenos Aires on December 2, precipitating a chain of unanticipated consequences. The officers of the Patricios invited Saavedra and other junta members to a celebratory dinner at their barracks, but a sentry turned Mariano Moreno away at the door. Moreno would never forgive this slight. Then, during the evening, a drunken officer ignited a second scandal by toasting Saavedra as "emperor and king of South America."[18] When informed, Moreno brought the matter to the full junta, which quickly published a regulation mandating complete equality among junta members and stripping Saavedra of his distinguishing honors as president, including his right to a military escort. In case Moreno's point was not clear, the regulation also banned all toasts that singled out any one member of the junta for praise.[19] The battle was now engaged.

This calculated humiliation of Saavedra proved a pyrrhic victory for Moreno. Little more than two weeks later, on December 18, Saavedra successfully advocated that the junta seat seven delegates, who were sent to

Buenos Aires by provincial governments, with full voting rights.[20] The creation of this Junta Grande strengthened Saavedra and led to Moreno's resignation and indirectly to his death. Moreno soon agreed to what was, in effect, voluntary exile by accepting the junta's appointment as a diplomat to Great Britain. While at sea Moreno became ill and died an agonizing death on March 4, 1811.[21] In a letter to Feliciano Antonio Chiclana written on January 15, 1811, Saavedra expressed that Moreno's resignation meant, "the disappearance of terrorism and the Robespierre system."[22] His judgment proved premature. Moreno's supporters were most visibly concentrated in two venues, a newly created regiment, the Star of the South (the regiment was also called América), commanded by Domingo French and in a popular location for political gossip and speechmaking, the Café de Marco in the city center. Saavedra and his allies now feared the possibility of a military mutiny led by the officers of the Star of the South supported by a popular demonstration provoked by the orators of the Café de Marco, a constellation of political actors not unlike that organized in opposition to Liniers by Álazaga in 1809 and in opposition to Cisneros by Saavedra's own supporters in May 1810.[23] Despite making a series of threatening gestures, including providing his regiment with powder and shot in the barracks, Domingo French and other opponents fatally held back.

Saavedra soon pressed his advantage. Beginning on the evening of April 5, 1811, thousands of laborers and artisans from the poorest suburban districts and from nearby farms and slaughter yards massed in the Plaza Victoria in front of the cabildo. Beruti remembered "an immense crowd" organized by *alcaldes de barrio*.[24] With the important exception of the Star of the South, most of the urban garrison joined the demonstration, reinforcing the massed civilian protestors in the plaza. This included many from the Patricios, Arribeños, and Pardos and Morenos.[25] In addition to the alcaldes de barrio, military officers known to be loyal to Saavedra were prominent among the leaders of this demonstration. Using the cabildo as an intermediary during this "popular" protest on April 6, the protestors' leaders forced the resignations and internal exile of Saavedra's remaining opponents in the junta as well as Domingo French and his second in command in the Star of the South regiment. It might be argued that the porteño plebe, in both its civilian and military manifestations, had once again collectively asserted its will at the center of the city's commercial and political life. Yet, this massed political performance had been drained of the spontaneity and class consciousness visible in the much more muscular and convincing demonstrations, for example, that previously forced Viceroy Sobremonte from office. As Ignacio de Gorriti, a deputy from Jujuy serving in the Junta Grande, remembered this "scandalous" event, Saavedra and other "rivals of Moreno were still not satisfied that they gained the exclusive superiority in the junta they desired" and therefore had organized this "popular" demonstration.[26]

But just as Moreno's apparent success in stripping Saavedra of his privileges and honors at the end of 1810 led to his fall, the elimination of Saavedra's key opponents following the demonstrations of April 5 and 6 foreshadowed his political eclipse. Once again the conflict in Alto Peru precipitated a reconfiguration of political power in Buenos Aires. On June 20, 1811, Juan José Castelli's forces suffered a devastating loss to Spanish loyalists at Huaqui. Pushed by his friends (and disingenuously by his enemies) Saavedra agreed to resign the presidency of the junta to go north to try to save the military situation.[27] In his absence the reconstituted junta floundered and was replaced in September by a three-person executive, the Triumvirate, composed of Feliciano Antonio Chiclana, who served as president, Juan José Paso, and Manuel de Sarratea (brother-in-law of Santiago de Liniers).[28] Fear of increased levels of crime, including break-ins by armed gangs, built support for these changes among the urban propertied classes, salaried workers, merchants, and professionals, and helped drive both the dismissal of Saavedra and the creation of the Triumvirate.[29]

One measure of the new government's desire to strike at the sources of Saavedra's power and constrain the independence and perceived lawlessness of the plebe that had reliably supported him was its decision to appoint Manuel Belgrano, recalled from command of junta forces in Paraguay by the demonstrators of April 5 and 6, as colonel and commander of the Patricios.[30] The dramatic last act of the political transition begun on April 5 and 6 occurred on December 6 and 7 when troops loyal to the new government crushed a mutiny by the enlisted ranks of units of the Patricios serving in the city's garrison. The regiment was also identified militarily as Regiment 1° in recognition of its heroic record.[31] Argentine historians have generally referred to this event as the *motín de las trenzas* (mutiny of the pigtails).

The regiment's heroic performance against the British in 1807 and its determining role on January 1, 1809, had set it apart from the city's other military units. From its formation in 1806 the regiment's enlisted men had

FIGURE 35 An officer of the Patricios. Published with the permission of the AGN, Buenos Aires, Argentina.

generally worn their hair in pigtails, and this habit had continued even after the professionalization of the military was initiated in 1810, a professionalization marked by reforms that included short haircuts as well as more severe discipline. Surviving evidence does not clearly indicate that the new commander, Manuel Belgrano, ordered the enlisted ranks of the Patricios to cut their hair. Testimony taken in the trials that followed the suppression of the mutiny indicates that one officer, exasperated by a lack of deference, had indeed threatened to cut the pigtails of some AWOL enlisted men. It also makes it clear that this threat was answered by an enlisted man who asserted it "would be easier to put him in chains than cut his pigtail."

It is telling that there was no mention of pigtails in the demands presented to the Triumvirate by the mutineers during negotiations. Instead, their first demand was that the soldiers of the Patricios be "treated like free citizens and not like troops of the line [regular soldiers]."[32] The regiment's heroic status, its long custom of electing officers, its ties to Saavedra (until recently the most powerful politician of the new era), and its recruitment base among the plebeian sectors present in every moment of collective political expression since the late 1790s exempted it from the early stages of professionalization imposed on lesser regiments. It may be that the pigtail was a symbol of this unique status, but the fact that enlisted ranks still presumed the right to influence the selection of officers and be exempted from flogging and other humiliating punishments for minor infractions is clearly what was meant when the mutineers demanded to be "treated like free citizens."

Their second demand was the replacement of Manuel Belgrano as commander by Juan Antonio Pereyra who had served as a captain in the unit from the earliest days. Although Pereyra had recently retired, he had a long and warm relationship with Saavedra and had played a prominent role at two historic moments in the city's history, the defeat of the January 1, 1809, coup attempt by the Álzaga faction and the May Revolution that brought the Primera Junta to power.[33] The mutineers also sought the replacement of Belgrano's second in command, Gregorio Perdriel. The two core objectives, the demand to be treated like citizens (not professional soldiers) and the strongly asserted right to select the unit's officers, reflected the experience of the plebe under arms in the period before 1810.

With the survival of Spanish rule in the South Atlantic at stake, the armed plebe had helped transform Buenos Aires politically. Dependent on this force to meet the British threat, Liniers and other commanders had accepted the election of officers by militia units. Subsequent events only enhanced the power of the plebeian enlisted ranks. As Saavedra and other militia commanders asserted their right to mediate every emergency (the 1809 coup attempt, the replacement of Liniers by Cisneros, and news of the fall of Seville and the creation of the Spanish Regency), they were forced to fulfill the expectations of the enlisted ranks on which their authority ultimately rested. Circumstances changed on May 25, 1810, with the creation of the junta. Once in power Saavedra and his supporters moved cautiously to professionalize the militia. They viewed ending the election of officers as a key to this process, leading ultimately to the imposition of Belgrano by the Triumvirate.

More interesting to our central concerns than the demands presented by the mutineers was the social character of the mutiny. After Colonel Belgrano made his final rounds on the evening of December 6, a large group of enlisted men and noncommissioned officers assembled and ejected the small number of officers still in the barracks. In the events that followed, noncommissioned officers were highly visible among the mutineers, but a number of privates brazenly confronted both their officers and the emissaries sent by the government to negotiate. Among the most visible was the English-born shoemaker Ricardo Norfres (perhaps his name is the Spanish version of Richard Murphy), who was remembered to have addressed an officer "with the most insolent and rude words."[34] He was not alone. In the negotiations that preceded the final armed confrontation the mutineers exhibited no signs of deference or subordination, regardless of the rank or status of the intermediaries.

Shortly after the enlisted men took control of the barracks, Belgrano returned to attempt to calm his men. When met with threats that included cries of "kill him," Belgrano retreated to notify the members of the Triumvirate. In the false calm of the next hours, the mutineers composed their demands as the Triumvirate's president, Chiclana, and other members of the government took measures to put the rest of the city garrison under arms and place loyal forces around the Patricios's barracks. When finally in receipt of the demands of the rebellious force, the government offered to discuss all of the demands if the mutineers put down their arms. The government also promised to pardon all the participants for their insubordination and threats. The leaders of the mutiny rejected this offer out of hand. The Triumvirate then initiated a succession of negotiations to end the standoff. The mutineers demanded to talk to Chiclana, who, at some risk, went to the barracks without affecting a compromise.

An effort by ecclesiastical authorities achieved the same result. Bishop Dr. Benito Lué y Riega of Buenos Aires and Bishop Rodrigo Antonio de Orellana of Córdoba met directly with the leaders of the mutiny and repeated the offer of an amnesty for the insubordination and mutiny if the soldiers put down their arms immediately.[35] As the ecclesiastics and their military escort retreated from this unsuccessful intervention, the mutineers unleashed a ragged volley of small arms and cannon fire that precipitated the final clash.[36] According to witnesses, the Englishman Norfres fired the first cannon shot, killing 1 and wounding 6 among the ranks of loyal troops. Because the rest of the city's garrison remained loyal the resulting conflict lasted less than half an hour, ending with the surrender of the mutinous Patricios, 380 men.[37] Government forces suffered 8 dead and 35 wounded. The mutineers suffered something like 9 dead and 39 wounded.

The government identified eleven leaders among the surrendered mutineers and executed ten—four sergeants, two corporals, and four privates. One of those identified as a ringleader escaped. The Triumvirate acting as a court heard the cases and assessed the exemplary punishments. In addition to those sentenced to death, another twenty enlisted men were sentenced to prison for terms ranging from two to ten years. All the regiment's sergeants and corporals present in the barracks during the mutiny not implicated were stripped of their rank. The Triumvirate also disbanded the three companies most involved in the mutiny, two grenadier companies and the unit's artillery company. It then attempted to break the pride of this prestigious and troublesome Patricios Regiment 1º. The government removed its preeminence in the regimental hierarchy, renumbering it as Regiment 5º and then removing the unit's claim to unique status by assigning the name Patricios to all the city's infantry units.[38]

On December 11, 1811, the members of the Triumvirate mobilized loyal troops to publicly condemn the "authors of the scandalous insurrection" that had exposed the nation to "the horrors of division." They promised clemency to the majority of those implicated in the mutiny but asserted the need for exemplary punishments that would "serve as a break on the passions."[39] The next day the sergeants Juan Ángel Colares, Domingo Acosta, Manuel Alfonso, and José Enríquez; the corporals Manuel Pinto, Agustín Quiñones, and Gregorio Ceballos; and the privates Agustín Castillo, Juan Herrera, Mariano Carmen, and Ricardo Norfres were all executed by order of the Triumvirate. The nearly complete absence of the honorific *Don* in the judicial proceeding brought against this group suggests the social character of the mutiny. As the execution date approached, the government provided the condemned men with an abundant and generous ration of food and drink that must have appeared luxurious to plebeians accustomed to minding their budgets.[40] This would be the only mercy enjoyed by the condemned. The following morning a firing squad carried out the execution of the mutineers. Their corpses were then hanged from a scaffold to serve as a lesson to the public as well as to other potential rebels within military ranks.

This was not the last mutiny or rebellion within the porteño military, but the crushing defeat of the mutineers on December 7 and the ten executions

FIGURE 36 The plaza in front of the cabildo, the scene of popular demonstration from 1806 until the 1811 confrontations between the followers of Cornelio Saavedra and the allies of Mariano Moreno. Source: C. E. Pellegrini, *Recuerdos del Río de la Plata* (Buenos Aires: Libreria L'Amateur, 1969). Published with the permission of the publisher, Librería L'Amateur, Buenos Aires.

five days later effectively marked the end of the era begun in 1806 when the Buenos Aires plebe embraced the military as an institution born of their collective identity and defined by their voluntary obligations.[41] Certainly the plebe's new military avocation had been prepared in no small measure by the nearly two decade long weakening of traditional structures, the cabildo's wholesale dismissal of corporate craft organization in 1799, and the combined assault of sinking real wages and the prospering slave trade after 1800. The incremental suppression of this earlier, more chaotic and democratic tradition begun by the junta and continued by the Triumvirate had propelled the Patricios towards mutiny, but the marginalization of Saavedra's faction in the preceding months played a role as well.[42] This explains the anger of the mutineers, expressed in the intentionally insulting words and gestures directed towards the Triumvirate, Episcopal authorities, and toward their own officers. It also explains why, in the end, the mutineers initiated the hopeless battle that led to their complete defeat.[43]

Notes

Preface

1. Among the early discussions see Caillet-Bois, *Ensayo sobre el Río de la Plata y la revolución francesa*; Lewin, "La 'conspiración de los Franceses' en Buenos Aires (1795)"; and E. Ortega, *El complot colonial*.

2. As is true of so much of Argentine historiography Tulio Halperín Donghi's was the first to explore the economic and political impact of militarization. See for example his "Revolutionary Militarization in Buenos Aires 1806–1815."

3. Tulio Halperín Donghi argues that military wages were particularly crucial for the local-born artisans and laborers, rather than for the Spanish immigrants. As a result, the militia units whose enlisted ranks were mostly filled with Spaniards pulled back from full time service quickly after the defeat of Beresford, while the native born remained in barracks on full salary. This persisted after the defeat of Whitelocke in 1807 and helped to determine the test of strength between Santiago Liniers and Martín de Álazaga in January 1809. See his *Politics, Economics, and Society in Argentina in the Revolutionary Period*, 143.

Introduction

1. The monthly wage of master shoemakers fluctuated between three and four pesos per month in Buenos Aires. This means that the alcalde sought to impose a fee equal to between four and five and a half months' income. AGN, División Colonia, Sección Contaduría, Culto de Buenos Aires, Mercedarios, Convento Grande de San Ramón, Libros de Gastos, libro III; and AGN, Culto de Buenos Aires, Bethlemitas, Convento y hospital de Santa Catalina, libro de gastos.

2. AGN, División Colonia, Sección Gobierno, Justicia, leg. 51, exp. 1461.

3. AGN, División Colonia, Sección Gobierno, Interior, leg. 54, exp. 3.

4. AGN, División Colonia, Sección Gobierno, Interior, leg. 55, exp. 5, 14–49.

5. Between 1791 and 1800 the Río de la Plata region took 2.7 percent of all slaves imported to the Americas. Between 1801 and 1810 the region received 6.3 percent. Jeremy Adelman used the universally respected estimates produced by

David Eltis to calculate this rising trajectory. See Adelman's *Sovereignty and Revolution in the Iberian Atlantic*, 76.

6. The classic discussion of these events is Roberts, *Las invasiones inglesas del Río de la Plata, 1806–1807*, but the most useful exploration is provided by Halperín Donghi's "Revolutionary Militarization in Buenos Aires 1806–1815."

7. The literature devoted to artisans and artisan production includes: Arteaga, *El artesano en la Cuenca colonial*; Santos Barreto, "A despeito do defeito"; Castro Gutiérrez, *La extinción de la artesanía gremial*; Domínguez Compañy, "Regulación municipal del trabajo libre de los oficios mecánicos, en Hispanoamérica colonial"; Mayor Mora, *Cabezas duras y dedos inteligentes*; Moyano, *La organización de los gremios en Córdoba*; Pérez Vila, "El artesanado."

8. Among the many useful books and articles on artisans in the transitional period. See Amaro Peñaflores, *Los gremios acostumbrados*; Pérez Toledo, *Los hijos del trabajo*; Gaviria Liévano, *El liberalismo y la insurrección de los artesanos contra el librecambio*; Quiroz, *La protesta de los artesanos, Lima-Callao, 1858*; García-Bryce, *Crafting the Republic*; Gazmuri Riveros, "Los artesanos de Santiago en 1850, y el despertar político del sector popular chileno"; and Sowell, *The Early Colombian Labor Movement*.

9. Among the books that reveal the urban plebe in convincing ways, see Cope, *The Limits of Racial Domination*; Di Meglio, ¡Viva el pueblo bajo!; and Milton, *The Many Meanings of Poverty: Colonialism, Social Compacts, and Assistance in Eighteenth-Century Ecuador*.

10. Levene, *Ensayo histórico sobre la Revolución de Mayo y Mariano Moreno*.

11. Mangan's *Trading Roles: Gender, Ethnicity, and the Urban Economy in Colonial Potosí* suggests the enormous potential of such a construction.

12. This is not the place to undertake a full examination of the Atlantic literature, but J. H. Elliott's *Empires of the Atlantic World* is a good place for anyone interested this synthetic literature to start. I particularly like the synthesis provided by Kenneth J. Andrien, "The Spanish Atlantic System," and Paquette, *Enlightenment, Governance, and Reform in Spain and Its Empire, 1759–1808*. Among the other useful titles, see Armitage and Braddick, *The British Atlantic World, 1500–1800*; Bailyn, *Atlantic History*; Benjamin, *The Atlantic World*; Breen and Hall, *Colonial America in an Atlantic World*; Cañizares-Esguerra and Seeman, *The Atlantic in Global History, 1500–2000*; Heywood and Thornton, *Central Africans, Atlantic Creoles, and the Foundation of the Americas, 1585–1660*; Knight and Liss, *Atlantic Port Cities*; Kraus, *The Atlantic Civilization*.

13. I am grateful to Ken Andrien who pushed me in the direction of an Atlantic framework with great patience and good sense, despite my initial pig-headed resistance to a good idea.

14. I would like to mention three books that engage these issues admirably: Sarah C.

Chambers, *From Subjects to Citizens: Honor, Gender, and Politics in Arequipa, Peru, 1780–1854* (University Park: Penn State University Press, 1999); Peter Guardino, *The Time of Liberty: Popular Culture in Oaxaca, 1750–1850* (Durham: Duke University Press, 2005); and Charles F. Walker, *Smoldering Ashes: Cuzco and the Creation of Republican Peru, 1780–1840* (Durham: Duke University Press, 1999).

15. The recent book by Di Meglio, ¡Viva el pueblo bajo!, is mostly focused on the period after May 25, 1810, but the first two chapters do examine the late colonial plebe.

16. See, for example, Falkner, *A Description of Patagonia and the Adjoining Parts of South America*, 63–64; and Davie, *Letters from Paraguay*, 59.

17. For a useful summary of institutional structures, see Martin Saint-Leon, *Historia de las corporaciones de oficio*. For a wonderful modern discussion of Spanish guilds, see MacKay, *Lazy and Improvident People*, esp. 111–201.

18. Anne Robert Jacques Turgot sought to abolish French guilds in 1776, the year of the Viceroyalty of Río de la Plata's creation, but failed and was driven from office in May of that year.

19. One of the most successful examples of this style of inquiry is Frank's *Dutra's World*.

20. One noteworthy exception to this pattern is Alberto Flores Galindo's *Aristocracia y plebe: Lima, 1760–1830* (Lima: Mosca Azul Editores, 1984).

21. For the Caribbean story, see Dubois, *A Colony of Citizens*.

22. For a sample of the documents, see Caillet-Bois, *Ensayo sobre el Río de la Plata y la revolución francesa*.

23. See Ortega, *El complot colonial*, 55–57. For an insightful discussion of how news from Saint-Domingue circulated through Caribbean ports, see Scott, "A Common Wind."

24. See the *pasquín* with the single word *Libertad* reprinted in AGN, División Colonia, Sección Gobierno, Interior, leg. 38, exp. 1.

1. Plebeian City

1. AGN, División Colonia, Sección Gobierno, Tribunales, leg. 85, exp. 10.

2. García Belsunce et al., *Buenos Aires*, anejo 2. In 1810, 313 artisans owned 1,110 slaves.

3. See an excellent summary of the viceregal period in Moutoukias, "Power, Corruption, and Commerce."

4. For this early period, see Saguier, "The Social Impact of a Middleman Minority in a Divided Host Society."

5. Samuel Hull Wilcocke in his *History of the Viceroyalty of Buenos Ayres*, 523, claimed that 50 percent of the city's trade was in the form of contraband. He

also suggested that American ships used the slave trade as a cover for the importation of a broad range of illegal goods (Wilcocke, *History of the Viceroyalty of Buenos Ayres*, 557).

6. For an indication of the growing complexity of late colonial trade relations, see Silva, "Hamburgo y el Río de la Plata."

7. As late as July 24, 1805, Viceroy Sobremonte was still trying to control the flow of contraband disguised by slave trade voyages. See Vieytes and Cerviño, *Seminario*, tomo 3:369.

8. Corruption of Spanish officials and contraband are discussed in Socolow, *The Bureaucrats of Buenos Aires, 1769–1810*, esp. 243–48. See also Cooney, "Oceanic Commerce and Platine Merchants, 1796–1806"; Galmarini, "Comercio y burocracia colonial, a propósito de Tomás Antonio Romero," esp. 410–26.

9. Falkner, *A Description of Patagonia and the Adjoining Parts of South America*, 63–64.

10. Davie, *Letters from Paraguay*, 59.

11. Sir Woodbine Parish described the carts, still in use in 1839, in his *Buenos Ayres and the Provinces of the Río de la Plata*, 14.

12. Urban modernizers installed two, long diagonal streets to direct traffic away from the nineteenth-century city center, but their plan forced a drastic trimming of the cabildo building, which remained one of the few consequential colonial-era buildings in the city center.

13. Juan Francisco de Aguirre, "Diario 1783," *Anales de la biblioteca* (Buenos Aires, 1905), 4:181.

14. See Biedma et al., *Acuerdos del extinguido cabildo de Buenos Aires*, serie 3, tomo 11, libro 57, 588–89. For the earlier period, see Silva's "El cabildo, el abasto de carne y la ganadería"; and Silva's "La grasa y el sebo."

15. In Decemeber 1789 the cabildo was forced to address the common practice of fishmongers who tossed unsold fish into the streets at the end of the day. See Biedma et al., *Acuerdos del extinguido cabildo de Buenos Aires*, serie 3, tomo 9, libro 50, 228–29. Later in July 1804 the cabildo returned to these issues of hygiene and public health and organized a garbage collection paid for by a tax on householders. See Biedma et al., *Acuerdos del extinguido cabildo de Buenos Aires*, serie 4, tomo 1, libro 58, 186.

16. Biedma et al., *Acuerdos del extinguido cabildo de Buenos Aires*, serie 3, tomo 9, libro 51, 414–15; tomo 10, libro 52, 30–31, 168; tomo 11, libro 55, 105.

17. Ibid., serie 3, tomo 10, libro 54, 455–57.

18. Mawe, *Travels in the Interior of Brazil*, 42.

19. Davie describes the city plan in the late eighteenth century in his *Letters from Paraguay*, 79.

20. AHPBA, Criminales, leg. 34-1-20. In this case a confrontation between a group

of journeymen tailors working outside in front of their master's shop and a *jornalero* looking for work leads to homicide.

21. Cayetano Catteneo quoted in de Lafuente Machain, *Buenos Aires en el siglo XVIII*, 42–43.

22. See the useful compendium of regulations and petitions collected in *Administración edilicia de la ciudad de Buenos Aires (1776–1805)*, introducción de Luis María Torres, Universidad de Buenos Aires, *Documentos para la historia Argentina*. See also Biedma et al., *Acuerdos del extinguido cabildo de Buenos Aires*, serie 3, tomo 8, libro 49, 620, for the communication of Viceroy Marquez de Loreto with the cabildo over the need to regulate construction.

23. Davie, *Letters from Paraguay*, 115.

24. Catteneo, quoted in de Lafuente Machain, *Buenos Aires en el siglo XVIII*, 42.

25. AGN, División Colonia, Sección Gobierno, Tribunales, leg. 85, exp. 10.

26. In 1774, the cabildo attempted to impose standard sizes on brick, roof tiles, and adobe bricks manufactured in the city, see AGN, División Colonia, Sección Gobierno, Cabildo de Buenos Aires, Bandos, libro 3, 25 February 1774, 304.

27. Aguirre, "Diario 1783," 4:157–81.

28. Radaelli, *Memorias de los virreyes del Río de la Plata*, 383–84.

29. The English merchant Tomas Kinder, who arrived in Buenos Aires following the failed British invasion of 1807, rented rooms from the powerful *porteño* merchant Tomás Antonio Romero. See Kinder's handwritten *Journal of a Voyage to the Río de la Plata, 1808–1810* at the JCBL.

30. For a very helpful discussion of the conflicts that inevitably flowed from these events, see Garavaglia, "El teatro del poder."

31. Biedma et al., *Acuerdos del extinguido cabildo de Buenos Aires*, serie 4, tomo 1, libro 58, 146–47.

32. The Recova was first proposed in July 1784. See Biedma et al., *Acuerdos del extinguido cabildo de Buenos Aires*, serie 3, tomo 7, libro 46, 379.

33. Throughout this period the cabildo's major source of income came from its administration of property seized from the Jesuits in 1769. See Torres, *La administración de temporalidades en el Río de la Plata*; and Hernández, *El extrañamiento de los Jesuitas de Río de la Plata y de las misiones del Paraguay por decreto de Carlos III*.

34. Biedma et al., *Acuerdos del extinguido cabildo de Buenos Aires*, serie 4, tomo 1, libros 58, 211; libro 59, 408, 425, and 541.

35. Ibid., serie 3, tomo 1, libro 58, 160–61.

36. Hanon, *Buenos Aires desde las quintas de Retiro a Recoleta*, 79–82.

37. See Biedma et al., *Acuerdos del extinguido cabildo de Buenos Aires*, serie 3, tomo 7, libro 49, 624–30. The cabildo applied a comprehensive ban on "bailes de los negros." After connecting the dances to the observance of African religious

practice the *procurador* rehearsed the expected objections — disorder, thefts from owners, the potential seduction of Christians — and he asserted that the dances encouraged insubordination and lack of respect for whites. Put simply the dances led slaves to forget their station and the respect due their betters. See also Di Meglio, *¡Viva el pueblo bajo!*, who focuses his discussion of black and casta experience on this neighborhood.

38. Rodríguez Molas, "Algunos aspectos del negro en la sociedad rioplatense del siglo XVIII," 92.

39. Garavaglia, "El pan de cada día," 8.

40. The U. S. Census Bureau's analysis of 1990 returns estimated that it had undercounted the black population by 4.4 percent and the Hispanic population by 5 percent. See this discussion, "Net Undercount and Undercount Rate for U.S. (1990)," summarized on the U.S. Census Bureau's website: http://www.census .gov/dmd/www/pdf/underus.pdf.

41. Aguirre, "Diario 1783," 4:169.

42. Radaelli, *Memorias de los virreyes*, 382.

43. This document is printed in full in Instituto de estudios historicos sobre la reconquista, *La Reconquista y Defensa de Buenos Aires*, "Documento 10," 234. One British visitor offered an estimate of 60,000 in 1807; see Mawe, *Travels in the Interior of Brazil*, 39.

44. The Popham and Doblas estimates are found in Marfany, *El cabildo de Mayo*, 8.

45. The crude birthrate is the number of births per one thousand of population in a given year. We can represent this as

$$\frac{\text{number of births/year}}{\text{total population}} \times 1{,}000 = \text{crude birth rate}.$$

46. Alberto B. Martínez estimated that at least fifty stillborn children of slaves were not recorded in the parochial records in his *Historia demográfica de Buenos Aires*, 3:316. The under registration of baptisms would have been a fraction of this number.

47. For Spain's birthrate, see Livi-Bacci, "Fertility and Population Growth in Spain in the Eighteenth and Nineteenth Centuries," 530; and for France's birthrate, see Mitchell, *European Historical Statistics, 1750–1970*, 104–6. Irish birthrate statistics are provided by Connell, *The Population of Ireland, 1750–1845*, 30.

48. This discussion is fully developed in my article, "Estimaciones de la población de Buenos Aires en 1744, 1778 y 1810." Even if the much higher fertility rate of 50 per thousand is used the city population would have reached 61,160, pushing Buenos Aires past Lima as the largest city in Spanish South America.

49. Parish provides an estimate of 60,000 taken from the Memorial of Viceroy

Nicolás de Arredondo in 1795 (*Buenos Ayres and the Provinces of Río de la Plata*, 24).

50. See AGN, División Colonia, Sección Gobierno, Padrones de Buenos Aires, ciudad y campaña, 1782–1807, for census of artisans with numerous examples of migrants from the interior. For the foreign population in 1776, see AGN, División Colonia, Sección Gobierno, Archivo del Cabildo, 1776, padrón de estranjeros.

51. The procurador of the cabildo dismissed casta migrants as beggars and potential criminals in 1791. See AGN, División Colonia, Sección Gobierno, Tribunales, leg. 116, exp. 33.

52. Socolow, *The Merchants of Buenos Aires, 1778–1810*, and *The Bureaucrats of Buenos Aires, 1769–1810*. See also Moutoukias, *Contrabando y control colonial en el siglo XVII*.

53. The best analysis of the 1810 census is found in García Belsunce et al., *Buenos Aires*, anexo 1.

54. See AGN, División Colonia, Sección Gobierno, Justicia, leg. 9, exp. 177.

55. In the 1744 census, 5 percent of urban residents had been born in the interior or other Spanish colonies, but birthplace was not recorded for 79.5 percent of the population. In 1810 interior migrants accounted for 15.4 percent of the population, but birthplace was not recorded for 31.2 percent of the population.

56. Díaz, "Las migraciones internas a la ciudad de Buenos Aires, 1744–1810." See also Díaz, "Migraciones y plebe urbana en Buenos Aires, 1744–1810," 78–79.

57. Díaz, "Las migraciones internas," 12–16.

58. Ibid., 17.

59. Portions of the 1810 census have disappeared and, as a result, my estimate of the percentage of the native born based on this census is less reliable than that for 1744. See García Belsunce, *Buenos Aires*, anexo 1.

60. Díaz, "Las migraciones internas," 19–21.

61. Ibid., 7.

62. See for example Biedma et al., *Acuerdos del extinguido cabildo de Buenos Aires*, serie 3, tomo 6, libro 40, 55, 130–31; tomo 7, libro 45, 239; tomo 7, libro 44, 15–17.

63. *Diario de Barcelona* 55 (24 febrero, 1793), 223, available on Biblioteca Virtual de Prensa Historica's website (http://prensahistorica.mcu.es). Biblioteca Virtual de Prensa Historica, Ministro de Cultura publishes the Real Orden of same day expanding the slave trade. Among the many inducements are the removal of duties on ships from Spanish America sailing directly to Africa, the use of foreigners in crews (up to 50 percent), and forgiveness of taxes on ships constructed in foreign shipyards and purchased for the slave trade.

64. Data for the last decade of the British *asiento* are fragmentary. See Scheuss de Studer, *La trata de negros en el Río de la Plata durante el siglo XVIII*.

65. For the Royal Order permitting foreigners to introduce slaves, see Universidad de Buenos Aires, *Documentos para la historia Argentina*, "Comercio de Indias," tomo 6, 474; and an older article focused more on Venezuela and Cuba by Torre Revello, "Origen y aplicación del código negrero en la América española (1788– 1794)." See also Rosal, "Artesanos de color en Buenos Aires, 1750–1850," 331–32.

66. These summary estimates for the slave trade are from Alex Boruki who has undertaken a careful reconstruction of slave trade numbers in the archives of Buenos Aires and Montevideo. See his table 1 in Acree and Boruki, *Jacinto Ventura de Molina y los caminos de la escritura negra en el Río de la Plata*, 23.

67. This was also the peak period in slave imports to Montevideo as well. See the two cities compared in Campagna Caballero, "La población esclava en ciudades puertos del Río de la Plata."

68. These sources clearly underrepresented actual arrivals. Some scholars have put the total for the period 1740–1822 at more than 45,000. The importance of the contraband slave trade is suggested by the altered racial distributions found in contemporary censuses. These sources indicate that the African-originated population of the city rose from 17 percent in 1744 to 29 percent in 1778. See Goldberg and Mallo, "La población africana en Buenos Aires y su campaña. Formas."

69. Bauss, "Rio Grande do Sul in the Portuguese Empire: The Formative Years, 1777–1808," 533.

70. Radaelli, *Memorias de los virreyes*, 394.

71. Cooney, "Oceanic Commerce," 515. Alex Boruki counted 12,243 in this decade, see Acree and Boruki, *Jacinto Ventura de Molina*, 23, table 1.

72. Goldberg, "La población negra y mulata de la ciudad de Buenos Aires, 1810– 1840."

73. See Johnson and Socolow, "Población y espacio en el Buenos Aires del siglo XVIII," especially 332–34; and see Garavaglia, "Los labradores de San Isidro (siglos XVII–XIX)" for a discussion of the growing reliance on slave labor in the countryside.

74. These sources among others are summarized in Coria, *Pasado y presente de los negros en Buenos Aires*, 46–51.

75. Major Alexander Gillespie, *Gleanings and Remarks: Collected During Many Months of Residence at Buenos Ayres* (Leeds: J. W. Whitely, 1818), 69–70.

76. This estimate developed by César García Belsunce and his collaborators is broadly compatible to the revised slave trade estimates produced by Alex Boruki. See García Belsunce, *Buenos Aires*, 76; and Acree and Boruki, *Jacinto Ventura de Molina*, 23, table 1.

77. One interrogation of the issues of racial identity is Alejandro Solomianski's *Identidades secretas*, esp. chapters 1 and 2.

78. Molas, "Algunos aspectos del negro en la sociedad rioplatense," 86.

79. Most of these sources suggest that only 20 percent of the urban population was white. The difference between the census counts and the perceptions of visitors to the city reflects the necessarily imprecise line that separated "white" from "mulatto" in colonial Buenos Aires. Where visitors saw mulattoes, locals often saw whites. See Goldberg and Mallo, "La población africana," 18.

80. Rosal, "El tráfico esclavista y el estado saniterio de la ciudad de Buenos Aires (1750–1810)." See also Biedma et al., *Acuerdos del extinguido cabildo de Buenos Aires*, serie 3, tomo 6, libro 53, 277–78.

81. Biedma et al., *Acuerdos del extinguido cabildo de Buenos Aires*, serie 4, tomo 1, libro 58, 213.

82. One baker owned thirty-seven slaves in 1810, for example. The concentrated nature of the distribution became very clear when the governing junta sought to conscript slaves during the independence struggle. See Goldberg de Flinchman and Jany, "Algunos problemas referentes a la situación del esclavo en el Río de la Plata."

83. Aparicio, "Relación de un viaje entre Mendoza y Buenos Aires en 1794," 236. He notes "various families that have no property other than their slaves."

84. Quotation of José de Espinoza and Felipe Bauza found in Fondebrider, *La Buenos Aires ajena*, 55.

85. AGN, Tribunales, leg. 254, exp. 62.

86. AGN, Escribanía, Registros 1–7, anos 1776–1810. Approximately 11 percent of all the manumissions granted during the viceregal period required that the slave continue making a weekly or monthly payment to the owner.

87. AGN, Interior, leg. 26, exp. 4, 25–25 vta.

88. "Reflexiones cristianas sobre los negros esclavos," Cabello y Mesa, *Telégrafo Mercantil*, tomo 2:191–96. This article is somewhat misleading on the price of recently arrived African slaves, *bozales*. During the last two decades of the colonial era, the price of African males in Buenos Aires fluctuated between two hundred and two hundred and fifty pesos. A slave who became a master artisan could bring as much as six hundred pesos.

89. This conclusion results from a close examination of a number of matriculations of artisans from 1780 that show residence arrangements. See the census of *albañiles*, for example, in AGN, Tribunales, leg. 66, exp. 15.

90. See García Belsunce, *Buenos Aires*, anexo 1.

91. This was true in the campo as well. See Gelman, *Campesinos y estancieros*, and his focused examination of labor, "Sobre esclavos, peones, gauchos y campesinos."

92. It is difficult to assert with confidence a manumission rate for Buenos Aires, or any other colonial city, but a close analysis of the surviving notary records indicates that by the last decades of the colonial period just under 1.5 percent of

the slave population gained freedom each year. See Johnson, "Manumission in Colonial Buenos Aires, 1776–1810." In addition to my article on manumission in Buenos Aires, see Schwartz, "The Manumission of Slaves in Colonial Brazil"; Kiernan, "Baptism and Manumission"; Mattoso, "A propósito de Cartas da Alforria na Bahia, 1779–1850." See also Bowser, "The Free Persons of Color in Lima and Mexico City"; Proctor, "Gender and Manumission of Slaves in New Spain."

93. Azara, *Viajes por la América Meridional*, 1:170.

94. The matricula of *tallistas, carpinteros, estatuarios, silleteros, toneleros, aserradores,* and *peineros* is in AGN, División Colonia, Sección Gobierno, Tribunales, leg. 13, exp. 15; the matricula of albañiles is in Tribunales, leg. 66, exp. 37; and barberos is in Interior, leg. 9, exp. 5; *sastres* are found in Justicia, leg. 9, exp. 177; *lomilleros, ʒapateros* and other leather trades are in Interior, leg. 9, exp. 5; *calafates* and carpinteros de ribera are in Tribunales, leg. 13, exp. 15. I have added *panaderos* and *plateros* from the census of 1778 to these matriculations to produce this table. The census in found in Universidad de Buenos Aires, *Documentos para la historia Argentina*, tomo 11, "Territorio y población, padrón de la ciudad de Buenos Aires (1778)," passim.

95. Vieytes and Cerviño, *Seminario*, 1:35.

96. Mawe, *Travels in the Interior of Braʒil*, 42.

2. Structures of a Working Life

1. AHPBA, Criminales, leg. 34-1-13.

2. AGN, División Colonia, Sección Gobierno, Archivo del Cabildo, 1784. Antonio Obligado serving in 1784 as *fiel ejecutor* estimated that the average baker earned more then one thousand six hundred pesos in profit per year. Large-scale producers earned four thousand pesos, and, in once case, a baker had earned thirty thousand pesos. As a comparison he mentioned that a captain of infantry earned only six hundred pesos per year.

3. See for example the regulations of the guild of shoemakers in Cádiz. A copy is found in AGN, División Colonia, Sección Gobierno, Interior, leg. 26, exp. 4.

4. This is a topic that is not adequately developed in the historical literature devoted to Spain and Spanish America. However, much can be learned by the analysis offered by historians of other European countries, see Scott, *The Classworkers of Carmaux*; Dobb, *Estudios sobre el desarrollo del capitalismo*, esp. 49–106; and Rudé, *La multitud en la historia*, esp. 201–44. For the colonies, see Carranca y Trujillo, *Las ordenanʒas de gremios de Nueva Espana*; Carrera Stampa, *Los gremios mexicanos*; Martin Saint-Leon, *Historia de las corporaciones de oficio*; Samayoa Guevara, *Los gremios de artesanos en la ciudad de Guatemala*; and Herr, *The Eighteenth-Century Revolution in Spain*, 124–28. In the early Americas, the 1540s and 1550s, guilds of chainmakers, cordmakers, painters, and shoemakers were

formed in Mexico City. In Lima, the first guilds were created in the 1550s, while in Guatemala guild formation occurred a little later in the 1580s. See Carrera Stampa, *Los gremios mexicanos*, 260, and Carranca y Trujillo, *Las ordenanzas de gremios de Nueva Espana*, 8–12.

5. See Susan Socolow's discussion of this in *The Merchants of Buenos Aires, 1778–1810: Family and Commerce*, 19–21.

6. Eighteenth-century reformers as well as many modern historians may have over estimated the self-perpetuating nature of guild recruitment. Michael Sonenscher convincingly argues that less than 50 percent of new masters in France were the sons of existing masters. See his *Work and Wages*, esp. chapter 4.

7. For the argument that emphasizes the closed nature of recruiting as a justification for the abolition of guilds in the reign of Louis XVI, see the discussion in Vardi, "The Abolition of Guilds During the French Revolution"; and Martin Saint-Leon, *Historia de las corporaciones de oficio*, 406–14.

8. Cornelio Saavedra, *procurador* of the cabildo of Buenos Aires, made this argument to justify his opposition to the organization of a guild of shoemakers in Buenos Aires in 1799. AGN, División Colonia, Sección Gobierno, Interior, leg. 55, exp. 5.

9. See Johnson, "The Racial Limits of Guild Solidarity." See also Lockhart, *Spanish Peru, 1532–1560*, esp. chapter 6; and Harth-Terre, "El artesano negro en la arquitechtura virreinal Limeña."

10. This is discussed in my article "The Silversmiths of Buenos Aires."

11. This is suggested by comparing the explicit racial data from a 1792 census of master shoemakers with the 1780 list. It appears that approximately 30 percent to 40 percent of those who claimed to be criollos in 1780 were identified as castas in the second, more closely scrutinized matriculation. Generalizing from this case, I conservatively corrected the 1780 data for apprentices by moving 25 percent of the criollos to the casta category. See AGN, División Colonia, Sección Gobierno, Tribunales, leg. 24, exp. 7, for the corrected racial data.

12. Biedma et al., *Acuerdos del extinguido cabildo de Buenos Aires*, serie 4, tomo 3, libro 62, 92 and libro 64, 475.

13. I searched the city's seven notary registers for the period 1776–1810 and found that 124 apprenticeships had been recorded. These records provide the basis for the following tables and analysis. More recently, two Argentine historians reexamined the notary records and found 6 additional apprenticeship contracts. See Aguirre and Petit, "La contratación de aprendices en la actividad artesanal en la ciudad de Buenos Aires durante el Virreinato.

14. AGN, División Colonia, Sección Gobierno, Tribunales, leg. 13, exp. 15.

15. The surviving registrations of the city's artisans are found in the following archival records. The matricula of *tallistas, carpinteros, estatuarios, silleteros, tone-*

leros, *aserradores*, and *peineros* is in AGN, División Colonia, Sección Gobierno, Tribunales, leg. 13, exp. 15. The matricula of *albañiles* is in Tribunales, leg. 66, exp. 37; and *barberos* in Interior, leg. 9, exp. 5. *Sastres* are found in Justicia, leg. 9, exp. 177. *Lomilleros*, *zapateros* and other leather trades are in Interior, leg. 9, exp. 5. *Calafates* and *carpinteros de ribera* are in Tribunales, leg. 13, exp. 15. I have added *panaderos* and *plateros* from the census of 1778 to these matriculations to produce this table. The census is found in Universidad de Buenos Aires, *Documentos para la historia Argentina*, vol. 11, "Territorio y población, padrón de la ciudad de Buenos Aires (1778)," passim.

16. Biedma et al., *Acuerdos del extinguido cabildo de Buenos Aires*, serie 4, tomo 3, libro 62, 92 and libro 64, 475.

17. AGN, División Colonia, Sección Gobierno, Tribunales, leg. 66, exp. 177.

18. The discussion of wages for artisans and other workers is based on AGN, Division Colonia, Sección Contaduría, Caja de Buenos Aires, 1770–1815, and División Colonia, Sección Gobierno, Archivo del Cabildo, 1770–1815; División Colonia, Sección Contaduría, Obras Publicas, Canal de San Fernando, 1770–1808; Cabildo de Buenos Aires, Obras, 1805–1806. I searched every annual account book and recorded every wage record.

19. There are fewer cases in this table than in table 3 because only cases where the relationship between signatory and apprentice was clear are counted.

20. AGN, División Colonia, Sección Contaduría, Escribanía, Registro 2, 1787, 434–36.

21. AGN, Escribanía, Registro 2, 1795, 69–71 vta. provides a case where the alcalde forces a formal contract to prevent the boy's mother from obligating her son to seek work as *jornalero*.

22. In 1810 Martín de Álzaga, serving as alcalde, removed a young boy from a shop where he served without a contract and placed him in the shop of Agustín Tadeo Aríza. AGN, Escribanía, Registro 2, 1810 477–78v.

23. AGN, Escribanía, Registro 5, 1792.

24. AGN, Escribanía, Registro 6, 1797.

25. AGN, Escribanía, Registro 5, 1806–1807.

26. AGN, Escribanía, Registro 5, 1790.

27. For an example of this common provision, see AGN, Escribanía, Registro 4, 1804–1807.

28. For contracts involving the master shoemaker Jose Labrador, see AGN, Escribanía, Registro 4, 1796–1797; Registro 4, 1798–1799; Registro 4, 1800–1801; and Registro 1, 1794–1795.

29. Ibid. Also see AGN, Escribanía, Registro 3, 1796, for the apprenticeship of Jose Vieyra, and AGN, Escribanía, Registro 2, 1795, for the apprenticeship of Pantaleon Costane.

30. AGN, Escribanía, Registro 1, 1796–1797. See also AGN, Escribanía, Registro 4, 1800–1801, for the apprenticeship of Josef Antonio Garcia for shoemaking; AGN, Escribanía, Registro 4, 1802–1803, for the apprenticeship of Eusebio Calderon for shoemaking; and AGN, Escribanía, Registro 1, 1798–1799, for the apprenticeship of Bartolo Jose Velásquez as a tailor.

31. AGN, Escribanía, Registro 1, 1792–1793. A similar case is in AGN Registro 1, 1792–1793, where Manuel Velasquez agreed to split all medical expenses incurred by his son with the master Pedro Rolon.

32. AGN, Escribanía, Registro 3, 1807.

33. AGN, Escribanía, Registro 1, 1804–1809.

34. The contract signed in 1807 by the master shoemaker Josef Vasquez and the father of his apprentice Marcelino Azocan provided that the father could end the contract, if his son was punished too severely.

35. AGN, Escribanía, Registro 2, 1810.

36. An example of this common provision can be found in AGN, Escribanía, Registro 3, 1805, where the master shoemaker Eugenio Yglesias obligates himself to "deliver his apprentices as a perfect journeyman" at the end of the three-year period.

37. See Thompson's discussion of the English case in *The Making of the English Working Class*, 252–53.

38. See the matricula of tallistas, carpinteros, estatuarios, silleteros, toneleros, aserradores y peineros in AGN, División Colonia, Sección Gobierno, Tribunales leg. 13, exp. 15.

39. AGN, Tribunales, leg. 66, exp. 37.

40. AGN, Justicia, leg. 9, exp. 177.

41. For the census of 1810, see AGN, División Colonia, Sección Gobierno, Censo de Buenos Aires, 1810. I searched all surviving *manzanas* (city blocks) to discover all households headed by artisans.

42. The cases in this section come from AGN, División Colonia, Sección Gobierno, Padrones de Buenos Aires, ciudad y campaña, 1782–1807.

43. AGN, División Colonia, Sección Gobierno, Bandos, libro 4, 1777–1790, 158–59.

44. The comparisons of artisan population are based on Universidad de Buenos Aires, *Documentos para la historia Argentina*, vol. 11, "Territorio y población, padrón de la ciudad de Buenos Aires" and the 1780 matriculations AGN, División Colonia, Sección Gobierno, Tribunales, leg. 13, exp. 15; Tribunales, leg. 66, exp. 37; Interior, leg. 9, exp. 5; Justicia, leg. 9, exp. 177; Interior, leg. 9, exp. 5; and Tribunales, leg. 13, exp. 15.

45. AGN, Division Colonia, Sección Contaduría, Caja de Buenos Aires, 1780.

46. See Ménétra, *Journal of My Life*, as a firsthand account of this way of life.

47. AGN, División Colonia, Sección Gobierno, Interior, leg. 38, exp. 1, 47 vta.

48. Michael Sonenscher points out that efforts to control the number of masters in the trades in eighteenth-century France were directly tied to the assumption that nearly every master was a married head of household (Sonenscher, *Work and Wages*, 116–17, 124–25).

49. The sources for this discussion is provided in note 15 above. I have added those sources for panaderos and plateros found in the census of 1778 to these matriculations to produce this table. The census in found in Universidad de Buenos Aires, *Documentos para la historia Argentina*, vol. 11, "territorio y población," *passim*.

50. AGN, División Colonia, Sección Gobierno, Interior, leg. 26, exp. 4, 22–22 vta.

51. Marisa M. Díaz, "Las migraciones internas a la ciudad de Buenos Aires, 1744–1810," *Boletín del instituto de historia Argentina y Americana, "Dr. Emilio Ravignani,"* Tercera serie 16–17 (1997–1998): esp. 22–25.

52. The data for this discussion is taken from the universe of surviving matriculations of artisans taken in 1780. These sources are provided in note 15.

53. AGN, División Colonia, Sección Gobierno, Archivo del Cabildo, 1788, 18–20 vta.

54. Ricardo Cicercchia, *Historia de la vida privada en la Argentina* (Buenos Aires: Troquel, 1998), 63.

55. Municipalidad de la Capital, *Documentos y planos relativos al periodo edilicio colonial de la ciudad de Buenos Aires* (Buenos Aires: Talleres Peuser, 1910), 2:85. The bishop noted that the vacated College of the Jesuits was temporarily being used but that the guards were seen entering the rooms of the women causing great scandal.

56. AGN, Sucesiones, 8415.

57. AGN, Escribanía, Registro 6, 117–21.

58. The best examination of the culture of honor in Spanish America is Ann Twinam's *Public Lives, Private Secrets*.

59. Richard Boyer discusses the topic of plebeian honor in colonial Mexico in his "Honor among Plebeians."

60. AGN, División Colonia, Sección Gobierno, Archivo del Cabildo, 1795, 318–26v, provides the case of Martín de Sagastume, a *maestro mayor* of ship carpenters who sought to be relieved of his office as *alcalde de barrio* because it interfered with his duties to his employer, the navy yard.

61. See AGN, División Colonia, Sección Gobierno, Interior, leg. 26, exp. 4, 25, for the cabildo's opinion that white parents hesitated to place their sons as apprentices with masters who trained or employed blacks.

62. Vieytes and Cerviño, *Seminario de agricultura, industria y comercio*, 12:233–38.

63. AHPBA, Criminales, leg. 34-1-18.

64. AHPBA, Criminales, leg. 34-1-12.

65. This is not an appropriate place to thoroughly review this literature, but a brief citation of some of the more important studies might be useful to the reader. See Pitt-Rivers, *The Fate of Shechem or the Politics of Sex*; Campbell, *Honour, Family, and Patronage*; Delaney, "Seeds of Honor, Fields of Shame." I also find Brandes's *Metaphors of Masculinity* to be very helpful.

66. AHPBA, Criminales, leg. 34–1–18. See also AHPBA, Criminales, leg. 34–1–10, for a similar case.

67. AHPBA, Criminales, leg. 34–1–10.

68. See my articles "Artisans" and "The Impact of Racial Discrimination on Black Artisans in Colonial Buenos Aires."

69. See Freud, *Civilization and Its Discontents*, 61.

70. Boyer, "Honor among Plebeians," 161–64.

71. AHPBA, Criminales, leg. 34–1–19.

72. AHPBA, Criminales, leg. 34–1–10. See also AHPBA, Criminales, leg. 34–1–20, for another case involving the murder of a slave in similar circumstances.

73. See AGN, División Colonia, Sección Goberierno, Comerciales, leg. 14, exp. 8, for a discussion of apprenticeship practice among silversmiths prior to the creation of a guild. For examination of journeymen, see AGN, División Colonia, Sección Goberierno, Archivo del Cabildo, 1790.

74. For a discussion of festivals in contemporary Chile, see Valenzuela Márquez, "Poder y pirotecnia, artesanos y mapuches."

75. The Cofradía de San Eloy, patron saint of silversmiths, functioned in Buenos Aires by 1743 and organized its members' celebration of the patron's feast day as well as participation in events like the celebration of the coronation of Charles III. See AGN, División Colonia, Sección Goberierno, Justicia, leg. 17, exp. 144.

76. For the best examination of the place of public ritual in the political capitals of Spanish America, see Curcio-Nagy's *The Great Festivals of Colonial Mexico City*. For a hint of the Buenos Aires case, see Urquiza, "Etiquetas y conflictos." For the most complete and compelling description of Corpus Christi in Buenos Aires, see Davie, *Letters from Paraguay*, 76–83.

77. This theme is developed in chapter 3 of this book and in my article "The Competition of Slave and Free Labor in Artisanal Production: Buenos Aires, 1770–1815." Urquijo makes this point convincingly in his excellent *La industria sombrerera porteña, 1780–1835*.

78. Azara, *Viajes por la América Meridional*, 1:168–69.

79. Quoted in Barreneche, *Crime and the Administration of Justice in Buenos Aires, 1785–1853*, 26.

80. While we only glimpse this world through criminal records or regulations in Buenos Aires, the importance of these settings to the culture of the plebe is illu-

minated clearly in a contemporary memoir written in France, see Ménétra, *Journal of My Life*.

81. Municipalidad de la Capital, *Documentos y planos*, 2:69.

82. Biedma et al., *Acuerdos del extinguido cabildo de Buenos Aires*, serie 3, tomo 5, libro 40, 731.

83. Pereira Salas, *Juegos y alegrias coloniales en Chile*, 63–108, provides a good general introduction to this topic. See also Torre Revello, *Crónicas del Buenos Aires colonial*, 179–200.

84. A very useful short summary is provided by Urquijo, *El virreinato del Río de la Plata en la epoca del Marques de Avilés*, 375–78.

85. Even after a permanent bullring had been constructed in Buenos Aires some extraordinary events were held in the Plaza Mayor, for example, between November 1795 and February 1796, fifteen *corridas* were staged to welcome the new viceroy, Pedro Melo de Portugal y Villena (Torre Revello, *Crónicas del Buenos Aires colonial*, 189). The original bullring was a wooden arena constructed in Plaza Monserrat at the end of the 1780s. The size of the construction distorted the plaza's earlier market function, leading the cabildo to license the construction of a larger brick bullring in Retiro in the late 1790s.

86. In one of the lesser-known versions of the bullfight, the bull was mounted by the bullfighter, typically dressed as a native, who exhausted the bull before dispatching him with a knife. The exemplar of this style was Mariano Ceballos, a free black from Buenos Aires, who eventually performed in Spain in the era of Charles III (see Torre Revello, *Crónicas del Buenos Aires colonial*, 198–99).

87. See Universidad de Buenos Aires, *Documentos para la historia Argentina*, tomo 9, "Administración edilicia de la ciudad de Buenos Aires," 279–342, for documents related to construction of bullrings.

88. See the discussion of a 1794 criminal case from Buenos Aires where a bullfighter, José María Troncoso, killed a neighbor who questioned his performance in the bullring in my article "Dangerous Words, Provocative Gestures, Violent Acts: The Disputed Hierarchies of Plebeian Life in Colonial Buenos Aires," 133. Ignacio Núñez claimed it was very rare to find a professional toreador "who had not committed great crimes," see his *Autobiografía*, 53–55.

89. Barreneche, *Crime and the Administration of Justice in Buenos Aires, 1785–1853*, 25.

90. Authorities responded by imposing penalties, work with street-paving crews, that signaled that the class origins of perpetrators had changed (see Urquijo, *El virreinato del Río de la Plata en la epoca del Marques de Avilés*, 380–81).

91. César, *El carnaval de Buenos Aires (1770–1850)*, 41–49.

92. Ibid., 87–88.

93. In a criminal case from 1795 Martín de Álzaga, acting as a special prosecutor, closely questioned a group of artisans suspected of conspiracy. In his effort to fully expose the conspirators he pushed the suspects to reveal the details of their leisure activities. Among these were nearly daily dinners together at food stalls and restaurants near the Plaza Mayor (see AGN, División Colonia, Sección Gobierno, Tribunales, leg. 60, exp. 6).

94. Universidad de Buenos Aires, *Documentos para la historia Argentina*, 2:91.

95. Ignacio Núñez wrote about his passion for billiards and the culture of leisure in his *Autobiografía*, 57. See also López Cantos, *Juegos, fiestas y diversiones en la América Española*, 269–87.

96. Radaelli, *Memorias de los virreyes del Río de la Plata*, 382. Arredondo notes that he has increased the number of alcaldes de barrio, a force created earlier by Vértiz but not expanded, and claimed that this enhanced presence reassured property owners.

97. AGN, División Colonia, Sección Goberierno, Bandos, libro 5, 123–25.

98. Kinder, *Journal of a Voyage to the Río de la Plata, 1808–1810*, JCBL, 124–27. Kinder claims that there was at least one murder each night on festival days and that four murders had been committed in a single night after his arrival.

99. López Cantos, *Juegos, fiestas y diversiones en la América Española*, 256–59.

100. Urquijo, *El virreinato del Río de la Plata en la epoca del Marques de Avilés*, 369–71. Among the many devices invented to control *bolos*, the viceroy granted a monopoly to a single investor who paid two thousand pesos per year during the duration of the contract.

101. Biedma et al., *Acuerdos del extinguido cabildo de Buenos Aires*, serie 3, tomo II, libro 55, 131.

102. Ibid., libro 55, 249–53. See also Pereira Salas, *Juegos y alegrias coloniales en Chile*, 139–48.

103. Torre Revello, *Crónicas del Buenos Aires colonial*, 279–92.

104. AGN, División Colonia, Sección Gobierno, Cabildo de Buenos Aires, Obras, 1805–1806, Relación de lo recaudado de los cafes, canchas, posadas, etc.

3. Remembered Scripts

1. AGN, Sección Colonial, Archivo del Cabildo, 1780–1783, 441–41 vta. Documents permit the identification of forty-two of the seventy-one signatories by birthplace and race. Twenty-two masters, or 52.4 percent, were born in Buenos Aires. The remaining 47.6 percent were immigrants. Of these, sixteen immigrants, or 38.2 percent, were born in Europe. Thirty-five masters, or 83.3 percent, were white. There were five morenos or pardos and two mestizos.

2. See Márquez Miranda, *Ensayo sobre los artificies de la platería en el Buenos Aires*

colonial, 84. He notes that despite this presumption the silversmiths of Buenos Aires enjoyed no special status.

3. AGN, Sección Colonial, Archivo del Cabildo, 1780–1783, 442.

4. See the coverage of these events in Barba, *La organización del trabajo en el Buenos Aires colonial*, esp. 49–53.

5. AGN, Sección Colonial, Archivo del Cabildo, 1780–1783, 443–43 vta. The shoemakers sought to sweeten the deal by suggesting that guild officers would facilitate the military's procurement of shoes and boots by dividing contracts among a number of shoemakers. They also claimed that the guild would stimulate an improved economic situation for its members, thereby increasing the government's tax base. All the quotations come from this initial petition.

6. Ibid., 1780–1783, 442 vta.

7. This was common practice for the prices of most consumer goods, including food and clothing. See Barba, *La organización del trabajo en el Buenos Aires colonial*, 37–48. *Aranceles* were in use in Córdoba in the seventeenth century. See a brief discussion in Furlong, *Artesanos Argentinos durante le dominación hispanica*, 79.

8. The ethnic composition of the artisan community is discussed in detail in chapter 1. The *matrículas* of artisans recorded in 1780 indicate that 41.2 percent of artisans residing in Buenos Aires were immigrants.

9. The best study of the development and organization of the European guild system is Martin Saint-Leon's *Historia de las corporaciones de oficio*.

10. AGN, Sección Colonial, Archivo del Cabildo, 1780–1783, 444.

11. Ibid., 1780–1783, 443 vta.

12. Biedma et al. *Acuerdos del extinguido cabildo de Buenos Aires*, serie 3, tomo 6, libro 42, 365.

13. See Biedma et al., *Acuerdos del extinguido cabildo de Buenos Aires*, serie 3, tomo 6, libro 42, 444.

14. AGN, División Colonia, Sección Gobierno, Criminales, leg. 13, exp. 31, sentence from 19 Marzo 1778.

15. Original document in AGN, División Colonia, Sección Gobierno, Archivo del Cabildo, 1780–1783, 444–52. It is reprinted in Barba, *La organización de trabajo en el Buenos Aires colonial*, 123–33.

16. AGN, Sección Colonial, Archivo del Cabildo, 1780–1783, 444.

17. Ibid., 1780–1783, 451–451 vta.; and Barba, *La organización del trabajo en el Buenos Aires colonial*, 135–37.

18. This function of corporate organization is well developed in Ruth MacKay, *Lazy and Improvident People*, esp. 111–201.

19. AGN, Sección Colonial, Archivo del Cabildo, 1780–1783, 446 vta.

20. Ibid., 1780–1783, 447 vta.

21. AGN, Sección Colonial, Archivo del Cabildo, 1780–1783, 447. See also my discussion in "The Role of Apprenticeship in Colonial Buenos Aires."

22. AGN, Sección Colonial, Archivo del Cabildo, 1780–1783, 445 vta.

23. Martin Saint-Leon, *Historia de las corporaciones de oficio*, 403–14. In his discussion of Tugot's attempt to abolish the Parisian guilds, Martin Saint-Leon provides an excellent synopsis of nepotism and discrimination in the European guild system.

24. AGN, Sección Colonial, Archivo del Cabildo, 1780–1783, 447 vta.

25. Ibid., 1780–1783, 453 vta.

26. The first examinations for master recorded for this craft were in 1635. See Márquez Miranda, *Ensayo sobre los artífices de la platería en el Buenos Aires colonial*, 65.

27. This story is told in greater detail in my article "The Silversmiths of Buenos Aires."

28. There is a substantial bibliography for this general topic. The following titles represent the most effective and reliable studies of the development of the guilds of silversmiths in the New World: Carrera Stampa, *Los gremios mexicanos*; Márquez Miranda, *Ensayo sobre los artífices de la platería en el Buenos Aires colonial*; Ravignani, "El cuerpo de plateros en el Río de la Plata"; Samayoa Guevara, *Los gremios de artesanos en la ciudad de Guetemala*; and Torre Revello, *El gremio de plateros en los Indias Occidentales* (Buenos Aires: Imprenta de la Universida, 1932).

29. Torre Revello, *El gremio de plateros en los Indias Occidentales*, 15–21.

30. See Curcio-Nagy, *The Great Festivals of Colonial Mexico City*, 97–98, for an idea of the wealth and the prestige of the silversmith's guild.

31. Márquez Miranda, *Ensayo sobre los artífices de la platería en el Buenos Aires colonial*, 53–54.

32. AGN, Cabildo de Buenos Aires, 1745–1752, leg. 3, 1748.

33. AGN, Tribunales, leg. P6, exp. 8, 1–15 vta.

34. Ibid., 15 vta.–16, 27.

35. From a letter dated March 13, 1758. See Biedma et al., *Acuerdos del extinguido cabildo de Buenos Aires*, serie 3, tomo 2, libro 31, 242–243.

36. Biedma et al., *Acuerdos del extinguido cabildo de Buenos Aires*, serie 3, tomo 2, libro 31, 306.

37. AGN, Justicia, leg. 17, exp. 444.

38. To see some of the work produced by these artisans, see Smithsonian Institution, *Silverworks from Río de la Plata, Argentina (18th and 19th centuries)*, works from the collection of the Issac Fenández Blanco Museum (1976).

39. AGN, Comerciales, leg. 14, exp. 25, 2 vta.

40. AGN, Justica, leg. 17, exp. 444.

41. Ibid. Callejas y Sandoval's *cofradía* met in the convent of Santa Catalina.

42. Ibid.

43. AGN, Hacienda, leg. 73, exp. 1929, 50–53. See the petition signed by "all of the silversmiths" naming Callejas y Sandoval as their representative.

44. AGN, Comercicales, leg. 14, exp. 8, 7–9.

45. The census is found in Universidad de Buenos Aires, *Documentos para la historia Argentina*, vol. 11, territorio y población, *passim*. The 1780 matriculation of Zapateros is found in AGN, Interior, leg. 9, exp. 5. I thoroughly searched the census of 1778 to locate every resident identified as either a shoemaker or silversmith.

46. Universidad de Buenos Aires, *Documentos para la historia Argentina*, vol. 11, "territorio y población," passim.

47. See my "Manumission in Colonial Buenos Aires, 1776–1810" for a fuller discussion of wage earning and manumission.

48. AGN, Interior, leg. 9, exp. 5. The matrícula reliably provide birthplace, craft status, and legal status of blacks and mulattoes. The census more reliably provides age, racial labels, addresses, and family and household information.

49. Ibid. The *escribano* who compiled the matrícula distinguished between "Negroes" and "mulattoes." For the purpose of this figure, I collapsed the two categories.

50. Azara, *Viajes por la América Meridional*, 2:161–162. Azara briefly discussed Spanish policy on slaves who escaped from foreign territories.

51. See my "Manumission in Colonial Buenos Aires, 1776–1810," 258–79.

52. AGN, Interior, leg. 26, exp. 4, 1–1 vta.

53. Ibid., exp. 4, 2–2 vta.

54. Ibid., exp. 4, 4.

55. AGN, Interior, leg. 26, exp. 4, 5 vta. The draft constitution written by Ramos Mexía in 1780 had also stipulated a prerequisite of six years of experience for the examination, but the earlier draft had reversed the time requirements so that the young artisan would only spend two years at the unpaid apprentice rank. The 1788 proposal was generated by the master shoemakers themselves, and this modification in the instructional program would provide them with two additional years of unpaid labor from each of their apprentices.

56. AGN, Interior, leg. 26, exp. 4, 7, 8.

57. Ibid.

58. Ibid., exp. 4, 9–14 vta. This is the copy of the draft constitution. All references to this draft are taken from these pages.

59. AGN, División Colonia, Sección Gobierno, Tribunales, leg. 9, exp. 4.

60. Although the guild of shoemakers had an extremely short duration, the notarized apprenticeship contract was common throughout the late colonial period.

Examples of these contracts can be found in AGN, Escribanía, Registro 1, 1798–1799, 23–23 vta., 94 vta.–95, and 184 vta.–185.

61. AGN, Interior, leg. 26, exp. 4, 13 vta., 14 vta.–15, and 16.

62. AGN, Interior, leg. 26, exp. 4, 23, 25.

63. I discuss this in detail in "The Competition of Slave and Labor in Artisanal Production: Buenos Aires, 1770–1815," *International Review of Social History* 40 (1996), 409–24.

64. AGN, Interior, leg. 26, exp. 4, 25–25 vta.

65. Ibid., exp. 4, 25 vta.

66. See Vieytes and Cerviño, *Seminario de agricultura, industria y comercio,* 4:233–38.

67. AGN, Interior, leg. 26, exp. 4, 26, 27–28 vta., and 29. The other suggestions from the cabildo were less controversial. They asked the shoemakers to increase the penalty for opening a shop without license, reduce the fees for examinations, and set maximum prices for all classes of shoes and boots.

68. AGN, Interior, leg. 26, exp. 4, 30, 32 vta., and 33–34.

69. Ibid., exp. 4, 39. Five of the six masters nominated for alcalde can be identified by birthplace. Juan Esteban Caro and Juan José Romero were Spaniards. Manuel Antonio Sustaeta, Agustín Marín, and José Farías were *porteños,* and Felix Sánchez cannot be identified. Joaquín Alvarez was Portuguese.

70. AGN, Interior, leg. 26, exp. 4, 40 vta.

71. AGN, Interior, leg. 26, exp. 4, 40, 44 vta.–42.

72. The signatories included two criollos, Agustín Marín and Luis de la Rosa, and two Spaniards, Juan Esteban Caro and Agustín de Zuasnabal.

73. AGN, Interior, leg. 26, exp. 4, 41 vta.–42.

74. Ibid., exp. 4, 43 vta.

75. Ibid., exp. 4, 45–45 vta.

76. I examine the ways in which slaves challenged their masters in legal proceedings in "'A Lack of Legitimate Obedience and Respect.'"

77. AGN, Interior, leg. 26, exp. 4, 47.

78. Ibid., exp. 4, 40.

79. Ibid., exp. 4, 15 vta.

80. The Madrid shoemakers' constitution was approved in November 1770 and therefore offers a good point of comparison with the porteño draft. See Barba, *La organización del trabajo en el Buenos Aires colonial,* 66–67.

81. AGN, Interior, leg. 26, exp. 4, 49 vta.–80 vta. All references to the Madrid constitution are drawn from these pages.

82. Martin Saint-Leon, *Historia de las corporaciones de oficio,* 364–65.

83. The Madrid ordinances also included a cofradía as a separate but integral part

of the corporate organization. The cofradía organized the religious observances of the corporate membership and maintained a separate chapel dedicated to the patron saints of the guild, Crispin and Crispiniano.

84. AGN, Interior, leg. 26, exp. 4, 84 vta.–85.

85. Ibid., exp. 4, 85 vta.–86.

86. Ibid., exp. 4, 86.

87. Ibid.

88. AGN, Interior, leg. 26, exp. 4, 100 vta.–101 vta.

89. Ibid., exp. 4, 111 vta. The first lawyer, Benito González Rivadavia, soon complained of ill health and withdrew.

90. Ibid., exp. 4, 153 vta. The draft appropriated many of the best-known social objectives advocated by Spanish intellectuals like Campomanes in his *Discurso sobre educación popular*. See also Barba, *La organización del trabajo en el Buenos Aires colonial*, 73–75, for his coverage of this story.

91. AGN, Interior, leg. 26, exp. 4, 117 vta.

92. Ibid., exp. 4, 117.

93. Ibid., exp. 4, 123 vta.

94. Ibid., exp. 4, 113–113 vta.

95. Ibid., exp. 4, 122.

96. Ibid., exp. 4, 122 vta.

97. Ibid., exp. 4, 123.

98. Ibid., exp. 4, 153 vta., 154 vta.–155, and 157 vta.

99. Following the publication of Paula Sanz's *bando* in 1788 the cabildo of Buenos Aires ordered the guild leadership to undertake a comprehensive *visita* of all silversmith shops to check on the credentials of masters, closing shops where the "master" had not served a five-year apprenticeship and two-year period as a journeyman. See Biedma et al., *Acuerdos del extinguido cabildo de Buenos Aires*, serie 3, tomo 8, libro 48, 553–56.

100. Some of the more impressive works of colonial-era silversmiths are illustrated and collected in the museum catalog, Smithsonian Institution, *Silverworks from the Río de la Plata, Argentina*.

101. See AGN, División Colonia, Sección Gobierno, Comerciales, leg. 14. exp. 8, for the case of Josef Bermúdez. The case of Cipriano Rodríguez from 1789 is similar in character, see AGN, División Colonia, Sección Gobierno, Tribunales, leg. 74, exp.29.

102. AGN, División Colonia, Sección Gobierno, Archivo del Cabildo, 1790, Sept.–Dic.

103. See Biedma et al., *Acuerdos del extinguido cabildo de Buenos Aires*, serie 3, tomo 9, libro 49, 63–64, for a dispute that drew the cabildo into guild affairs over the right of Josef Bermúdez to open a shop.

104. AGN, División Colonia, Sección Gobierno, Tribunales, leg. G17, exp. 1.

105. The visitas are described in detail in the resulting legal disputes. See AGN, División Colonia, Sección Gobierno, Tribunales, leg. 74, exp. 29.

106. AGN, División Colonia, Sección Gobierno, Tribunales, leg. 131, exp. 12.

107. Elements of this process are provided in Márquez Miranda, *Ensayo sobre los artificies de la platería en el Buenos Aires colonial*, 101–30. One of the documents is provided on 36–38 in apéndice no. 4.

108. AGN, División Colonia, Sección Gobierno, Tribunales, leg. 131, exp. 12.

109. AGN, División Colonia, Sección Gobierno, Tribunanles, leg. P12, exp. 31, 1–15.

110. Carroll, *Through the Looking-Glass*, 117.

111. Félix de Azara, a Spanish officer who led the expedition to determine Paraguay's boundary with Brazil, was a careful observer of social forms and noted that the three founding races had "mixed with facility one with the other." This he stated "results in mixed individuals that are called *gentes de color* (pardos)." His suggestion was that pardo was a word so elastic that it was assigned to every mixed group. See Azara, *Viajes por la América Meridional*, 1:156–57.

112. AGN, División Colonia, Sección Gobierno, Tribunales, leg. Z4, exp. 7, 1.

113. Barba, *La organización del trabajo en el Buenos Aires colonial*, 85–90. Barba has reprinted the matrícula of shoemakers compiled by García López and found in AGN, Tribunales, leg. Z4, exp. 7. This list, however, is literally sandwiched between portions of a visita of master shoemakers undertaken by García López and the newly elected officers of the guild on December 14–15, 1792. Barba, apparently believing the lists identical, has ignored the visita. A close comparison, however, reveals a discrepancy of twenty-nine masters. In the light of a later dispute over the accuracy of the census by the guildsmen themselves, I have chosen to collapse the two lists. Where the data from the two lists have conflicted for race, birthplace, or civil state, I have used the following criteria: (1) conflicts in race were resolved by selecting the least prestigious as probably the most accurate; (2) birthplace conflicts were settled in favor of the more explicit designation; and (3) conflicting information on civil state was resolved by selecting explicit information (for example, either *casado* or *soltero*) over no designation and married over single, since the compilers would probably have used single, rather than married, in cases where they were not sure.

4. Collective Obligations

1. AGN, División Colonia, Sección Gobierno, Interior, leg. 54, exp. 3, 3–4 vta.

2. AGN, División Colonia, Sección Gobierno, Interior, leg. 26, exp. 4, 103–104 vta.

3. This pattern was not unusual in the world of guilds. See MacKay, *Lazy, Improvident People*, esp. 140–50.

4. The constitution was officially published in Buenos Aires by order of the viceroy

on June 9, 1792. See AGN, División Colonia, Sección Gobierno, Interior, leg. 26, exp. 4, 157 vta.

5. AGN, División Colonia, Sección Gobierno, Tribunales, leg. z4, exp. 7, 7–7 vta.

6. Ibid., exp. 7, 8.

7. AGN, División Colonia, Sección Gobierno, Interior, leg. 25, exp. 4, 158 vta.–159. The letter is undated and is included in a suit asking the *fiscal* of the *audiencia* to rule against charging the guild for the cost of the census by the alcalde, García López. Antonio Porra, Nicolás Riguy, José Labrador, José Canepa, and Marin Porra signed this note.

8. AGN, División Colonia, Sección Gobierno, Interior, leg. 33, exp. 7, 7 vta.–8.

9. Ibid., exp. 7, 3–3 vta.

10. Ibid., exp. 7, 3 vta.–4.

11. Ibid., exp. 7, 4 vta., 5.

12. Ibid., exp. 7, 5, 5 vta.–6.

13. AGN, División Colonia, Sección Gobierno, Interior, leg. 33, exp. 16. Romero dismissed this protest and Baquero avoided it because they feared that this claim undermined their narrower defense of Baquero and his closest allies. The point claimed by the protestors, however, that identity was determined by bureaucratic decision, not biology, had been the everyday reality among the Buenos Aires plebe prior to the guild movement.

14. AGN, División Colonia, Sección Gobierno, Interior, leg. 33, exp. 7, 7–7 vta.

15. Ibid., exp. 7, 9, 9 vta.–10.

16. Ibid., exp. 7, 11–12.

17. Francisco Baquero was certainly a remarkable character willing to confront both colonial authorities and the most powerful members of his craft. But his origins were probably quite humble as is indicated by his illiteracy. See AGN, División Colonia, Sección Gobierno, Tribunales, leg. v8, exp. 23. His son Joseph signed a letter to the alcalde for his father, acknowledging his illiteracy.

18. AGN, División Colonia, Sección Gobierno, Tribunales, leg. v8, exp. 23, 16, 16 vta.–17.

19. Ibid., exp. 23, 20–20 vta, 22 vta.–23, 23 vta., and 25–25 vta.

20. Ibid., exp. 23, 26 vta., 27.

21. AGN, División Colonia, Sección Gobierno, Interior, leg. 33, exp. 16, 1–3 vta.

22. AGN, División Colonia, Sección Gobierno, Interior, leg. 33, exp. 7, 31 vta.

23. The report to the audiencia was filed on January 11, 1793. See AGN, División Colonia, Sección Gobierno, Interior, leg., 53, exp. 2, 109 vta.

24. Ibid., exp. 2, 109.

25. See AGN, División Colonia, Sección Gobierno, Interior, leg. 34, exp. 18, for a dispute among shoemakers over the location of their *cofradía*. On September 4, 1793, the newly elected guild leadership turned to the cabildo to settle this con-

flict. Guild officers had initially decided to establish the cofradía at the church of San Francisco, but later some guild officials had reached a verbal agreement to locate the cofradía at the church of Santo Domingo. The cabildo's alcalde, Manuel de Cerro Sáenz, sided with the majority, noting that San Francisco had been selected by a clear majority of the guild officers, "in a meeting, that proceeded with the order and solemnity provided by His Majesty for these cases." Placed in the context of the endemic factional strife and oft-required interventions by the government, this dispute demonstrated again that the shoemakers were unable to resolve factional struggles without recourse to the colonial bureaucracy.

26. The king's decision arrived in Buenos Aires in early 1794, see AGN, División Colonia, Sección Gobierno, Interior, leg. 54, exp. 3, 3 vta.–4, 4–4 vta. See also AGN, División Colonia, Sección Gobierno, Reales Cédulas, Decretos, leg. 27, 1793–1795.

27. AGN, División Colonia, Sección Gobierno, Interior, leg. 54, exp. 3, 5–6, 7 vta., 9–9 vta.

28. AGN, División Colonia, Sección Gobierno, Interior, leg. 4, exp. 14, 6 vta.

29. AGN, División Colonia, Sección Gobierno, Interior, leg. 54, exp. 2, 1–1 vta.

30. Ibid., exp. 2, 3–4 vta., 4 vta.

31. Ibid., exp. 2, 4 vta.–5 vta.

32. Ibid., exp. 2, 7, 8–8 vta.

33. Ibid., exp. 2, 10.

34. Ibid., exp. 2, 12 vta.–13, 15 vta., and 24 vta.–25.

35. Ibid., exp. 2, 30, 33–41 vta.

36. This letter is found in two separate expedientes: AGN, Interior, leg. 41, exp. 14, 1; and AGN, Interior, leg. 54, exp. 3, 10. See also the discussion of Francisco Baquero's advocacy in Madrid in Barba, *La organización del trabajo en el Buenos Aires colonial*, 95–97.

37. AGN, División Colonia, Sección Gobierno, Interior, leg. 41, exp. 14, 1. The black and casta shoemakers paid 155 pesos to the Madrid *apoderado*. See also AGN, Tribunales, leg. z4, exp. 7.

38. AGN, División Colonia, Sección Gobierno, Interior, leg. 41, exp. 14, 2, 2–2 vta.

39. AGN, División Colonia, Sección Gobierno, Interior, leg. 41, exp. 14, 3.

40. Another example of Baquero's aggressiveness is found in AGN, División Colonia, Sección Gobierno, Interior, Leg, 54, exp. 3, 31–47 vta. He accused the *escribano* Basavilvaso of deliberately withholding portions of the royal decree suspending the guild. The escribano asked the fiscal to clear his name and reputation of the slurs generated by Baquero and his associates. The fiscal stated that the escribano had precisely fulfilled his obligations and ordered that Baquero's "slanders" be removed from all public records.

41. AGN, División Colonia, Sección Gobierno, Interior, leg. 41, exp. 14, 2–2 vta.

42. AGN, División Colonia, Sección Gobierno, Interior, leg. 54, exp. 3, 43–43 vta.

43. Many of the details of this story are provided in Barba, *La organización del trabajo en el Buenos Aires colonial.*

44. AGN, División Colonia, Sección Gobierno, Interior, leg. 54, exp. 3, 43–43 vta.

45. AGN, División Colonia, Sección Gobierno, Interior, leg. 55, exp. 5, 2 vta.

46. AGN, División Colonia, Sección Gobierno, Interior, leg. 34, exp. 12.

47. In the census of 1778 Troncoso was listed as a Spaniard. In the guild census of 1788 he was identified as a "natural de Buenos Aires," see Márquez Miranda, *Ensayo sobre los artificies de la platería en el Buenos Aires colonial,* 223.

48. See AGI, Audiencia de Buenos Aires, leg. 294, numero 1, for Jorge Troncoso's February 1796 letter to the king seeking permission to form a guild and compose ordinances. The lawyer from Madrid hired to represent the silversmiths, Juan Pablo Fretes, presented the letter and request to the court.

49. AGN, División Colonia, Sección Gobierno, Tribunales, leg. 131, exp. 12.

50. AGN, División Colonia, Sección Gobierno, Tribuanles, leg. G17, exp. 1, 1–25.

51. See AGN, División Colonia, Sección Gobierno, Comerciales, leg. 15, exp. 16, for another case where disputed *limpieza de sangre* was pursued in the courts.

52. See the similar case of Leon Recolde who in 1795 the cabildo ordered to be examined by the guild, which it resisted. AGN, División Colonia, Sección Gobierno, Interior, leg. 36, exp. 6.

53. This case dragged on for two years until the viceroy ordered the guild to provide the examination. See Márquez Miranda, *Ensayo sobre los artifices de platería en el Buenos Aires colonial,* 112 n.2.

54. AGN, División Colonia, Sección Gobierno, Interior, leg. 41, exp. 7.

55. AGN, División Colonia, Sección Gobierno, Tribunales, leg. G17, exp. 1.

56. Márquez Miranda, *Ensayo sobre los artifices de platería en el Buenos Aires colonial,* 128.

57. AGN, División Colonia, Sección Gobierno, Interior, leg. 4, exp. 14, 6 vta., 7.

58. Ibid., exp. 14, 7.

59. AGN, División Colonia, Sección Gobierno, Interior, leg. 55, exp. 5, 2 vta.

60. AGN, División Colonia, Sección Gobierno, Interior, leg. 41, exp. 14, 9 vta.

61. Ibid., exp. 14, 11–17 vta. This provides all the statistical information discussed below.

62. AGN, División Colonia, Sección Gobierno, Interior, leg. 41, exp. 14, 18, 19 vta.–20.

63. AGN, División Colonia, Sección Gobierno, Interior, leg. 55, exp. 5, 4.

64. Ibid., exp. 5, 4 vta.–5, 5–5 vta., 6–6 vta.

65. Ibid., exp. 5, 8.

66. Ibid., exp. 5, 7–7 vta.

67. The conflict between shoemakers and the trade in ready-to-wear shoes conducted by *pulperos* is found in AGN, División Colonia, Sección Gobierno, Interior, leg. 53, exp. 2, 112–51 vta.

68. In January 1793 the newly elected leadership of the united guild successfully petitioned Viceroy Arredondo to publish the sections of the guild constitution that banned the sale of shoes in *pulperías*. See AGN, División Colonia, Sección Gobierno, Bandos, libro 7, 114–17 vta.

69. In September 1794 the fiscal required the shoemakers to pay thirty-two pesos to the pulperos for the confiscated ready-made shoes, effectively ending any effort to control or prohibit the manufacture and sale of ready-to-wear shoes. AGN, División Colonia, Sección Gobierno, Interior, leg. 53, exp. 2, 141–51.

70. AGN, División Colonia, Sección Gobierno, Interior, leg. 55, exp. 5, 8 vta.

71. Ibid., exp. 5, 9.

72. This was not unique to Buenos Aires, a similar pattern arose in France, see Sonenscher, *Work and Wages*, 101–2.

73. See John R. Commons, "American Shoemakers, 1648–1895: A Sketch of Industrial Evolution," *Quarterly Journal of Economics* 24.1 (November 1909): 39–83, for a discussion of the relationship between the marketplace and the means of production.

74. AGN, División Colonia, Sección Gobierno, Interior, leg. 55, exp. 5, 1 vta.–2.

75. See for example AGN, División Colonia, Sección Gobierno, Justicia, leg. 17, exp. 144, for the Governor Intendant Francisco de Paula Sanz's support for the collection of guild dues.

76. The Sindico Procurador Ramón Ximenez y Navia granted the guild leadership formal approval to formulate ordinances on January 24, 1797. See AGN, División Colonia, Sección Gobierno, Interior, leg. 41, exp. 7, 6–6 vta.

77. The leader of the dissident faction, Salvador Grande, was also the silversmith most often penalized for adultered goods. See AGN, División Colonia, Sección Gobierno, Tribunales, leg. P12, exp. 31, 1 vta.–2. See also Torre Revello, *El gremio de plateros en las Indias Occidentales*, 27–29.

78. AGI, Audiencia de Buenos Aires, leg. 214 (19); and AGN, División Colonia, Sección Gobierno, Hacienda, leg. 73, exp. 1927. As late as November 1799 the widow of a silversmith who had had goods embargoed in 1791 was still seeking the return of the goods. See AGN, División Colonia, Sección Gobierno, Tribunales, leg. 74, exp. 29.

79. AGN, División Colonia, Sección Gobierno, Interior, leg. 34, exp. 12. See also Ravignani, "El cuerpo de plateros en el Río de la Plata," 314–15; and Márquez Miranda, *Ensayo sobre los artífices de la platería en el Buenos Aires colonial*, 128.

80. AGN, División Colonia, Sección Gobierno, Hacienda, leg. 73, exp. 1927.

81. AGN, División Colonia, Sección Gobierno, Comerciales, leg. 14, exp. 8. Despite this crushing blow to the guild, silversmiths continued to supervise formal examinations for master status to the end of the colonial period. See AGN, Archivo del Cabildo, 1809, for the cabildo's order to administer an exam on December 19, 1809.

82. AGN, División Colonia, Sección Gobierno, Interior, leg. 53, exp. 2, p. 109 vta.

83. AGN, División Colonia, Sección Gobierno, Interior, leg. 54, exp. 3, pp. 43–43 vta.

84. AGN, División Colonia, Sección Gobierno, Interior, leg. 55, exp. 5, 1 vta.–2.

85. These conflicts poisoned private business arrangements as well. The criollo Nicolás Riera agreed to sell his shop to the Italian immigrant Salvador Vareti (or Bareti) for 635 pesos in 1799. The arrangement stipulated that Riera would continue to work as the new owner made the transition. In court, Riera alleged that he was being persecuted by a "conspiracy of foreigners," who sought to "usurp the bitter drops of sweat from his labor." See AGN, División Colonia, Sección Gobierno, Tribunales, leg. b8, exp. 22.

86. Ravignani, "El cuerpo de plateros en el Río de la Plata," 314–15.

87. Saavedra's opinion and the place of this opinion in an emerging economic consensus favoring market freedom was recognized and examined by an earlier generation of Argentine historians. See Barba, *La organización del trabajo en el Buenos Aires colonial*, 108–17; and Levene, "Investigaciones acerca de la historia económica del virreinato del Río de la Plata," in *Obras de Ricardo Levene*, 3 vols. (Buenos Aires: Comisión Nacional Ejecutiva del 150 Aniversario de la Revolución de Mayo, 1962), 1:373–75; and Ruiz-Guiñazu, *El Presdidente Saavedra y el pueblo soberano de 1810*, 42–47.

88. Barba, *La organización del trabajo en el Buenos Aires colonial*, 113–14.

89. AGN, División Colonia, Sección Gobierno, Interior, leg. 55, exp. 5, 14–14 vta.

90. Barba believes that this section follows closely the opinion of the Spanish jurist and intellectual Gaspar Melchor de Jovellanos (Barba, *La organización del trabajo en el Buenos Aires colonial*, 111).

91. AGN, División Colonia, Sección Gobierno, Interior, leg. 55, exp. 5, 15.

92. Ibid., exp. 5, 17 vta.–18.

93. Ibid., exp. 5, 18, 18 vta., 21 vta., 18.

94. Ibid., exp. 5, 15 vta.

95. In 1810 the *Correo de comercio* hosted an exchange between anonymous authors on the issue of forming guilds as a way of promoting industry and regulating standards. After the publication of a positive opinion, the issue of June 2, 1810, published a rebuttal that reiterated the Saavedra opinion. The author argued that

this would end in "retardando los progresos de los mas aplicados" (see Academia Nacional de la Historia (Argentina), *Correro de comercio*, 115–17).

96. See Biedma et al., *Acuerdos del extinguido cabildo de Buenos Aires*, serie 3, tomo 6, libro 42, 444.

97. AGN, División Colonia, Sección Gobierno, Interior, leg. 55, exp. 5, 26–26 vta. See also Barba, *La organización del trabajo en el Buenos Aires colonial*, 114.

98. They also cited the abolition of guilds in Florence, noting "there has been a notable increase in the industry of that district." See AGN, División Colonia, Sección Gobierno, Interior, leg. 55, exp. 5, 28–33 vta.

99. AGN, División Colonia, Sección Gobierno, Interior, leg. 55, exp. 5, 33–33 vta.

100. Ibid., exp. 5, 34.

101. This compromise had been prepared in July 1797 when white and black masters had agreed to seek a racially unified cofradía in which nonwhite masters would have full participatory rights. The fiscal accepted the proposal tentatively the following month. Despite the agreement, the proposed cofradía of shoemakers was never realized. See AGN, División Colonia, Sección Gobierno, Interior, leg. 55, exp. 5, 48 vta.–49.

102. In fact the king repeated his order to the viceroy in October 1799: put the two guilds in place. Instead the proposals went to the Fiscal Márquez de la Plata, who decided in May 1800 that "no hay lugar" (see Barba, *La organización del trabajo en el Buenos Aires colonial*, 118).

103. See AGN, División Colonia, Sección Gobierno, Interior, leg. 55, exp. 5, for the costs assessed the white guild, and see AGN, División Colonia, Sección Gobierno, Tribunales, leg. z4, exp. 7, for the costs borne by the black and casta guild. Among black and casta masters, legal fees had reached 1,037 pesos (or 15 pesos per master) in 1803.

104. Between July 1792 and June 1794 the pardo and moreno masters had accumulated a debt of 272 pesos for legal costs. Another 130 pesos were spent by September 1797. AGN, División Colonia, Sección Gobierno, Tribunales, leg. z4, exp. 7, 20–25 vta.

5. "French Conspiracy" of 1795

1. This and related documents are found in Caillet-Bois, *Ensayo sobre el Río de la Plata y la revolución francesa*, apéndices 110–11.

2. AGN, División Colonia, Sección Gobierno, Tribunales, leg. z4, exp. 7, visita de maestros zapateros, July 24, 1792. See also the letter to the *fiscal* of October 23, 1792, signed by Manuel Antonio Sustaeta, Francisco Baquero and others in AGN, División Colonia, Sección Gobierno, Interior, leg. 33, exp. 7. The 1780 census of shoemakers was compiled by order of Viceroy Vértiz, Sustaeta is described

as a married master shoemaker living in a rental with his wife. He had six years of experience in 1780, see AGN, División Colonia, Sección Gobierno, Interior, leg. 9, exp. 5.

3. A useful short summary of these events is found in Lewin, "La 'conspiración de los Franceses' en Buenos Aires (1795)." For a more dramatic and colorful version, see Ortega, *El complot colonial*. The first scholar to take up this topic was Caillet-Bois in *Ensayo sobre el Río de la Plata y la revolución francesa*.

4. A shorter version of this chapter is published as "The French Conspiracy of 1795: Paranoia and Opportunism on the Eve of Independence in Buenos Aires" in *War, Empire and Slavery, 1770–1830*, eds. Richard Bessel, Nicholas Guyatt, and Jane Rendall (Basingstoke: Palgrave Macmillan, 2010), 106–20.

5. See Besio Moreno, *Buenos Aires*. Total burials recorded in parish registers rose to 1,320 from 812 in 1793.

6. For the effects of these large changes on the broader regional economy, see Garavaglia, "Economic Growth and Regional Differentiations." Garavaglia argues that the regional economy grew by 59 percent between 1786 and 1802 (57).

7. See AGN, Cabildo de Buenos Aires, Correspondencia con el virrey, 1795–1796, 10 Diciembre 1795. The cabildo, "finding in this city a notable shortage of wheat," notes the ongoing wheat shortage and high prices and tells the viceroy that wagons should be sent to Luján and more distant Santiago del Estero.

8. Viceroy Arredondo provided a breakdown of slave imports for 1792 that suggests the enduring importance of Brazil. He stated that from February 11, 1792, to March 16, 1793, the city received 2,689 slaves, 425 directly from Africa and the rest from Brazil, see Radaelli, *Memorias de los virreyes de Río de la Plata*, 394.

9. Aparicio, "Relación de un viaje entre Mendoza y Buenos Aires en 1794," 3:236.

10. This topic is fully developed in my article "'A Lack of Legitimate Obedience and Respect.'"

11. Bareneche, *Crime and the Administration of Justice in Buenos Aires, 1785–1853*, 24–25.

12. AGN, División Colonia, Sección Gobierno, Bandos, libro 7, 133–37.

13. Ibid., libro 7, 131–132.

14. The *alcaldes de barrio* and others wrote to request assistance between January 1794 and February 1795, see AGN, División Colonia, Sección Gobierno, Cabildo de Buenos Aires, Correspondencia con el virrey, 1794 and 1795, 448–49.

15. Fiscal officials in Buenos Aires registered 9,013 legal slave imports in the 1790s. For the Royal Order permitting foreigners to introduce slaves, see Universidad de Buenos Aires, *Documentos para la historia Argentina*, "Comercio de Indias," tomo 6, 474. Volume then increased in the last decade of colonial rule with the arrival of 13,256 slaves. See also, Campagna Caballero, "La población esclava en ciudades puertos del Río de la Plata."

16. Biedma et al., *Acuerdos del extinguido cabildo de Buenos Aires*, serie 4, tomo 9, libro 50, 221.

17. This topic is discussed in two works by Rodríguez Molas, "Esclavitud africana, religión y origen étnico," and "Algunos aspectos del negro en la sociedad rioplatense del siglo XVIII," esp. 103–6.

18. Rodríguez Molas, "Esclavitud africana, religión y origen étnico," 140–44.

19. AGN, División Colonia, Sección Gobierno, Cabildo de Buenos Aires, Correspondencia con el Virrey, 1795. See also two works by Néstor Ortiz Oderigo, "Orígenes etnoculturales de los negros argentinos" and "Las 'naciones' africanas"; see also Rodríguez Molas, "Esclavitud africana, religión y origen étnico," 130.

20. Biedma et al., *Acuerdos del extinguido cabildo de Buenos Aires*, serie 3, tomo 9, libro 50, 229. See also División Colonia, Sección Gobierno, Correspondencia con el Virrey, 1795–1796, for the case of *pulpero* Juan Estevan Sosa, who was fined ten pesos for allowing afterhours gambling in his *pulpería*. The three men arrested with him included two slaves and a free pardo.

21. Biedma et al., *Acuerdos del extinguido cabildo de Buenos Aires*, serie 4, tomo 1, libro 59, 409.

22. For discussion of the role of commerce and shipping in the transmission of revolutionary ideas, see Linebaugh and Rediker, *The Many-Headed Hydra*, esp. chapter 5.

23. For a brief examination of the ways that news of revolutionary events in France and Haiti spread in the Caribbean and beyond, see Dubois, *A Colony of Citizens*, 104–5. For a longer discussion, see Scott, "A Common Wind."

24. Radaelli, *Memorias de los virreyes de Río de la Plata*, 375.

25. AGN, División Colonia, Sección Gobierno, Interior, leg. 26, exp. 4, 69.

26. Caillet-Bois, *Ensayo sobre el Río de la Plata y la revolución francesa*, 32–46.

27. The captain, Alejandro Duclos Guyot, and the crew were detained at least until 1796. Duclos Guyot was back in the Río de la Plata at the time of the British invasions, probably as a Napoleonic agent, and he was made an aide de camp by Santiago de Liniers. See Caillet-Bois, *Ensayo sobre el Río de la Plata y la revolución francesa*, 60–75.

28. The pasquines are briefly discussed in Corcuera Ibáñez, *Santiago Liniers*, 47–48. This work is a generally reliable summary of secondary and essential primary sources, but it is marred by the absence of citations.

29. My weighted index of commodity prices rose from 85.2 in 1794 to 110 in 1795 (in 1776 it was 100). See my full discussion in chapter 6.

30. See this pasquín in AGN, División Colonia, Sección Gobierno, Interior, leg. 38, exp. 1.

31. See Ortega, *El complot colonial*, 55–57.

32. For a short summary, see Puentes, *Don Francisco Javier de Elío en el Río de la Plata*, 13–16.

33. Caillet-Bois, *Ensayo sobre el Río de la Plata y la revolución frances*, 60–61.

34. While "French" bakers were a small minority of this trade, they were highly visible among those cited by the *fiel ejecutor* for violations of municipal regulations. The ongoing struggle between the cabildo's chief regulators, the fiel ejecutor and *sindico procurador*, and the *panaderos* led to a new round of regulations and threatened fines in 1794. The fiel ejecutor was Gregorio Ramos Mexía, the regidor in 1780 who had dismissed the shoemakers as drunkards. On this occasion the new regulations were carried to each *panadería* and the baker was forced to read them and sign his name. Both Juan Luis Dumont and Antonio Grimau, arrested in 1795, were among those represented on the list. See AGN, División Colonia, Sección Gobierno, Archivo del Cabildo, 1794, 388–92 vta.

35. AGN, División Colonia, Sección Gobierno, Hacienda, leg. 76, exp. 2002.

36. See Caillet-Bois, "La américa española y la revolución francesa," 203.

37. Caillet-Bois, *Ensayo sobre el Río de la Plata y la revolución francesa*, 75.

38. These and many other testimonies are collected in AGN, División Colonia, Sección Gobierno, Interior, leg. 38, exp. 1–19 vta.

39. Ibid., exp. 1, 29 vta.

40. Caillet-Bois, *Ensayo sobre el Río de la Plata y la revolución francesa*, 76.

41. AGN, División Colonia, Sección Gobierno, Interior, leg. 38, exp. 1, 33.

42. Ibid., exp. 1, 36 vta.

43. AGN, División Colonia, Sección Gobierno, Tribunales, leg. 60, exp. 6. In the final stage of this judicial process one of the defense lawyers reminded the *audiencia* that "public opinion had clamored incessantly for the discovery, arrest, and punishment" of those attempting to raise an insurrection in Buenos Aires.

44. AGN, División Colonia, Sección Gobierno, Archivo del Cabildo, 1791, 261–61 vta. Antonio Grimau was fined more than twenty pesos for underweight bread.

45. It is useful to place the numerous voluntary testimonies and denunciations that fueled the 1795 investigation in Buenos Aires in the recent literature devoted to the politics and cultural meanings of denunciations in European history. A very helpful introduction is found in a special issue of the *Journal of Modern History* 68.4 (1996), see esp. Colin Lucas "The Theory and Practice of Denunciation in the French Revolution," 768–85.

46. AGN, División Colonia, Sección Gobierno, Interior, leg. 38, exp. 1, 8.

47. Ortega, *El complot colonial*, 86–87.

48. AGN, División Colonia, Sección Gobierno, Interior, leg. 38, exp. 1, 9 vta.–10 vta.

49. Ortega, *El complot colonial*, 127.

50. AHPBA, Real Audiencia, Criminales, leg. 104.

51. While the connections cannot be made conclusively, Barbarín may have had

ties to Saint-Domingue in the years prior to the rebellion. The French merchant family Reynaud, also known as Reynaud de Barbarin or Barbarin, were active in Saint-Domingue after 1778 with one son, Jean-Baptiste Barbarin, important in commercial affairs in the early 1780s. See Thésée, *Négociants bordelais et colons de Saint-Domingue*, 30–34.

52. The case of José Díaz is found in AGN, División Colonia, Sección Gobierno, Interior, leg. 38, exp. 1, but the full court record is found in the AHPBA, 7.103.16, Real Audiencia, Criminales, leg. 103 (quotations are from the La Plata legajo except when specified).

53. AHPBA, 7.103.16, Real Audiencia, Criminales, leg. 103, 1–13.

54. AGN, División Colonia, Sección Gobierno, Interior, leg. 38, exp. 1.

55. AHPBA, (Real Audiencia) Criminal Provincial, leg. 103, 1–38 vta. See also the discussion in Lewin, "La 'conspiración de los Franceses' en Buenos Aires (1795)," 26–30.

56. The Franciscan's name is not found in the documents. The physician Bernardo Nogué would be present for the two tortures of Díaz and later Santiago Antonini. At the end of the judicial process he demanded that his fees be paid by the prisoners. See AGN, División Colonia, Sección Gobierno, Tribunales, leg. 60, exp. 6.

57. Gabriel Di Meglio covers this component of the 1795 investigation very briefly, but mixes Luis Dumont, the French baker, with his slave Juan Pedro, see ¡Viva el bajo pueblo!, 78–79.

58. AGN, División Colonia, Sección Gobierno, Tribunales, leg. 60, exp. 6, 1–4.

59. AGN, División Colonia, Sección Gobierno, Interior, leg. 38, exp. 1, 110–12.

60. AGI, Casa de Contratación, pasajeros a indias, informaciones y licencias, 8 Febrero 1780. This is a license for Juan Prevost and his family, accompanied by two servants to migrate to Louisiana abroad the polacro (ship rigged like a bergantine) *Nuestra Señora de las Mercedes* sailing first to Havana. Juan Luis Dumont, sixteen years old, was one of the two servants. So, it appears that Dumont, like Grimau, had some experience in the wider world before arriving in Buenos Aires.

61. See Lokke, "French Designs On Paraguay in 1803." Henri de Liniers, the Conde, had been in Spanish South America from 1790 after having served as a colonel in the Spanish Army. He pursued numerous commercial schemes including the production of dried beef for the Spanish Navy that led to purchase of the *quinta* where the conspirators were alleged to have met in 1795. He also imported slaves. In 1803 he proposed to Napoleon that France lead a military force to seize control of what he believed to be rich mineral properties near Maldonado, thus anticipating his younger brother Santiago's brief flirtation with Napoleon in 1806 and 1807.

62. Santiago de Liniers was married to the daughter of Don Martín de Sarratea one of the city's wealthiest merchants and a founding member of the Consulado of Buenos Aires. Álzaga sent his agents to Liniers's quinta during the night of March 8 where they arrested Bloud, the foreman, Pedro Mayte, the cook, and an unnamed female servant. AGN, División Colonia, Sección Gobierno, Cabildo de Buenos Aires, Correspondencia con el virrey, 1795–1796.

63. AGN, División Colonia, Sección Gobierno, Cabildo de Buenos Aires, Correspondencia con el virrey, 1795–1796, letter from Martín de Álzaga to Nicolás de Arredondo, March 12, 1795.

64. One of the group, Juan Borien, a wigmaker, was absent from the city but was tracked down and arrested in Montevideo. See AGN, División Colonia, Sección Gobierno, Interior, leg. 38, exp. 1.

65. Juan Luis Dumont testified that he had known Santiago Antonini in Cádiz before they both emigrated and that he had given Antonini a loan of one hundred pesos when he arrived in Buenos Aires. See AGN, División Colonia, Sección Gobierno, Tribunales, leg. 60, exp. 6.

66. Two soldiers corroborated the testimony about the bribe. See Lewin, "La 'conspiración de los Franceses' en Buenos Aires (1795)," 44–45.

67. AGN, División Colonia, Sección Gobierno, Tribunales, leg. 60, exp. 6. Testimony provided Álzaga alleged that Dumont had offered a toast upon news of the execution of Louis XVI in the pulpería of Polovio.

68. Álzaga was so sure of Antonini's involvement in the conspiracy that he prevented letters from the clockmaker's wife and parents from being delivered to him in jail. See AGN, División Colonia, Sección Gobierno, Cabildo de Buenos Aires, Correspondencia con el virrey, 1795–1796, doc. 228.

69. AGN, División Colonia, Sección Gobierno, Cabildo de Buenos Aires, Correspondencia con el virrey, 1795–1796.

70. Ibid. Álzaga pushed to move the process rapidly toward convictions. He initially gave defense lawyers only four days to review the testimonies and other documents, but finally he agreed to allow them eight days.

71. Ibid. In fact both Álzaga and the audiencia had hesitated to fully embrace the story offered to them by Juan Pedro. Before Antonini's second torture Álzaga had asked the court's permission to question Juan Pedro under torture as well. The court refused, but did allow Álzaga to question Juan Pedro as he showed him the instruments of torture. While Juan Pedro was shaken, he stuck to his story, and Antonini faced his second torment.

72. AGN, División Colonia, Sección Gobierno, Tribunales, leg. 60, exp. 6.

73. Radaelli, *Memorias de los virreyes de Río de la Plata*, 375. Viceroy Arredondo's memoir at the end of his viceregency notes that these cases were sent to Spain for "final resolution."

74. AGN, División Colonia, Sección Gobierno, Solicitudes Civiles, libro F–G, 272–73.

75. AGI, Estado, 79, numero 104, letter sent 14 Thermidor (December 8, 1795).

76. AGN, División Colonia, Sección Gobierno, Tribunales, leg. P12, exp. 18, tracks the growing controversy with the city's bakers. By the middle of 1790 authorities doubled fines for poor quality or light-weight bread to forty pesos, and three bakers unable to pay the fines were placed in jail.

77. Caillet-Bois, *Ensayo sobre el Río de la Plata y la revolución francesa*, 76–77.

78. AGN, División Colonia, Sección Gobierno, Interior, leg. 38, exp. 1.

79. Ibid., exp. 1, 9 vta.–10 vta.

6. Reproduction of Working-Class Life

1. The probate record for Juan Antonio Callejas y Sandoval is found in AGN, Sucesiones, 5343. His testament is AGN, División Colonia, Sección Gobierno, Escribanía, Registro 5, 1786.

2. The testament of Juan Felix Duarte is found in AGN, División Colonia, Sección Gobierno, Escribanía, Registro 5, 1793.

3. AGN, Sucesiones, 3917, testamentaria de Pascual Braga.

4. For a similar case see AGN, Sucesiones, 7778, testamentaría de Pedro del Río. This unmarried casta migrant from Santa Fe slept in a rented room near the Plaza Mayor, sharing the space with seven other laborers. The appraised value of his estate was just thirty-seven pesos.

5. AGN, División Colonia, Sección Contaduría, Culto de Buenos Aires, Mercedarios, Hospicio de San Ramón de las Conchas, libros 1, 3, and 5; Culto de Buenos Aires, Bethlemitas, Convento y hospital de Santa Catalina; Culto de Buenos Aires, Mercedarios, Convento Grande de San Ramón, Libro de Gastos, 1775–1815. While it is preferable to use a single source for price history, no single source provided monthly prices for all eight commodities for the entire period. I combined prices from all sources to create a single series for the eight commodities once an examination of the separate sources revealed that all institutions purchased these goods in city markets in similar volumes and paid similar prices.

6. AGN, División Colonia, Sección Contaduría, Caja de Buenos Aires, 1770–1815.

7. For an effort to measure changes in the standard of living of the working class of contemporary Philadelphia, see Smith, "The Material Lives of Laboring Philadelphians, 1750–1800."

8. Ruggiero Romano argued that prices in late colonial Buenos Aires were stagnant in a series of small monographs and articles in the 1960s. He never published a price index. This made it impossible to calculate a cost of living index or real wages. See his "Movimiento de los precios y desarrollo económico," esp.

32–34. Romano and I exchanged views in 1992, see Romano and Johnson, "Una polémica sobre la historia de precios en el Buenos Aires virreinal." Juan Carlos Garavaglia also examined the region's price history in his "Precios de los productos rurales y precios de la tierra en la campaña de Buenos Aires." Garavaglia uses values for a range of rural products, including wheat, estimated in the probate process in rural districts. That is, these are not market prices that can be used to directly estimate urban consumer costs, but his clear explication of these prices over a long term is of great value to economic historians. He also confirms in a general way my price estimates, while suggesting that Romero's broad assumptions about price stability may be more plausible with an earlier base year.

9. For estimates of food expenditures as a percentage of total expenditures in Great Britain, see Tucker, "Real Wages of Artisans in London, 1729–1935," 75; Gilboy, "The Cost of Living and Real Wages in Eighteenth Century England"; and more generally Ashton, "The Standard of Life of the Workers in England, 1790–1830"; and Smith, "Material Lives of Laboring Philadelphians, 1750–1800," esp. 167–72. For a similar effort by economists dealing with eighteenth-century material, consult David and Solar, "A Bicentenary Contribution to the History of the Cost of Living in America," 15–22.

10. Thompson, *The Making of the English Working Class*, 315.

11. George Rudé illuminated this area of popular protest. See his *La multitud en la historia*, esp. 55–70.

12. See Cope, *Limits of Racial Domination*, for the connections between corn prices and an urban riot. See also Florescano, "Las crisis agrícolas de al época colonial y sus consecuencias económicas."

13. See the discussion of diet in Octavio C. Battolla, *La sociedad de antaño* (Buenos Aires: Emecé Editores, 2000), esp. 77–89.

14. Florescano, *Precios de maíz y crisis agrícolas en México, 1708–1910*; and Tandeter and Wachtel, *Precios y producción agraria*.

15. Universidad de Buenos Aires, *Documentos para la historia Argentina*, tomo 4, "*abastos*," 166–168. See also AGN, División Colonia, Sección Gobierno, Archivo del Cabildo, 1805, 294–95; and 1810, 194–97.

16. Alexander Gillespie stated that "the abundance of food prevents starvation, but the poverty of the lower classes is always apparent in their garments and their filth." *Gleanings and Remarks*, 87.

17. Biedma et al., *Acuerdos del extinguido cabildo de Buenos Aires*, serie 4, tomo 1, libro 58, 143.

18. The military emergency of 1806–1807 led the government to impose a new tax on bread, but it proved impossible to enforce. See AGN, División Colonia, Sección Gobierno, Bandos, libro 8, 363, for Liniers's decision to revoke this tax.

I have discussed efforts by the cabildo to hold down bread prices in "The Entrepreneurial Reorganization of an Artisan Trade: The Bakers of Buenos Aires."

19. A typical *arancel* for bread is published in Universidad de Buenos Aires, *Documentos para la historia Argentina*, "Real Hacienda," 1:72–73.

20. The work on Spanish grain prices is summarized by Juan Plaza Prieto, *Estructura económica de España en el siglo XVIII*, 251–53. See also Hamilton, *War and Prices in Spain, 1651–1800*.

21. Enrique Tandeter pointed out the effects of this region-wide natural disaster based on his reading of the letters of Gaspar Santa Coloma (see AGN, División Colonia, Sección Gobierno, Coleccion Gaspar de Santa Coloma) and his research on the price history of Potosí.

22. AGN, División Colonia, Sección Gobierno, Archivo del Cabildo, 1801–1802.

23. Plaza Prieto, *Estructura económica de España en el siglo XVIII*, 933.

24. Many of the city's most important merchants, like Tomás Antonio Romero and Pedro Duval, were involved in trade with Havana, the major source of the sugar consumed in Buenos Aires. See AGN, División Colonia, Sección Gobierno, Resguardo, 1800–1802.

25. Braudel, *Civilization and Capitalism, 15th–18th Century*, vol. 1, *The Structure of Everyday Life*, esp. 224–27.

26. Azara stated that during the period 1792–1796 Buenos Aires received an average of 196,000 arrobas per year. Azara, *Viajes por la América Meridional*, 2:187.

27. AHPBA, Criminales, leg. 34–1–10. As part of the testimony in a criminal case it was stated that local custom required the master artisan to provide yerba twice a day.

28. AHPBA, Criminales, leg. 34–1–12 and leg. 34–1–11. See also Rodríguez Molas, *Las pulperías*, 8. The cabildo and the viceregal government attempted (unsuccessfully) to control the sale of alcoholic beverages in a long series of unenforceable laws. See AGN, División Colonia, Sección Gobierno, Bandos, libro 5, 133–39. One measure of the importance of alcohol in the local diet was the popular protest against the imposition of a new tax on *aguardiente*. See Biedma et al., *Acuerdos del extinguido cabildo de Buenos Aires*, serie 4, tomo 3, libro 63, 154–55.

29. Probably both factors played a role in determining the level of alcohol consumption. In contemporary England the workingman "took small beer with each main meal of the working day and ale, in no small measure, whenever he had occasion to celebrate" (see Ashton, "Standard of Life of the Workers in England," 30).

30. AHPBA, Criminales, leg. 34–1–12.

31. AGN, División Colonia, Sección Gobierno, Bandos, libro 7, 154–56, June 2, 1794; Bandos, libro 8, 46–50, September 6, 1800; and Bandos, libro 8, 365–69, April 17, 1809.

32. Braudel, *Structures of Everday Life*, 236–37.

33. AHPBA, Criminales, leg. 34–1–9, leg. 34–1–19, leg. 34–1–11, and leg. 34–1–12.

34. Brown, *A Socioeconomic History of Argentina, 1776–1860*, 33–35.

35. Gillespie, *Gleanings and Remarks*, 78–79.

36. Azara, *Viajes por la América Meridional*, 2:186–87. He also notes a substantial amount of sugar imported from Lima.

37. Furlong, *Los industrias en el Río de la Plata desde la colonización hasta 1778*, 22–27; and Gillespie, *Gleanings and Remarks*, 78–79.

38. Socolow, *The Merchants of Buenos Aires, 1778–1810*, 63.

39. AGN, División Colonia, Sección Gobierno, Tribunales, leg. z4, exp. 11.

40. See AHPBA, Criminales, leg. 34–1–10, for an example of the mixing of workers from different backgrounds and legal statuses.

41. In this price series I have only included years with a minimum of ten rental payments to increase the reliability of this series. A group of eleven apartments owned by the cabildo provided the longest rental series (1770–1806), see AGN, División Colonia, Sección Gobierno, Cabildo de Buenos Aires, Propios, 1770–1806. These records were supplemented for 1798, 1801, and 1804 with a group of apartments similar in location, size, and price owned by the Convent of San Ramón, see AGN, División Colonia, Sección Contaduría, Convento y iglesia de San Ramón de Buenos Aires, Inventorio de los bienes, muebles y inmuebles, 1788–1792. Rents for the period 1808–1812 are for forty single rooms located in the municipally owned Recova, a large, multistory commercial structure located just south of the central plaza, see AGN, División Colonia, Sección Gobierno, Cabildo de Buenos Aires, Propios, 1808–1812.

42. AGN, División Colonia, Sección Gobierno, Cabildo de Buenos Aires, Propios, 1810–1811, docs. 7–10.

43. AGN, División Colonia, Sección Contaduría, Convento y iglesia de San Ramón de Buenos Aires, Inventorio de los bienes, muebles y inmuebles, 1788–1792.

44. Wages used in this discussion are public sector wages found in the colonial government treasury accounts. See AGN, División Colonia, Sección Contaduría, Caja de Buenos Aires, 1770–1815. I searched annual accounts for the entire period and produced mean and median wages for each occupation and skill level.

45. Mawe, *Travels in the Interior of Brazil*, 39.

46. AGN, Sucesiones, 3468, Testamentaria de Victoriano Arias de Andrade, 1800; and Sucesiones, 8414, Testamentaria de Agustín Sagari, 1793.

47. Gillespie, *Gleanings and Remarks*, 118. He notes, "The houses in the suburbs of Buenos Aires, in every direction, are mean, but penetrate little into the country."

48. Davie, *Letters from Paraguay*, 89, 115.

49. See my "Estimaciones de la población de Buenos Aires en 1744, 1778 y 1810," esp. 116–19, for a discussion of undercounting in colonial censuses.

50. AGN, División Colonia, Sección Contaduría, Convento y Iglesia de San Ramón de Buenos Aires, Inventorio de los bienes y muebles, inmuebles, 1788–1792. *Esquinas* owned by the convent rented for an average of ten pesos per month. This was three pesos more than other apartments in the same buildings. When the municipal commercial spaces of the Recova were completed, one-room spaces rented for an average of eight and a half pesos per month. After 1810 rent increased to twelve pesos, see AGN, División Colonia, Sección Gobierno, Cabildo de Buenos Aires, Propios, 1808–1812.

51. From 1785 to 1789 Buenos Aires received a net transfer (*situado*) of 6,597,241 pesos. In the period 1796–1800 it received 7,162,330 pesos. We must suspect that the transfer of sums this large (1 to 2 million pesos per year) had at least some inflationary effect on both wages and prices in a city of around 60,000 residents, see Grafe and Irigoin, "The Spanish Empire and Its Legacy," tables 3 and 4.

52. The estimation of reliable weights is a common problem, confronted by every historian who attempts to construct a cost of living index. Among the useful examples are Smith, "Material Lives of Laboring Philadelphians, 1750–1800," 167–72; Gilboy, "Cost of Living and Real Wages in Eighteenth Century England," 135; and Marcelo Carmanagni, *El salariado minero en Chile colonial*, 74–78.

53. AGN, División Colonia, Sección Gobierno, Cabildo de Buenos Aires, Propios, 1805–1806. A nearly identical diet was provided for the men hauling rock used in constructing a new seawall, see AGN, División Colonia, Sección Gobierno, Cabildo de Buenos Aires, Obras, 1805–1806.

54. For a summary discussion of food expenditure by members of the laboring classes, see Shammas, "Food Expenditures and Economic Well-being in Early Modern England."

55. This workforce consisted of eleven prisoners, a guard, twenty-four *peones*, and a *capataz*, see AGN, División Colonia, Sección Gobierno, Cabildo de Buenos Aires, Obras 1805–1806. A similar diet was provided for the Spanish garrison in Havana, see AGI, Indiferente General, 1581.

56. AGN, División Colonia, Sección Contaduría, Temporalidades, Obra de la Real Universidad, 1783.

57. This is the common shopping practice noted by Gillespie, *Gleanings and Remarks*, 118.

58. AGN, División Colonia, Sección Contaduría, Buenos Aires, Temporalidades, 1783–1788, Obra de la Real Universidad. Standard practice, although there was variety among dioceses, was for 150 meatless days per year or 41 percent of the year.

59. Because fish prices increased during days when meat was religiously restricted, the cabildo sought permission from the bishop to permit the poor to eat beef in

1782, see Biedma et al., *Acuerdos del extinguido cabildo de Buenos Aires*, serie 3, tomo 7, libros 44, 27.

60. Gilboy, "Cost of Living and Real Wages," 136; Smith, "Material Lives of Laboring Philadelphians, 1750–1800," 168–71.

61. Johnson, "Entrepreneurial Reorganization of an Artisan Trade," 149.

62. Thompson, *Making of the English Working Class*, 315.

63. Gillespie, *Gleanings and Remarks*, 119; and YUL, David Curtis Deforest Papers, Journals and Letterbooks, vol. 2, 140. See also AGN, División Colonia, Sección Gobierno, Archivo del Cabildo, 1806, 767–67v, for examples of bakers using high fuel costs to explain their violations of the arancel.

64. See AHPBA, Criminales, leg. 34–1–11 and leg. 34–1–13, for an example.

65. Domínguez Ortiz, *La sociedad española en el siglo XVIII*, 211–12; and Ringrose, *Madrid and the Spanish Economy, 1560–1850*, 112–14.

66. The weights proposed above are very similar to those used in a broad array of studies of cost of living and real wages for early modern European societies. The most respected effort to estimate the expenditures of English laborers claims that between 40 and 50 percent of weekly wages were devoted to the purchase of bread and other grain products. Animal products consumed another 20 percent while fuel and light, beverages and condiments, and clothing each consumed an estimated 10 percent.

67. AGN, División Colonia, Sección Gobierno, Tribunales, leg. B8, exp. 22.

68. Members of this class owned approximately thirty pesos worth of clothing at the time of their deaths.

69. AGN, División Colonia, Sección Gobierno, Tribunales, leg. L9, exp. 4; Tribunales, leg. B8, exp. 22; AGN, División Colonia, Sección Gobierno, Buenos Aires 1783–1788.

70. Gillespie, *Gleanings and Remarks*, 87.

71. AHPBA, Criminales, 34–1–19.

72. Gillespie notes that the abundance of food prevented starvation (*Gleanings and Remarks*, 87), but he also underlined the high cost of bread (77).

73. Dietary necessities are largely defined by culture, and consumers attempt to eat traditional staples even as prices rise, despite the availability of lower-priced substitutes. Marx noted this tendency when he wrote, "Our wants and pleasures have their origin in society; we therefore measure them in relation to the objects which serve for their gratification. Since they are of a social nature, they are of a relative nature" (quoted in David and Solar, "A Bicentenary Contribution to the History of the Cost of Living in America," 10).

74. The crude death rate was calculated from burial records and population estimates provided by Alberto B. Martínez, *Historia demográfica de Buenos Aires*, Dirreccíon General de Estadística Municipal, vol. 3 (Buenos Aires, 1910).

Nicolás Besio Moreno also provided an annual summary of deaths in *Buenos Aires*.

75. A thorough search of surviving records for late colonial Buenos Aires discovered 103 testaments and 89 probate inventories for artisans and a small number of laborers. I have found the work of Alice Hanson Jones and Gloria Main useful models. See Main's *Tobacco Colony*. Her "Appendix C: Probate Records as a Source for Historical Investigation," 282–92, is a brief and intelligent introduction to the topic. The discussion of methodological issues in Alice Hanson Jones's *Wealth of a Nation to Be* (New York: Columbia University Press, 1980) is well worth the attention of any investigator using these materials.

76. Estate inventories and testaments are two of the most reliable sources available, but estate inventories are clearly superior because they provide itemized lists of a decedent's household and capital goods compiled by court-appointed appraisers. Testaments, on the other hand, are far less reliable in estimating the value, size, and composition of an estate, since the individual testator provided a personal assessment of the value of real estate, consumer goods, and financial assets. Testaments do have a compensatory value. They offer a wider range of pertinent biographical information than probate inventories, including birthplace, occupation, and important elements of family history.

77. For some exceptions to this pattern, mainly examples of silversmiths whose estates had high levels of inventory, see AGN, Sucesiones, 7708, Manuel Antonio Pimienta, inventorio de sus bienes, 1796; Sucesiones, 7151, Manuel Milton, inventorio de sus bienes, 1799; and Sucesiones, 6777, Vicente Monferrer, inventorio de sus bienes, 1809.

78. A good short summary of the major features of the colonial economy is offered by Brown, *Socioeconomic History of Argentina*, 9–49. Brown's intent is descriptive, not analytical, but the general character of the economy is visible. The major weakness is his failure to appreciate the role played by public sector expenditures.

79. Gillespie reported that while a horse cost two pesos, it cost five pesos to have the horse shoed by a competent smith (*Gleanings and Remarks*, 70).

80. AGN Sucesiones, 5904, Isidro Gonzalez, inventorio de sus bienes, 1809.

81. AGN Sucesiones, 8734, Andres Vibas, inventorio de sus bienes, 1776.

82. AGN, División Colonia, Sección Gobierno, Escribanía, Registro 4, 1784–1788, folios 58v–83v, Capital de Don Estevan Villanueva.

83. AGN, Escribanía, Registro 6, 1776, 54–56, testamento de Thomas Batlla. This pattern functioned on a smaller scale as well. See AGN, Sucesiones, 4837, Manuel Brebet.

84. AGN, Escribanía, Registro 6, 1786, 499–501, testamento de Juan Antonio Callejas y Sandoval. Callejas y Sandoval played an important role in the effort

to create a guild of silversmiths. See my article "The Silversmiths of Buenos Aires: A Case Study in the Failure of Corporate Social Organization."

85. AGN, Escribanía, Registro 2, 1796, folios 148v–51, testamento de Tiburcio López de Heredia.

86. AGN, Escribanía, Registro 2, 1800, folios 237–39v, testamento de José Yanes.

87. AGN, Escribanía, Registro 2, 1803, folios 434v–38v, testamento de José Melendes.

88. AGN, Escribanía, Registro 2, 1791, Testamento Francisco Ibarzabal.

89. This may have been a common characteristic throughout the Western Hemisphere. Alice Hanson Jones found that 56 percent of artisans and small manufacturers in the thirteen British colonies of North America owned real estate. She also found that the average value of the real estate accounted for approximately 67 percent of the wealth held by members of this class (*Wealth of a Nation to Be*, 223–27).

90. AGN, Sucesiones, 7709, Pedro Palavecino, inventorio de sus bienes, 1799.

91. AGN, Sucesiones, 8141, Ramón Saran, inventorio de sus bienes, 1807.

92. AGN, Sucesiones, 8133, Antonio Rodriquez, inventorio de sus bienes, 1779.

93. AGN, Sucesiones, 5589, Joaquin Estevez de la Guy, inventorio de sus bienes, 1811.

94. AGN, Sucesiones, Manuel de Ortega, inventorio de sus bienes, 1804.

95. See also the inventories of the shoemaker Nicolás Riguy, a Spaniard, and the baker María Josefa Oreyro, a *porteña*, as examples of large investments in household goods, AGN, Sucesiones, 8137 and 7371, inventorio de sus bienes.

96. Although there is some evidence that the city occasionally experienced a shortage of specie, it is clear that business was conducted on a cash basis. Gillespie states that "cash is the only medium of their dealings" (*Gleanings and Remarks*, 71).

97. AGN, Sucesiones, 7709, Pedro Palavecino, inventorio de sus bienes, 1799.

98. For two examples of artisans losing their jobs when they were unable to pay off a debt, see AGN, División Colonia, Sección Gobierno, Tribunales, leg. s10, exp. 6, for a silversmith who pledged his tools as collateral; and AGN, Sección Gobierno, Tribunales, leg. B5, exp. 22, for a similar case involving a pastry cook.

99. AGN, División Colonia, Sección Gobierno, Tribunales, leg. v8, exp. 23. For similar cases involving bad debts, see AGN, División Colonia, Sección Gobierno, Tribunales, leg. B5, exp. 22; and Tribunales, leg. 118, exp. 22.

100. The largest debt was registered by the criollo María Josefa Oreyro who along with her husband Sebastian Rodriquez owned one of the city's largest bakeries. Although this debt was exceptional among members of the skilled working class, nearly every baker owed debts well above the class average.

101. See AGN, Sucesiones, 7709, Pedro Palavecino, and 7371, Sebastian Rodríguez,

inventorio de sus bienes, 1799 and 1786, for two cases of loans contracted in Europe.

102. The occupational categories are (the number of individuals found in each occupation in the probate records are provided in parenthesis): indoor trades, including shoemakers (twelve), armorers (one), silversmiths (six), turners (one), coopers (three), combmakers (one), harness makers (one), clock makers (one), painters (one), pot makers (one); outdoor trades, including blacksmiths (ten), carpenters (twenty-seven), tanners (one), bricklayers (two), bronze makers (three); and small manufacturers, including millers (five), carters (one), brickmakers (five), tile makers (three).

103. AGN, División Colonia, Sección Gobierno, Escribanía, Registro 6, 1801, folios 129v–31v, testamento de Jacobo Padin.

104. AGN, Escribanía, Registro 6, 1781, folios 159–61, testamento de Juan Ignacio de Echeberria.

105. AGN, Escribanía, Registro 5, 1787, folios 369–72v, testamento de Joseph Gomez Belmundes.

106. AGN, Escribanía, Registro 2, 1805, folios 123v–26, testamento de Rogue Antonio Angelino.

107. AGN, Escribanía, Registro 6, 1802, folios 112–14v, testamento de Francisco Abrego.

108. AGN, Sucesiones, 7706, Basilia Antonia Pinto.

109. AGN, Sucesiones, 8141, Francisca Salinas.

110. AGN, Escribanía, Registro 6, 1784, testamento de Rafael Salomón (the largest inheritance).

111. AGN, Escribanía, Registro 2, 1791, testmento de Francisco Ibazarbal.

112. AGN, Escribanía, Registro 6, 1776, testmento Thomas Batlla.

113. AGN, Escribanía, Registro 2, 1792, folios 198v–201, testamento de Juan Verois.

114. AGN, Escribanía, Registro 6, 1798–1799, folios 251–53, testamento de Antonio da Costa Almeyda. See also the case of Tiburcio López de Heredia in AGN, Escribanía, Registro 2, 1796, folios 148v–51.

7. Working-Class Wages

1. We do not have a comprehensive study of the administration of Jesuit properties after their expulsion, but Torres, *La administración de temporalidades en la Río de la Plata* still offers a good introduction. This case is found in AGN, División Colonia, Sección Contaduría, Temporalidades, 1787.

2. See, for example, Biedma et al., *Acuerdos del extinguido cabildo de Buenos Aires*, serie 3, tomo 7, libro 44, 181.

3. In the last decades of the colonial era there were numerous complaints by civil authorities about the laziness and unreliability of both the urban and rural labor-

ing classes. See, Vieytes and Cerviño, *Seminario de agricultura, industria y comercio*, 12:233–38 for an example of this argument.

4. I think that R. Douglas Cope's illumination of the urban masses of late-seventeenth-century Mexico City is a particularly useful example of what can be revealed by the colonial documents. See *The Limits of Racial Domination*. The publication of Ruth MacKay's *Lazy, Improvident People* is a very welcome edition to this literature.

5. Although there are a handful of useful price histories for colonial Latin America, the process of establishing the region's wage history has hardly begun. Important exceptions to this general rule are Carmanagni's *El salariado minero en Chile colonial*; and Lahmeyer Lobo, Canavarros et al., "Estudo das categorias socioprofissionais, dos Salarios e do custo da alimentacao no Rio de Janeiro de 1820 a 1930," 129–76.

6. Historians have debated issues of method and sources for decades. See for example Chance and Taylor, "Estate and Class in a Colonial City"; and the response of McCaa, Schwartz, and Grubessich, "Race and Class in Colonial Latin America." A final series of exchanges occurred in response to Seed and Rust, "Estate and Class in Colonial Oaxaca Revisited."

7. Enrique Tandeter's study of labor in Potosí is an important exception to this general rule. Although focusing on the *mita*, he also illuminates the role of free labor in the mines. See "Forced and Free Labour in Late Colonial Potosí," *Past and Present* 93 (November 1981): 98–136.

8. Cope, *The Limits of Racial Domination*, one of the best studies of the urban plebe, reduces these issues to the level of subtext in a narrative largely focused on ethnicity.

9. AGN, División Colonia, Sección Contaduría, Caja de Buenos Aires, 1770–1815. Each year's accounts were searched and each wage recorded.

10. AGN, División Colonia, Sección Gobierno, Archivo del Cabildo, 1770–1815; Obras Publicas, Canal de San Fernando, 1770–1808; Cabildo de Buenos Aires, Obras, 1805–1806. AGN, División Colonia, Sección Contaduría, Culto de Buenos Aires, Mercedarios, Hospicio de San Ramón de las Conchas, libros 1, 3, and 5; Culto de Buenos Aires, Mercedarios Convento, gastos, libros 1, 2, and 3; Culto de Buenos Aires, Bethlemitas, Convento y hospital de Santa Catalina; Culto de Buenos Aires, Mercedarios, Convento Grande de San Ramón, Libro de Gastos, 1775–1815.

11. A careful comparison of wages paid to laborers by the municipality, the Mercedarian and Bethlemites convents, and by the Hospital of Santa Catalina indicated that these records could be blended successfully into a single series. Not only were annual median wages paid to laborers by these three institutions simi-

lar to those paid by municipal and colonial governments, but they also moved cyclically in a close pattern over the entire period.

12. AGN, División Colonia, Sección Gobierno, Cabildo de Buenos Aires, Obras, 1805–1806. Record is for the month of January 1805.

13. For the salaries of bureaucrats see AGN, División Colonia, Sección Contaduría, Caja de Buenos Aires, Real hacienda, Sueldos de Empleados, 1797. For the salaries of military officers see Halperín Donghi, *Guerra y finanzas en los origenes del estado Argentino, 1791–1850*, 35.

14. AGN, División Colonia, Sección Contaduría, Temporalidades de Buenos Aires, 7 Julio 1787. Doctor Antonio Bacilio Rodríguez, a doctor of canon law, was paid three hundred pesos per year. Don Francisco de Berea, a teacher in the College of San Carlos, received two hundred and fifty pesos.

15. The evidence clearly suggests that the high wage levels of the period 1806–1815 were maintained into the Rosas period. See Romero, *Buenos Aires*, 13; and Burgin, *The Economic Aspects of Argentine Federalism, 1820–1852*, 28 n. 24. For the continuation of labor shortages and high wages after the fall of Rosas, see Sabato, *Trabajar para vivir o vivir para trabajar*.

16. For the Cevallos expedition, consult Barba, *Don Pedro de Cevallos*; and Alden, "The Undeclared War of 1773–1777."

17. Roberts, *Las invasiones inglesas del Río de la Plata, 1806–1807*, 87.

18. The distortions of the local economy in the years following 1806 are detailed by Halperín Donghi in *Guerra y finanzas en los origenes del estado Argentino, 1791–1850*, 73–91. He found that in the period 1807–1809 alone the military salary bill reached 700,000 pesos. He also estimated that approximately 30 percent of the city's adult male population was under arms by 1810 (84).

19. Immigrant French hatmakers in Buenos Aires in 1818 claimed that while a worker in France would receive two reales, a worker in Buenos Aires earned ten reales plus a food allowance. See Urquijo, "La mano de obra en la industria porteña (1810–1835)."

20. Halperín Donghi, *Guerra y finanzas en los origenes del estado Argentino, 1791–1850*, 25–91.

21. Universidad de Buenos Aires, *Documentos para la historia Argentina*, tomo 4, "*Abastos de la cuidad y campaña de Buenos Aires*," 161–65.

22. These efforts were repeated nearly every December and January as noted in the *bandos* of the cabildo, see AGN, División Colonia, Sección Gobierno, Cabildo de Buenos Aires, Libros de Bandos, 4, 5, 8, 1782–1806.

23. See, for example, Tucker, "Real Wages of Artisans in London, 1729–1935"; or the commonly cited Phelps Brown and Hopkins, "Seven Centuries of Building Wages," which presents the wage data as index numbers.

24. For a discussion of the early history of this industry, see Furlong, *Los industrias en el Río de la Plata desde la colonizacion hasta 1778*, esp. 87–91.

25. In 1792 Viceroy Arredondo wrote to ask the Spanish government to send a maestro mayor and "six to eight" journeymen to help with the improvement of defenses because of the "very poor quality of artisans in these trades in this country," see AGI, Duplicado de Arredondo, leg. 108.

26. These novel terms were never used in records of private-sector employees or in the records of the municipal and ecclesiastical establishments. See AGN, División Colonia, Sección Contaduría, Culto de Buenos Aires, Mercedarios, Convento Grande de San Ramón, Libro de Gastos, 1775–1815.

27. For the slave trade, see Scheuss de Studer, *La trata de negros en el Río de la Plata durante el siglo XVIII*. The early introduction of compulsory labor for rural workers is noted in Garavaglia, "Comercio colonial." The use of Paraguayan Indians during the harvest is found throughout the records of the Cabildo of Buenos Aires, see, for example, AGN, División Colonia, Sección Gobierno, Bandos, libro 5; and Biedma et al., *Acuerdos del extinguido cabildo de Buenos Aires*, serie 3, tomo 8, libro 48, 227; and serie 4, tomo 2, libro 60, 145–46. For an example of urban workers forced to harvest grain, see Levene, *Obras de Ricardo Levene*, vol. 2, *Investigaciones acerca de la historia economica del virreinato del Plata*, 328–29.

28. AGN, División Colonia, Sección Gobierno, Cabildo de Buenos Aires, Obras, 1805–1806.

29. On the disruption of labor supply provoked by increased military needs, see Halperín Donghi, *Guerra y finanzas en los origenes del estado Argentino, 1791–1850*, 73–117.

30. Some urban workers did receive at least one meal per day as a part of their compensation. Bricklayers working for the colonial government in 1783 received a noon meal. This record suggests a more varied and nutritious diet than that generally provided to rural laborers, see AGN División Colonia, Sección Contaduría, Temporalidades, Obra de la Real Universidad, 1783. However, we cannot presume that urban wage earners, the majority of whom worked without this type of compensation, were able to consume this diet regularly. Before any final judgment can be accepted on the relative nutrition in the diets of urban and rural workers much new research will have to be undertaken.

31. Private-sector wages were developed from the notary records. All of the following notary copybooks were searched and every wage payment recorded. Most commonly, wage data were provided in contracts for new construction or in the preprobate management of a decedent's real estate holdings, see AGN, División Colonia, Sección Gobierno, Escribanía, Registro 1: Años 1770, 1778–79, 1780–81, 1783–85, 1790–91, 1794–95, 1796–97, 1798–99, 1804–09; Regi-

stro 2: Años 1778–79, 1780, 1786, 1789–90, 1793, 1805–09; Registro 3: Años 1778–79, 1788–89, 1790–93, 1802, 1804; Registro 4: Años 1784–88, 1790, 1796; Registro 5: Años 1787, 1794–95, 1796–97; Registro 6: Años 1798, 1802, 1806.

32. In 1797 master and journeyman bricklayers working for the Mercedarian Convent of San Ramón were commonly paid the same wage, six reales per day. By 1800 the Mercedarians were commonly paying a small premium, one or two reales, to masters. However, there were three times during the year when masters were paid less than journeymen working on the same job, see AGN, División Colonia, Sección Contaduría, Culto de Buenos Aires, Mercedarios, Convento Grande de San Ramón, Libro de Gastos (4 tomos), 1775–1815.

33. AGN, División Colonia, Sección Gobierno, Tribunales, leg. 9, exp. 4.

34. AGN, División Colonia, Sección Contaduría, Culto de Buenos Aires, Mercedarios, Convento Grande de San Ramón, Libro de Gastos (4 tomos), libro 4.

35. AGN, División Colonia, Sección Gobierno, Tribunales, leg. P12, exp. 31.

36. See Gillespie, *Gleanings and Remarks*, 115.

37. AGN, División Colonia, Sección Contaduría, Culto de Buenos Aires, Mercedarios, Convento Grande de San Ramón, Libro de Gastos, libro 3; and AGN, Culto de Buenos Aires, Bethlemitas, Convento y hospital de Santa Catalina.

38. During the period 1775–1810 there were only twelve apprenticeship contacts registered by the city's tailors. All notary copybooks were searched and every apprenticeship recorded. Escribanía, Registros 1–7 (1775–1810).

39. AGN, División Colonia, Sección Contaduría, Culto de Buenos Aires, Bethlemitas, Convento y hospital de Santa Catalina; Culto de Buenos Aires, Mercedarios, Convento Grande de San Ramón, Libro de Gastos, 1775–1815.

40. For the development of this industry, see Johnson, "The Entrepreneurial Reorganization of an Artisan Trade."

41. Some scholars have put total slave imports for the period 1740–1822 at more than 45,000. The importance of the contraband slave trade is suggested by the altered racial distributions found in contemporary censuses. These sources indicate that the African-originated population of the city rose from 17 percent in 1744 to 29 percent in 1778. See Goldberg and Mallo, "La población africana en Buenos Aires y su campaña." For the Royal Order permitting foreigners to introduce slaves, see Universidad de Buenos Aires, *Documentos para la historia Argentina*, vol. 4, "Comercio de Indias," 474. This was also the peak period in slave imports to Montevideo as well. See the two cities compared in Campagna Caballero, "La población esclava en ciudades puertos del Río de la Plata."

42. According to Jeremy Adelman, the Río de la Plata region took 2.7 percent of all slaves imported to the Americas between 1791 and 1800. The region then received 6.3 percent between 1801 and 1810. See Adelman's *Sovereignty and Revo-*

lution in the Iberian Atlantic, 76. Adelman's discussion is based on the universally respected estimates of David Eltis in *The Rise of African Slavery in the Americas.*

43. This topic is covered in greater detail in my article "The Competition of Slave and Free Labor in Artisanal Production."

44. Slave values are discussed briefly in Johnson, "Manumission in Colonial Buenos Aires, 1776–1810."

45. García Belsunce et al., *Buenos Aires.* See the table "tenencia de esclavos" in anejo 1.

46. The impact of slavery on wages in Rio de Janeiro is discussed briefly by Harold B. Johnson Jr. in "A Preliminary Inquiry into Money, Prices, and Wages in Rio de Janeiro, 1763–1823."

47. See my "Salarios, precios y costo de vida en el Buenos Aires colonial tardío" for a preliminary analysis of wages.

48. These problems are discussed by Donald Woodward in his analysis of the English preindustrial working class. See Woodward's "Wage Rates and Living Standards in PreIndustrial England."

49. See AGN, División Colonia, Sección Contaduría, Caja de Buenos Aires, Impuesto, numeros 1–272, for examples of blacksmiths hired by the colonial government that demonstrate this pattern.

50. AGN, División Colonia, Sección Contaduría, Caja de Buenos Aires, Impuesto, numeros 1–542.

51. AGN, Sección Colonia, División Contaduría, Caja de Buenos Aires, 1780.

52. AGN, Sección Colonia, División Contaduría, Caja de Buenos Aires, 1800.

53. AGN, Sección Colonia, División Contaduría, Caja de Buenos Aires, 1785.

54. AGN, Sección Colonia, División Contaduría, Caja de Buenos Aires, 1775.

55. AGN, División Colonia, Sección Gobierno, Hacienda, leg. 42, exp. 1071.

56. For this case see AGN, División Colonia, Sección Contaduría, Temporalidades, 1787. See also Torres, *La administración de temporalidades en la Río de la Plata,* for a general discussion of the administration of these properties.

57. Rock, *Artisans of the New Republic,* 296–98. Rock offers a good, short summary of drinking habits, in particular the celebration of "Saint Monday." For another view, see Gutman, *Work, Culture, and Society,* 19–21. Similar behavior among English workers is noted in Hobsbawm, *Industry and Empire,* 85.

58. For Campomanes's estimate, see Plaza Prieto, *Estructura económica de España en el siglo XVIII,* 694.

59. Urquijo, "La mano de obra en la industria porteña," 616.

60. Religious holidays were provided in almanacs published in the late colonial period. For example, see *Almanak y kalendario general diario de quartos de Luna,* which indicated eighteen days, or *Almanak o calendario y diario de quarto de Luna,* which indicated twenty-four days.

61. Paul A. David and Peter Solar discuss the issue choosing leisure in place of income in "A Bicentenary Contribution to the History of the Cost of Living in America," 6–7. The cabildo tried repeatedly to restrict access to drink and gaming as a means of pushing reluctant labor into the marketplace.

62. See, for example, Biedma et al., *Acuerdos del extinguido cabildo de Buenos Aires*, serie 3, tomo 7, libro 44, 181.

63. As suggested earlier, this is the major weakness of the article by Chance and Taylor, "Estate and Class in a Colonial City," 454–60.

64. See Kicza, *Colonial Entrepreneurs*, 207–26.

65. Actually, one real per day might be a better estimate. In 1802 the cabildo paid one real per day for the food given to laborers employed for street paving, see Universidad de Buenos Aires, *Documentos para la historia Argentina*, tomo 4, "Abastos," 163.

66. AGN, División Colonia, Sección Contaduría, Temporalidades, Obra de la Real Universidad, 23 Junio 1783.

67. AGN, División Colonia, Sección Contaduría, Culto de Buenos Aires, Mercedarios, Convento, Gastos, libros 1, 2, and 3.

68. AGN, División Colonia, Sección Gobierno, Tribunales, leg. B7, exp. 18. This is a case of the bricklayer Pedro Blanco selling materials wholesale. AGN, División Colonia, Sección Gobierno, Tribunales, leg. B8, exp. 6, presents a case of five carpenters in a partnership that purchased timber in Paraguay for resale in Buenos Aires.

69. Rawls, *A Theory of Justice*, 62, 302.

70. Levene, *Ensayo histórico sobre la revolución de Mayo y Mariano Moreno*, 1:231–32. Levene developed index numbers for twenty-two common imported goods that show an increase from one hundred to two hundred in this period.

71. Biedma et al., *Acuerdos del extinguido cabildo de Buenos Aires*, serie 4, tomo 1, libro 59, 449–50.

72. Ibid., serie 4, tomo 2, libro 60, 141.

73. Mawe, *Travels in the Interior of Brazil*, 42.

74. Williamson and Lindert, *American Inequality*, 281–91.

75. See a discussion of the North American case in Montgomery, "The Working Classes of the Pre-Industrial American City, 1780–1830," 12. He argues that "the unskilled American enjoyed a premium of 80 percent over his British counterpart."

76. Williamson and Lindert, *American Inequality*, 12.

77. Susan M. Socolow used my consumer price index to deflate an index of salaries paid to bureaucrats employed by the colonial government of Buenos Aires. She found this group to be significantly disadvantaged relative to both skilled and unskilled workers.

78. Samuel Amaral examines this tension between free and slave labor for the countryside in "Rural Production and Labour in late Colonial Buenos Aires." He summarizes that "it was therefore more convenient for the landowner to employ forced labour for permanent jobs" (272).

8. An Empire Lost

1. Manuel Barbarín was married to Simona Sarratea, a former slave of Martín de Sarratea, the father-in-law of Santiago de Liniers. See Estrada, *Argentinos de orígin Africano*, 81.

2. *La Gaceta Mercantil*, May 24, 1836. The Hispanic Division of the Library of Congress, Washington, D.C., has the full run of this journal. The poem celebrating the life of Manuel was published in *La Gaceta Mercantil* on March 14. For more details about his social position and for the details of the division of his estate, see AGN, Sucesiones, 3931. His widow inherited property and goods valued at 1,759 pesos and each child inherited 293 pesos.

3. This story is summarized in Estrada, *Argentinos de orígin Africano*, 81–84. This source was the basis for an interesting essay more broadly focused on the black population of Argentina, see also Bernard, "Entre pueblo y plebe," 75–76.

4. The colonial government also used a lottery to distribute pensions among the widows and orphans of those who lost their lives in defense of the city. In the end a total of eighteen pensions were funded for a total of two hundred pesos per year by the cabildo and church, see Ricardo Rodolfo Caillet-Bois, *Mayo documental*, 12 tomos (Buenos Aires: Universidad de Buenos Aires, Facultad de Filosofía y Letras, 1961), 6:238–41.

5. Estrada, *Argentinos de orígin Africano*, 81.

6. This summary follows closely Groussac, *Santiago Liniers*, 53–61. Groussac's work was originally published in 1907, but I have relied on a new edition.

7. The plans and ambitions of the British naval commander, Admiral Sir Home Riggs Popham, and his connections to Francisco Miranda and to the British government is revealed in the collection of documents in Grainger, *The Royal Navy in the River Plate, 1806–1807*, 1–108.

8. See Lozier Almazán, *Beresford Governador de Buenos Aires*, 63–143, for a very reliable summary of this period. The military force that took Buenos Aires in 1806 was sent first to take the Dutch Cape Colony. Once this task was accomplished the commanding officer, Admiral Sir Home Riggs Popham, acting on a long-contemplated British scheme, crossed the Atlantic to conquer Buenos Aires.

9. This is well described in Lozier Almazán, *Liniers y su tiempo*, 82–84.

10. One eyewitness, Francisco Saguí, claimed that Sobremonte's flight had led to panic and the collapse of the city's defense, see his *Los últimos cuatro años*, 13.

11. Nearly every contemporary account of this event excoriated Sobremonte's apparent concern to save the treasury rather than defend the city, but the meaning of this decision is not as clear as it appears at first glance. Sobremonte had notified the cabildo to prepare its funds for quick removal in case of an attack on December 18, 1805, well before the actual attack, and the cabildo had expressed no reservations. See Biedma et al., *Acuerdos del extinguido cabildo de Buenos Aires*, serie 4, tomo 2, libro 60, años 1805–1807, 186–87.

12. The confusion and helplessness of the city's leadership in the wake of the viceroy's flight is described in a firsthand account by Mariquita Sánchez de Thompson available in a modern collection, Sánchez de Thompson, *Intimidad y política, diario, cartas y recuerdos*, 150–55.

13. This letter to Don Zacarías Pereyra is found in Williams Álzaga, *Martín de Álzaga Cartas (1806–1807)*, 114. The reference to wolves is found in a letter to Don Pasqual Dubois dated August 30, 1806 (127).

14. See Museo Historico Nacional and Carranza, *Memorias y autobiografías*, 1:96–97.

15. Beruti, *Memorias curiosas*, 46–47. This is a modern edition of Beruti's wonderful memoir published earlier in a facsimile edition in 1942 in the *Revista de la Biblioteca Nacional*. Beruti was born in Buenos Aires in 1777 and began his diary when he was thirteen years old. He wrote his last notes in 1855 just months before his death.

16. Levene, "Escritos de Mariano Moreno sobre las Invasiones Inglesas," 33.

17. Sánchez de Thompson, *Intimidad y política*, 151. Ignacio Núñez looked back dismissively on the viceroy, referring to him as a "gross dwarf" and his wife as "pretentious and ugly." See Núñez, *Autobiografía*, 52–53. He also mentions that while some called him a traitor, he was more precisely a coward (see 88–89, 106).

18. After Beresford surrendered one volunteer unit, the Voluntarios Patriotas de la Unión organized by the Junta de Catalanes, a powerful group of Spanish merchants led by Álzaga, revealed to Liniers that they had earlier tunneled under the fortress and prepared an explosive charge to destroy the British force without consulting him, see Williams Álzaga, *Fuga del General Beresford*, 71–74.

19. Ibid., 50–51.

20. For a very engaging discussion of the invasion and the reaction of local groups to the threat and opportunities presented by the British, see Gillespie, *Gleanings and Remarks*.

21. The division of the captured treasury among British officers and enlisted men is explained in Elissalde, *Historias ignoradas de las invasiones Ingleses*, 175. For a contemporary account, see Fairburn, *Authentic and Interesting Description of the City of Buenos Ayres and the Adjacent Country*.

22. News of Liniers's victory reached London on December 23, 1806. See Segreti, *Bernardino Rivadavia*, 167.

23. Juan Martín de Pueyrredón, for example, created a light cavalry, militia force called the Husares de Pueyrredón, recruiting the men, arming them, and paying their wages; see Museo Mitre, *Documentos del archivo de Pueyrredón*, 1:51–54.

24. Saguí, *Los últimos cuatro años*, 36.

25. With the fall of Montevideo, even regular enlisted men, like the Spanish sailors who retreated to Buenos Aires, demanded the right to elect officers in imitation of the militia units they served with. The results of these elections often led to factionalism and a lack of discipline. As a result, the political authorities attempted to reform the process by giving superior officers the right to vet candidates in June 1807. See Salas, *Diario de Buenos Aires, 1806–1807*, 389, 459. For a discussion of the election of officers in the Arribeños, see AGN, División Colonia, Sección Gobierno, Invasiones Inglesas, Solicitudes civiles y militares, propuestas, nombramientos, relaciones, cédulas de premios, certificados de servicio, libro 7, for a letter from Jorge Roberedo to the military commander.

26. Cornelio Saavedra, commander of the Patricios and later president of the Junta of May 25, 1810, describes this process in his memoirs. See his "Memoria autografa de Cornelio Saavedra," 31–32. See also Manuel Belgrano's critical discussion in Museo Historico Nacional and Carranza, *Memorias y autobiografías*, 1:98–101.

27. Saguí remembered that the militarized plebe thought of "nothing but the war and the exercises with weapons" (*Los últimos cuatro años*, 31).

28. On January 3, 1807, Juan del Pino, a lieutenant in a calvary unit, wrote to the cabildo to praise the patriotism of "600 men of the classes Indios, Pardos, y Morenos," who had acted with heroism in the Reconquest. See Biedma et al., *Acuerdos del extinguido cabildo de Buenos Aires*, serie 4, tomo 2, libro 61, años 1805–1807, 386.

29. Many of the most useful documents describing these events are collected in *La reconquista y defensa de Buenos Aires*, Instituto de Estudios Historicos sobre la Reconquista y Defensa de Buenos Aires, 1806–1807 (Buenos Aires: Peusar, 1947). This section is based on the letter sent to the king by the cabildo on August 20, 1806 (234–41).

30. Ignacio Núñez quotes Liniers as saying that as the formal attack began his force was joined by a "multitud de pueblo" that fought as "un cuerpo inmenso de guerreros." See his *Autobiografía*, 167–68.

31. Saguí remembered that the popular force advanced towards the plaza "with knives in their hands" and "without order or discipline" (*Los últimos cuatro años*, 20).

32. Pedro Fernández Lalanne, *Los Álzaga y sus épocas* (Buenos Aires, 2005), 56; and Salas, *Diario de Buenos Aires*, 165.

33. See, for example, Gillespie, *Gleanings and Remarks*, 103–6.

34. Despite this patriotic rush to enlist, the cabildo supported an appeal from the "commanders of the forces" to order a general enlistment of "all able to serve." See Biedma et al., *Acuerdos del extinguido cabildo de Buenos Aires*, serie 4, tomo 2, libro 61, años 1805–1807, 346–48.

35. One eye witness remembered that "days were filled with military drills and nights with dancing" (Núñez, *Autobiografía*, 128–29).

36. Pueyrredón, *1810 La revolución de Mayo*, 29.

37. Mario Corcuera Ibáñez ably summarizes this period in his popular biography of Liniers, *Santiago Liniers*, 123–38.

38. The cabildo called the event a "Junta General" in its letter of August 14, 1806, informing Viceroy Sobremonte of the decision to give Liniers political and military authority. See *La reconquista y defensa*, 255. On August 18 Sobremonte wrote to Liniers and used the term "cabildo abierto" to describe the same event (261).

39. See Biedma et al., *Acuerdos del extinguido cabildo de Buenos Aires*, serie 4, tomo 2, libro 61, años 1805–1807, 265–69, for the official cabildo record of the decisions.

40. Viceroy Sobremonte had attempted to restrain Liniers from attacking, and knowledge of this intention had helped fuel popular hostility to the viceroy in the days following Beresford's surrender (Saguí, *Los últimos cuatro años*, 25). He later refers to Sobremonte as "so inept and cowardly" (28).

41. Lozier Almazán, *Martín de Álzaga*, 269. See also the discussion in Álzaga, *Fuga del General Beresford*, 93–95. In addition to those present as representatives of civilian, military, and ecclesiastical institutions, forty-five of the city's richest and most influential men were present as well (Fernández Lalanne, *Los Álzaga*, 57–58).

42. Sobremonte's response to cabildo is found in Biedma et al., *Acuerdos del extinguido cabildo de Buenos Aires*, serie 4, tomo 2, libros 59, 60, 61, 62, años 1805–1807, 294. See also Lozier Almazán, *Liniers y su tiempo*, 109.

43. Lozier Almazán, *Liniers y su tiempo*, 108. Lozier Almazán claims in summary of this remarkable meeting, "the seed of May [the cabildo abierto of May 25, 1810 that signals the first step towards independence] was planted."

44. Historians have estimated a crowd of four thousand or more. See, for example, Segreti, *Bernardino Rivadavia*, 25.

45. Public knowledge of the scandalous affair of Queen María Luisa and Goday informed many of the angry demonstrations against Sobremonte when angry cries against the royal favorite were mixed with demands for the dismissal of the viceroy (see Núñez, *Autobiografía*, 135).

46. Ibid., 141. Núñez confirms the estimated crowd size at four thousand.

47. *La reconquista y defensa*, 261, letter from Marques de Sobremonte to Santiago de Liniers, August 18, 1806.

48. Shortly after August 14 Juan Martín de Pueyrredón met with Sobremonte and passed on his opinion that "it would be very dangerous" for the viceroy to enter Buenos Aires, see Pueyrredón, *1810 La revolución de Mayo*, 32–33, citing a now missing manuscript held by the Biblioteca Nacional.

49. Lozier Almazán, *Liniers y su tiempo*, 108.

50. Ignacio Núñez caught the political and personal complexities of this moment for Liniers, noting that Liniers was caught between his "desire to seize all the advantages of his position [after the Reconquest] . . . and the desire to avoid responsibility for any abuse [perceived] by the viceroy or the Spanish Court" (*Autobiografía*, 140).

51. *La reconquista y defensa*, 261, 262–263, letter from Santiago de Liniers to Marques de Sobremonte, August 22, 1810.

52. Saguí summarized the general opinion of Sobremonte in the wake of these disasters in his memoir. He stated, "Este hombre, capaz del mando supremo en plena paz por sus virtudes y buena capacidad, carecia por desgracia de las mas preciosas calidades en un mandatario de su rango para una época como aquella: carecia de valor y de pericia military" (*Los últimos cuatro años*, 10).

53. Biedma et al., *Acuerdos del extinguido cabildo de Buenos Aires*, serie 4, tomo 2, libro 61, años 1805–1807, 408–9. The decision to send the force to relieve Montevideo was taken by what might be appropriately called another cabildo abierto where the cabildo membership was supplemented with leaders of Spanish colonial and ecclesiastical authorities as well as wealthy *vecinos*. See Núñez, *Autobiografía*, 186–87, for a firsthand account of this event.

54. See Beruti, *Memorias curiosas*, 56–57. The events in Montevideo are summarized by Lozier Almazán, *Liniers y su tiempo*, 121–24.

55. A brief summary of the career of Marqués de Sobremonte is provided by John Lynch in *Spanish Colonial Administration, 1782–1810*, 299–300. Sobremonte remained in Buenos Aires until he returned to Spain, where he was charged with neglecting his duty. He was tried and absolved in Cádiz in 1813 and then promoted to field marshal in 1815. He died in Cádiz in 1827 at the age of eighty-one.

56. Viceroy Sobremonte's actions during the British attack on Montevideo are provided in detail in a very useful contemporary account; see Núñez, *Autobiografía*, 173–89. See also Salas, *Diario de Buenos Aires*, 353–54.

57. Quoted in Salas, *Diario de Buenos Aires*, 371–72.

58. For the act that stripped Sobremonte of his authority see *Reconquista y Defensa*, doc. 39, 293. See also Biedma et al., *Acuerdos del extinguido cabildo de Buenos Aires*, serie 4, tomo 2, libro 61, años 1805–1807, 440–50, for the original actions

of the cabildo. The proclamation is printed in Levene, *Ensayo histórico sobre la revolución de Mayo y Mariano Moreno*, 2:18–20.

59. See the preliminary action of the cabildo on February 6 in Biedma et al., *Acuerdos del extinguido cabildo de Buenos Aires*, serie 4, tomo 2, libro 61, años 1805–1807, 432–35.

60. This was strongly asserted in Núñez, *Autobiografía*, 160.

61. Found in YUL, David Curtis Deforest Papers, Journals and Letterbooks, vol. 6, January 29, 1807. See also Saguí, *Los últimos cuatro años*, 49; and Pueyrredón, *1810 La Revolución de Mayo*, 36.

62. The audiencia notified the cabildo of its decision to remove Sobremonte on February 20, 1807. See Biedma et al., *Acuerdos del extinguido cabildo de Buenos Aires*, serie 4, tomo 2, libro 61, años 1805–1807, 460–61.

63. For a firsthand account see Beruti, *Memorias curiosas*, 58–59. This is also mentioned in an anonymous contemporary memoir written by an enlisted soldier in the Patricios. See Comisión Nacional Ejecutiva, *Diario de un soldado*, 147–48.

64. Most male residents had enlisted in the immediate wake of the defeat of Beresford, but on February 5, 1807, after the surrender of Montevideo militia commanders asked the cabildo for permission to "collect all unenlisted men for the services" (see Biedma et al., *Acuerdos del extinguido cabildo de Buenos Aires*, serie 4, tomo 2, libro 61, años 1805–1807, 430–32).

65. Comisión Nacional Ejecutiva, *Diario de un soldado*, 147–49. A lower estimate of 11,300 is found in Beruti, *Memorias curiosas*, 72–73. José de María, chief of the armed slave force created during the Reconquest, wrote to the cabildo to claim he could recruit up to four thousand slaves if they provided knives and lances (Salas, *Diario de Buenos Aires*, 370).

66. Beresford's victory in 1806 had initially excited the slaves of Buenos Aires with hope of emancipation. Many slaves fled their masters and many more expressed their belief that they would now be free. To quiet this agitation and gain the support of slave owners, Beresford issued a bando that responded to "mulatto and black slaves . . . attempting to escape subjugation . . . and lacking in obedience to their masters." He ordered slaves "to maintain absolute subordination" (see Elissalde, *Historias ignoradas de las invasiones Ingleses*, 181).

67. Biedma et al., *Acuerdos del extinguido cabildo de Buenos Aires*, serie 4, tomo 2, libro 61, años 1805–1807, 476–77. For the discussion of the abolition of slavery in the French Caribbean during the revolutionary era, see Dubois, *A Colony of Citizens*.

68. Defeated on the outskirts of the city, Liniers seemed to lose confidence and nearly surrendered when this was proposed by the British. But Álzaga and other military leaders put some steel in his spine, and Liniers then returned to the city to help organize remaining forces (see Saguí, *Los últimos cuatro años*, 65).

69. Salas, *Diario de Buenos Aires*, 476–510.

70. The role of small groups in defending the city is described by Saguí, *Los últimos cuatro años*, 67.

71. Ibid., 484–512.

72. Ibid., 88. Saguí mentioned the heroic efforts of "four Africans" in defending the barracks of the Arribeños from an English force.

73. Biedma et al., *Acuerdos del extinguido cabildo de Buenos Aires*, serie 4, tomo 2, libro 61, años 1805–1807, 611–23, provides the cabildo's summary of events. See also Beruti, *Memorias curiosas*, 61–64. Liniers's description of the defense is available in full in Gallo, *Las invasiones Inglesas*, 111–21. For a modern summary see Lozier Almazán, *Liniers y su tiempo*, 150–61.

74. See Anonymous, *Buenos Ayres, Truth and Reason Versus Calumny and Folly*, esp. 9–33.

75. These and other issues were the basis for Whitelocke's court martial in 1808. See the testimony in *Trial at Large of Lieutenant General Whitelocke Late Commander in Chief of the Forces in South*.

76. Salas, *Diario de Buenos Aires*, 167.

77. Saguí noted that nearly every class of laborer and artisan was devoted to military exercises, leaving behind their jobs and businesses (see *Los últimos cuatro años*, 31–32). As discussed in chapter 7, the real wage index rose from 62.2 in 1805 to 102.1 in 1810.

78. At the end of 1806 with British forces pressing the defenses of Montevideo, the majority of the Buenos Aires militia units were granted a salary of twelve pesos per month. Nearly all the native-born units, especially the Patricios, Arribeños, and Pardos and Morenos, were fully militarized. Spanish units, among them the Vicaínos and Catalanes, remained part time and did not receive wages (Salas, *Diario de Buenos Aires*, 361–62).

79. Any discussion of these topics must begin with Tulio Halperín Donghi's "Revolutionary Militarization in Buenos Aires 1806–1815." He points out that the military salary bill rose to a million pesos per year in this period (106).

80. Among the heroes who lost their lives in the streets of Buenos Aires was Juan de Dios Campuzano, captain of the Pardos and Morenos. He had earlier been elected as one of two Indian vocales of the shoemakers in 1792 (along with Francisco Baquero) and was registered as a pardo in a later guild census (Salas, *Diario de Buenos Aires*, 510). José Baudrix, active in the creation of the Guild of Pardo and Moreno shoemakers, commanded the sixth company of that same militia during the street fighting of 1807 (426).

81. An anonymous member of the Patricios regiment noted this in his diary on May 20, 1809 (see Comisión Nacional Ejecutiva, *Diario de un soldado*, 247). With the bad feelings generated by the failed *golpe de estado* of January 1, 1809,

still raw, the Spanish-dominated cabildo was unwilling to let this recognition pass without protest, writing to the junta to suggest that this title suggested that Liniers and his heirs would have some seigniorial claim on the city's income (see Lozier Almazán, *Liniers y su tiempo*, 213–14). Formal notice of this reward was announced to the people in a printed bando on May 15, 1809, see JCBL, *Documentos 1807–1809*, Bando, May 15, 1809.

82. Núñez claims that before the French invasion of Spain Napoleon was viewed as a giant both in Spain and the colonies (*Autobiografía*, 147).

83. David Curtis DeForest claimed in a letter to another merchant that contraband had become in effect a parallel commercial system and that some English merchants had opened shops in the city; see YUL, David Curtis Deforest Papers, Journals and Letterbooks, vol. 3, DeForest to Nathaniel Lucas, March 25, 1809. Thomas Kinder, a British merchant resident in Buenos Aires at about the same time, confirmed DeForest's opinion. Kinder rented a room from Tomás Antonio Romero, one of the wealthiest merchants, and was well informed. He claimed in his journal that "contraband is so profitable that every merchant here is a decided enemy of free trade," see JCBL, Kinder, *Journal of a Voyage to the Río de la Plata, 1808–1810*, 122–23.

84. Edberto Oscar Acevedo, *Funcionamiento y quiebra del sistema* virreinal (Buenos Aires: Editorial Ciudad de Buenos Aires, 2004), 114–23. Liniers's poverty led the cabildo to provide a financial gift in 1806. See Biedma et al., *Acuerdos del extinguido cabildo de Buenos Aires*, serie 4, tomo 2, libro 61, años 1805–1807, 499. His circumstances were little changed in 1808 when he wrote to the Junta Central in Spain to ask for a subsidy for his three daughters (he had five sons as well) (see Caillet-Bois, *Mayo documental*, 6:247).

85. News of the French invasion of Spain arrived in Buenos Aires on July 15, 1808.

86. There is no doubt about the scale of Napoleon's ambitions in 1808. He believed he could appropriate many if not all of Spain's colonies. He pursued this end by diplomacy, sending agents to meet with Spanish colonial officials, and by direct action, sending arms and promoting insurrections in the colonies (Caillet-Bois, *Mayo documental*, 1:216, 224–33, 235, 249–50, for examples of these actions).

87. The size of this burden is clear in the budget of 1807. The viceroyalty's income was 2,047,248 while the budget for military salaries and related expenses was approximately 3 million pesos; see Biedma, *Documentos referentes de la guerra*, 187.

88. The cabildo and colonial fiscal authorities used various short-term measures to try to cover the costs of defense, including the use of lapsed salaries from bureaucratic positions and, finally, taking a percentage of the salaries of civil officials; see Biedma et al., *Acuerdos del extinguido cabildo de Buenos Aires*, serie 4, tomo 2, libro 61, años 1805–1807, 532–33.

89. Tulio Halperín Donghi convincingly argues that this was a crucial distinction that contributed to the political divisions that led to independence; see Halperín Donghi, *Politics, Economics, and Society in Argentina in the Revolutionary Period*, 143. See also Segreti, *Bernardino Rivadavia*, 26–27, for the case of the Gallegos. The pressure to satisfy the expectations of these units is indicated by the decision of the region's supreme military commander, Pasqual Ruiz Huidobro, to reclassify the Pardos and Morenos as "provinciales" to maintain them at full salary, despite Spanish military regulations that banned paying casta units as "veteranos" (AGN, División Colonia, Sección Gobierno, Invasiones Inglesas, Correspondencia y varios, Julio–Diciembre 1807–1809).

90. Saavedra, "Memoria autografa de Cornelio Saavedra," 41–42. Spain, following the French invasion, was pressing for funds at the same time. On August 23, 1808, the frigate *Prueba* put in to Maldonado carrying news from the Junta de Galicia of the alliance with Britain and the demand that the local government send to Spain "todos los caudales pertenecientes a S. M. que haya en toda la extension del Vireynato de V. E." (JCBL, *Imprenta de Niños Expositos*, Documentos 1807–1809). The *Prueba* finally sailed with 170,054 pesos in donations, not treasury funds (JCBL, *Imprenta de Niños Expositos*, Documentos 1807–1809, *Proclama*, February 20, 1809).

91. Cornelio Saavedra solicited this wage for the Patricios during training before the second invasion ("Memoria autografa de Cornelio Saavedra," 348–50). See also Salas, *Diario de Buenos Aires*, 405, 526, for comments on military wages and efforts to reduce them.

92. This report is quoted in Salas, *Diario de Buenos Aires*, 530. In a private correspondence the Argentine historian Alejandro Rabinovich said that many members of the Arribeños were recruited from among the large numbers of cart drivers and drovers who hovered in the outskirts of the city awaiting commissions to carry goods to the interior. These social and occupational origins were reflected in the unit's armament. Francisco Saguí remembers them as armed with lances, rather firearms, in the defense of the city in 1807. This probably explains why they had the highest casualty rate (Saguí, *Los últimos cuatro años*, 63–64). Ignacio Núñez confirmed that the Arribeños were recruited among migrants from the interior and cart drivers (Núñez, *Autobiografía*, 150).

93. Biedma et al., *Acuerdos del extinguido cabildo de Buenos Aires*, serie 4, tomo 2, libro 61, años 1805–1807, 355.

94. Anonymous, *Truth and Reason*, 54.

95. Halperín Donghi, *Politics, Economics, and Society in Argentina*, 129.

96. Quoted in ibid., 128. It is important to remember that this dismissive categorization followed Álzaga's failed effort to remove Liniers on January 1, 1809, when militia units loyal to the viceroy intervened.

97. Beruti, *Memorias curiosas*, 196–98. Among those singled out by Beruti was Cornelio Saavedra.

98. This quotation is found in an appendix authored by an anonymous informant and published in Mawe, *Travels in the Interior of Brazil*, 342.

99. In fact black and casta enlisted men were found in large numbers in "Spanish" units. On January 1, 1809, one "Spanish" unit, the Andaluces, did not turn out in the plaza in support of Álzaga's golpe de estado. Thomas Kinder who witnessed the event first hand stated that the commander of that unit had held back "probably doubting his corps which contains, at least, half its number of blacks distrustful of the success of their efforts" (JCBL, Kinder, *Journal of a Voyage to the Río de la Plata*, JCBL, 142).

100. In the period before the second British attack militia soldiers were often in the streets with weapons without any supervision by officers. As a result, the elite complained repeatedly to the cabildo and to Liniers about acts of violence and petty robberies carried out by armed enlisted men (Salas, *Diario de Buenos Aires*, 447, 449–50, 452, and 454). An anonymous member of the Patricios noted an attack on an officer by an enlisted man from the Montañeses militia on March 3. See Comisión Nacional Ejecutiva, *Diario de un soldado*, 154.

101. AGN, División Colonia, Sección Gobierno, Invasiones Inglesas, Solicitudes civiles y militares, propuestas, nombramientos, relaciones, cédulas de premios, certificados de servicio, libro 7.

102. Ibid., certificados de servicio, libro 4. See the letter from Don Manuel Palomares, who solicited recognition for his heroic actions. He noted that he had entered the battle "with my slaves."

103. Saguí, *Los últimos cuatro años*, 95–96, provides a fulsome appreciation to the heroic actions of the slave community in defense of the city.

104. Comisión Nacional Ejecutiva, *Diario de un soldado*, 513, 521.

105. Biedma et al., *Acuerdos del extinguido cabildo de Buenos Aires*, serie 4, tomo 2, libro 61, años 1805–1807, 476.

106. Salas, *Diario de Buenos Aires*, 500.

107. These first efforts to manage the expectations of the slave community are found in Biedma et al., *Acuerdos del extinguido cabildo de Buenos Aires*, serie 4, tomo 2, libro 62, años 1805–1807, 694–95. Other funds were found to provide a small pension for slave women widowed by the deaths of husbands in the combat (701). The widows of free blacks and castas who died during the military action received six pesos per month, one half the amount allocated for white widows. See Salas, *Diario de Buenos Aires*, 522.

108. Given the complex relations that pertained between slaves and masters, a small minority of the servile population determined to remain with masters despite the implicit promise of emancipation offered during the recruit of slaves for

military service. Manuel Antonio Picavea asked to have his name removed from the lottery because his seventy-year-old mistress was extremely poor and sick and depended completely on his earnings. See Biedma et al., *Acuerdos del extinguido cabildo de Buenos Aires*, serie 4, tomo 2, libro 62, años 1805–1807, 712.

109. The cabildo paid for the manumissions of twenty-five of this total; see Roberts, *Las invasions Inglesas*, 396–97. For a brief, firsthand account, see Comisión Nacional Ejecutiva, *Diario de un soldado*, 196. Manumissions continued at a much reduced rate after this event. In 1808, for example, the cabildo spent another 2,477 pesos to free slave volunteers and then another 984 pesos in 1809. See JCBL, "Estado General Que de Orden del Excmo. Cabildo de Esta Capital Forma su Contaduría para Demonstrar los Caudales," Documentos 1807–1809.

110. AGN, Invasiones Inglesas, Solicitudes civiles y militares, propuestas, nombramientos, relaciones, cédulas de premios, certificados de servicio, libro 7.

111. AGN, Invasiones Inglesas, Solicitudes civiles y militares, propuestas, nombramientos, relaciones, cédulas de premios, certificados de servicio, libro 5.

112. For descriptions of this event, see Beruti, *Memorias curiosas*, 78–82; and Comisión Nacional Ejecutiva, *Diario de un soldado*, 196.

113. This patriotic effusion addressed to the city's slaves is published in full in Gallo, *Las invasiones Inglesas*, 122–24.

114. Quotation is found in Barreneche, *Crime and the Administration of Justice in Buenos Aires, 1785–1853*, 37. Almost at the same time the cabildo decided to stop recruiting slaves until such time that the military commanders decided it was unavoidable. See AGN, Invasiones Inglesas, Solicitudes civiles y militares, libro 7.

115. Salas, *Diario de Buenos Aires*, 172–174.

116. Ignacio Núñez commented on the public nature of the affair between Liniers and La Perichóna in his *Autobiografía*, 135.

117. Ibid., 162.

118. Major Alexander Gillespie claimed that he saw Liniers in the company of "French officers" at the time of Beresford's surrender (Gillespie, *Gleanings and Remarks*, 97, 104).

119. This document is found in Caillet-Bois, *Mayo documental*, 6:334–35.

120. Biedma et al., *Acuerdos del extinguido cabildo de Buenos Aires*, serie 4, tomo 2, libro 61, años 1805–1807, 304.

121. Caillet-Bois, *Ensayo sobre el Río de la Plata y la revolución francesa*, 61–63.

122. Both Perichón de Vandueil and Duclos Guyot were in Spain before the French invasion and both sought to have French Ambassador Beauharnais lobby Carlos IV for pensions and other benefits based on their actions against the British. See Caillet-Bois, *Mayo documental*, 1:158–63.

123. Argentina, Congreso de la Nación, *Biblioteca de Mayo, Diarios y cronicas*, mem-

oir de General Tomás Guido, tomo V (Buenos Aires: Imprenta Nacional, 1960), 4,311.

124. In the wake of the election, a *pasquín* celebrated Álzaga as the "father of his nation" (see Comisión Nacional Ejecutiva, *Diario de un soldado*, 199).

125. Gabriel A. Puentes discusses Elío's role in these events in, *Don Francisco Javier de Elío en el Río de la Plata*, 196–215.

126. Relations between Liniers and Álzaga worsened in the last months of 1808. In this environment where every action had political meaning, Liniers challenged the Spanish leadership of the cabildo by pushing for the appointment of Bernardino Rivadavia, the son of an ally and benefactor, as *alférez real*. The cabildo replied by dismissing the young Rivadavia as "incapaces" and as a "joven sin ejercicio." Álzaga's faction simultaneously went on the attack complaining to the Junta Central that Liniers had violated both the law and precedent by agreeing to the marriage of his daughter with Juan Bautista Perichón, a French national, militia officer, and brother of his mistress (see Segreti, *Bernardino Rivadavia*, 36–37).

127. Saguí, *Los últimos cuatro años*, 107–19.

128. Cornelio Saavedra remembered long after these events that Álzaga and his allies had developed this plot over months and that he had advance notice, since he had posted spies near the cabildo and bishop's residence. See Saavedra, "Memoria autografa de Cornelio Saavedra," 34, 42–51.

129. Letter from Felipe Contucci to the Portuguese court, November 4, 1808, quoted in Williams Álzaga, *Dos revoluciones*, 210.

130. The larger intentions of the conspirators are still unresolved. Among contemporaries who saw this event as undermining Spanish authority was Manuel Belgrano. See Museo Historico Nacional and Carranza, *Memorias y autobiografías*, 1:102–3.

131. The full poem is published in Jorge L. R. Fortín, *Liniers (1808–1810)* (Buenos Aires, 2000), 93–95.

132. The text of this renunciation is published in full in ibid., 86–87.

133. By January 1 Álzaga and his faction believed that Liniers was weak, corrupt, and dangerous. The depth of their resentment is suggested in Moreno, *Memorias de Mariano Moreno*, 77–79.

134. Even before the successful defense of the city in 1807, the Patricios had had a number of confrontations with both Spanish militias and regular army units. On the eve of the defense a group of Spaniards provoked the Patricios by dressing a figure of Judas in the uniform of the regiment prior to setting this image on fire (see Saguí, *Los últimos cuatro años*, 93 note a).

135. One British observer of the events of May 25, 1810, reported that the interim viceroy had prepared for these events by his cultivation of the native militia commanders. See this discussion in the appendix in Mawe, *Travels in the Interior*

of Brazil, 342. José Manuel de Goyeneche astutely analyzed these events in a letter to the Junta Central on April 22, 1809. See Caillet-Bois, *Mayo documental*, 8:228–29.

136. Saavedra suggests the new political style emerging in Buenos Aires when he affirmed in his memoirs that "no other voice was heard in the plaza," a formulation suggesting a popular political action rather than the military test that actually occurred (see Saavedra, "Memoria autografa de Cornelio Saavedra," 53). This version of events was confirmed by Martín Rodríguez in his memoir, "Memorias de General Martín Rodríguez," 132–33.

137. In the tense stand off two or three people were killed and another five or six were wounded. An anonymous eyewitness provided this casualty estimate. See Fortín, *Liniers (1808–1810)*, 79–81.

138. In the aftermath of the confrontation a mob entered the homes of some of the better-known plotters and, in one case, appropriated a very large sum of money (three hundred thousand pesos). See Saguí, *Los últimos cuatro años*, 121.

139. Senado de la Nación, Biblioteca de Mayo, *Diarios y cronicas, memoir de General Tomás Guido*, 5:4,311. He stated "la autoridad del virrey [Liniers] vino a quedar bajo la única salvaguardia de los batallones nacionales."

140. The letter from Diego Ponce de León Junta to Count Floridablanca on behalf of the Montevideo junta was sent February 10, 1809. See Caillet-Bois, *Mayo documental*, 8:111–15. The characterization made by Francisco Javier Elío in a letter to Eusebio Bardaxí y Azara on December 4, 1810, is quoted at length in Williams Álzaga, *Dos revoluciones*, 213. Martín Rodríguez, Saavdra's chief lieutenant, similarly dismissed Álzaga's civilian supporters as "chusma." See Museo Historico Nacional and Carranza, *Memorias y autobiografías*, 1:123–25.

141. Letter from Matías de Cires to the king in Caillet-Bois, *Mayo documental*, 8:22.

142. The full document is found in Caillet-Bois, *Mayo documental*, 8:208.

143. Thomas Kinder, an English merchant, resident in Buenos, and a friend of Liniers, asserted this point in his journal (JCBL, Kinder, *Journal of a Voyage to the Río de la Plata*, JCBL, 185–86). Manuel Belgrano also reported this discussion in his *Autobiografía*. See Museo Historico Nacional and Carranza, *Memorias y autobiografías*, 1:103–5. The cabildo of Buenos Aires on July 13 formally noted that Cornelio Saavedra and other militia commanders had met on July 11 to discuss resistance to the transfer of power to Cisneros (Levene, *Ensayo histórico sobre la revolución de Mayo y Mariano Moreno*, 3:204–11).

144. Before the arrival of Cisneros in the viceroyalty, Liniers continued to publicly attack Napoleon's duplicity in invading Spain and warned the population of Buenos Aires to be vigilant for French propaganda, noting optimistically that "Bonaparte y sus satellites marchan precipitamente a la tumba" (JCBL, Documentos 1807–1809, Proclama de Santiago de Liniers, May 13, 1809).

145. The timidity and cautiousness of Cisneros quickly provoked anger among other Spanish authorities in Buenos Aires, including the audiencia and bishop. A series of prickly letters sent by the audiencia and bishop to Cisneros are printed in full in the documentary collection Caillet-Bois, *Mayo documental*, 9:150–56.

146. JCBL, Kinder, *Journal of a Voyage to the Río de la Plata*, JCBL, 185. Kinder writes, "The commanders of the several corps held frequent counsels and Saavedra and others strongly urged General Liniers to continue at their head" (185).

147. JCBL, Documentos 1807–1809, Proclama(s), Baltasar Hidalgo de Cisneros, July 15, 1809 and August 23, 1809.

148. JCBL, Kinder, *Journal of a Voyage to the Río de la Plata*, JCBL, 185, 187.

149. The negotiation between Cisneros and Liniers proved difficult. Liniers avoided returning to Spain, despite the direct order of the Spanish junta, and purchased a rural property in Córdoba, Alta de Gracia. A sharp exchange of letters between Cisneros and Liniers is printed in full in Fortín, *Liniers (1808–1810)*, 97–99. See also the exchange of letters between Cisneros and Liniers in July 1809 published in Caillet-Bois, *Mayo documental*, 9:165–67.

150. JCBL, Baltasar Hidalgo Cisneros to "Las Tropas Voluntarios de Buenos Ayres," Documentos 1807–1809, September 11, 1809.

151. Spain's Regency Council confirmed Cisnero's pardon of Álzaga in 1810. See Caillet-Bois, *Mayo documental*, 10:265.

152. Williams Álzaga, *Dos revoluciones*, 212–17.

153. JCBL, Documentos 1807–1809, Bando, April 17, 1809.

154. Anonymous, *An Authentic Narrative of the Proceedings of the Expedition Under the Command of Brigadier General Crauford, until its arrival at Monte Video; With an Account of the Operations against Buenos Ayres under the Command of Lieutenant General Whitelocke* (London: printed by the author, 1808).

155. Similarly, desertions, charges of insubordination, and even common crimes committed by soldiers increased dramatically as well. See AGN, Invasiones Inglesas, Solicitudes civiles y militares, libro 4–7, for militiamen sentenced to whippings, prison time in chains, or other punishments in 1809 and early 1810.

156. JCBL, Bando, September 18, 1809, Documentos 1807–1809.

157. AGN, Invasiones Inglesas, Correspondencia y varios, Julio–Diciembre, 1807–1809, order signed by Pasqual Ruiz Huidobro, November 3, 1808.

158. A useful short summary of this debate is found in Puiggrós, *Los caudillos de la revolución de Mayo*, 20–32. Moreno's "Representación de los Hacendados" is printed in Biedma, *Documentos referentes a la guerra de la independencia y emancipación de la República Argentina*, 1:228–47.

159. Levene, *Ensayo histórico sobre la revolución de Mayo y Mariano Moreno*, 1:298.

160. Ibid., 294.

161. AGN, Tribunales, leg. 24, exp. 7. The debt continued to accumulate even during

the invasions. In December 1806 the black and casta masters were still appealing for relief (AGN, Justicia, leg. 51, exp. 1461).

162. Among the scores to make this transition was the shoemaker Juan Nepomuceno, who had served as a sergeant in the militia of Pardos and Morenos since 1792. After the two British invasions Nepomuceno actively pursued a military career. See his request to assume the rank of *alferez* in September 1807 in AGN, Invasiones Inglesas, Solicitudes civiles y militares, libro 4.

163. Cornelio Saavedra's 1799 opinion on the creation of a guild of shoemakers is printed in full in Levene, *Ensayo histórico sobre la revolución de Mayo y Mariano Moreno*, 3:214–18.

164. Saguí, *Los últimos cuatro años*, 141.

165. Marfany, *La semana de Mayo, diario de un testigo*, 9–10.

166. One contemporary, Ignacio Núñez, wrote that his political allies had to "almost drag" Saavedra back to the city from his rural estate, quoted in Lozier Almazán, *Martín de Álzaga*, 194.

167. The effect of accumulating bad news on the plebe is suggested in Lozier Almazán, *Martín de Álzaga*, 293–94, where the anonymous author wrote, "each day things are getting worse."

168. Lozier Almazán, *Martín de Álzaga*, 63.

169. Pueyrredón, *1810 La revolución de Mayo*, 248.

170. For a recent discussion of the Atlantic context for these events see Adelman, *Sovereignty and Revolution in the Iberian Atlantic*, esp. 208–10, for Buenos Aires.

171. Letter from Maestro Fray Gregorio Torres, original publication found in Senado de la Nación, Biblioteca de Mayo, *Diarios y cronicas, memoir de General Tomás Guido*, 5:4,294.

172. For Cornelio Saavedra's memories of these events, see his "Memoria autografa de Cornelio Saavedra," 64–67.

173. Marfany, *La semana de Mayo, diario de un testigo*, 40.

174. Marfany, *El cabildo de Mayo*, 34–35.

175. Marfany provides a list of those attending the May 22 *cabildo abierto* in *El cabildo de Mayo*, 38–42.

176. Quote found in Pueyrredón, *1810 La revolución de Mayo*, 588.

177. Roberto Marfany closely examined these events in "La Primera Junta de Gobierno de Buenos Aires (1810)." For a firsthand account that asserts a larger role for the plebe, see the "Informe" of Francisco de Orduña, subinspector of artillery, in Argentina, Congreso de laNación, *Biblioteca de Mayo, Diarios y cronicas, memoir de General Tomás Guido*, 5:4,325–26.

178. Pueyrredón, *1810 La revolución de Mayo*, 278–79.

179. When the cabildo failed to publish the results of the cabildo abierto of May 22 by nightfall, Cornelio Saavedra demanded an explanation and discovered that

Cisneros had been named president of the junta. As a result, partisans of independence had a full day to plan their response before the official announcement on the 24; see Saavedra, "Memoria autografa de Cornelio Saavedra," 65–67.

180. News of these events only reached the Spanish Regency on August 31 in the form of a letter from the Montevideo cabildo announcing its loyalty to the regency and its refusal to send a representative to Buenos Aires. See *Gazeta extraordinaria de la Regencia de España é Indias*, 607–10. Available on the website for Ministerio de Cultura de España, Biblioteca Virtual de Prensa Historica, http://prensahistorica.mcu.es/.

181. One British eyewitness to the events of May made the logical connection to the removal of Sobremonte by "an extraordinary Junta of the people, who assembled in the Cabildo." See the description of the May Revolution by an anonymous witness in the appendix of Mawe, *Travels in the Interior of Brazil*, 338.

182. Roberto Marfany carefully examined the evidence and claimed that the crowd numbered in the hundreds, not thousands, and that Beruti and French directed them. See Marfany, "El pronunciamiento de Mayo." Tulio Halperín Donghi provides a valuable alternative to Marfany's deflation of popular opinion; see his *Politics, Economics, and Society*, 153–56.

183. Marfany quotes the *sindico procurador* of the cabildo who asked, "where are the people?" (Marfany, "La Primera Junta de Gobierno," 233–34).

184. Saguí describes these events in *Los últimos cuatro años*, 156–61.

185. Argentina, Congreso de laNación, *Biblioteca de Mayo, Diarios y cronicas, memoir de General Tomás Guido*, 5:4308.

186. This statement by an unknown informant was included in Mawe, *Travels in the Interior of Brazil*, 337.

187. JCBL, Documentos 1807–1809, Bando, Santiago Liniers and Oidores, April 17, 1809.

188. See Bak and Paczuski, "Complexity, Contingency, and Criticality." The sandpile paradigm is discussed on 6691.

189. JCBL, Documentos 1810–1819, Junta Provisional, "Cuerpos Militares de Buenos Ayres," May 29, 1810.

190. See Saavedra's testimony in "Memoria autografa de Cornelio Saavedra," 67–69.

Epilogue

1. Senado de la Nación, Argentina, Congreso de laNación, *Biblioteca de Mayo*, "Apuntes sobre la repercusion de la revolución de Mayo en Córdoba," *Diarios y cronicas, memoir de General Tomás Guido*, tomo V, (Buenos Aires: Imprenta Nacional, 1960) 5:4334–35. In this memoir Presbítero Alcántara Giménez recounts that Cisneros wrote to Liniers on May 25 and that his letter reached the former viceroy three days later.

2. Liniers made this clear in a letter to his father in law Martín de Sarratea. Bernardo Lozier Almazán quotes this letter at length in his *Liniers y su tiempo* (Buenos Aires: Emecé Editores, 1990), 240–41.

3. Needless to say, the authors of nearly every Liniers biography cover this period in detail. Among those worth reading are Lozier Almazán, *Liniers y su tiempo*, esp. 243–251; Ortega, *Santiago de Liniers*, esp. 270–98; and the still interesting Groussac, *Santiago Liniers*, now available in a modern edition. For a more fanciful treatment, see Salduna, *El ultimo virrey*.

4. The Buenos Aires junta determined to establish its control over the north in large measure because of the city's long dependence on the Potosí *situado*, which had averaged more than a million pesos a year during the last fifteen years of the colonial era, as well as to deal with the loyalists centered in Córdoba. For the necessity of guarding access to the mining region, see Irigoin, "Gresham on Horseback."

5. Despite many generations of new research, Groussac's *Santiago Liniers*, published first in two parts in 1897 and 1904, remains a valuable resource for these events. See the discussion on the capture and execution in the version published in the series Biblioteca de Clásicos Argentinos, edited by Julio Noé, vol. 11 (Ediciones Estrada, 1943), 379–95. According to Groussac, his captors seized thirty thousand silver pesos along with personal effects.

6. Even on August 14 the official periodical, *Gaceta de Buenos Ayres*, prepared the ground for this harsh sentence, saying that Liniers had "sworn the ruin and extermination of a generous people that with the blood of its sons had produced the crown of his glories" (Academia Nacional de la Historia, *Gaceta de Buenos Aires*). The *Gaceta de Buenos Ayres* (the article written most likely by Moreno) returned to this theme on October 11, long after the executions, to claim that "an eternal opprobrium will cover the ashes of Don Santiago Liniers" (Academia Nacional de la Historia, *Gaceta de Buenos Aires*).

7. Tomás Guido, "Reseña historica," in *Biblioteca de Mayo, colección de obras y documentos para la historia Argentina, Diarios y cronicas, memoir de General Tomás Guido*, tomo V, 5:4,311.

8. Every member of the junta, with the exception of Manuel Alberti who was a cleric, signed the death sentence. Massot, *Matar y morir*, 36.

9. The *sargento mayor* of the Cuerpo de Arribeños, Ildefonso Pasos, wrote to Liniers to urge that his unit, recruited among casta laborers and journeymen from the interior provinces, continue to receive military wages, noting "the majority of the men would be indigent . . . [and] if deprived of this income would likely turn to robberies" (Salas, *Diario de Buenos Aires, 1806–1807*, 530).

10. Numerous authors have discussed these events and almost all rely on the same

short list of contemporary sources. Julio A. Sierra provides a good short version of these events in his *Fusilados*, 69–83.

11. Exequiel César Ortega quotes correspondence between Moreno and Chiclana at length, demonstrating Moreno's sense of urgency and his fears that the presence of the former viceroy in Buenos Aires could lead to political problems. See Ortega, *La primera pena de muerte resulta por la junta de Mayo*, 111–14.

12. A lone memoir claims that the firing squad was selected from British deserters now serving in the Buenos Aires militia because the officers could not rely on the willingness of native-born troops to carry out the execution. See "Relación de los ultimos hechos del General Liniers," in *Biblioteca de Mayo, colección de obras y documentos para la historia Argentina, Diarios y cronicas, memoir de General Tomás Guido*, tomo V, 5:4,368.

13. Juan Manuel Beruti, *Memorias curiosas*, 148.

14. Relying on the secondhand accounts of Spaniards in Montevideo, Ortega claims that Liniers suffered the "near destruction of his right side" in the first volley (*Santiago de Liniers*, 297).

15. Lozier Almazán, relying on the memoir of Dámaso Uriburu, claims the battalion of Patricios then quartered in Córdoba nearly mutinied when informed of the execution (*Liniers y su tiempo*, 251).

16. Beruti, *Memorias curiosas*, 147–48.

17. Historians have struggled with the efficacy of the term Jacobin to describe Moreno and his closest collaborators. I like the discussion in Goldman, "Los 'Jacobinos' en el Río de la Plata."

18. In addition to the provocation of the toast, another officer took a crown of "sugar" from a pastry and handed that to Saavedra's wife Saturnina Otárola who then passed it on to her husband as the crowd applauded. The event and its fallout is discussed in Ruiz-Guiñazu, *El Presdidente Saavedra y el pueblo soberano de 1810*, 358–64.

19. Beruti describes this event and its aftermath in detail; see *Memorias curiosas*, 152–57.

20. This decision was announced in the official publication, the *Gaceta de Buenos Ayres* on December 26 (Academia Nacional de la Historia, *Gaceta de Buenos Aires [1810–1821]* [Buenos Aires: Compañía sud-americana de billetes de banco, 1810]). See the partisan but revealing discussion by Manuel Moreno in his memoir of his brother's life, *Memorias de Mariano Moreno*, 201–8. See Beruti, *Memorias curiosas*, 154–55, for the full text of the regulation.

21. From the nineteenth century some have speculated that Mariano Moreno was poisoned. See a modern version of this argument in Vicente Massot, *Matar y morir*, 53–54. Manuel Moreno witnessed his brother's illness and death on board

the English ship. He describes in detail both the physical and psychological symptoms that afflicted his brother. It is his description of the ship captain's ministrations that has served as the chief evidence of poisoning (see *Memorias de Mariano Moreno*, 212–15).

22. Enrique Ruiz-Guiñazu produced a photograph of the original letter in his *El Presidente Saavedra* (388–91), and notes that it is in his "collection." I was unable to find the document in the AGN.

23. Ibid., 378–84.

24. Beruti, *Memorias curiosas*, 164–67.

25. Mitre, *Historia de Belgrano y de la independencia*, 151.

26. Gorriti is quoted by Ernesto J. Fitte, *El motín de las trenzas* (Buenos Aires:Editorial Fernández Blanco, 1960), 30–31. Beruti made a similar argument, placing Saavedra at the heart of an intrigue; see *Memorias Curiosas*, 166–67.

27. Cornelio Saavedra never took up command of the forces in Alto Peru. He was relieved of command before arriving and then suffered a long period of exile from Buenos Aires. See his description of this period in his "Memoria autografa de Cornelio Saavedra."

28. Beruti, *Memorias curiosas*, 182–83, records the creation of this "Junta Ejecutiva" on September 23, noting that in addition to the three vocals the body included three secretaries José Julián Pérez, Bernardino Rivadavia, and Vicente López. While Manuel de Sarratea was related to Liniers through marriage, his presence in the Triumvirate indicates unambiguously that his views were at least compatible with those of the anti-Saavedra faction.

29. Gabriel Di Meglio discusses crime in the two decades following May 25, 1810, in his "Ladrones." See the contemporary account of Pedro José Agrelo, a judge, in Museo Histórico Nacional and Carranza, *Memorias y autobiografías*, 2:232–34.

30. The popular demonstration of April 5 and 6 in which the Patricios had been highly visible had successfully demanded that Manuel Belgrano be recalled from his command of forces in Paraguay and the Banda Oriental. Supporters of Saavedra saw his appointment to the command of the Patricios as another insult by the Triumvirate (Mitre, *Historia de Belgrano*, 164–65).

31. Vicente Massot provides a good short summary in his *Matar y morir*, 54–60; but Gabriel Di Meglio's ¡Viva el pueblo bajo!, 116–22, situates his summary, mostly based on Fitte, in the social context explored here.

32. This discussion follows closely the only full study of the event; see Fitte, *El motín de las trenzas*, 90–97.

33. Ibid., 95–99.

34. Ibid., 102.

35. Beruti, *Memorias curiosas*, 192.

36. Bishop Orellana of Córdoba had been condemned to death by the junta along

with Liniers in 1810. Fearful of mass protest, the junta imposed a sentence of internal exile. When the Triumvirate took power in September 1811 it commuted this sentence, explaining the presence of the bishop in Buenos Aires in December. Among others attempting to end the mutiny were Domingo French, Moreno ally and former commander of the Regiment Estrella (or América), and Juan José Castelli. French had been sent to internal exile as a result of the April 6 demonstration and then been pardoned by the Triumvirate. Castelli had returned to Buenos Aires in disgrace after his defeat by Spanish forces at Huaqui. Beruti, *Memorias curiosas*, 105–8.

37. The regiment's full complement was between 1,100 and 1,200 enlisted men and officers. Scores of men fled the barracks when the mutiny started. Some climbed across the roof to the barracks of the Pardos and Morenos located next door. It is also likely that at least one battalion of 300 men was in the field sent north as part of an expedition in March (Beruti, *Memorias curiosas*, 163).

38. Ibid., 191–94.

39. The Triumvirate still feared popular mobilization as indicated by its decision to force civilians to turn over all weapons under the pain of one hundred strokes of the whip in the streets of Buenos Aires; see JCBL, Documentos, El Gobierno Superior de las Provincias Unidas de Río de la Plata a nombre del Señor Don Fernando Septimo, January 16, 1812.

40. The thirty-six pesos and five reales (roughly two and a half months wages for an enlisted man) expended by the government purchased six bottles of *aguardiente*, six bottles of wine, and three pesos worth of cigars. In addition they provided beef, chicken, rice, garbanzos, bread, sugar, and chocolate. Preparation of the execution site, including gallows and blindfolds cost roughly the same amount, thirty-one pesos and six reales; see Fitte, *El motín de las trenzas*, 132–37.

41. JCBL, Documentos, El Gobierno a las Tropas, December 11, 1811.

42. Juan Manuel Beruti was opposed to the Saavedra faction and strongly supportive of the Triumvirate in late 1811. He went out of his way to characterize Cornelio Saavedra as "cruel and tyrannical," (*Memorias curiosas*, 176). He also claimed Saavedra's supporters, "these perverse ones" were the authors of both the April uprisings and the mutiny by the Patricios. In fact, he claimed that September 23, the replacement of the junta by the Triumvirate, was more "memorable" than May 25, 1810, a truly remarkable judgment, (194–97). Nine days after suppressing the mutiny, the Triumvirate ordered the provincial deputies, allied previously with Saavedra in the Junta Grande, to leave the city.

43. See Academia Nacional de la Historia, *Gaceta de Buenos Ayres*, viernes, 13 Diciembre 1811.

Bibliography

Archival Sources

ARCHIVO GENERAL DE INDIAS (AGI), SEVILLE, SPAIN

Audiencia de Buenos Aires, leg. 156, 214

Audiencia de Buenos Aires: Duplicados del Virrrey, leg. 78–97

Cartas y Expedientes, leg. 263–90

Casa de Contratación, pasajeros a indias, informaciones y licencias, 8 febrero 1780

Correspondencia con los Virreyes, leg. 37, 38, 39, 40

Duplicados del Virrey Marques de Sobremonte, leg. 134–39

Duplicados del Virrey Nicolás de Arredondo, leg. 108–21

Estado, 75, numero 15, 48, 110

Estado, 79, numeros 1, 2, 12, 80, 104

Estado 80, numero 30

Estado 81, numero 17

Estado, 82, numero 106, 127

Expedientes del Consulado y Comercio, leg. 584–89

Expedientes de Real Hacienda, leg. 473–484

Expedientes de Real Hacienda y de partes, leg. 489–508

Expedientes e instancias de partes, leg. 301–18

Expedientes pendientes de informes, leg. 294–99

Indiferente General, leg. 1526, 1527, 1581

ARCHIVO GENERAL DE LA NACIÓN (AGN),
BUENOS AIRES, ARGENTINA

División Colonia, Sección Contaduría

Caja de Buenos Aires, 1770–1815

Caja de Buenos Aires, Impuesto, numeros 1–272

Caja de Buenos Aires, Impuesto, numeros 1–542

Caja de Buenos Aires, Real hacienda, Sueldos de Empleados, 1797

Convento y iglesia de San Ramón de Buenos Aires, Inventorio de los bienes, muebles y inmuebles, 1788–1792

Culto de Buenos Aires, Mercedarios, Convento Grande de San Ramón, Libro de Gastos, 1775–1815

Culto de Buenos Aires, Mercedarios, Hospicio de San Ramón de las Conchas, libros 1, 3, and 5.

Culto de Buenos Aires, Bethlemitas, Convento y hospital de Santa Catalina

Obras Publicas, Canal de San Fernando, 1770–1808; Cabildo de Buenos Aires Obras, 1805–1806

Temporalidades, 1787

Temporalidades de Buenos Aires 1787

Temporalidades, Obra de la Universidad, 1783

División Colonia, Sección Gobierno

Archivo del Cabildo, 1770–1815

Archivo del Cabildo, 1776, padrón de estrangeros

Bandos, libro 4

Bandos, libro 5

Bandos, libro 6

Bandos, libro 7

Bandos, libro 8

Cabildo de Buenos Aires, 1745–1752, leg. 3 (1748)

Cabildo de Buenos Aires, Correspondencia con el virrey, 1794 and 1795

Cabildo de Buenos Aires, Correspondencia con el virrey, 1795–1796

Cabildo de Buenos Aires, Obras, 1805–1806

Cabildo de Buenos Aires, Obras, 1805–1806, Relación de lo recaudado de los cafes, canchas, posadas, etc.

Cabildo de Buenos Aires, Propios, 1770–1806

Cabildo de Buenos Aires, Propios, 1805–1806

Cabildo de Buenos Aires, Propios, 1808–1809

Cabildo de Buenos Aires, Propios, 1810–1811

Censo de Buenos Aires, 1810

Comerciales, leg. 14, exp. 8

Comerciales, leg. 14, exp. 25

Comerciales, leg. 15, exp. 16

Criminales, leg. 13, exp. 31

Escribanía, Registros 1-7 (1775–1810)

Hacienda, leg., 17, exp. 389

Hacienda, leg. 42, exp. 1071

Hacienda, leg., 62, exp. 1621

Hacienda, leg. 69, exp. 1836

Hacienda, leg. 73, exp. 1927

Hacienda, leg. 73, exp. 1929

Hacienda, leg. 76, exp. 2002

Interior, leg. 4, exp. 14

Interior, leg. 9, exp. 5

Interior, leg. 25, exp. 4

Interior, leg. 26, exp. 4

Interior, leg. 33, exp. 7

Interior, leg. 33, exp. 16

Interior, leg. 34, exp. 12

Interior, leg. 34, exp. 18

Interior, leg. 36, exp. 6

Interior, leg. 38, exp. 1

Interior, leg. 41, exp. 7

Interior, leg. 41, exp. 14

Interior, leg. 53, exp. 2

Interior, leg. 54, exp. 2

Interior, leg. 54, exp. 3

Interior, leg. 55, exp. 5

Invasiones Inglesas. Correspondencia y varios (1807–09)

Invasiones Inglesas. Solicitudes civiles y militares, propuestas, nombramientos, relaciones, cédulas de premios, certificados de servicio: (A–B, C–F, G–L, M–P, Q–R, S–Z), libro 7, libro 8

Justicia, leg. 9, exp. 177

Justicia, leg. 17, exp. 4

Justicia, leg. 17, exp. 144

Padrones de Buenos Aires, ciudad y campaña, 1782–1807

Reales Cédulas, Decretos, leg. 27, 1793–1795

Resguardo, 1800–1802

Solicitudes Civiles, libro F–G

Tribunales, leg. 9, exp. 4

Tribunales, leg. 13, exp. 15

Tribunales, leg. 24, exp. 7

Tribunales, leg. 60, exp. 6

Tribunales, leg. 66, exp. 37

Tribunales, leg. 74, exp. 29

Tribunales, leg. 116, exp. 33

Tribunales, leg. 131, exp. 12

Tribunales, leg. 254, exp. 62

Tribunales, leg. B5, exp. 22

Tribunales, leg. B7, exp. 18

Tribunales, leg. B8, exp. 6

Tribunales, leg. B8, exp. 22

Tribunales, leg. G17, exp. 1

Tribunales, leg. L9, exp. 4

Tribunales, leg. P6, exp. 8

Tribunales, leg. P12, exp. 18

Tribuanles, leg. P12, exp. 31

Tribunales, leg. S5, exp. 10

Tribunales, leg. S10, exp. 6

Tribunales, leg. V8, exp. 23

Tribunales, leg. Z4, exp. 7

Tribunales, leg. Z4, exp. 11

Sucesiones

Sucesiones, 3468

Sucesiones, 3863

Sucesiones, 3865

Sucesiones, 3866

Sucesiones, 3867

Sucesiones, 3916

Sucesiones, 3917

Sucesiones, 3918

Sucesiones, 3931

Sucesiones, 4308

Sucesiones, 4833

Sucesiones, 4837

Sucesiones, 4838

Sucesiones, 5340

Sucesiones, 5341

Sucesiones, 5343

Sucesiones, 5589

Sucesiones, 5673

Sucesiones, 5687

Sucesiones, 5871

Sucesiones, 5872

Sucesiones, 5873

Sucesiones, 5903

Sucesiones, 5904

Sucesiones, 5905

Sucesiones, 6258

Sucesiones, 6260

Sucesiones, 6316

Sucesiones, 6376

Sucesiones, 6447

Sucesiones, 6478

Sucesiones, 6497

Sucesiones, 6725

Sucesiones, 6727

Sucesiones, 6730

Sucesiones, 6774

Sucesiones, 6777

Sucesiones, 7151

Sucesiones, 7152

Sucesiones, 7153

Sucesiones, 7154

Sucesiones, 7273

Sucesiones, 7371

Sucesiones, 7384

Sucesiones, 7705

Sucesiones, 7706

Sucesiones, 7708

Sucesiones, 7709

Sucesiones, 7758

Sucesiones, 7776

Sucesiones, 7778

Sucesiones, 7780

Sucesiones, 8133

Sucesiones, 8135

Sucesiones, 8137

Sucesiones, 8139

Sucesiones, 8141

Sucesiones, 8413

Sucesiones, 8414

Sucesiones, 8415

Sucesiones, 8456

Sucesiones, 8559

Sucesiones, 8575

Sucesiones, 8734

ARCHIVO HISTORICO DE LA PROVINCIA DE
BUENOS AIRES (AHPBA), LA PLATA, ARGENTINA
(Real Audiencia) Criminales, leg. 34–1–9
Criminales, leg. 34–1–10
Criminales, leg. 34–1–11
Criminales, leg. 34–1–12
Criminales, leg. 34–1–13
Criminales, leg. 34–1–18
Criminales, leg. 34–1–19
Criminales, leg. 34–1–20
Criminal Provincial, leg. 103
Criminal Provincial, leg. 104

JOHN CARTER BROWN LIBRARY (JCBL),
PROVIDENCE, RHODE ISLAND
"Estado General Que de Orden del Excmo. Cabildo de Esta Capital Forma su
    Contaduría para Demonstrar los Caudales," Documentos 1807–1809
Gazeta de Buenos Ayres
Gazeta Ministerial de Gobierno de Buenos Ayres
Imprenta de Niños Expositos
Documentos 1807–1809
Documentos 1810–1819
Thomas Kinder, *Journal of a Voyage to the Río de la Plata, 1808–1810*. Hand-written
    manuscript

MUSEO MITRE (MM), BUENOS AIRES, ARGENTINA
Guia de Foresteros; 1792: 20/1/44; 1797: 44/3/34; 1803: 20/1/44
Matrículas: Arm. B, C. 23, P.2, N⁰ de Ord. 18
Esclavos: Arm. B, C. 24, P.1, N⁰ de Ord. 41

YALE UNIVERSITY LIBRARY (YUL),
NEW HAVEN, CONNECTICUT
David Curtis Deforest Papers, Journals and Letterbooks

Published Primary Sources

Academia Nacional de la Historia (Argentina). *Correro de Comercio*. Facsimile
    edition. "Introducción" by Ernesto J. Fitte, 1970.
————. *Gaceta de Buenos Aires (1810–1821): Reimpresión facsimilar dirigida por la
    Junta de historia y numismática americana en camplimiento de la ley no. 6286 y por*

resolución de la comisión nacional del centenario de la revolución de mayo. Buenos Aires: Compañía sud-americana de billetes de banco, 1910.

Aguirre, Juan Francisco de. "Diario 1783." *Anales de la biblioteca* (Biblioteca Nacional) 4 (1905). Introduction by Paul Groussac.

Almanak o calendario y diario de quarto de Luna, segun Meridiano de Buenos Ayres para el año de 1809. Buenos Aires: Real Imprenta de Niños Expósitos, 1809.

Almanak y kalendario general diario de quartos de Luna, segun el Meridiano de Buenos Ayres para el año del señor de 1797. Buenos Aires: Real Imprenta de Niños Expósitos, 1797.

Almanaque político y de comercio de la ciudad de Buenos Ayres para el año de 1826. Facsimile ed. Buenos Aires: Ediciones de la Flor, 1968.

Anonymous. *Buenos Ayres, Truth and Reason Versus Calumny and Folly in which the Leading Circumstances of General Whitelocke's Conduct in South America Are Explained.* London: Kerby and Bowdery, 1807.

Aparicio, Francisco de. "Relación de un viaje entre Mendoza y Buenos Aires en 1794." In *Anales del instituto de etnografía Americana*, volume 4, edited by Salvador Canals Frau. Mendoza: Universidad Nacional de Cuyo, 1943.

Argentina, Congreso de la Nación, Senado de la Nación. *Biblioteca de Mayo, colección de obras y documentos para la historia Argentina.* 9 volumes. Buenos Aires: Imprenta Nacional, 1960.

Azara, D. Félix de. *Viajes por la América Meridional.* 2 volumes. Edited by C. A. Walckenaér. Translated by Francisco de las Barras de Aragon. Buenos Aires: Calpe, 1923.

Barba, Enrique M. "Prologue." In *Almanaque político y de comercio para 1826.* Buenos Aires: Ediciones de la Flor, 1968.

Belgrano, Manuel. *Correo de comercio [3 de Marzo de 1810–6 de Abril de 1811].* Buenos Aires: Academia Nacional de la Historia, 1970.

Beruti, Juan Manuel. *Memorias curiosas.* Buenos Aires: Emecé Editores, 2001.

Biedma, José Juan. *Documentos referentes de la guerra de la independencia y emancipación política de la República Argentina y de otras secciones de América a que cooperó desde 1810 a 1828 [Antecedentes políticos, económicos y administrativos de la revolución de Mayo de 1810; 1776–1812].* Buenos Aires: Archivo General de la Nación Argentina, 1914.

Buenos Aires (Argentina). *Documentos y planos relativos al periodo edilicio colonial de la ciudad de Buenos Aires.* 5 volumes. Buenos Aires: Talleres Peuser, 1910.

Buenos Aires (Argentina), José Juan Biedma, Augusto S. Mallié, Eugenio Corbet France, and Héctor C. Quesada. *Acuerdos del extinguido cabildo de Buenos Aires.* Buenos Aires, 1907.

Cabello y Mesa, Francisco Antonio. *Telégrafo Mercantil; rural, político-económico e historiógrafo del Río de la Plata ([1 Abr.] 1801–[17 Oct.] 1802.)*. Buenos Aires: Compañia sud-americana de billetes de banco, 1914.

Caillet-Bois, Ricardo Rodolfo. *Mayo documental*. 12 volumes. Buenos Aires: Universidad de Buenos Aires, Facultad de Filosofía y Letras, 1961.

Comisión Nacional Ejecutiva. *Diario de un soldado*. 150 Aniversario de la Revolución de Mayo. Buenos Aires: Ministro del Interior, 1960.

Concolorcorvo. *El Lazarillo de Ciegos Caminantes desde Buenos Aires hasta Lima (1773)*. Buenos Aires: Ediciones Solar, 1942.

Davie, John Constanse. *Letters from Paraguay: Describing the Settlements of Montevideo an[d] Buenos Ayres*. London: G. Robinson, 1805.

Fairburn, John. *Authentic and Interesting Description of the City of Buenos Ayres Adjacent Country; Situated on the River Plate on the East Side of South America Shewing the Manners, Customs, and Commerce of that Most Important and Invaluable Country*. London: John Fairburn, 1806.

Falkner, Thomas. *A Description of Patagonia and the Adjoining Parts of South America: Containing an Account of the Soil, Produce, Animals, Vales, Mountains, Rivers, Lakes, etc., of the Countries. . . .* London: C. Pugh, 1774.

Gillespie, Alexander. *Gleanings and Remarks: Collected During Many Months of Residence at Buenos Ayres*. Leeds: J. W. Whitely, 1818.

Instituto de estudios historicos sobre la reconquista y defensa de Buenos Aires. *La Reconquista y Defensa de Buenos Aires 1806–1807*. Buenos Aires: Peusar, 1947.

Konetzke, Richard, ed. *Colección de documentos para la historia de la formación social de Hispanoamérica, 1493–1810*. 3 volumes. Madrid: Instituto Jaime Balmes, 1953–1962.

Mawe, John. *Travels in the Interior of Brazil, Particularly in the Gold and Diamond Districts of that Country by Authority of the Prince Regent of Portugal, Including a Voyage to the Río de la Plata and an Historical Sketch of the Revolution of Buenos Ayres*. London: Longman, Hurst, Rees, Orme, and Brown, 1812.

Museo Histórico Nacional (Argentina), and Adolfo P. Carranza, ed. *Memorias y autobiografías*. Buenos Aires: Impr. de M.A. Rosas, 1910.

Museo Mitre. *Documentos del archivo de Pueyrredón*. 4 volumes. Buenos Aires: Impr. de Coni hermanos, 1912.

———. *Documentos del archivo de San Martín*. Buenos Aires: Impr. de Coni hermanos, 1910.

Núñez, Ignacio. *Autobiografía*. Buenos Aires: Comisión de Cultura del Senado de la Nación, 1996.

Parish, Sir Woodbine. *Buenos Ayres and the Provinces of the Río de la Plata: From Their Discovery and Conquest by the Spaniards to the Establishment of Their Political Independence. With Some Account of Their Present State, Trade, Debt,* etc.; *An Appendix of Historical and Statistical Documents; and a Description of the Geology and Fossil Monsters of the Pampa.* London: John Murray, 1839.

Popham, Home Riggs. *A Full and Correct Report of the Trial of Sir Home Popham Including the Whole of the Discussions which Took Place between that Officer and Mr. Jervis, the Counsel for the Admiralty.* London: Printed for J. and J. Richardson, C. Chapple, 1807.

Radaelli, Sigfrido Augusto. *Memorias de los virreyes del Río de la Plata.* Buenos Aires: Editorial Bajel, 1945.

Rodríguez, Martín. "Memorias de General Martín Rodríguez." In *Los sucesos de Mayo contados por sus actores. prologo por Dr. Ricardo Levene.* Buenos Aires: El Ateneo, 1928.

Saavedra, Cornelio. "Memoria autografa de Cornelio Saavedra." In *Los sucesos de Mayo contados por sus actores, prologo por Dr. Ricardo Levene.* Buenos Aires: El Ateneo, 1928.

Saguí, Francisco. *Los últimos cuatro años de la dominación Española en el antiguo virreinato del Río de la Plata desde 26 de Junio de 1806 hasta 25 de Mayo de 1810, memoria historica familiar.* Buenos Aires: Imprenta Americana, 1874.

Trial at Large of Lieutenant General Whitelocke Late Commander in Chief of the Forces in South America by A General Court Martial Held at Chelsea Hospital on Thursday, January 28, 1808. London: R. Faulder and Son, 1808.

Universidad de Buenos Aires. *Documentos para la historia del Virreinato del Río de la Plata.* Buenos Aires: Compañia Sud-Americana de Billetes de Banco, 1912.

Universidad de Buenos Aires, Facultad de Filosofía y Letras, Instituto de Historia Argentina, "Doctor Emilio Ravignani." *Documentos para la historia Argentina.* 24 volumes. Buenos Aires: Compañía Sud-Americana de Billetes de Banco, 1913.

Vieytes, Juan Hipólito, and Pedro Antonio Cerviño. *Seminario de agricultura, industria y comercio; reimpresión facsímile publicada por la Junta de historia y numismática americana. Tomos 1–5 (núm. 1–218), 1 Sept. 1802–11 Feb. 1807.* Buenos Aires: G. Kraft Ltda, 1928.

Wilcocke, Samuel Hull. *History of the Viceroyalty of Buenos Ayres: Containing the Most Accurate Details Relative to the Topography, History, Commerce, Population, Government, etc. etc. of that Valuable Colony.* London: H. D. Symonds, 1807.

Secondary Sources

Acevedo, Edberto Oscar. *Funcionamiento y quiebra del sistema virreinal.* Buenos Aires: Editorial Ciudad de Buenos Aires, 2004.

Acree, William G., Jr., and Alex Boruki, eds. *Jacinto Ventura de Molina y los caminos de la escritura negra en el Río de la Plata.* Montevideo: Linardi y Risso, 2008.

Adelman, Jeremy. *Sovereignty and Revolution in the Iberian Atlantic.* Princeton: Princeton University Press, 2006.

Aguirre, Susana, and Marta Petit. "La contratación de aprendices en la actividad artesanal en la ciudad de Buenos Aires durante el Virreinato," *Temas de historia Argentina* (Universidad Nacional de La Plata, Facultad de Humanidades y Ciencias de la Educación) 16 (1994–1997): 7–15.

Alden, Dauril. "The Undeclared War of 1773–1777: Climax of Luso-Spanish Platine Rivalry." *HAHR* 41.1 (1961): 55–74.

———, ed. *Colonial Roots of Modern Brazil*. Berkeley: University of California Press, 1974.

Amaral, Samuel. "Rural Production and Labour in late Colonial Buenos Aires." *Journal of Latin American Studies* 19.2 (1987): 235–78.

Amaro Peñaflores, René. *Los gremios acostumbrados: los artesanos de Zacatecas, 1780–1870*. Zacatecas: Universidad de Zacatecas, 2002.

Andrien, Kenneth J. "The Spanish Atlantic System." In *Atlantic History: A Critical Appraisal*, edited by Jack D. Greene and Philip D. Morgan, 55–80. Oxford: Oxford University Press, 2009.

Armitage, David, and Michael J. Braddick, eds. *The British Atlantic World, 1500–1800*. London: Palgrave Macmillan, 2002.

Arteaga, Diego. *El artesano en la Cuenca colonial: 1557–1670*. Cuenca: Centro Americano de Artesanias, 2000.

Ashton, J. S. "The Standard of Life of the Workers in England, 1790–1830." *Journal of Economic History* 9 (1949): S19–S38.

Bailyn, Bernard. *Atlantic History: Concept and Contours*. Cambridge: Harvard University Press, 2005.

Bak, Per, and Maya Paczuski. "Complexity, Contingency, and Criticality." *Proceedings of the National Academy of Sciences* 92 (1995): 6,689–96.

Barba, Enrique M. *Don Pedro de Cevallos*. Buenos Aires: Biblioteca Humandades, 1978.

———. *La organización del trabajo en el Buenos Aires colonial*. La Plata: Universidad Nacional de La Plata, 1944.

Barreneche, Osvaldo. *Crime and the Administration of Justice in Buenos Aires, 1785–1853*. Lincoln: University of Nebraska Press, 2006.

Battolla, Octavio C. *La sociedad de antaño*. Buenos Aires: Emecé Editores, 2000.

Bauss, Rudy. "Rio Grande do Sul in the Portuguese Empire: The Formative Years, 1777–1808." *Americas* 39.4 (1983): 519–35.

Benjamin, Thomas. *The Atlantic World: Europeans, Africans, Indians, and Their Shared History, 1400–1900*. Cambridge, UK: Cambridge University Press, 2009.

Bernard, Carmen. "Entre pueblo y plebe: patriotas, africanos en Argentina (1790–1852)." In *Blacks, Coloureds, and National Identity in Nineteenth-Century Latin America*, edited by Nancy Priscilla Naro, 60–80. London: University of London, Institute of Latin American Studies, 2003.

Besio Moreno, Nicolás. *Buenos Aires: Puerto del Río de la Plata, capital de la Argentina, estudio critico de su población, 1536–1936.* Buenos Aires: Talleres Gráficos Tuduri, 1939.

Bowser, Frederick. "The Free Persons of Color in Lima and Mexico City: Manumission and Opportunity, 1580–1650." In *Race and Slavery in the Western Hemisphere: Quantitative Studies,* edited by Stanley L. Engerman and Eugene D. Genovese, 331–68. Princeton: Princeton University Press, 1974.

Boyer, Richard. "Honor among Plebeians." In *Faces of Honor: Sex, Shame, and Violence in Colonial Latin America,* edited by Lyman L. Johnson and Sonya Lipsett-Rivera, 152–78. Albuquerque: University of New Mexico Press, 1998.

Brandes, Stanley. *Metaphors of Masculinity: Sex and Status in Andalusian Folklore.* Philadelphia: University of Pennsylvania Press, 1980.

Braudel, Fernand. *Civilization and Capitalism, 15th–18th Century.* 3 volumes. New York: Harper and Row, 1979.

Breen, T. H., and Timothy Hall. *Colonial America in an Atlantic World.* New York: Longman Publishing Group, 2003.

Brown, Jonathan C. *A Socioeconomic History of Argentina, 1776–1860.* Cambridge, UK: Cambridge University Press, 1979.

Burgin, Miron. *The Economic Aspects of Argentine Federalism, 1820–1852.* New York: Russell and Russell, 1971.

Caillet-Bois, Ricardo Rodolfo. "La américa española y la revolución francesa." *Boletín de la Academia Nacional Historia* 13 (1940): 159–216.

———. *Ensayo sobre el Río de la Plata y la revolución francesa.* Buenos Aires: Facultad de Filosofía y Letras, 1929.

Campagna Caballero, Ernesto. "La población esclava en ciudades puertos del Río de la Plata: Montevideo y Buenos Aires." In *Actas, História e población, estudios sobre America Latina,* 218–25. Brazil: Congreso en Ouro Preto, 1989.

Campbell, J. K. *Honour, Family, and Patronage: A Study of Institutions and Moral Values in a Greek Mountain Community.* Oxford: Oxford University Press, 1964.

Cañizares-Esguerra, Jorge, and Erik R. Seeman, eds. *The Atlantic in Global History, 1500–2000.* Upper Saddle River: Prentice Hall, 2007.

Carmagnani, Marcelo. *El salariado minero en Chile colonial.* Santiago: Universidad Nacional de Chile, 1963.

Carranca y Trujillo, Raul. *Las ordenanzas de gremios de Nueva Espana.* Mexico: Crisol, 1932.

Carrera Stampa, Manuel. *Los gremios mexicanos.* Mexico: Edición y Distribución Ibero Americana de Publicaciones, 1954.

Carroll, Lewis. *Through the Looking-Glass, and What Alice Found There.* New York: Harper and Row, 1902.

Castro Gutiérrez, Felipe. *La extinción de la artesanía gremial*. México: Universidad Nacional Autónoma de México, Instituto de Investigaciones Históricas, 1986.

César, Romeo. *El carnaval de Buenos Aires (1770–1850): El bastión sitiado*. Buenos Aires: Editorial de las Ciencias, 2005.

Chance, John K., and William B. Taylor. "Estate and Class in a Colonial City: Oaxaca in 1792." *Comparative Studies in Society and History* 19.4 (1977): 454–87.

Comité Argentino Para el Bicentenario de la Revolución Francesa. *Imagen y Recepción de la Revolución Francesa en la Argentina. Jornadas Nacionales*. Buenos Aires: Grupo Editor Latinoamericano, 1990.

Connell, K. H. *The Population of Ireland, 1750–1845*. Oxford: Oxford University Press, 1950.

Cooney, Jerry W. "Oceanic Commerce and Platine Merchants, 1796–1806: The Challenge of War." *Americas* 45.4 (1989): 509–24.

Cope, R. Douglas. *The Limits of Racial Domination: Plebeian Society in Colonial Mexico City, 1660–1720*. Madison: University of Wisconsin Press, 1994.

Corbière, Emilio P. *El terrorismo en la revolución de Mayo*. Buenos Aires: Editorial La Facultad, 1937.

Corcuera Ibáñez, Mario. *Santiago Liniers: Primera víctima de la violencia política Argentina*. Buenos Aires: Librería Histórica, 2006.

Coria, Juan Carlos. *Pasado y presente de los negros en Buenos Aires*. Buenos Aires: Editorial J. A. Roca, 1997.

Curcio-Nagy, Linda A. *The Great Festivals of Colonial Mexico City: Performing Power and Identity*. Albuquerque: University of New Mexico Press, 2004.

David, Paul A., and Peter Solar. "A Bicentenary Contribution to the History of the Cost of Living in America." In *Research in Economic History*, volume 2, edited by Paul Uselding, 1–80. Greenwich: JAI Press, 1977.

de Lafuente Machain, R. *Buenos Aires en el siglo XVIII*. Buenos Aires: Municipalidad de Buenos Aires, 1946.

Delaney, Carol. "Seeds of Honor, Fields of Shame." In *Honor and Shame and the Unity of the Mediterranean*, edited by David D. Gilmore, 35–48. Washington: American Anthropological Association, 1987.

Díaz, Marisa M. "Las migraciones internas a la ciudad de Buenos Aires, 1744–1810," *Boletín del instituto de historia Argentina y Americana "Dr. Emilio Ravignani,"* Tercera serie (1997 y 1998): 7–32.

———. "Migraciones y plebe urbana en Buenos Aires, 1744–1810," Thesis, Licenciatura en Historia, Universidad Nacional de Luján, 1996.

Di Meglio, Gabriel. "Ladrones. Una aproximanción a los robos en la ciudad de Buenos Aires, 1810–1830." *Andes* (Universidad Nacional de Salta), no. 17, (2006): 1–5.

———. *¡Viva el pueblo bajo! La plebe urbana de Buenos Aires y la política entre la revolución de Mayo y el Rosismo*. Buenos Aires: Prometeo Libros, 2006.

Dobb, Maurice. *Estudios sobre el desarrollo del capitalismo*. Translated by Luis Etcheverry. Buenos Aires: Siglo XXI, 1971.

Domínguez Compañy, Francisco. "Regulación municipal del trabajo libre de los oficios mecánicos, en Hispanoamérica colonial." *Revista de Historia de América* 103 (1987): 75–106.

Domínguez Ortiz, Antonio. *La sociedad española en el siglo XVIII*. Madrid: Instituto Balmes de Sociologia, 1955.

Dubois, Laurent. *A Colony of Citizens: Revolution and Slave Emancipation in the French Caribbean, 1787–1804*. Chapel Hill: University of North Carolina Press, 2006.

Elissalde, Roberto L. *Diario de Buenos Aires 1810*. Buenos Aires: Aguilar, Altea, Taurus, Alfaguarta, S. A. de Ediciones, 2009.

———. *Historias Ignoradas de las Invasiones Inglesas*. Buenos Aires: Aguilar, Altea, Taurus, Alfaguara, S. A. de Ediciones, 2006.

Elliott, J. H. *Empires of the Atlantic World*. New Haven: Yale University Press, 2006.

Eltis, David. *The Rise of African Slavery in the Americas*. Cambridge, UK: Cambridge University Press, 1999.

Estrada, Marcos de. *Argentinos de orígin Africano*. Buenos Aires: Editorial Universitaria de Buenos Aires, 1979.

Fernández Lalanne, Pedro. *Los Álzaga y sus épocas*. Buenos Aires, 2005.

Florescano, Enrique. "Las crises agrícolas de al época colonial y sus consecuencias económicas." *Cuadernos Americanos* 27 (1968): 180–95.

———. *Precios de maíz y crisis agrícolas en México, 1708–1910*. Mexico: El Colegio de Mexico, 1969.

Fondebrider, Jorge, ed. *La Buenos Aires ajena: Testimonios de extranjeros de 1536 hasta hoy*. Buenos Aires: Emecé Editores, 2001.

Frank, Zephyr. *Dutra's World: Wealth and Family in Nineteenth-Century Rio de Janeiro*. Albuquerque: University of New Mexico Press, 2004.

Freud, Sigmund. *Civilization and Its Discontents*. Edited and translated by James Strachey. New York: W. W. Norton, 1961.

Furlong, Guillermo S. J. *Artesanos Argentinos durante le dominación hispanica*. Buenos Aires: Editorial Huarpes, 1946.

———. *Los industrias en el Río de la Plata desde la colonización hasta 1778*. Buenos Aires: Academia Nacional de la Historia, 1978.

Gallo, Klaus. *Las invasiones Inglesas*. Buenos Aires: Eudeba, 2004.

Galmarini, Hugo R. "Comercio y burocracia colonial. A propósito de Tomás Antonio Romero." *Investigaciones y ensayos* 28 (1980): 387–424.

Garavaglia, Juan Carlos. "Comercio colonial: expansion y crisis." *Polemica, Numero* 5 (1970): 122–40.

———. *Construir el Estado, inventar la Nación: El Río de la Plata, siglos XVIII–XIX*. Buenos Aires: Prometeo Libros, 2007.

———. "Economic Growth and Regional Differentiations: The River Plate Region at the End of the Eighteenth Century." *HAHR* 65.1 (1985): 51–89.

———. "Los labradores de San Isidro (siglos XVII–XIX)." *Desarrollo Económico* 32 (1993): 513–42.

———. "El pan de cada día: El Mercado del trigo en Buenos Aires, 1770–1820." *Boletín del instituto de historia Argentina y Americana "Dr. E. Ravignani."* Tercera serie 4 (1991): 7–29.

———. "Precios de los productos rurales y precios de la tierra en la campaña de Buenos Aires: 1750–1826." *Boletín del instituto de historia Argentina y Americana "Dr. Emilio Ravignani."* Tercera serie 11 (1995): 65–112.

———. "El teatro del poder: ceremonias, tensiones y conflictos en el estado colonial." *Boletín del instituto de historia Argentina y Americana "Dr. Emilio Ravignani."* Tercera serie 14 (1996): 7–30.

García Belsunce, César., et al. *Buenos Aires: su gente, 1810–1830*. Buenos Aires: Emecé, 1976.

García-Bryce, Iñigo L. *Crafting the Republic: Lima's Artisans and Nation Building in Peru, 1821–1879*. Albuquerque: University of New Mexico Press, 2004.

Gaviria Liévano, Enrique. *El liberalismo y la insurrección de los artesanos contra el librecambio: primeras manifestaciones socialistas en Colombia*. Bogotá: Universidad de Bogotá, 2002.

Gazmuri Riveros, Cristián. "Los artesanos de Santiago en 1850, y el despertar político del sector popular chileno." *Revista de Indias* 5.192 (1991): 397–416.

Gelman, Jorge. *Campesinos y estancieros*. Buenos Aires: Editorial Los Libros del Riel, 1998.

———. "Sobre esclavos, peones, gauchos y campesinos: el trabajo y los trabajadores en una estancia colonial rioplatense." In *Estructuras Sociales y Mentalidades en América Latina: Siglos XVII y XVIII*, edited by Torcuato Di Tella, 241–79. Buenos Aires: Fundación Simón Rodríguez, 1990.

Gilboy, Elizabeth W. "The Cost of Living and Real Wages in Eighteenth Century England." *Review of Economic Statistics* 18.3 (1936): 135–37.

Goldberg, Marta B. "La población negra y mulata de la ciudad de Buenos Aires, 1810–1840." *Desarrollo Económico* 16.61 (1976): 75–99.

Goldberg, Marta B., and Silvia C. Mallo. "La población africana en Buenos Aires y su campaña. Formas de vida y de subsistencia (1750–1850)." *Temas de Africa y Asia* (Facultad de Filosofia y Letras, Universidad de Buenos Aires) 2 (1993): 15–70.

Goldberg de Flinchman, Marta B., and L. B. Jany. "Algunos problemas referentes a la situación del esclavo en el Río de la Plata." *IV Congreso Internacional de Historia de América* (Academia Nacional de la Historia) 6 (1966): 61–75.

Goldman, Noemí. "Los 'Jacobinos' en el Río de la Plata: Modelo, discursos y practicas (1810–1815)." In *Imágen y recepción de la Revolución Francesa en la Argentina*, edited by Comité Argentino para el Bicentenario de la Revolución Francesa, 7–26. Buenos Aires: Grupo Editor Latinoamericano, 1990.

Grafe, Regina, and María Alejandra Irigoin. "The Spanish Empire and Its Legacy: Fiscal Redistribution and Political Conflict in Colonial and Post-Colonial Spanish America." *Journal of Global History* 1 (2006): 241–67.

Grainger, John D., ed. *The Royal Navy in the River Plata, 1806–1807*. Cambridge, UK: Scholar Press for The Navy Records Society, 1996.

Groussac, Paul. *Santiago Liniers: Conde de Buenos Aires*. Buenos Aires: El Elefante Blanco, 1998.

Gutman, Herbert. *Work, Culture, and Society*. Oxford: Basil Blackwell, 1977.

Halperín Donghi, Tulio. *Guerra y finanzas en los origenes del estado Argentino, 1791–1850*. Buenos Aires: Editorial de Belgrano, 1982.

———. *Politics, Economics, and Society in Argentina in the Revolutionary Period*. Cambridge: Cambridge University Press, 1975.

———. "Revolutionary Militarization in Buenos Aires 1806–1815." *Past and Present* 40 (1968): 84–107.

Hamilton, Earl J. *War and Prices in Spain, 1651–1800*. Cambridge: Harvard University Press, 1947.

Hanon, Maxine. *Buenos Aires desde las quintas de Retiro a Recoleta*. Buenos Aires: Editorial El Jagüel, 2000.

Hanson Jones, Alice. *Wealth of a Nation to Be*. New York: Columbia University Press, 1980.

Harth-Terre, Emilio. "El artesano negro en la arquitectura virreinal Limana." *Revista del Archivo del Peru* 25 (Julio–Dic. 1961): 360–430.

Hernández, Pablo José. *El extrañamiento de los Jesuitas de Río de la Plata y de las misiones del Paraguay por decreto de Carlos III*. Madrid: V. Suarez, 1908.

Herr, Richard. *The Eighteenth-Century Revolution in Spain*. Princeton: Princeton University Press, 1958.

Heywood, Linda M., and John K. Thornton. *Central Africans, Atlantic Creoles, and the Foundation of the Americas, 1585–1660*. Cambridge: Cambridge University Press, 2007.

Hobsbawm, E. J. *Industry and Empire*. London: Penguin Books, 1990.

Irigoin, María Alejandra. "Gresham on Horseback: The Monetary Roots of Spanish American Political Fragmentation in the Nineteenth Century." *Economic History Review* 62.3 (2009): 551–75.

Johnson, Harold B., Jr. "A Preliminary Inquiry into Money, Prices, and Wages in Rio de Janeiro, 1763–1823." In *Colonial Roots of Modern Brazil*, edited by Dauril Alden, 231–83. Berkeley: University of California Press, 1974.

Johnson, Lyman L. "Artisans." In *Cities and Society in Colonial Latin America*, edited by Louisa Schell Hoberman and Susan Migden Socolow, 227–50. Albuquerque: University of New Mexico Press, 1986.

———. "The Competition of Slave and Free Labor in Artisanal Production: Buenos Aires, 1770–1815." *International Review of Social History* 40 (1996): 409–24.

———. "Dangerous Words, Provocative Gestures, Violent Acts: The Disputed Hierarchies of Plebeian Life in Colonial Buenos Aires." In *The Faces of Honor. Sex, Shame, and Violence in Colonial Latin America*, edited by Lyman L. Johnson and Sonya Lipsett-Rivera, 127–51. Albuquerque: University of New Mexico Press, 1998.

———. "The Entrepreneurial Reorganization of an Artisan Trade: The Bakers of Buenos Aires." *Americas* 32. 2 (1980): 139–60.

———. "Estimaciones de la población de Buenos Aires en 1744, 1778 y 1810." *Desarrollo Económico* 73.19 (1979): 107–19.

———. "The Impact of Racial Discrimination on Black Artisans in Colonial Buenos Aires." *Social History* 6.3 (1981): 301–16.

———. "'A Lack of Legitimate Obedience and Respect': Slaves and Their Masters in the Courts of Late Colonial Buenos Aires." *HAHR* 87.4 (2007): 631–57.

———. "Manumission in Colonial Buenos Aires, 1776–1810." *HAHR* 59.2 (1979): 258–79.

———. "The Racial Limits of Guild Solidarity: An Example from Colonial Buenos Aires." *Revista de Historia de America* 99 (1985): 7–26.

———. "The Role of Apprenticeship in Colonial Buenos Aires." *Revista de Historia de América* 103 (1987): 7–30.

———. "Salarios, precios y costo de vida en el Buenos Aires colonial tardío." *Boletín del instituto de historia Argentina y Americana* "Dr. E. Ravignani." Tercera serie 1 (1990): 133–58.

———. "The Silversmiths of Buenos Aires: A Case Study in the Failure of Corporate Social Organization." *Journal of Latin American Studies* 8.2 (1976): 181–213.

Johnson, Lyman L., and Sonya Lipsett-Rivera, eds. *The Faces of Honor. Sex, Shame, and Violence in Colonial Latin America*. Albuquerque: University of New Mexico Press, 1998.

Johnson, Lyman L., and Susan M. Socolow. "Población y espacio en el Buenos Aires del siglo XVIII." *Desarrollo Económico* 20.79 (1980): 329–50.

Kicza, John E. *Colonial Entrepreneurs: Families and Business in Bourbon Mexico City.* Albuquerque: University of New Mexico Press, 1983.

Kiernan, James Patrick. "Baptism and Manumission: Paraty, 1789–1822," *Social Science History* 3.1 (1978): 56–71.

Knight, Franklin, and Peggy K. Liss, eds. *Atlantic Port Cities: Economy, Culture, and Society in the Atlantic World, 1650–1850.* Knoxville: University of Tennessee Press, 1991.

Kraus, Michael. *The Atlantic Civilization: Eighteenth-Century Origins.* Ithaca: Cornell University Press, 1949.

Lahmeyer Lobo, Eulalia Maria, and Octavio Canavarros et al. "Estudo das categorias socioprofissionais, dos salarios e do custo da alimentação no Rio de Janeiro de 1820 a 1930." *Revista brasileira de economia* 27. 4 (1973): 129–76.

Levene, Ricardo. *Ensayo histórico sobre la revolución de Mayo y Mariano Moreno.* 3 volumes, fourth edition. Buenos Aires: Ediciones Peusar, 1960.

———. "Escritos de Mariano Moreno sobre las Invasiones Inglesas." In *La Reconquista y Defensa de Buenos Aires.* Instituto de Estudios Historicos sobre la Reconquista y Defensa de Buenos Aires, 1806–1807. Buenos Aires: Peusar, 1947.

———. *Obras de Ricardo Levene.* 3 vols. *Investigaciones acerca de la Historia Economica del Virreinato del Plata.* Buenos Aires: Comisión Nacional Ejecutiva del 150 Aniversario de la Revolución de Mayo, 1962.

Lewin, Boleslao. "La 'conspiración de los Franceses' en Buenos Aires (1795)." *Anuario* 4.4 (1960): 9–57.

———. *Rousseau y la independencia Argentina y América.* Buenos Aires: Editorial Universitaria de Buenos Aires, 1967.

Linebaugh, Peter, and Marcus Rediker. *The Many-Headed Hydra: Sailors, Slaves, Commoners, and the Hidden History of the Revolutionary Atlantic.* Boston: Beacon Press, 2000.

Livi-Bacci, Massimo. "Fertility and Population Growth in Spain in the Eighteenth and Nineteenth Centuries." *Historical Population Studies*, special issue, *Daedalus* 97.2 (1968): 523–35.

Lockhart, James. *Spanish Peru, 1532–1560.* Madison: University of Wisconsin Press, 1968.

Lokke, Carl Ludwig. "French Designs on Paraguay in 1803." *HAHR* 8.3 (1928): 392–405.

López Cantos, Ángel. *Juegos, fiestas y diversiones en la América Española.* Madrid: Editorial Mapfre, 1992.

Lozier Almazán, Bernardo. *Beresford Governador de Buenos Aires.* Buenos Aires: Editorial Galerna, 1994.

———. *Liniers y su tiempo.* Buenos Aires: Emecé Editores, 1990.

————. *Martín de Álzaga: historia de una trágica ambición*. Buenos Aires: Ediciones Ciudad, 1998.

Lynch, John. *Spanish Colonial Administration, 1782–1810: The Intendant System in the Viceroyalty of the Río de la Plata*. New York: Greenwood Press, 1969.

MacKay, Ruth. *Lazy and Improvident People: Myth and Reality in the Writing of Spanish History*. Ithaca: Cornell University Press, 2006.

Main, Gloria. *Tobacco Colony: Life in Early Maryland, 1650–1720*. Princeton: Princeton University Press, 1982.

Mangan, Jane E. *Trading Roles: Gender, Ethnicity, and the Urban Economy in Colonial Potosí*. Durham: Duke University Press, 2005.

Marfany, Roberto H. *El cabildo de Mayo*. Buenos Aires: Ediciones Theoria, 1961.

————. "La Primera Junta de Gobierno de Buenos Aires (1810)." *Estudios Americanos* 19.102 (1960): 223–34.

————. "El pronunciamiento de Mayo." *Historia, Revista Trimestral de Historia Argentina* 3.12 (1958): 61–126.

————. *La semana de Mayo, diario de un testigo*. Buenos Aires: privately published, 1955.

Márquez Miranda, Fernando. *Ensayo sobre los artifices de la platería en el Buenos Aires colonial*. Buenos Aires: Imprenta de la Universidad, 1933.

Martin Saint-Leon, Étienne. *Historia de las corporaciones de oficio*. Translated by Alfredo Cepeda. Buenos Aires: Editorial Partenon, 1947.

Martínez, Alberto B. *Historia demográfica de Buenos Aires*. Volume 3. Dirección General de Estadística Municipal. Buenos Aires, 1910.

Martiré, Eduardo. *1808 La clave de emancipación hispanoamericana*. Buenos Aires: Elefante Blanco, 2002.

Massot, Vicente. *Matar y morir. La violencia política en la Argentina (1806–1980)*. Buenos Aires: Emecé, 2003.

Mattoso, Katia M. Queiros. "A proposíto de Cartas da Alforria na Bahia, 1779–1850." *Anais de Historia* 4 (1972): 23–25.

Mayor Mora, Alberto. *Cabezas duras y dedos inteligentes: estilo de vida y cultura técnica de los artesanos colombianos del siglo XIX*. 2nd ed. Medellín: Hombre Nuevo Editores, 2003.

McCaa, Robert, Stuart B. Schwartz, and Arturo Grubesich. "Race and Class in Colonial Latin America: A Critique." *Comparative Studies and History* 21.3 (July 1979): 421–33.

Ménétra, Jacques-Louis. *Journal of My Life*. Translated by Arthur Goldhammer, introduction and commentary by Daniel Roche. New York: Columbia University Press, 1986.

Milton, Cynthia E. *The Many Meanings of Poverty: Colonialism, Social Compacts, and Assistance in Eighteenth-Century Ecuador*. Stanford: Stanford University Press, 2007.

Mitchell, B. R. *European Historical Statistics, 1750–1970*. New York: Columbia University Press, 1975.

Mitre, Bartolomé. *Historia de Belgrano y de la independencia Argentina*. Buenos Aires: Editorial Suelo Argentino, 1959.

Montgomery, David. "The Working Classes of the Pre-Industrial American City, 1780–1830." *Labor History* 9.1 (1968): 3–22.

Moreno, Manuel. *Memorias de Mariano Moreno*. Buenos Aires: Carlos Pérez Editor, 1968.

Moutoukias, Zacarias. *Contrabando y control colonial en el siglo XVII*. Buenos Aires: Centro Editor de America Latina, 1988.

———. "Power, Corruption, and Commerce: The Making of the Local Administrative Structure in Seventeenth-Century Buenos Aires." *HAHR* 68. 4 (1988): 771–801.

Moyano, Hugo. *La organización de los gremios en Córdoba: sociedad artesanal y producción artesanal, 1810–1820*. Córdoba: Centro de Estudios Históricos, 1986.

Ortega, Exequiel César. *El complot colonial*. Buenos Aires: Editorial Ayacucho, 1947.

———. *La primera pena de muerte resulta por la junta de Mayo*. Buenos Aires: Editorial Lumen, 1954.

———. *Santiago de Liniers: Un hombre del antiguo regimen*. La Plata: Universidad Nacional de la Plata, 1946.

Ortiz Oderigo, Néstor. "Las 'naciones' africanas." *Todo es Historia* 162 (1980): 28–34.

———. "Origenes etnoculturales de los negros argentinos." *Historia* 7 (1982): 100–113.

Paquette, Gabriel. *Enlightenment, Governance, and Reform in Spain and Its Empire, 1759–1808*. Houndsmills: Palgrave Macmillian Press, 2008.

Pereira Salas, Eugenio. *Juegos y alegrias coloniales en Chile*. Santiago: Empresa Editora Zig-Zag, 1947.

Pérez Toledo, Sonia. *Los hijos del trabajo: los artesanos de la ciudad de México, 1780–1853*. Mexico: Colegio de México, 1996.

Pérez Vila, Manuel. "El artesanado: la formación de una clase media propiamente americana, 1500–1800." *Boletín de la Academia Nacional de la Historia* (Caracas) 69.274 (1986): 327–44.

Phelps Brown, E. H., and Sheila V. Hopkins. "Seven Centuries of Building Wages." *Economica* (New Series) 22.3 (1955): 195–206.

Pitt-Rivers, Julian. *The Fate of Shechem or the Politics of Sex: Essays in the*

Anthropology of the Mediterranean. Cambridge, UK: Cambridge University Press, 1977.

Plaza Prieto, Juan. *Estructura económica de España en el siglo XVIII.* Madrid: Confereración Española de Cajas de Ahorros, 1975.

Pozzi Albornoz, Ismael R. *El ataque británico al Plata indiano, 1806: ocupación y reconquista de Buenos Aires.* Buenos Aires: Editorial Nueva Militaria Argentina, 2009.

Proctor, Frank. "Gender and Manumission of Slaves in New Spain." *HAHR* 86.2 (2006): 309–36.

Puentes, Gabriel A. *Don Francisco Javier de Elío en el Río de la Plata.* Buenos Aires: Ediciones Esnaola, 1966.

Pueyrredón, Carlos A. *1810 La revolución de Mayo segun amplia documentación de la época.* Buenos Aires: Ediciones Peusar, 1953.

Puiggrós, Rodolfo. *Los caudillos de la revolución de Mayo.* Buenos Aires: Editorial Contrapunto, 1971.

Quesada, Héctor C. *El alcalde Álzaga, la tragedia de su vida.* Buenos Aires: Editorial El Ateneo, 1936.

Quiroz, Francisco. *La protesta de los artesanos, Lima-Callao, 1858.* Lima: Universidad Nacional Mayor de San Marcos, 1988.

Ravignani, Emilio. "El cuerpo de plateros en el Río de la Plata." *Nosotros* (Sept. 1916): 305–15.

Rawls, John. *A Theory of Justice.* Cambridge: Harvard University, Belknap Press, 1971.

Ringrose, David R. *Madrid and the Spanish Economy, 1560–1850.* Berkeley: University of California Press, 1983.

Roberts, Carlos. *Las invasiones inglesas del Río de la Plata, 1806–1807.* Buenos Aires: Emecé Editores, 2000.

Rock, Howard B. *Artisans of the New Republic.* New York: New York University Press, 1979.

Rodríguez Molas, Ricardo. "Algunos aspectos del negro en la sociedad rioplatense del siglo XVIII." *Anuario* 3. 3 (1958): 81–106.

———. "Esclavitud africana, religión y origen étnico." *Ibero-amerikanisches Archivo* 14 (1988): 128–29.

———. *Las pulperías: La vida de nuestro pueldo.* Buenos Aires: Centro Editor de America Latina, 1982.

Romano, Ruggiero. "Movimiento de los precios y desarrollo económico: el caso de Sudamérica en el siglo XVIII." *Desarrollo Económico* 3.1–2 (1963): 31–43.

Romano, Ruggiero, and Lyman L. Johnson. "Una polémica sobre la historia de precios en el Buenos Aires virreinal." *Boletín del instituto de historia Argentina y Americana "Dr. Emilio Ravignani".* Tercera serie 6 (1992): 149–72.

Romero, Luis Alberto. *Buenos Aires: La sociedad criolla, 1810–1850.* Buenos Aires: Centro de Investigaciones Sociales sobre el Estado y la Administración, 1980.

Rosal, Angel Miguel. "Artesanos de color en Buenos Aires, 1750–1850." *Bolétin del instituto de historia Argentina y Americana "Dr. Emilio Ravignani"* 17.27 (1982): 331–54.

———. "El tráfico esclavista y el estado saniterio de la ciudad de Buenos Aires (1750–1810)." *Jornadas de Historia de la Ciudad de Buenos Aires,* La salud en Buenos Aires, 2 (1985): 231–40.

Rudé, George. *La multitud en la historia.* Translated by Ofelia Castillo. Buenos Aires: Siglo XXI, 1971.

Ruiz-Guiñazu, Enrique. *El Presidente Saavedra y el pueblo soberano de 1810.* Buenos Aires: Estrada Editores, 1960.

Sabato, Hilda. *Trabajar para vivir o vivir para trabajar: Empleo ocasional y escasez de obra en Buenos Aires, cuidad y compaña, 1850–1880.* Buenos Aires: Centro de Investigaciones Sociales sobre el Estado y la Administración, 1983.

Sabsay, Fernando L. *Hombres de la revolución: segundo centenario.* Buenos Aires: Librería Histórica, 2006.

Saguier, Eduardo. "The Social Impact of a Middleman Minority in a Divided Host Society: The Case of the Portuguese in Early Seventeenth-Century Buenos Aires." *HAHR* 65.3 (1985): 467–91.

Salas, Alberto Mario. *Diario de Buenos Aires, 1806–1807.* Buenos Aires: Editorial Sudamericana, 1981.

Salduna, Horacio. *El ultimo virrey.* Buenos Aires: Ediciones Valdez, 1987.

Samayoa Guevara, Hector Humberto. *Los gremios de artesanos en la ciudad de Guatemala.* Guatemala: Universidad de San Carlos de Guatemala, 1962.

Sánchez de Thompson, Mariquita. *Intimidad y política, diario, cartas y recuerdos.* Edited by María Gabriela Mizraje. Buenos Aires: Adriana Hidalgo Editora, 2003.

Santos Barreto, Daniela. "A despeito do defeito: artesãos na cidade do Rio de Janeiro, c. 1690-c. 1750." *Acervo* (Rio de Janeiro) 15.2 (2002): 69–86.

Schell Hoberman, Louisa, and Susan M. Socolow. *Cities and Society in Colonial Latin America.* Albuquerque: University of New Mexico Press, 1986.

Scheuss de Studer, Elena F. *La trata de negros en el Río de la Plata durante el siglo XVIII.* Buenos Aires: Libros de Hispanoamerica, 1984.

Schwartz, Stuart B. "The Manumission of Slaves in Colonial Brazil: Bahia, 1684–1745." *HAHR* 54.4 (1974): 603–35.

Scott, Joan Wallach. *The Classworkers of Carmaux.* Cambridge: Harvard University Press, 1974.

Scott, Julius S. "A Common Wind: Currents of Afro-American Communication in the Age of the Haitian Revolution." PhD diss., Duke University, 1986.

Seed, Patricia, and Philip F. Rust. "Estate and Class in Colonial Oaxaca Revisited." *Comparative Studies in Society and History* 25.4 (1983): 703–10.

Segreti, Carlos S. A. *Bernardino Rivadavia*. Buenos Aires: Planeta, 1999.

Shammas, Carole. "Food Expenditures and Economic Well-being in Early Modern England." *Journal of Economic History* 43.1 (1983): 89–100.

Sierra, Julio A. *Fusilados. Historias de condenados a muerte en la Argentina*. Buenos Aires: Sudamericana, 2008.

Silva, Hernán Asdrúbal. "El cabildo, el abasto de carne y la ganadería: Buenos Aires en la primera mitad del siglo XVIII." *Investigaciones y Ensayos* 3 (1967): 393–462.

———. "La grasa y el sebo: dos elementos vitals para la colonia; Buenos Aires en la primera mitad del siglo XVIII." *Revista de Historia Americana y Argentina* (Mendoza) 8.15 (1970): 39–53.

———. "Hamburgo y el Río de la Plata: Vinculaciones económicas a fines de la época colonial." *Jahrbuch für Geschichte von Staat, Wirtschaft und Gesellschaft Lateinamerikas* (Köln, Germany: Böhlau Verlag) 21 (1984): 189–209.

Smith, Billy G. "The Material Lives of Laboring Philadelphians, 1750–1800." *William and Mary Quarterly* 38.2 (1981): 163–202.

Smithsonian Institution. Traveling Exhibition Service, American Revolution Bicentennial Administration. *Silverworks from the Río de la Plata, Argentina (18th and 19th centuries)*. Washington: The Service, 1976.

Socolow, Susan M. *The Bureaucrats of Buenos Aires, 1769–1810*. Durham: Duke University Press, 1987.

———. *The Merchants of Buenos Aires, 1778–1810: Family and Commerce*. Cambridge, UK: Cambridge University Press, 1978.

Solomianski, Alejandro. *Identidades secretas: la negritude Argentina*. Buenos Aires: Beatriz Viterbo Editora, 2003.

Sonenscher, Michael. *Work and Wages: Natural Law, Politics and the Eighteenth-Century French Trades*. Cambridge, UK: Cambridge University Press, 1989.

Sowell, David. *The Early Colombian Labor Movement: Artisans and Politics in Bogotá, 1832–1919*. Philadelphia: Temple University Press, 1992.

Tandeter, Enrique, and Nathan Wachtel. *Precios y produccíon agraria: Potosí y Charcas en el siglo XVIII*. Buenos Aires: El Centro de Estudios de Estado y Sociedad, 1983.

Thésée, Françoise. *Négociants bordelais et colons de Saint-Domingue*. Liaisons D'Habitations Paris: Société Française D'histoire D'Outre-Mer, 1972.

Thompson, E. P. *The Making of the English Working Class*. New York: Pantheon Books, 1964.

Torre Revello, José. *Crónicas del Buenos Aires colonial*. Buenos Aires: Taurus, 2004.

————. *El gremio de plateros en las Indias Occidentales*. Buenos Aires: Imprenta de la Universida, 1932.

————. "Origen y aplicación del código negrero en la América española (1788–1794)." *Bolétin de Investigaciones Historicas* 15.53 (1932): 42–50.

Torres, Luis María. *La administración de temporalidades en el Río de la Plata*. Buenos Aires: Talleres Gráficos, 1917.

Tucker, Rufus S. "Real Wages of Artisans in London, 1729–1935." *Journal of American Statistical Association* 31.193 (1936): 73–85.

Twinam, Ann. *Public Lives, Private Secrets: Gender, Honor, Sexuality, and Illegitimacy in Colonial Spanish America*. Stanford: Stanford University Press, 1999.

Urquijo, José M. Mariluz. *La industria sombrerera porteña, 1780–1835*. Buenos Aires: Instituto de Investigaciones de Historia del Derecho, 2002.

————. "La mano de obra en la industria porteña (1810–1835)." *Academia Nacional de la Historia Boletín* 33 (1962): 617–18.

————. *El virreinato del Río de la Plata en la epoca del Marques de Avilés*. Buenos Aires: Academia Nacional de la Historia, 1964.

Urquiza, Fernando. "Etiquetas y conflictos. El virrey, el obispo y el cabildo en el Río de la Plata en la segunda mitad del siglo XVIII." *Anuario de Estudios Americanos* 50.1 (1993): 55–100.

Valenzuela Márquez, Jaime. "Poder y pirotecnia, artesanos y mapuches: apogeo barroco de proclamaciones reales de Chile, 1760–1789." *Colonial Latin American Historical Review* 14.1 (2005): 49–78.

Vardi, Liana. "The Abolition of Guilds during the French Revolution." *French Historical Studies* 15.4 (1988): 704–17.

Williams Álzaga, Enrique. *Álzaga 1812*. Buenos Aires: Emecé Editores, 1968.

————. *Dos Revoluciones*. Buenos Aires: Emecé Editores, 1963.

————. *Fuga del General Beresford*. Buenos Aires: Emecé Editores, 1965.

————, ed. *Martín de Álzaga Cartas (1806–1807)*. Buenos Aires: Emecé Editores, 1972.

Williamson, Jeffrey G., and Peter H. Lindert. *American Inequality: A Macroeconomic History*. New York: Academic Press, 1980.

Woodward, Donald. "Wage Rates and Living Standards in PreIndustrial England." *Past and Present* 91 (1981): 28–46.

Index

guild and, 135–41; political empowerment of, 264–66; racial tensions and, 51–52; in shoemakers' guild, 96–98, 105–10, 119–26, 150–51; shoemakers' guild formation by, 126–32, 150–51; in silversmiths' guild, 96–98, 141–46; as slave owners, 18; trade liberalization and empowerment of, 275

Castelli, Juan José, 277, 286–88, 290, 364n36

Castillo, Agustín, 294

Castro, Tadeo, 62

Catana, Bartolo, 135

Cavenagoy, Lorenzo, 192

Ceballos, Gregorio, 294

Ceballos, Mariano, 312n86

cedaẓero (slaughtering tool artisan), 61

census statistics: housing fluidity of artisans reflected in, 63–65; pardo and moreno shoemakers' guild and, 135–41; population demographics for Buenos Aires and, 28–31, 303n59; for shoemakers' guild, 113–16, 319n113; on silversmiths and shoemakers, 94–98; slave trade and underestimates in, 37–39, 302n46, 304nn66–68; undercounting in, 29–31, 302n40

Cerro Sáenz, Manuel de, 320n25

Cevallos, Josef Nicolás, 59–61

Cevallos, Pedro de, 220–21, 227

Charles IV (king of Spain), 260, 266, 288

Charlevoix, Padre, 37

Chiclana, Feliciano Antonio, 286–87, 289–90, 293–95, 362n11

Cisneros, Baltasar Hidalgo de (viceroy), 5, 292, 359n149; exile of, 284–87; militarization and, 261–62; political activities of, 271–79, 358n144, 359n145, 359n149

class structure: of artisan workers, 52–53; cultural practice and vocational formation and, 53–61; culture of honor and, 68–75; militarization of Buenos Aires and alteration of, 253–57, 271; shoemakers' guild regulations and influence of, 88–90

clothing, cost-of-living fluctuations and ownership of, 194–97, 336n66

cockfighting, popularity among plebeians of, 80–82

Cofradía de San Eloy, 92–94, 311n75

cofradías (lay brotherhoods): black artisans' formation of, 28; in colonial era, 10; religious and civic activities of, 76, 311n75; for shoemakers' guilds, 107–10, 125–26, 317n83, 320n25, 325n101; of silversmiths, 93–94. *See also hermandades*

Colares, Juan Ángel, 294

colonialism: economic conditions of plebeians and, 197–208; guild formation and, 10, 54–61; silversmiths' guilds and, 91–94

commercial integration: guild formation threatened by, 2–3; plebe history and role of, 14

commissary records, cost-of-living fluctuations and, 191–97

Concolorcorvo. *See* Carrió de la Vandera, Alonso (Concolorcorvo)

Conde de Liniers family, 170–77, 329n61. *See also* Liniers, Don Santiago de

construction trades: earnings vs. wages in, 235–43; wages and occupational categories in, 218–32. *See also* brick

Garavaglia, Juan Carlos, 331n8

García, Don Baltasar, 159–60

García López, Antonio, 113, 119–23, 319n113

García Martinez de Caceres y Garre, Don Josef, 175

gender issues: culture of honor and masculine identity, 69–75; labor trends and, 11–12; migration patterns to Buenos Aires and, 33–35

gente decente: apprenticeships and importance of, 12; in late colonial Buenos Aires, 23–24; ready-to-wear shoes for, 141; slave ownership by, 38–39, 152

geopolitics: French Conspiracy of 1795 and, 177–78; impact in Buenos Aires of, 154–57; militarization of Buenos Aires and, 260–62; political transformation in Buenos Aires and, 280–81

Gillespie, Alexander, 37, 194–95, 356n118

Gómez Belmundes, Joseph, 209–10

González Silba, Manuel, 120

Gorriti, Ignacio de, 290

government expenditures, wage increases linked to, 220–32

Grande, Salvador, 111, 323n77

Great Britain: invasions by, of Buenos Aires, 3–4, 8, 15–16, 250–62, 288, 346n8; Spanish relations with, 261–62

Grimau, Antonio, 328n34, 328n44

Guatemala City, guild formation in, 10

Guild of Pardo and Moreno Shoemakers, formation of, 89–90, 105–10, 114–18, 126–41, 319n111

guild system: in colonial Buenos Aires, 10; earnings vs. wages and, 240–43; ethnic tensions within, 11; in Europe, 54–61, 87–90, 118–19, 307n6, 310n48, 315n23; migrant hierarchy within, 44–47; pardo and moreno shoemakers' guild and models of, 114–18, 126–32, 135–41; as political and legal tool, 3–4; political transformation and demise of, 280–81; racial segregation in, 2, 98–102; shoemakers' guild model and, 1–2, 57–61; social origins and cultural practice in, 52–53; upward mobility through, 94–98; vocational formation and cultural initiation through, 53–61. *See also specific guilds*

Guillermo, José, 32

Gutierrez, Cayetano, 62

Gutiérrez de la Concha, Juan, 283–87

Guzman, Joaquin, 264

Haitian slave rebellion, 151, 154–57, 164, 171. *See also* Saint-Domingue slave rebellion

Halperín Donghi, Tulio, 222, 297nn2–3

heavy industry in Buenos Aires, 201–8

hermandades, 76, 160–62. *See also cofradías* (lay brotherhoods)

Herrera, Juan, 294

historiography: concerning Buenos Aires, 8–9, 297n2; labor history and interdisciplinary research of, 6–7

homeownership among artisan community, 66–68; social determinants of success and, 208–12; wealth accumulation through, 179–82, 203–8. *See also* real estate

honor, culture of: construction of masculinity and, 68–75; guild formation and, 11–12; in plebeian community, 51–83 household goods, scarcity of, for plebeians, 205–8

housing arrangements of artisans, 62–65, 215–16; culture of honor and masculine identity and, 71–75; earnings vs. wages and, 240–43; militarization and housing allowances and, 263–66; patterns of, 187–90. *See also* homeownership among artisan community

housing construction in Buenos Aires, 24–26; culture of honor and masculine identity and, 72–75; living arrangements of artisan workers and, 62–65; for pardo and moreno shoemakers, 117–18

Huidobro, Pasqual Ruiz, 354n89

Ibárzabal, Francisco, 203, 211

Ignacia, María, 166

immigrants in Buenos Aires: artisan community and, 32–35, 314n8; credit access of, 207–8; culture of honor and masculine identity and, 73–75; in late colonial Buenos Aires, 19–28, 31–35, 49–50; political empowerment of, 270–71; real wages and influx of, 245–47. *See also* internal migration to Buenos Aires, patterns of

income patterns: of artisan workers, 52–53, 182–87; earnings vs. wages and, 240–43; rent fluctuations and, 187–90; wages and occupations and, 216–32

indigenous peoples: apprenticeship barriers for, 54–61; migration patterns to Buenos Aires of, 34–35

indios, shoemakers' guild formation and, 95–98, 114–15, 120, 122–26

inheritance, wealth accumulation through, 210–12

integration of slave and free labor, 24, 42–43, 50, 82–83; culture of honor and masculine identity and, 73–75; international trade and, 154–57; shoemakers' guild regulations barring, 100–102, 319n111

internal migration to Buenos Aires, patterns of, 32–35, 303n55; apprenticeship accessibility and, 55–61; artisan community and, 44–47; marriage and family habits and, 66–68; silversmiths and shoemakers and, 96–98; wages and workforce participation and, 232–33

inventories of plebeians, valuations for, 199–208, 337nn75–76

job instability, fluidity of housing arrangements for workers and, 63–65

John Carter Brown Library, xiii

jornaleros (day laborers), 11–12; apprenticeship system and, 58–61; in artisan community, 43–47

journeyman workers: apprenticeship accessibility and, 55–61; black and casta shoemakers as, 136–41; earnings vs. wages for, 234–43; food rations for, 193–97; housing arrangements for, 62–65, 190; integration of slave and free labor and, 42–43; marriage and family patterns for, 65–68; of migrant workers, 45–47, 49–50; shoemakers' guild formation and, 87–90, 100–102; in silversmiths' and shoemakers' guilds, 97–98; wages and skill levels of, 217–32; wealth accumulation for, 198–208

Orellano, Rodrigo Antonio de (Bishop), 283–87, 293–95, 364n36
Orrega, José Antonio, 74–75
Ortega, Manuel, 205
outdoor trades: alliances with other artisans in, 65; cabildo regulation of, 24, 27; census underestimates of, 29, 55–56; cost-of-living fluctuations and, 191–97; decline in late colonial era of, 5–6; decline of apprenticeships in, 58–59; earnings of, 14, 68, 306n2; integration of free and slave labor in, 24, 41–42, 50; locally born artisans in, 45; slave ownership by, 39, 42, 58–59, 68; urban congestion in Buenos Aires and, 24–28; wages and occupational categories for, 216–32; work patterns in, 215
out-migration, in colonial Buenos Aires, 9

Padín, Jacobo, 208–9
Palavecino, Pedro, 204
papel de venta, slave ownership transfer and, 39–40, 152
Paraguay, migration to Buenos Aires from, 33–35
pardos: apprenticeship accessibility and, 55–61; culture of honor and masculine identity and, 71–75; failure of guilds and, 117–18; migration patterns to Buenos Aires of, 34–35; political empowerment through militarization, 263–66, 270–71, 352n78, 354n89, 360n162, 365n37; shoemakers' guild formation and, 89–90, 105–10, 114–18, 126–41, 319n111; as silversmiths and shoemakers, 94–95
Pasos, Ildefonso, 263, 362n9

Pasos, Juan José, 277, 290
pasquines, distribution of, 155–56, 257
Patricios military unit: militarization of Buenos Aires and, 269–70, 351n64, 352n78, 354n91, 355n100; mutiny in, 288–95, 357n134, 363n15, 364n30, 365n37, 365n40
Paula Sanz, Francisco de, 92–94, 98, 113, 288, 318n99
peinero (comb maker), 62
Pellizar, Sebastian, 153
pelota, popularity of, 81–82
pension lotteries, 346n4, 355nn107–8
peones, apprenticeship system and, 58–61
Peralta, Valentín, 61
Perdriel, Gregorio, 292
Pereda, Don Carlos, 81–82
Pereyra, Juan Antonio, 292–95
Pérez, Alberto, 135
Pérez, José Julián, 364n28
Perichón, Juan Bautista, 266–69, 356n122, 357n126
Perichón de O'Gorman, Ana, 262, 266, 356n116
Perignon, Dominique-Catherine, 176
personalist politics, ascendancy of, 281–82
Picavea, Manuel Antonio, 355n108
Pimienta, Manuel Antonio, 205
Pino, Juan del, 348n28
Pino y Rozas, Joaquín, 27, 245
Pinto, Basilia Antonia, 210
Pinto, Manuel, 294
Pintos, Manuel, 91
plebeians: in artisan community, 43–47; Cabildo Abierto of 1810 and, 275–79; classification of, 6; colonialism and, x; consumption patterns of, 182–87; cost-of-living fluctuations

and, 191–97; earnings vs. wages for, 233–43; economic conditions for, xi, 12–14; environment of, x; expansion of, in late colonial period, 18; French Conspiracy and, xi; guild creation and, x; homeownership and real estate acquisition by, 203–8; income increases for, 49–50; Junta Grande and, 290–95; in late colonial Buenos Aires, 7–8; leisure activities of, 77–82; masculinity and culture of honor for, 11–12, 51–83; militarization and transformation of, xii, 3, 12, 252–62, 297n3; political and legal skills of, 3–4; political empowerment following militarization of, 262–74, 275–82; real wages during drought and war for, 243–47; religious and civic activities of, 76–82; slavery rebellion and transformation of, ix; social and economic environment for, xi, 3–5; social determinants of success for, 208–12; standard of living for, xi; trade liberalization and empowerment of, 274–75; wages and occupational categories for, 216–32; wealth accumulation by, 179–82, 197–208; work patterns for, 215–16

politics: Cabildo Abierto of 1810 and, 275–79; empowerment of plebeians following militarization and, 262–66; loyalists in Buenos Aires and, 284–87; militarization of Buenos Aires and transformation of, 255–62, 271–74

Polovio, Juan, 173

Ponce de León, Diego, 263

Popham, Home Riggs (Sir), 29, 346n7, 347n8

population estimates for Buenos Aires, 28–31, 48–50; slave trade and, 37–39

Porra, Antonio, 120, 125

Porra, Martín, 120, 125, 127–30

porteño plebe: silversmiths and shoemakers as, 96–98. *See* plebes

Portuguese community in Buenos Aires, 32–35; silversmiths' guild formation and role of, 91–94, 111–16; Spanish campaign against, 220–21

prices: aranceles (prices) for shoes and boots, 88–90, 314n7; in colonial period, xi; consumption and income patterns of plebeians and, 182–87, 331n5; cost-of-living fluctuations and, 191–97, 331n8, 334n41; geopolitics and increases in, 156–57; plebeian history and role of, 7; real wages and, 243–47; for slaves, decline in, 40–43, 305n88; trade liberalization and, 275; wage declines and, 220–21. *See also aranceles* (fixed prices)

Primera Junta, 283–84, 292

private-sector employment, wages in, 228–32, 342n31

probate inventories: housing patterns of plebeians and, 189–90; marriage patterns of artisans and, 67–68; occupational categories in, 339n102; plebe history and role of, 7; plebeian wealth accumulation and, 13, 179–82, 331n4; wealth accumulation information from, 179–82

producer goods: values of, 198–208; wealth accumulation and, 179–82

public-sector employment, wage increases linked to, 222–32, 342n26

Pueyrredón, Juan Martín, 252–53, 256, 266, 348n23, 350n48

pulperos and *pulperías*, 6; debt accounts of, 207–8; as leisure activity location, 239–43, 344n57; plebeian leisure activities and, 75–82, 153–54, 327n20; ready-to-wear shoe trade and, 139–41, 323nn68–69

Quebedo, Don Francisco de, 158
Quiñones, Agustín, 294
Quiros, Baltasar de, 91
Quito, guild formation in, 10

race: apprenticeship systems and role of, 54–61, 307n111; culture of honor and masculine identity and, 68–75; demise of shoemakers' guild and, 119–26, 132–48; guild formation and, 2, 98–102, 112–16, 146–48; integration of slave and free labor and, 42–43; pardo and moreno shoemakers' guild and, 114–18, 126–32, 135–41; shoemakers' guild appointments and issues of, 95–98, 103–10, 113–16; silversmiths' guild and, 95–98; wages and occupations and role of, 218–32; working conditions for plebes and, 51–52. *See also* ethnicity
Ramos Mexía, Gregorio, 88–90, 98, 145, 316n55, 328n34
Ravignani, Emilio, 37
Ravina, Antonio, 62
Rawls, John, 243
ready-to-wear shoes, black and casta shoemakers and trade in, 139–41
real estate: social determinants of success and acquisition of, 208–12, 338n89; wealth accumulation through, 203–8. *See also* homeownership among artisan community
real wages: changes in, between 1775–

1811, 244; competition from slave labor, 150; economic crisis and impact on, 216; index of, in colonial period, xi–xii, 246; militarization of Buenos Aires and, 243–47, 260–62
Recova, construction of, 27–28, 48–50, 335n50
religious instruction for apprentices, 60–61
rent fluctuations, housing of plebeians and, 187–90, 334n41
revolutionary ideology, ascendancy of, in Buenos Aires, 156–57
Reyes, Micaela, 60
Reyes, Miguel Moreno, 91
Reynaud de Barbarín family, 328n51
Riera, Nicolás, 324n85
Riguy, Nicolás, 98, 101, 120, 125–26
Río, Pedro del, 331n4
Río de la Plata viceroyalty: black masters during, 73–75; Buenos Aires and establishment of, 8–9, 18–19, 297n5; economic change following, 48–50; guild formation, 94–98, 146–48; marriage and family patterns of, 66–68; militarization of Buenos Aires and, 261–62; population estimates following creation of, 30–31; real wages during, 245–47; slave trade during, 36–39; wage mobility under, 220–32
Rivadavia, Bernardino, 364n28
Rivas, Pedro, 135
Robespierre, Maximilien, 15, 154–55, 159–60, 178
Rocha, Antonio, 60
Rodríguez, Antonio, 204
Rodríguez, Bautista, 235
Rodríguez, Cipriano, 92
Rodríguez, Juan Roberto, 62

Lyman L. Johnson is a professor of history at the
University of North Carolina, Charlotte.

Library of Congress Cataloging-in-Publication Data
Johnson, Lyman L.
Workshop of revolution : plebeian Buenos Aires and
the Atlantic world, 1776–1810 / Lyman L. Johnson.
p. cm.
Includes bibliographical references and index.
ISBN 978-0-8223-4966-2 (cloth : alk. paper)
ISBN 978-0-8223-4981-5 (pbk. : alk. paper)
1. Buenos Aires (Argentina)—History—18th
century. 2. Buenos Aires (Argentina)—History—
19th century. 3. Working class—Argentina—Buenos
Aires—History—18th century. 4. Working class—
Argentina—Buenos Aires—History—19th century.
I. Title.
F3001.3.J64 2011
982'.11—dc22   2010041585